KW-271-957

Civil Liability for Environmental Damage

Energy and Environmental Law & Policy Series Supranational and Comparative Aspects

VOLUME 23

Editor

Kurt Deketelaere

Professor of Law, University of Leuven, Belgium,
Honorary Chief of Staff, Flemish Government
Honorary Professor of Law, University of Dundee, UK
Secretary – General, League of European Research Universities (LERU), Belgium

Editorial Board

Dr Philip Andrews-Speed, Associate Fellow, Chatham House
Professor Michael Faure, University of Maastricht
Professor Günther Handl, Tulane University, New Orleans
Professor Andres Nollkaemper, University of Amsterdam
Professor Oran Young, University of California

The aim of the Editor and the Editorial Board of this series is to publish works of excellent quality that focus on the study of energy and environmental law and policy.

Through this series the Editor and Editorial Board hope:

- to contribute to the improvement of the quality of energy/environmental law and policy in general and environmental quality and energy efficiency in particular;
- to increase the access to environmental and energy information for students, academics, non-governmental organizations, government institutions, and business;
- to facilitate cooperation between academic and non-academic communities in the field of energy and environmental law and policy throughout the world.

Civil Liability for Environmental Damage

Comparative Analysis of Law and Policy in Europe and the US

Second Edition

Mark Wilde

Wolters Kluwer
Law & Business

PLYMOUTH UNIVERSITY

9 U09284938

Published by:
Kluwer Law International
PO Box 316
2400 AH Alphen aan den Rijn
The Netherlands
Website: www.kluwerlaw.com

Sold and distributed in North, Central and South America by:
Aspen Publishers, Inc.
7201 McKinney Circle
Frederick, MD 21704
United States of America
Email: customer.service@aspenpublishers.com

Sold and distributed in all other countries by:
Turpin Distribution Services Ltd
Stratton Business Park
Pegasus Drive, Biggleswade
Bedfordshire SG18 8TQ
United Kingdom
Email: kluwerlaw@turpin-distribution.com

Printed on acid-free paper.

ISBN 978-90-411-3233-8

© 2013 Kluwer Law International BV, The Netherlands

DISCLAIMER: The material in this publication is in the nature of general comment only. It is not offered as advice on any particular matter and should not be taken as such. The authors expressly disclaim all liability to any person with regard to anything done or omitted to be done, and with respect to the consequences of anything done or omitted to be done wholly or partly in reliance on the basis of any matter contained in this volume without first obtaining professional advice regarding the particular facts and circumstances at issue. Any and all opinions expressed herein are those of the particular author, they are not necessarily those of the publisher of this volume and they do not reflect the views of any institution or organization.

All rights reserved. No part of this publication may be reproduced, stored in a retrieval system, or transmitted in any form or by any means, electronic, mechanical, photocopying, recording, or otherwise, without written permission from the publisher.

Permission to use this content must be obtained from the copyright owner. Please apply to: Permissions Department, Wolters Kluwer Legal, 76 Ninth Avenue, 7th Floor, New York, NY 10011-5201, USA. Email: permissions@kluwerlaw.com

Printed and Bound by CPI Group (UK) Ltd, Croydon, CR0 4YY.

Table of Contents

List of Abbreviations

ABI	Association of British Insurers
ACA	Anglers' Cooperative Association
ADAS	Agricultural and Advisory Service
ATCA	Alien Tort Claims Act (US)
AWE	Atomic Weapons Establishment
BAT	Best Available Technique
BATNEEC	Best Available Technology Not Entailing Excessive Cost.
BREF	Best Available Technique (BAT) Reference Documents
BGB	Das Bürgerliches Gesetzbuch (German Civil Code)
BNFL	British Nuclear Fuels Limited
BOP	Blow-Out Preventer
BVD	Bowel Virus Diarrhea
CCS	Carbon Capture and Storage
CERCLA	Comprehensive Environmental Response Compensation and Liability Act (US)
CGL	Comprehensive General Liability
CO2	Carbon Dioxide
CVM	Contingent Valuation Method
DEFRA	Department for the Environment, Food and Rural Affairs
EIL	Environmental Impairment Liability
ELA	Environmental Liability Act (Germany)
ELD	Environmental Liability Directive
EA	Environment Agency (UK)
EPA	Environmental Protection Agency (US and Australia)
ESP	Electro-Static Precipitator
EURATOM	European Atomic Energy Community

FCS	Fat Cow Syndrome
FOE	Friends of the Earth
GLO	Group Litigation Order
GMO	Genetically Modified Organism
HMIP	Her Majesty's Inspectorate of Pollution
ICCOP	International Convention on Civil Liability for Oil Pollution Damage
IOPC	International Oil Pollution Compensation Fund
IPPC	Integrated Pollution Prevention and Control
ITIA	International Tanker Indemnity Association
MNC	Multinational Corporation
NGO	Non-Governmental Organization
NRPB	National Radiological Protection Board
OPA	Oil Pollution Act (US)
PAH	Polycyclical Aromatic Hydrocarbons
PCB	Polychlorinated Biphenyls
PCE	Perchloroethene
PHAH	Polyhalogenated Aromatic Hydro-carbons
PPI	Parental Pre-conception Irradiation
SAC	Special Area of Conservation
SEA	Single European Act
TCDD	Tetrachlorodibenzo-p-dioxin
UNICE	Union of Industrial and Employers' Confederations of Europe
WRA	Water Resources Act (Germany)
WTAC	Willing to Accept Compensation
WTP	Willing to Pay

Preface

The first edition of this book stemmed from postgraduate studies commenced in 1995. By the early 1990s, environmental law had matured into a distinct topic with its own textbooks, law reports and distinctive regulatory techniques. As stated in the preface to the first edition, the prevailing view has long been that environmental damage is a matter for state regulation necessitating the use of public law 'command and control' mechanisms such as emission limits and planning controls. However, the potential role of private law, in the shape of tort, was also a predominant theme. In the UK, the seminal case of *Cambridge Water v. Eastern Counties Leather* highlighted the limitations of conventional torts as a means of environmental protection. The House of Lords recoiled from delivering a judgment which would have thrown the costs of historic pollution onto current operators. Thus, although it was acknowledged that the successful assertion of private law rights could occasionally result in some collateral environmental benefit, the law of tort did not appear well suited to achieving public interest objectives such as environmental protection. Nevertheless, throughout the common law world it was clear that no matter how sophisticated and comprehensive one's environmental controls are, there will always be accidents and unforeseen consequences. In the US, the Exxon Valdez disaster and the subsequent twenty years of litigation threw the private consequences of environmental disasters into sharp relief.

Meanwhile, moves were afoot in the European Community (EC) (as it then was) to harness private law in pursuit of environmental objectives. By this stage, the EC was the main driver of environmental law and policy in Europe. However, there was a poor record of compliance amongst EC Member States and enforcement difficulties undermined efforts to secure reductions in pollution. The EC Commission formed the view that by linking environmental standards with the ability to pursue civil claims for infractions, the enforcement of EC environmental laws could be enhanced. To this end, early proposals for a Directive on civil liability for damage caused by waste were published, although these were quickly superseded by proposals for a more far-reaching environmental liability regime.

It was against this background that the research culminating in the first edition of this book was undertaken. I sought to draw the desperate threads of the debate together and to clarify just what the proper role for tort should be in an environmental context. The book essentially operated on two levels. First, there was an attempt to establish a theoretical and conceptual basis for the use of tort in an environmental context. To this end, the book assembled a theoretical framework using historical, philosophical and economic components. This led to the conclusion that the pursuit of public interest objectives is a proper goal of tort. Second, there was an examination of the extent to which the main elements of tort could be manipulated so as to facilitate the attainment of environmental objectives. For example, adjusting causation rules and adopting stricter forms of liability.

Much of the first edition focused on the aforementioned EC initiatives which contemplated the introduction of an EC-wide civil liability regime designed to enhance the enforcement of environmental laws. This would have necessitated building more civil liability components into environmental measures with the result that breaching a statutory duty would trigger rights to compensation in addition to administrative and criminal penalties. However, just as the proofs for the first edition had been returned, the EC Commission published a draft environmental liability directive which was very different from the White Paper which preceded it. Rather than focusing on the role of private law, as the White Paper had done, the draft Directive set out a regulatory cost recovery system to be administered by public bodies. The draft Directive (which subsequently passed into law) was hurriedly included in an appendix to the first edition, although it was not entirely clear how it followed on from the previous policy initiatives and how it fitted in with the themes of the book. Indeed, for a time it looked as though the role of private law in environmental protection was no longer regarded as a pressing issue and that the book would be the first and last edition.

However, from my perspective, it is fortunate that reports of the premature demise of the environmental tort proved to be unfounded. Although the EU (as we can now call it regardless of the area of policy we are dealing with) has now moved its focus away from the development of an EU-wide tort-based environmental liability regime, events over the past ten years have demonstrated that tort still forms a very important part in the matrix of environmental law. A number of high profile cases have emerged which serve to underscore the point that 'accidents will happen' no matter how sophisticated one's environmental controls happen to be. In the UK, for example, a number of claimants were awarded damages in the high profile Corby Group Litigation case, which concerned birth abnormalities attributable to prenatal exposure to toxic substances released during the reclamation of a former steelworks site. Across the Atlantic, the Deepwater Horizon oil spill superseded Exxon Valdez as one of the worst environmental disasters in North American history. Moreover, a number of courageous litigants are currently stretching tort to its limits and beyond by endeavouring to sue polluters in respect of the mother of all environmental problems – climate change. Finally, those charged with administering international agreements on environmental damage continue to ponder the potential role of tort in transboundary pollution matters.

All this has provided an abundance of material to update the first edition and to develop the theoretical framework with a view to drawing some new conclusions and insights regarding the role of tort in an environmental context; although, as a result of the above developments, the focus has inevitably moved away from the EU. The first observation to be made in this respect is that in the first edition, I may have been unduly conservative in the conclusions I drew regarding the potential scope of liability in tort. Events such as Deepwater Horizon show that tort may play far more than a niche role confined to the localized consequences of relatively small-scale events. Tens of billions of dollars have been set aside to deal with the environmental damage costs and the economic losses suffered by businesses. Second, as noted above, concerted efforts are being made to hold major emitters of greenhouse gases liable for property damage and personal injuries caused by climate change. This issue was not touched upon in the first edition as such claims appeared far-fetched. Indeed, those actions which have been launched are struggling to overcome initial hurdles. Nevertheless, they clearly demonstrate that litigants will still turn to tort where there is a perceived lack of activity on the regulatory front.

Notwithstanding these dramatic developments on the international stage, one must not overlook the continuing role which tort plays as a means of dealing with the more localized consequences of 'traditional' pollution type problems. As previously noted, despite the sophistication of environmental controls in most developed countries, it is noteworthy that old-fashioned nuisance type disputes still come before the courts on a regular basis. With any book, there has to come a cut-off point at which proofs are submitted; it is inevitable that an important case will emerge just when it is too late to make alterations. For example, it is with some regret that I could not include discussion of cases such as *Anslow v. Norton Aluminium* which raises some fascinating issues regarding causation in nuisance law. These cases demonstrate that one should never lose sight of the important role which tort plays in protecting those private interests which may have been overlooked by the broad sweep of the regulatory regime. Aside from examining new cases, I have re-evaluated certain older cases with a view to ascertaining what they can tell us about the extent to which tort serves to correct 'regulatory failure' of this nature. For example, a reappraisal of the standard textbook case of *Allen v. Gulf Oil Refining Ltd*, concerning the defence of statutory authority in nuisance, reveals that the tort action stemmed from a failure of the planners and regulators to anticipate or act upon the harm.

Thus, the fact that the EU now appears to have moved away from the policy of adopting a tort-based liability regime, has not served to lessen or undermine the role of tort. Rather, the emphasis of the debate has shifted somewhat. Whereas the first edition of this book focused on the use of tort as a means of strengthening the enforcement of environmental regulations (an instrumentalist approach), this edition focuses more on the use of tort as a counterbalance to public law based regulation. In this respect, one of the main insights generated by the second edition is that linking tort too closely with environmental regulations is a bad thing. Thus legislatures should be slow to oust conventional torts where statutory definitions of harm rule out many of the ongoing low level harms which form the mainstay of nuisance claims. We can see this effect in the narrow way in which harm has been interpreted under the nuclear liability regime in the UK.

Given the dynamic and ever changing nature of tort and the creativity of litigants and their lawyers, I am more hopeful of further editions than I was ten years ago.

Much has changed during the course of the ten years since the publication of the first book but the patience and support of my parents, Myra and Peter has been a constant. One major change has been my marriage to Charlotte whose support and encouragement has been invaluable in bringing this project to fruition. And the birth of our daughter Florence Rose, whose arrival exactly coincided with the publication of this edition. Many thanks also to all at Kluwer for asking me to write this second edition and for their speedy and efficient production process.

Mark Wilde
December 2012

Part I: Introductory Issues

CHAPTER 1

The Law of Tort and the Environment: An Introduction to the Debate and Foundational Issues

§1.01 INTRODUCTION

Environmental regulation has been an important political issue since the latter part of the twentieth century. Attention has been focused on the extent to which law may provide a solution to the problem and has given rise to the development of environmental law.[1] Although environmental law has only become a discreet area of study in comparatively recent times,[2] its origins may be traced back several centuries.[3] However, until the nineteenth century attempts to deal with pollution by regulation were rare.[4] Thus, in cases where pollution caused loss or discomfort to an individual, it was necessary to have recourse to existing principles of private law governing disputes

---

1. However, environmental law is not a self-contained branch of law comprising unique principles. Rather, it is a banner under which those areas of law, which may be used to control environmentally harmful activities, are loosely grouped. See Stuart Bell & Donald McGillivray, *Environmental Law*, Ch. 1 (7th ed., OUP 2008).
2. Harrison C. Dunning may be credited with running the first, if not *the* first, courses entitled 'Environmental Law' at the University of Southern California in 1969. See Harrison C. Dunning, *Notes for an Environmental Law Course*, 55 Cornell L. Rev. 804 (1969–70).
3. In a celebrated incident in 1584 William Shakespeare's father was prosecuted by the town council for allowing a dung heap to accumulate outside his house in Henley Street. Moreover, an ordinance issued in 1610 by James I prohibited the burning of sea coal within a mile of 'our city of Westminster'; See J.F. Garner, *Environmental Law – a Real Subject?*, 142(6580) N.L.J. 1718 (1992). See also David Woolley et al. (eds.), *Environmental Law*, Ch. 1 (2d ed., OUP 2009).
4. This is due to the fact that until the nineteenth century there was not a regulatory machine in place capable of assimilating data and drafting an administrative response to problems such as pollution. See Patrick S. Atiyah, *The Rise and Fall of Freedom of Contract*, Ch. 5 (Clarendon Press 1979).

between neighbours, such as the common law of England. However, these mechanisms proved ineffectual in the face of the industrial revolution with the result that, during the nineteenth and twentieth centuries, there has been a systematic attempt by most industrialized nations to control pollution by means of regulation.[5] This has led to the marginalization of tort in this context.[6]

In the light of these considerations the issue which this book addresses concerns the role of tort in the context of environmental regulation. The original debate was prompted by a number of European Union (EU) and Council of Europe initiatives proposing the introduction of measures designed to adapt tort as a means of environmental protection. Indeed, much of the first edition of this book was preoccupied with these initiatives. As will be seen below, various means were suggested of overcoming, by way of statutory intervention, the particular difficulties which face a claimant when attempting to establish liability for environmental damage. In the event, EU policy took a rather different direction and the regime which emerged from these deliberations focused on administrative mechanisms for recovering the cost of pollution or for taking preventative action. Nevertheless, the role of tort in an environmental context remains of critical importance as demonstrated by events such as the Deepwater Horizon Disaster in 2010. Moreover, a number of individual states and international bodies have continued to develop tort based liability regimes for environmental damage.

The book considers those factors which have limited the efficacy of tort as a means of environmental protection in the past and critically analyses means of overcoming these difficulties. However, this is set against consideration of a much wider issue, namely, the *purpose* of tort in this context. Traditionally, the law of tort has been primarily concerned with the protection of private interests, whereas, environmental protection constitutes a public interest objective.[7] The main conceptual problem which has to be overcome concerns the extent to which tortious liability can accommodate both private and public interests. To this end it is necessary to determine whether it is practically and conceptually possible to develop tort in this manner and, furthermore, how such an approach interrelates with the regulatory responses which are already in place. Much of the debate has lacked an appreciation of these issues and

---

5.   The developments which allowed this to take place, such as the evolution of a new professional class, are reviewed by Atiyah, ch. 5.

6.   Consequently doubt has often been expressed regarding whether the common law any longer has a useful role to fulfil as a means of formulating responses to new problems. See Guido Calabresi, *A Common Law for the Age of Statutes*, 163 (Harvard University Press 1982): 'It is unrealistic to expect that courts will be able to play the kind of law making role they once played. For there will be too many situations in which, for example, the writing of a new law will simply be beyond the capacity of a court and in which, nonetheless, a new law must be promulgated all at once.'

7.   In this case the focus is on the collective interests of society rather than the private interests of any individuals concerned. The same act, such as theft, may simultaneously cause loss to an individual and threaten a societal interest. However, the law has traditionally considered public interests as being divisible from private interests and has protected them through separate mechanisms, such as the criminal law. Thus, in the case of theft, the victim must protect his property through the tort of trespass to chattels, whereas, the state may seek to protect the public from anti-social behaviour through the criminal law. In due course it will become apparent that it is difficult to draw rigid demarcations between the realms of public and private law.

has failed to adequately identify the theoretical underpinnings of tort as a means of environmental protection. It is only by considering existing and proposed specialist tort based liability systems in the light of these wider theoretical perspectives, regarding the function of tort, that a deeper understanding can be gained of the true purpose of tort in this context.

Before proceeding to a more detailed overview of the main issues addressed and the structure of the book, it is necessary to place the subject in context by identifying the reasons for the ecological crisis and the role of environmental law in general.

§1.02 THE NEED FOR ENVIRONMENTAL LAW

[A] Growing Awareness of Environmental Damage

As stated above, the latter part of the twentieth century has seen a dramatic increase in public concern regarding environmental damage. Two hundred years of industrialization has left indelible scars on landscapes and resulted in the release of billions of tonnes of noxious substances into the environment.[8]

Until comparatively recent times there appeared to be a belief that man was in some sense distanced from the environment.[9] Thus, the environment could be used as a form of receptacle for the harmful by-products of his industrial activities. However, there has been an increasing realization that man is part of the environment[10] and that, by releasing noxious substances, he is thereby inflicting harm upon himself. A very clear recent example is provided by the *Corby Group Litigation* case[11] in the UK where damages were sought in respect of upper limb deformities occurring in children born to mothers exposed to toxic dust churned up by the reclamation of a former steelworks site. Moreover, given that much of the environment is made up of individual parcels of land belonging to particular persons, environmental damage is often manifested as damage to private property such as a farmer's crops. In the absence of physical damage a person's ability to use and enjoy his property may nevertheless be adversely affected by pollution.

---

8. See Thomas Berry, *The Dream of the Earth*, xiii (Sierra Club Books 1990): 'we have changed the very chemistry of the planet, we have altered the biosystems, we have changed the topography and even the geological structure of the planet, structures and functions that have taken hundreds of millions and even billions of years to bring into existence.'
9. This may in part be due to the anthropocentric nature of Judeo-Christian dogma which places man at the centre of the universe. According to White, this promoted the belief that 'no item in the physical creation had any purpose save to serve man's purposes. And although man's body is made of clay, he is not simply part of nature: he is made in God's image.' See L. White Jr., *The Historical Roots of Our Ecological Crisis*,155 (3767) Science 1203 (1967). See also Alexander Gillespie, *International Law, Policy and Ethics*, Ch. 1 (Clarendon Press 1999).
10. See Sean McDonagh, *To Care for the Earth: A Call to a New Theology*, 102 (Cassell 1986): 'To pretend that we have no organic connection with the rest of creation is to overlook the greater part of 20 billion years of the story of the universe.'
11. [2009] EWHC 1944 (TCC), [2010] Env. L.R. D2. See §2.06[B][2], below.

More recently there has been an increasing recognition of the fact that pollutants do not respect political boundaries. This has brought the problem of transboundary pollution to the fore and the problem of how to seek redress where the pollution stems from another jurisdiction. On a global scale the phenomenon of climate change, resulting from anthropogenic emissions of greenhouse gases, has now been accepted as scientific fact.[12] Claims that such changes may threaten the long time survival prospects of our species may appear somewhat far-fetched.[13] Nevertheless, there is no doubt that even a marginal increase in sea levels would cause incalculable damage.[14]

[B]   The Source of the Environmental Problem

The root of the environmental problem lies in the manner in which natural resources are utilized. If the parties competing for the use of a resource fail to cooperate, the resource will eventually be destroyed. In order to demonstrate this problem, in his notable article entitled *The Tragedy of the Commons*,[15] Hardin used the example of the overgrazing of common pastures in the Western United States. Before deciding to increase the size of his herd, a herdsman must conduct a simple cost-benefit analysis. The herdsman knows that, when the time comes to sell the additional cattle, he will receive all the proceeds of the sale. The costs relate to the additional burden which the extra cattle will place on the common pastures. However, the herdsman also knows that these costs will be shared amongst all those who have access to the commons. Thus, the fact that the herdsman will only have to bear a small percentage of these costs means that they will only amount to a fraction of the potential benefits. This leads the herdsman to the inevitable conclusion that he should acquire the additional cattle. However, this conclusion will also have been reached by every other herdsman with access to the commons with the result that herds will increase in size until the commons can no longer sustain them, thus:

> Each man is *locked in* to a system that compels him to increase his herd without limit – in a world that is limited. Ruin is the destination toward which all men rush,

---

12. For a review of the key research findings in the area see Andrew E. Dessler and Edward A. Parson, *The Science and Politics of Global Climate Change: A Guide to the Debate* (2d ed., CUP 2010).
13. See James E. Lovelock, *Gaia: A New Look at Life on Earth* (OUP 1979). At the risk of over-simplification the theory can be summarised as follows. Lovelock proposes that Earth should be regarded as a single ecological entity of which homo sapiens are only one component. Furthermore, the system has the ability to regulate its climate so as to rid itself of any species which threatens the long term survival of the ecosystem as a whole. Thus, although the planet may allow us to destroy the habitat which humans need to survive, it will ensure that other forms of life may continue; thus, Lovelock states at 132, '[a] system as experienced as Gaia is unlikely to be easily disturbed.'
14. The total damage costs caused by climate change are hotly debated but in any event are thought to amount to trillions of dollars: see P. Watkiss (ed.), *The Climate Cost Project Final Report: the Impacts and Economic Costs of Climate Change in Europe and the Costs and Benefits of Adaptation* (Stockholm Env. Inst. 2011).
15. G. Hardin, *The Tragedy of the Commons*, 162 (3859) Science 1243 (1968).

each pursuing his own best interest in a society that believes in the freedom of the commons. *Freedom in a commons brings ruin to all.*[16]

Hardin argues that this analysis can also be applied to the problem of pollution; the only difference is that, rather than taking something from the commons (i.e., the environment[17]), man is putting something into the commons. The result is the same in that the commons will ultimately be damaged or rendered useless for certain activities such as agriculture. The cost – benefit analysis which a person may perform before deciding to discharge wastes into the environment, as opposed to purifying them or recycling them, is essentially the same as that performed by the herdsmen, thus:

> The rational man finds that his share of the cost of the wastes he discharges into the commons is less than the cost of purifying his wastes before releasing them. Since this is true for everyone, we are locked into a system of 'fouling our own nest', so long as we behave only as independent, rational, free-enterprisers.[18]

[C]   The Purpose of Environmental Law

Hardin continues that the tragedy of the commons analogy, 'as a food basket' is averted by private property. This enables a person to ring-fence an area of land and protect it from exploitation by others. However, as regards the pollution application of the analogy, property rules are not always conducive to environmental protection. One problem is that pollution does not respect property boundaries; as Hardin points out, 'the air and waters surrounding us cannot readily be fenced.'[19] A more fundamental difficulty is that the same rules which prevent others from damaging a resource may enable the owner to damage the resource himself:

> Indeed, our particular concept of private property, which deters us from exhausting the positive resources of the earth, favors [sic] pollution. The owner of a factory on the bank of a stream – whose 'property' extends to the middle of the stream – often has difficulty seeing why it is not his natural 'right' to muddy the waters flowing past his door. The law, always behind the times, requires elaborate stitching and fitting to adapt it to this newly perceived aspect of the commons.[20]

Accordingly, it has been necessary to develop a range of coercive laws or taxing measures the purpose of which is to render it more expensive to discharge pollutants into the environment as opposed to treating them first. Such measures have given rise to the body of law which is now loosely termed 'environmental law'.

Given the fact that, according to Hardin's analysis, private law may actually be antipathetic to environmental protection it is not immediately apparent whether tort has any useful role to fulfil in this context. This returns us to the central issue, to use

---

16.   Hardin, 1244.
17.   The environment may be equated with the 'commons' in that everyone has access to it.
18.   Hardin, 1245.
19.   *Ibid.*
20.   *Ibid.*

Hardin's phraseology, to what extent is it possible to stitch and fit tort so as to adapt it to this new objective?

§1.03   THE LAW OF TORT AND THE ENVIRONMENT

At this point it would be useful to clarify what is meant by tort. As will become apparent in due course it is impossible to arrive at an all-encompassing explanation which defines all its attributes and functions. Thus, it is more profitable to concentrate on the purpose and functions of tort. The function of tort varies, according to the particular tort and the circumstances of the case, however, in broad terms we can say that is concerned with loss allocation. Losses are bound to occur in any society, whether they stem from a failure to exercise due care or wilful conduct of some description. In some cases rules may operate so as to allocate responsibility to the party or parties who caused the loss; in other cases the loss may be left to lie where it falls. Clearly, not every loss is actionable; a tort is an act or omission which constitutes a breach of duty fixed by law. The reasons why certain acts and omissions are deemed actionable may be founded on an idea of justice or the need to allocate losses in a certain manner. This is an issue which is discussed in more detail below in the context of the philosophy of tort.

Historically, tort has served as a means of private dispute resolution; in this respect it has not been expressly concerned with securing third party objectives such as environmental protection. Nevertheless, it is recognized that tort has an environmental dimension. For example, a private assertion of property rights under nuisance may result in some collateral environmental benefit. This would be the case if a householder, troubled by noxious fumes, succeeded in enjoining the responsible activity. This has given rise to the so-called 'toxic tort' which is has been defined by Pugh and Day as follows:

> The term 'toxic tort' is a shorthand phrase ... for any claim that has, at its base, the prospect that an individual has suffered damage to person, property or to the quiet enjoyment of his/her property, or there has been damage caused to the local environment as a result of environmental pollution. The term therefore covers damage resulting from industrial waste pumped into the environment, whether into the air, the sea, the rivers ... It covers chemical and radioactive waste. It also covers claims for nuisance resulting from noise, dust etc. Finally it covers damage to the environment itself.[21]

The afore-mentioned Corby litigation provides a very clear recent example of the toxic tort in operation.[22]

Other torts are also relevant in an environmental context. Certain hazardous substances which are solid and tangible, such as sheets of asbestos, could constitute a trespass to land if left on another person's property. Where the polluter is culpable and there has been property damage or personal injury it may be possible to establish

---

21.   Charles Pugh and Martyn Day, *Toxic Torts*, 2 (Cameron May 1992).
22.   See n. 11, above.

liability under negligence. Emissions from certain installations may constitute a breach of statutory duty.

However, the role of tort, in this context, has been limited by factors which were succinctly summarized by Hughs, in an early edition of his work, as follows:

> [A]ctions at common law are time-consuming and expensive, fraught with complex technicalities and, in general, only on an individual, rather than a class, basis. A person cannot be the plaintiff [now claimant][23] in an action at common law unless he has a vested interest in the subject matter of the action; so in an action in tort the plaintiff must be the person injured by the wrongdoer.[24]

This encapsulates the main issues addressed in subsequent chapters. The technical difficulties, to which Hughs referred, have limited the role of tort as a means of environmental protection in the past. As will be seen below, they include such matters as the need to establish a causal link between environmental damage and a certain activity with a high degree of certainty. However, the latter difficulties highlighted by Hughs touch on a much wider issue, namely, the purpose of tort. The fact that the claimant must have a vested interest in the subject matter of the action highlights the fact that tort is primarily concerned with the resolution of private disputes. As stated above, one of the most important issues which has to be addressed concerns the extent to which the focus of tort can encompass both private interests and public concerns. Ultimately, this may require a reassessment of what constitutes a 'vested interest in the subject matter of the action'. These wider issues must be addressed before dealing with the detail of specific doctrinal developments which could expand the role of tort in an environmental context.

§1.04 AN OVERVIEW OF TORTIOUS LIABILITY FOR ENVIRONMENTAL DAMAGE

The subject of civil liability for environmental damage involves several areas of law and raises a multitude of issues. In order to clarify the main arguments, the material has been marshalled into the following structure which leads one through the issues in a logical manner. The operation of tort in an environmental context and the main difficulties which face a claimant, when attempting to establish liability for environmental damage, are dealt with in Part II, Chapters 2 and 3. This Part adopts a largely Anglo-American common law perspective, although the experience of other common law world jurisdictions is also drawn upon. This is because the common law provides a useful case study for illustrating the main issues associated with the use of tort in an environmental context. The common law is inextricably interrelated with the problem of land use conflict and the need to balance competing interests regarding the use of natural resources. In the absence of statutory guidance, the common law courts have

---

23. Following the civil justice reforms introduced in England and Wales in 1999 the term plaintiff was replaced with claimant. It is proposed to use the term plaintiff in respect of other common law jurisdictions and in respect of case law which precedes the reforms.
24. David Hughs, *Environmental Law*, 37 (3d ed., Butterworths 1989).

had the task of developing legal rules which are capable of balancing these interests. Practically all issues regarding the limitations of tort in an environmental context can be traced to the experience of the common law courts in resolving these difficulties. Thus illuminating comparisons can be made between how common law courts have dealt with environmental disputes in centuries past and how more recent initiatives would endeavour to resolve similar difficulties. For example, issues of causation have vexed English Courts since the nineteenth century when the sudden proliferation of environmentally harmful activities, spawned in the wake of the industrial revolution, rendered it increasingly difficult to trace damage pathways to one particular polluter. Law and policy makers are still grappling with this thorny issue and useful comparisons can be drawn between these developments and the experience of the courts in endeavouring to achieve a common law solution. Furthermore, the advantage of the common law is that, as it is effectively 'judge made' law, judgments must fully articulate the difficulties and the mode of resolution. In this respect, the decisions of courts in common law jurisdictions often provide an extremely in depth analysis of the difficulties. In this respect the judgments of US courts can be particularly enlightening as judges have not shied from confronting the underlying economic dilemmas which run throughout the subject.

In the light of the limitations of tort as a means of redress for environmental damage, Part III, comprising Chapters 4 and 5, focuses on the fundamental issue of whether tort has a useful role to play within a mix of environmental protection measures. To this end Chapter 4 considers whether it is conceptually and practically possible to develop tort so as to enhance its role in this context and, furthermore, whether such a development would serve a useful purpose. Much of the impetus for the development of tort as a means of environmental protection has stemmed from pollution issues which have a transfrontier element. Part IV considers specific means by which the role of tort in the field of environmental protection could be enhanced. Some doctrinal developments have already occurred as a result of case law developments in various states. More radical changes have been implemented by way of statutory intervention. To this end a comparative study is undertaken of issues such as strict liability, easing the burden of proof on causation, standing and various other elements of tort based liability. The implications of such developments in terms of the theory of tort based liability, as outlined in Chapter 4, are also carefully considered. Part V sets out some conclusions regarding how tort currently operates in an environmental context and the ramifications of extending this form of liability still further. At this point it is worth expanding on some of these themes.

[A]   Current Limitations of Tort

The general difficulties of establishing liability in tort for environmental damage have already been outlined above. Chapter 2 provides an overview of the main torts which are of relevance in an environmental context and how they have been applied in this field. Chapter 3 analyses in detail those factors which have limited the use of tort as a means of environmental protection. These include technical difficulties associated with establishing fault and causation. Furthermore, it is noted that, as tort has been principally concerned with the protection of private interests, there is a limited notion of standing in civil matters. Related to this problem is the fact that remedies awarded by the courts tend to reflect the loss incurred by the individual rather than the damage sustained by the environment.

[B] The Role of Tort in an Environmental Context

Chapter 4 addresses the fundamental issue of the role of tort. As stated above, much of the debate has lacked an appreciation of the theory of tort and its role in a modern society. Unless these issues are addressed it is difficult to justify the use of tort as a means of environmental protection or to define how it should operate. The object of the chapter is to ascertain whether there is a sound theoretical basis which justifies the use of tort as a specific means of environmental protection. To this end the chapter considers the following issues.

[1] The Philosophy of Tort

In order to understand the fundamental objectives of tort it is necessary to consider the theoretical basis of tort and its role in a modern society. In this respect the 'philosophy' of tort can be used to clarify those objectives and suggest means by which they may be achieved.[25] There are two main schools of thought. The economic view, of which one of the main proponents in recent years has been Posner,[26] proposes that the purpose of tort should be to ensure an efficient allocation of resources. The more traditional view, which finds favour amongst most legal scholars, is that tort is founded upon justice and the need to restore the *status quo ante* where one party has been wronged by another.

The economic view argues that the courts should bear in mind the respective economic values of competing land uses when, for example, deciding whether to grant an injunction in favour of a person who has suffered a nuisance. This approach is considered but ultimately rejected as a sound basis for a public interest model of tort. The main problem with the economic analysis is that it takes a very narrow view of the value of natural resources. The value of a resource is priced in monetary terms in accordance with economic criteria; this includes the value of the potential use of the property. The monetary value of commercial uses is always likely to outweigh the value of conservatory uses. The ecological value of a natural resource cannot be quantified in this manner; indeed, there is some evidence to suggest that, even the most

---

25. D.G. Owen, *Why Philosophy Matters to Tort Law*, 13–14, in *Philosophical Foundations of Tort Law* (D.G. Owen ed., Clarendon Press 1995): 'The subject of tort might fairly be said to involve the nature and extent of an actor's legal responsibility to a victim for causing harm. If so, then one important preliminary question for tort law must be how responsibility for causing harm should be defined and limited. Should it rest upon the actor's moral desert, limited by notions of blameworthiness for acting upon choices that are by some measures bad, as viewed ex ante? Or should the concept of tort responsibility be widened to embrace the harmful consequences of the actor's conduct, including victim needs ex post?'
26. See, for example, Richard A. Posner, *Economic Analysis of Law* (Little, Brown & Co. 1986).

ardent proponents of the economic approach, now accept its limitations in this context. The ecological value of conserving natural resources must be made in accordance with wider social and political preferences.

Thus, the chapter goes on to consider the extent to which a public interest model of tort can be founded upon notions of justice. At this point a distinction between the concepts of 'corrective' and 'distributive' justice has to be considered.[27] Whereas corrective justice focuses entirely on the respective rights of the individuals in a dispute, distributive justice admits societal preferences regarding who should bear the loss. The proponents of the latter approach argue that tort is now inextricably linked with distributional issues. They point to the fact that strict liability and insurance are realities which affect the decision of the court to apportion liability on a certain party.[28] However, a system based wholly upon distributive principles is problematic in that it operates as a blunt means of loss allocation which is not related in any way to the conduct of the defendant.[29] There is a place for such systems in certain circumstances, however, they should not entirely replace tort.[30] One of the potential strengths of tort is that, by defining a standard of conduct to which the defendant should adhere, the system provides an incentive to reduce the costs of his activity. However, a system which is entirely founded on corrective principles is also problematic in that it requires the claimant to establish fault and imposes a heavy burden of proof on causation. Furthermore, a corrective model of tort examines the dispute purely from the perspective of the individuals concerned and precludes consideration of public interest issues such as the desirability of environmental protection. Thus, the chapter concludes that the modern law of tort should seek to attain a balance between corrective and distributive justice. Furthermore, it is argued that there is a philosophical basis which can support such an approach.[31]

[2]   The Role of Tort in an Environmental Context

The specific role of tort as a means of environmental protection is considered in the light of this philosophical background. The fact that a public interest model of tort is possible in conceptual terms does not mean that a specialist environmental liability regime would necessarily augment traditional regulatory responses. Thus it is necessary to identify a gap in the enforcement of environmental law which tort may be capable of reducing.

---

27. See, for example, Izhak Englard, *The Philosophy of Tort Law*, Ch. 2 (Dartmouth Publishing 1993).
28. *Ibid.*
29. An example of such a system would include a no fault social security fund financed by general taxation or a special tax on a specific sector. The New Zealand Government introduced a scheme of this type under the Accident Compensation Act 1972; the scheme is currently goverened by the Accident Compensation Act 2001.
30. A case in point concerns contaminated land. This matter is discussed in ch. 4.
31. A particularly elegant explanation, which shall be discussed in ch. 4 is provided by I. Englard, *The Idea of Complementarity as a Philosophical Basis for Pluralism in Tort Law* in, *Philosophical Foundations of Tort* (D.G. Owen ed., Clarendon Press 1995).

The main potential benefit of tort is that it affords private individuals and bodies a means of participating in the enforcement of environmental standards. An individual, who has been affected by pollution, may be motivated to pursue the matter in cases where a regulatory authority has chosen not to act. In this sense tort has the potential to increase the penetration of environmental law.

Related to this issue of private enforcement is the matter of whether tort may provide an effective incentive for risk management. When considering incentives there is a temptation to make direct comparisons with the criminal law. On the face of it, criminal penalties may appear to provide a superior incentive for risk management in that they seek to punish breaches of regulations. Provided such regulations are adequately enforced, the stigma and adverse publicity associated with a prosecution may pray on the corporate mind of image conscious enterprises.[32] Furthermore, directors and senior officers, who may incur personal criminal liability,[33] have a personal interest in ensuring that regulations are observed. This may lead to the conclusion that an effective tort regime would not add to the incentives which are already provided by regulatory penalties. However, direct comparisons of this type are misleading. Provided that it is accompanied by effective remedies, the prospect of civil liability may provide equally effective incentives for risk management, although, the manner in which they influence the corporate mind is entirely different. Rather than punishing a breach of duty, tort may require the polluter to pay for the actual costs of clean-up. Furthermore, by the use of injunctive relief, it can be used prospectively to prevent the continuance of pollution. This provides an *economic* incentive for risk management. Rather than appealing to the conscience of the organization, tort converts pollution into a cost of production which the business will seek to reduce much like any other cost. Thus, in cold business terms, tort has the capacity to make it more expensive not to take abatement measures. By providing a different form of incentive, tort has the potential to augment regulatory penalties in pursuit of the common goal of environmental protection.

The possible use of tort as a means of privately enforcing environmental standards is linked with a wider theme, namely, the possible development of a concept of 'environmental rights'. This necessitates consideration of property law and the extent to which a private interest in land entitles one to disregard the effects of that land use on others. To a large extent, the environment has become inextricably linked with the private interests which vest in it. Thus, unless an individual suffers personal injury or property damage, the right to be free from noxious vapours, for example, is contingent upon that individual having a sufficient interest in property. Certain academics have argued in favour of widening the concept of property so as to afford private individuals a form of equitable proprietary interest in the 'goods of life';[34] this can include the environment.[35] Such an approach would separate the environment

---

32. For an analysis of the efficacy of criminal penalties see, for example, M.A. Cohen, *Criminal Penalties* in T.H. Tietenberg (ed.), *Innovation in Environmental Policy* (Edward Elgar 1992).
33. See, for example, section 157 Environmental Protection Act 1990.
34. C.A. Reich, *The New Property*, 73(5) Yale L.J. 733 (1964); C.B. Macpherson, *Human Rights as Property Rights*, 24 Dissent 72 (1977).
35. See K. Gray, *Equitable Property*, 47(2) CLP 157 (1994).

from the private interests which vest in it and designate it as a form of public space in which the public are afforded an interest. Chapter 4 considers whether a civil liability regime could provide the practical means of enforcing that interest.

Another key theme which emerges from this analysis is that tort does not necessarily have to be assimilated with regulatory regimes in order to serve an important purpose in this context. Much of the debate has focused upon using tort in an instrumentalist's manner by means of, for example, inserting provisions on civil liability into environmental legislation. Such provisions establish liability for breach of statutory duty in addition to criminal and administrative penalties. However, existing torts, such as the law of nuisance, may serve an equally important function, notwithstanding the fact that they focus on the private interests concerned in isolation from any public law responses to the problem. In short, from time to time it transpires that the impact of an activity on individual rights and interests may not have been foreseen by the legislature. For example, a narrow statutory definition of harm may have been adopted which does not encompass the type of harm suffered by an individual. Any private causes of action for breach of statutory duty, established under the legislation in question, would provide no answer for the complainant in that they would share the same statutory definition of actionable harm. Existing torts may have a useful role to play in providing redress for private harms stemming from what can be described as, at best, regulatory oversights and, at worst, regulatory failures. For this reason, it is concluded that the legislature should be slow to oust existing remedies when contemplating the inclusion of civil liability components in statutory regimes.

[3]   The Effect of Insurance on the Role of Tort

The role of tort cannot be considered in isolation from the effect of insurance. As noted above, the growth in insurance since the nineteenth century has increased the distributional component in tort in that it has a bearing on which party is in the best position to bear the loss. Although few judges have used the existence of insurance as a specific ground for allocating the loss to the insured party,[36] insurance has undoubtedly influenced the manner in which tort has developed.

Thus the decision to proceed with a specialist environmental liability regime must take into account the insurance implications of extending liability in this manner. Environmental impairment has caused particular difficulties for insurers due to the fact that it is difficult to calculate risk. A polluting incident may cause long term contamination, the full effects of which, may not manifest themselves for several years (long tail risks). This may expose an insurer to costs which are far in excess of those contemplated when the policy was originally drafted. In the past, this has led insurers to withdraw cover for pollution, however, the industry has begun to develop policies capable of absorbing this type of liability. As a result, the chapter concludes with an

---

36. An exception is Lord Denning who sometimes expressly referred to the existence of insurance as being a material consideration when apportioning liability. See, for example *Nettleship v. Weston* [1971] 2 Q.B. 691.

assessment of the insurability of environmental damage and how this might affect the development of tort.

It is also considered whether the availability of insurance would undermine the incentives provided by tort to reduce the risks of activities by absolving polluters from financial responsibility.

[C]   International and EU Initiatives

As stated above, the current debate regarding the use of tort as a means of environmental protection was initially generated by various EU and Council of Europe initiatives. Although the EU has been active in the field of environmental protection since the publication of its First Action Programme in 1973,[37] it is only in the last twenty years or so that it has contemplated intervention in the field of civil liability for environmental damage.

In 1989[38] a draft directive on civil liability for damage caused by waste was introduced; this was subsequently amended in 1991.[39] However, these proposals were superseded by the publication of a Green Paper[40] which discussed the merits of a general environmental liability regime covering a wider range of activities. This was followed by consultations with industry and environmental interest groups. In 1993 the Council of Europe introduced its 'Convention on Civil Liability for Damage resulting from Activities Dangerous to the Environment' (the *Lugano* Convention). Furthermore, certain Member States of the EU pressed ahead with their own specialist environmental liability regimes. In 2000 the EU Commission published a White Paper on the subject[41] which appeared to lay the groundwork for an EU tort based environmental liability regime. However, the Directive which emerged did not constitute a logical progression from the White Paper and instead implemented an administrative regime for preventing pollution or recovering the costs after the event.[42]

Nevertheless, the debate as to whether the law of tort could and should play a greater part in environmental protection continues and it is noteworthy that much of the impetus now stems from developments on the international stage. To this end Chapter 5 is devoted to an analysis of European and international attempts to get to grips with such problems with particular reference to the law of tort. First, there is an overview of the conflict of laws issues which may result from transfrontier pollution and the sometimes audacious attempts which have been made to overcome them. The litigation pursued against the Nigerian subsidiary of Shell is a notable example in this

---

37. Declaration of the Council of the European Communities and of the representatives of the Governments of the Member States meeting in the Council of 22 November 1973 on the programme of action of the European Communities on the environment [1973] OJ C112/1.
38. OJ C251/4 (1989).
39. OJ C192/6 (1992).
40. *Communication from the Commission to the Council and Parliament on Environmental Liability*, COM(93) 47 final.
41. EC Commission, *White Paper on Environmental Liabiliy*, COM(2000) 66 final.
42. European Parliament and Council Directive (EC) 2004/35 on environmental liability with regard to the prevention and remedying of environmental damage [2004] OJ L143/56.

respect. Second, there is an analysis of international attempts to establish internationally recognized tort based principles for dealing with the aftermath of accidents in, for
example, the oil and nuclear industries.

[D]   Enhancing the Role of Tort as a Means of Environmental Protection

Part IV considers how specific doctrinal developments may serve to enhance the role of
tort as a means of environmental protection. This Part has two main objectives which
are dealt with simultaneously. The first objective is to consider whether such a role is
consistent with the philosophical rationale for an environmental application of tort as
discussed in Chapter 4. The second objective is to consider whether the proposals
provide practical solutions to the problems of establishing civil liability discussed in
Chapter 3.

Certain EU Member States have already implemented civil liability regimes for
environmental damage. Clearly, these systems provide a rich source of comparative
material. Developments at a European and International level are contrasted with
principles which have already been adopted under these regimes. This invites a
comparative approach in analysing the solutions adopted under these regimes and
certain jurisdictions outside the EU.

Comparative law[43] serves a number of purposes in this context. Zweigert and
Kötz[44] argue that the primary function of comparative law is knowledge. The process
of attempting to find a legal solution to a particular problem is a scientific endeavour.
When viewed in these terms it appears folly to ignore solutions adopted in other
jurisdictions simply because they are foreign; as Zweigert and Kötz point out, 'no study
deserves the name of a science if it limits itself to phenomena arising within national
boundaries.'[45] Thus:

> If one accepts that legal science includes not only the techniques of interpreting the
> texts, principles, rules, and standards of a national system, but also the discovery
> of models for preventing or resolving social conflicts, then it is clear that the
> method of comparative law can provide a much richer range of model solutions
> than a legal science devoted to a single nation, simply because the different
> systems of the world can offer a greater variety of solutions than could be thought
> up in a lifetime by even the most imaginative jurist who was corralled in his own
> system. Comparative law is an 'école de vérite' which extends and enriches the
> 'supply of solutions' and offers the scholar of critical capacity the opportunity of
> finding the 'better solution' for his time and place.[46]

---

43. Comparative law must be distinguished from 'private international law' (or 'conflict of laws').
    The latter applies in international disputes and is used to determine which of several systems
    should be used to resolve the matter. Comparative law merely compares those systems without
    any specific dispute in mind; the object is a purely scientific exercise designed to contrast
    approaches to solving a particular problem. See Konrad Zweigert & Hein Kötz, *An Introduction
    to Comparative Law*, 6 (Tony Weir trans., 2d ed., Clarendon 1987).
44. Zweigert & Kötz, 15.
45. Zweigert & Kötz, 14.
46. Zweigert & Kötz, 15.

As such comparative law provides an invaluable tool for legislators when attempting to formulate a legal response to a particular problem.[47] Indeed, the English courts are now beginning to look beyond the common law to find solutions to new problems.[48]

Such an approach is adopted in Part IV. For example, when considering means of easing the burden of proof on causation, the solution adopted under the German Environmental Liability Act(ELA) 1991 (*UmweltHG*) is examined. As regards the issue of affording standing to environmental pressure groups to pursue actions in tort, developments in the Netherlands are investigated.

Part IV draws together the themes which emerge in the preceding chapters. Means of increasing the role of tort are considered in the light of the philosophical perspectives set out in Chapter 4 and the objectives of the EU identified in Chapter 5.

[E]   The Outer Limits of Tort

Since the first edition of this book was published we have seen attempts to use tort as a means of providing redress in respect of some of the greatest environmental problems of our age. Notable examples included the Deepwater Horizon disaster and the on-going saga of oil pollution in the Niger Delta region and the difficulties of holding global corporations to account. At the time of writing cases are afoot, largely in the US courts, which are endeavouring to use tort as a means of tackling the greatest and most extreme environmental problem ever to face humanity, that of climate change. This is a far cry from the localized disputes in which the key elements of tort were forged, such as malodorous emissions from pigsties and fumes from smelters. A recurrent theme addressed in the book concerns the extent to which tort provides a viable means of dealing with the consequences of such large scale issues. Aside from the practical difficulties of pursuing these actions, it must be asked whether there is a rational basis for apportioning such liabilities according to tort based principles.

[F]   Concluding Remarks

Part V consolidates the issues and ideas developed above and draws conclusions regarding whether it is possible to devise a workable model of tort for use as a means of environmental protection. The chapter closes with consideration of the wider implications of a civil liability regime, namely, the extent to which it may serve to promote the idea of the environment as a 'public good' capable of protection through the institutions of private law.

---

47.   Zweigert & Kötz, 15–17.
48.   For example in *Hunter v. Canary Wharf Ltd.* [1997] W.L.R. 684, one of the issues which fell to be determined concerned whether an interference with television reception was a sufficiently serious inconvenience to constitute a nuisance. Lord Goff, at p. 690, referred to a German decision (*G. v. City of Hamburg*, Oct. 21, 1983; Decisions of the Federal Supreme Court in Civil Matters, vol. 88, 344) in which such an interference was deemed actionable.

§1.05   CONCLUSION

The subject of civil liability for environmental damage continues to pose fascinating, albeit extremely complex problems. The subject raises a multitude of issues and several seemingly disparate areas of law. From the above it will be apparent that these include the philosophy of law, economics of law, property law, insurance law, public law, comparative law, EU and international law. To some extent this has led to the compartmentalization of the debate and has, perhaps, made it difficult to 'see the wood for the trees'. The aim of this book has been to draw these disparate areas together and to ascertain how they might interrelate so as to provide a solid foundation for an environmental application of tort. Much of the first edition focused on the EU proposals of the late 1980s and early 1990s. Although these initiatives were not pursued, the role of tort in an environmental context continues to excite much comment and debate, especially in the light of events such Deepwater Horizon and attempts to bring major emitters of greenhouse gases before the courts. By developing the themes set out in the first edition in the light of such developments, it is hoped that the second edition will continue to make a valuable contribution to this on-going debate.

Part II: Traditional Tort Based Remedies and Environmental Protection: A Common Law Perspective

CHAPTER 2

Conventional Tort Based Approaches to Environmental Harm

---

§2.01 INTRODUCTION

The purpose of this chapter is to consider the traditional role of tort in an environmental context. As noted in the introduction, this topic shall be considered by reference to Common Law jurisdictions, principally in the UK and US. Common law systems provide useful case studies for highlighting the main issues associated with the use of tort in an environmental context. This is because the case law is inextricably linked with changing social and economic conditions. For example, in the Industrial Revolution there was an increased societal and economic pressure for land to be used for industrial as opposed to agricultural purposes. The common law courts were not impervious to such pressures and had to adapt tort rules in a manner which would reach a compromise between competing land uses. Indeed, the problem of land use conflict is at the heart of this debate regarding the role of tort in an environmental context. The manner in which common law tort rules have evolved in response to these issues clearly illuminates the main issues which must be addressed by any specialist environmental liability regime of the nature discussed in subsequent chapters. The chapter also considers the tort of breach of statutory duty. This is not a common law based tort as it is created by statute rather than the courts; however, it is significant in that it assimilates tortious remedies with public law remedies which could include administrative or civil penalties. As will be seen in subsequent chapters the merits, or otherwise, of assimilating private and public remedies in this manner is an important theme.

To this end the chapter identifies the main torts which are relevant in an environmental context with a view to ascertaining in what circumstances a claimant may establish a prima facie cause of action. Procedural difficulties in bringing such claims are dealt with in the next chapter.

Save for comparatively recent torts, such as breach of statutory duty, English common law derives from the medieval *forms of action*.[49] These were early procedures which could be invoked by a plaintiff in order to restore some right of which he had been wrongfully disseised. Each procedure was instigated by a different writ according to the nature of dispute. Use of an incorrect procedure would prove fatal to a claim; the common law emerged as the substantives rules for determining which writ should be used.[50] The forms of action have long since been dissolved,[51] however, to some extent, the common law remains moulded in their image like a 'petrified forest'.[52] The most obvious legacy of the forms of action is that direct incursions of tangible matter are actionable under trespass whereas indirect incursions by intangible phenomena, such as noise or fumes, are actionable under nuisance. The resulting compartmentalized nature of tort remains in other common law jurisdictions although, as we shall see, the distinctions have been eroded in the US to a certain extent.

§2.02   TRESPASS TO LAND

[A]   Type of Harm

Trespass has its origins in a *form of action* designed to provide redress for forcible and direct incursions upon a person's property, namely, the writ of trespass *vi et armis* (with force and arms).[53] Originally, the writ also encompassed aggravating incidents which were often associated with a trespass to land, namely, assaults on the person and asportation of chattels. During the course of the thirteenth century these ancillary incidents evolved into distinct heads of trespass which became actionable, in their own right, irrespective of whether they had been associated with a trespass to land.[54]

Such incursions were treated seriously by the courts due to their inflammatory nature. The need to establish force was eventually dispensed with,[55] however, it is still necessary to show that an entry upon land was direct in order to found an action in

---

49. See Frederick William Maitland, *The Forms of Action at Common Law: A Course of Lectures*, (A.H. Chaytor and W.J. Whittaker (eds.), CUP 1936).
50. 'So great is the ascendancy of the law of actions in the infancy of the courts of justice, that substantive law has at first the look of being gradually secreted in the interstices of procedure': H.J.S Maine, *Early Law and Custom*, 389 (John Murray 1883).
51. The Common Law Procedure Act 1852, superseded by the Judicature Act 1872, replaced the old writs with a single writ which is applicable in all circumstances.
52. Bob Hepple and Glanville L. Williams, *Foundations of the Law of Tort*, 33 (Butterworths 1976).
53. See C.H.S. Fifoot, *History and Sources of the Common Law: Tort and Contract*, Ch. 3 (Stevens and Sons 1949).
54. In *Lombe v. Clopton* (1276) S.S. vol. 55, 30, Lombe successfully brought a writ in trespass against five defendants who seriously assaulted him at the fair of St. Ives although the assault was not carried out in connection with any trespass to land.
55. In two anonymous cases reported in 32 and 33 Ed. 1 (R.S.) 258–259 Chief Justice Bereford declared that the words *vi et armis* were superfluous and mere formalities. In the first case the jury had originally found in favour of the defendants on the grounds that although they had taken and imprisoned the plaintiff, they had not beaten or wounded him. In the second case the jury found that although the defendants had entered upon the plaintiff's land and chopped down trees, they had not done so with force and arms. See Fifoot, ch. 3.

trespass. This denotes a physical incursion be it in person,[56] by wandering animals,[57] or the placing of some object on land.[58] It is also necessary to show that the incursion was the inevitable result of the defendant's actions whether such actions constitute an immediate and deliberate entry, or, the setting in motion of a chain of events which must inevitably lead to an unauthorized entry upon the claimant's property. Thus, a strong and direct causal link must be established between the claimant's actions and the trespass. It is this requirement which limits the use of trespass in an environmental context. Many forms of pollution lack a substantial physical presence and take the form of fumes, smoke, heat or noise. In addition such forms of pollution are subject to the effect of wind and currents; therefore, any intrusion upon neighbouring property cannot be said to be the inevitable consequence of the defendant's conduct. These limitations can be demonstrated by reference to the few cases in the area.

In *Jones v. Llanrwst Urban District Council*,[59] the defendants were responsible for a sewerage outfall which discharged raw sewage into a stream which flowed past fields owned by the plaintiff. This resulted in the accumulation of faecal matter on the banks of the stream abutting the fields. It was held that the plaintiff could sustain an action in trespass. Parker J. stated:

> I am of the opinion that anyone who turns faecal matter or allows faecal matter collected by him or under his control to escape into a river in such a manner or under such conditions that it is carried, whether by current or the wind, on to his neighbours land is guilty of a trespass.[60]

A more restrictive interpretation of direct entry was applied by the Court of Appeal in *Southport Corporation v. Esso Petroleum Co. Ltd.*[61] In this case, a small tanker, the *S.S. Inverpool*, had been attempting to negotiate a narrow channel, in heavy seas, on her approach to Preston. Unbeknown to the master and crew, the steering mechanism had failed. At one point the vessel veered sharply off course and grounded across a revetment wall. This placed her in danger of breaking her back and put the lives of the crew in jeopardy. No attempt could be made to reverse the vessel as the propeller had become fouled. The master decided that the only option was to discharge some of the cargo in order to lighten the vessel thereby preventing her from being broken across the wall. The discharged oil was carried by the action of the wind and tides onto foreshore owned by Southport Corporation who claimed in public and private nuisance, trespass and negligence. As regards trespass, Denning L.J. stated that:

> In order to support an action for trespass to land the act done by the defendant must be a physical act done by him directly onto the plaintiff's land.[62]

---

56. See, for example, *Davis v. Lisle* [1939] 3 All E.R. 213.
57. See, for example, *League Against Cruel Sports v. Scott* [1986] Q.B. 240.
58. See, for example, *Holmes v. Wilson* (1839) 10 A. & E. 503.
59. [1908–1910] All E.R. 922.
60. *Ibid.*, 926 E-F.
61. [1954] 2 Q.B. 182.
62. *Ibid.*, 195.

He then went on to state that this distinguished trespass from the old action of *case*[63] where the interference was the consequential result of an activity carried out on the defendant's land. The distinction was set out in the *Prior of Southwark's* case.[64]

Applying this to the facts of the present case, Denning L.J. was of the opinion that the discharge was remote from the foreshore and, had it not been for the action of the wind and tide, the oil may never have come ashore at that location. Thus the pollution was consequential as opposed to the direct result of the master's actions:

> Applying this distinction, I am clearly of opinion that the Southport Corporation cannot here sue in trespass. This discharge of oil was not done directly onto their foreshore, but outside in the estuary. It was carried by the tide on to their land, but that was only consequential, not direct. Trespass, therefore does not lie.[65]

On appeal this approach was approved by the House of Lords.[66] The assertion by Parker J. in *Jones v. Llanwrst Urban District Council* that the action of wind and currents would not break the direct link between the original emission and the trespass was not accepted. Parker J.'s comments were obiter in that the intervention of such factors had not been an issue in this case. The fact that the sewage had been directly discharged into a narrow stream running past the plaintiff's property meant that it was inevitable that some of the solid matter would accumulate on the banks of the stream.

The US courts seem rather less hidebound by these historic distinctions and no longer differentiate between trespass and nuisance to the same extent as UK courts. For example, in *Bradley v. American Smelting & Refining Co.*,[67] the deposit of microscopic particles from a copper smelter was found to constitute a trespass. In the UK it is likely that the courts would have found that the particles lacked sufficient physical presence to amount to a trespass and would be susceptible to the effect air currents. Very often, the same contamination may give rise to an action in both trespass and nuisance. As Kitchens and Stevens explain, in relation to the case of *Hoffman v. Atlantic Gas Light Co.*:[68]

> the ongoing spread of hydrocarbon contamination from a broken petroleum pipeline is both a continuing nuisance, because of its ongoing interference with the use of land, and a continuing trespass because of the continuing invasion of land.[69]

---

63. The *form of action* from which negligence derives; this is explained in more detail below.
64. (1498) Y.B. 13 Hen. 7, f. 26, pl. 4. In this case the defendant was a glover and had dug a lime pit for the purpose of preserving calf skins. The pit polluted a nearby stream which led to the pollution of the plaintiff's property. It was held that if the lime pit had been dug in the plaintiff's soil, trespass would be the appropriate form of action. If, however, the pit had been dug on the defendant's land, case would have been the appropriate form of action.
65. [1954] 2 Q.B. 182, 196.
66. *Esso Petroleum Co. Ltd. v. Southport Corporation Ltd.* [1956] A.C. 218, 242: 'Certainly I do not regard such decisions as *Jones v. Llanwrst* and *Smith v. Great Western Railway Co.* as having any real bearing on the circumstances of this case in which the oil was jettisoned at sea, committed to the action of wind and wave, with no certainty, so far as appears, how, when or under what conditions it might come to shore.' per Lord Radcliffe.
67. 709 P.2d 782 (Wash. 1985).
68. 426 S.E.2d 387 (Ga. App. 1992).
69. W.H. Kitchens & M.P. Stevens, *Environmental Toxic Torts: An Overview of Developments In American Law*, Env. Liability 45, 48 (1996).

[B]   Trespass and Fault

Trespass to chattels and trespass to the person were assimilated with negligence[70] as they overlapped in most areas where they were applicable;[71] thus it is necessary to establish fault on the part of the defendant in respect of trespass claims for personal injuries[72] and damage to personal property.[73] Liability for trespass to land remains strict in that the purpose of the tort is to protect ones right to exclusive possession.[74] However, liability cannot be described as absolute[75] since a person will have a defence if the incursion was involuntary[76] or if he acted out of necessity.[77]

[C]   The Defence of Necessity

Necessity may provide a complete defence if the defendant can show that the trespass was necessary in order to prevent some greater harm. Thus, it is at least conceivable for a polluter to argue that the emission of a polluting substance was necessary because it was the lesser of two evils. There was some obiter consideration of this issue in the Court of Appeal decision in *Southport Corporation v. Esso Petroleum*.[78] For the reasons outlined above it was held that trespass was inapplicable in this case. Nevertheless, it was noted that, even if it had been possible to bring an action in trespass, a defence of necessity would have been available on the grounds that discharging the oil prevented the ship from breaking her back and jeopardizing the lives of the crew.[79] However, it was also noted that any suggestion of negligence on the part of the defendant would preclude the defence from operating.[80]

One must always bear in mind that the property torts can operate so as to protect the interests of the alleged polluter rather than the victims of pollution. It is interesting to note that in at least one notable case the boot has been on the other foot in that environmental protestors have sought to justify incursions onto an alleged polluter's land on the basis of necessity. However, the defence can be difficult to apply in such circumstances in that it is designed to deal with immediate threats to life and limb. Many environmental risks are long term and diffuse in nature and there may be

---

70. The essence of negligence is discussed below.
71. A particularly pronounced overlap occurred in cases involving accidents on the highway and collisions at sea. At one time the courts had to draw fine distinctions between acts which were wilful and direct and acts which were unintentional. The former sounded in trespass, whereas, the latter sounded in *Case* (or later negligence). See M.J. Prichard, *Trespass, Case and The Rule in Williams v. Holland*, CLJ 234 (1964).
72. *Stanley v. Powell* [1891] 1 Q.B. 86.
73. *N.C.B. v. Evans* [1951] 2 All E.R. 310.
74. Thus in *League Against Cruel Sports v. Scott* [1986] 1 Q.B. 240 the plaintiffs obtained a declaration that the straying of hounds, taking part in a stag hunt, into sanctuaries which they operated constituted a trespass and an injunction to prevent future incursions.
75. See P.H. Winfield, *The Myth of Absolute Liability*, 42 L.Q. Rev. 37 (1926).
76. *Smith v. Stone* (1647) Style 65.
77. *Handcock v. Baker* (1800) 2 Bos & P 260.
78. *Esso Petroleum v. Southport Corporation* [1954] 2 QB 182.
79. *Ibid.*, at 194 per Singleton LJ
80. *Ibid.*, at 197–198 per Denning LJ.

scientific disagreement regarding the nature of the threat. Thus in *Monsanto v. Tilley*,[81] in which demonstrators opposed to Genetically Modified (GM) crops ripped up plants at a trial site, the defence failed on the basis that there was no immediate risk to life or limb. Furthermore, the ripping up of a few plants did not show a concerted effort to remove a real and immediate threat; rather, it was designed to attract publicity and to invite prosecution leading to 'potential martyrdom' of the protestors.[82] In any case, it was held that the courtroom was not the proper place to settle scientific debates regarding the environmental and health effects of the technology.[83] By way of contrast, juries in criminal trials have adopted a far more flexible approach to the issue of necessity. In a case which received much media publicity, climate change protestors were acquitted of causing criminal damage during the course of a protest at the Kingsnorth coal-fired power station in Kent.[84]

§2.03   NUISANCE

[A]   Type of Harm

[1]   Protection of Rights in Land

Nuisance derives from a *form of action* known as the *assize of nuisance* and was designed to restore ancillary rights, associated with land ownership, without which the freehold would be sterile.[85] As Professor Newark explained in his seminal article, this encompassed interference with rights derived from agreements (*ab homine*), such as easements and profits, and natural rights which were conferred by law (*a jure*).[86] The latter category included the right to wholesome air and unpolluted water. The origins of these rights are lost in custom and appear to have been recognized in the earliest days of common law. In *Aldred's Case*, Wray C.J. equated the right to wholesome air with the Biblical right to light.[87] Interference with these rights was actionable on the grounds that it impaired the ability of the land holder to use his property in the ordinary way. This constituted a total or partial disseisin of a right associated with land-holding. In Stephen's Commentaries it was stated:

> If a person keeps his hogs or other noisome animals so near the house of another, previously built and inhabited, that the stench of them incommodes him, and

---

81. [2000] Env LR 313.
82. *Ibid.*, [25] (Stuart-Smith LJ).
83. *Ibid.*, [26] (Stuart-Smith LJ).
84. For an account of how the case was won by the defence see M Wolkind *How we Won Acquittal of Kingsnorth Six*, Guardian (London May 31, 2009), http://www.guardian.co.uk/environment/cif-green/2009/may/31/kingsnorth-defence-lawyer (accessed Mar. 4, 2010).
85. See Fifoot (n. 53), ch. 1.
86. F.H. Newark, *The Boundaries of Nuisance*, 65 L.Q. Rev. 480, 482 (1949).
87. (1611) 9 Coke Rep. f. 57b. Wray C.J. quoted Solomom in Ecclesiast. 11.7, '*Dulce lumen est et delectable oculis videre solem* ... ' See Fifoot (n. 53) 101.

makes the air unwholesome, this is a nuisance, as it tends to deprive him of the use and benefit of his house.[88]

In modern parlance this would be termed an interference with the right to use and enjoyment of one's property although the meaning is essentially the same. *Forms of action* served to restore such rights to the plaintiff; these rights became generic and were eventually hardened into the *sic utere tuo ut alienum non laedas* maxim (so use your property as not to injure your neighbour's). The types of land use amounting to rights, which may be protected from interference, do not comprise a closed category and may be added to in accordance with changing social conditions and expectations.[89]

Nuisance actions resulting from pollution considerably pre-date the onset of the industrial revolution. For example, actions were brought in respect of corruption of the wholesome air resulting from the emissions of lime kilns,[90] dye houses,[91] tallow furnaces,[92] and smiths' forges.[93] As regards the torts to land, nuisance has continued to be more widely used than trespass, in this context, in that most forms of pollution consist of vapours, gases, heat, particles or diffuse chemicals. These elements lack the physical presence needed for a trespass.

It is also important to remember that the essence of private nuisance is that the activity must emanate from a neighbouring parcel of land. From its earliest origins the purpose of nuisance has been to settle disputes between neighbours. This point was reiterated in the case of *Southport Corporation v. Esso Petroleum* in which Denning L.J. stated that no action could be founded in private nuisance because the discharge of oil resulted from the use of a ship at sea and not neighbouring land.[94]

[2]   Personal Injuries

Much pollution can give rise to adverse health effects in addition to environmental damage. The issue of whether private nuisance can be used to found a claim in respect of damage to health has given rise to much academic and judicial debate. Newark

---

88.   4th ed., vol. 3, 491, 492.
89.   For example, in *Bridlington Relay Ltd v. Yorkshire Electricity Board* [1965] Ch. 436, Buckley J. did not consider that the ability to receive television signals was of sufficient importance to justify an action in nuisance in respect of any activity which interfered with reception. However, in *Hunter v. Canary Wharf Ltd* [1997] 2 W.L.R. 684, 688F-G, Lord Goff stated that, for many people, television now 'transcends the function of mere entertainment' and that reception is now of sufficient importance to warrant protection at common law.
90.   *Aldred's Case* (n. 87).
91.   *Jones v. Powell* (1629) Hutton, 136, Palmer, 539.
92.   *Morley v. Pragnell* (1638) Cro. Car. 510.
93.   *Bradley v. Gill* (1688) 1Lutw. 69.
94.   [1954] 2 Q.B. 182, 196. Devlin J., had stated, obiter, that it was not necessary to show that the pollution stemmed from land owned or occupied by the defendant. Although Lord Denning clearly rejected this view, it has been followed in Canada. See, for example, *Bridges Bros. Ltd. v. Forest Protection* (1976) 72 D.L.R. (3d) 335., which concerned crop damage caused by drifting insecticide sprayed by an aircraft, ' ... it matters not whether there is any relationship between an aircraft which a nuisance emanates from and the owner of the land beneath the air space where the nuisance originates. A nuisance is created by the discharge of a deleterious substance from an aircraft if that substance is wrongfully caused or allowed to escape on to the land of another.'

asserted that damage to health, in effect a claim for personal injuries, has no place in private nuisance in that such loss cannot be regarded as an interference with property rights. In fact he went so far as to declare that it was a 'heresy' to assert that private nuisance was a suitable vehicle for pursuing personal injuries claims.[95] Newark's thesis has been cited with approval by the House of Lords on a number of occasions including the case of *Hunter v. Canary Wharf*[96] concerning various nuisances arising from the redevelopment of the London Docklands area in the late 1980s and early 1990s. Palmer[97] makes a compelling argument that Newark's thesis is historically and doctrinally flawed. In fact, protection of one's health was historically regarded as an integral aspect of land ownership and indivisible from lesser harms such as minor inconveniences or annoyances. In fact, the right to be protected from certain health threats went to the very core of nuisance in its early development due to the belief that fumes, smoke and smells brought with them ill health:

> What may be lost on a modern audience is that at this time the mere smell of fumes was considered an agent of harm. It was believed that unwholesome or corrupted air, when breathed in, was the source of ill-health. This was an age of miasma theory, in which odours were linked causally with disease. Placing these cases on the context of miasma theory strengthens the interpretation of case law as incorporating, from its original conception, remedies for ill-health.[98]

Nevertheless, there are still strong policy reasons for excluding personal injuries from the scope of private nuisance. Could it be right, for example, that a householder could rely on the stricter standard of liability offered by nuisance when a lodger in the same premises would have to establish negligence in respect of an identical harm?[99] These are jurisprudential questions which one day will have to be answered by the new Supreme Court as successor to the House of Lords. However, Palmer cautions against placing further restrictions on the scope of private nuisance purely as a consequence of the dominance of negligence.[100] Negligence is rather like a tide which rushes in to fill any voids left by damning off nuisance, trespass or other torts; yet the need to establish fault in the sense demanded by negligence may not always be desirable (see the example of maritime oil pollution referred to below). In subsequent chapters it will be argued that the stricter standards of liability offered by torts such as nuisance are essential in the interests of environmental protection. In other words, personal injuries arising from such harms may have special features which justify a stricter standard of liability than that offered by negligence. These issues are discussed at more length in Chapter 4 on theoretical perspectives and the rationale for strict liability.

---

95. Newark (n. 86), 489.
96. [1997] A.C. 655. As regards personal injuries and nuisance Lord Goff cites Newark extensively at 687–692.
97. R.C. Palmer, *Personal Injury in Private Nuisance: the Historical Truth about Actionability of 'Bodily Security'*, 21 Envtl. L. Mgt. 302 (2009).
98. *Ibid.*, 307–308.
99. [1997] A.C. 655; see 707H–708A (Lord Hoffmann).
100. Palmer (n. 97), 310–311.

[3]   Duration of Harm

Private nuisance is typically associated with a state of affairs which has existed over a period of time; whether the harm is on-going or occurred in the past. However, the courts have never determined how long a state of affairs should endure before it sounds in nuisance. In *Colour Quest Ltd v. Total Downstream UK Plc*[101] it was held that an explosion at a petroleum storage depot was actionable in private nuisance. This is counterintuitive in that an explosion is by its very nature a sudden event, although the consequences may be longstanding. Furthermore, it erodes the distinction between nuisance and strict liability under *Rylands v. Fletcher*; this aspect of the case is dealt with more fully below in the context of *Rylands* liability.

[4]   The Need for a Physical Dimension to the Harm

Despite these limitations and areas of uncertainty regarding scope, nuisance has advantages over negligence in that, as a property tort, damages can be recovered in respect of diminution in the market value of property irrespective of whether this stems from perceptible damage. Thus, as Dobbs notes in relation to the US common law position in this issue:

> A plume of contamination deep under the plaintiff's land is an invasion, and if permanent and serious enough, can count as a nuisance, even though the landowner cannot directly perceive it and is harmed only because the value of her land is reduced by its presence.[102]

Of course, not all activities, which have an environmental impact, are caused by an actual invasion of property. However, in the absence of this tangible element there is a possibility that the harm will be regarded as merely aesthetic. Historically, the common law has proved reluctant to provide a remedy in respect of the amenity value of landscapes and outlooks due to the subjective nature of the harm. In Aldred's case Wray CJ held:

> for prospect, which is a matter only of delight, and not of necessity, no action lies for stopping thereof and yet it is a great commendation of a house if it has a long and large prospect, *unde dicitur, laudaturque domus longos qui prospicit agros*. But the law does not give an action for such things of delight.[103]

In more recent times the problem of aesthetic harms has been brought to the fore in a number of US cases involving the proliferation of huge onshore wind farms.[104] This is very much a twenty-first century environmental problem. Wind farms are a response to climate change and provide a clean alternative to the burning of fossil fuels. Yet their

---

101. [2009] EWHC 540 (Comm); [2009] 2 Lloyd's Rep. 1.
102. Dan B. Dobbs, *The Law of Torts*, 1330 (West 2001).
103. *Aldred's Case*, (n. 87).
104. See S.H. Butler, *Headwinds to a clean energy future: Nuisance Suits Against Wind Energy Projects in the United States*, 97(5) CLR 1337 (2009); K. Culley, *Has Texas Nuisance Law Been Blown Away by the Demand for Wind Power?*, 61 Baylor L. Rev. 943 (2009).

relentless march across the landscape may still cause environmental problems, albeit of a very different type. Although they do not belch smoke and fumes wind farms are undoubtedly an invasive addition to the landscape and disrupt the lives of residents. However, in *Rankin v. FPL Energy LLC*[105] the claimant's concerns were largely dismissed as aesthetic and thus in-actionable. Nevertheless, from the claimant's point of view the harm was far from imagined in that the wind farm seriously reduced the value of her property. This raises the issue of economic loss which shall be discussed in due course.

There can be a fine line between matters of pure amenity or aesthetic value and actual interference with the use and enjoyment of property. As regards the afore-mentioned example of wind farms, claimants now typically attempt to find a tangible element to the harm such as noise, vibration or the strobe effect caused by the shadows of the rotating blades at dawn and dusk (although such claims were dismissed in *Rankin* as insignificant or unsubstantiated). Perhaps cases involving light, of which the strobe effect is an example, are at the fringes of tangibility. Glare caused by the sun reflected off a glass building has been found to be actionable[106] and there is no doubt that glare from overly bright lights or industrial processes sounds in nuisance.[107] The latter incommodes neighbours in the use and enjoyment of their property in a tangible manner.

[5]   Nuisance Verses Negligence: The Scope of Harm

Overall, in terms of the type of harm covered, it can be argued that nuisance has certain major advantages over negligence in that it can be used in respect of a wide range of environmental problems aside from those which cause immediate and tangible physi-cal damage. However, it is limited by the fact that it can only be invoked by those with a sufficient interest in property. One's right to the undisturbed use and enjoyment of property is thereby generally limited to the immediate vicinity.

[B]   The Locality Doctrine

Prior to the Industrial Revolution, courts were clearly of the opinion that any adverse interference with natural rights would give rise to an action in nuisance; this approach was characterized by the maxim *sic utere tuo ut alienum non laedas*, referred to above. After the industrial revolution, the courts were faced with the issue of whether it was proper to continue asserting natural rights in such an uncompromising manner.[108]

The Industrial Revolution resulted in new challenges for the common law in that the creation of large industrial towns created a conflict between industrial and conservatory land uses. The common law judges were undoubtedly aware of the

---

105. LLC, 266 S.W.3d 506, 512 (Tex. App. 2008).
106. *Bank of New Zealand v. Greenwood* [1984] 1 N.Z.L.R. 525.
107. *Murdoch v. Glacier Metal Ltd* [1998] Env. L.R. 732.
108. See J.P.S. Mclaren, *Nuisance Law and the Industrial Revolution: Some Lessons from Social History*, 3(2) O. J. Leg. Stud. 155, 169–190 (1983).

economic arguments in favour of allowing industrial at the expense of conservatory uses of land. The courts did not operate in a vacuum and were aware that rigidly asserting natural rights in the face of large scale developments would have ramifications for the new industrial economy. As McLaren states:

> An appreciation of political and social philosophy and economics was part of the 'intellectual baggage' of educated people of that age, including the judges.[109]

In *St. Helens Smelting v. Tipping*[110] the House of Lords set about arriving at a solution which would facilitate the economic benefits of industrialization yet limit externalities to acceptable levels. The nuisance in this case was caused by the defendant's copper smelting plant, fumes from which killed off trees in the plaintiff's orchard. It was held that for an activity to result in an actionable nuisance, it must *visibly* diminish the value of the property and the use and enjoyment of it.[111] In ascertaining whether the utility of the property had been visibly diminished, regard must be had to all the circumstances of the case including the nature of the locality and its utility to the community as a whole.[112] This shows that it was recognized that the character of large areas of land had been changed forever with the result that there was no alternative but to re-define natural rights in accordance with changing circumstances. However, the traditional approach was not entirely abandoned; Lord Westbury added an important proviso to the effect that tangible damage could never be reasonable and would continue to be actionable per se.[113] This approach has also been adopted in the United States where the character of the neighbourhood test has been preserved as an aspect of determining liability in nuisance. Thus:

> When the nuisance is invasive and seriously affects the physical integrity of the land itself, as where toxic chemicals percolate into the groundwater, it may be a nuisance as a matter of law and without regard to the neighbourhood's character.[114]

In the UK the courts have continued to adhere to the locality doctrine. In *Halsey v. Esso Petroleum Ltd*,[115] a claim in nuisance was brought in respect of noise, fumes and damage to cars and laundry by acid smuts from an oil storage and distribution depot in Fulham, London. The non-tangible harms, namely fumes and noise, were regarded as excessive and hence actionable notwithstanding the mixed residential and industrial character of the neighbourhood. The tangible damage to laundry and cars was clearly actionable per se.

The environmental implications of the locality doctrine are obvious in that it operates as a crude means of zoning areas for industrial or other types of invasive

---

109. *Ibid.*, 192.
110. (1865) 11 H.L.C. 642.
111. *Ibid.*, at 650–653.
112. *Ibid.*
113. *Ibid.*, 651–652 (Lord Westbury).
114. Dobbs (n. 102).
115. [1961] 1 W.L.R. 683.

development. Thus in *Murdoch v. Glacier Metal Company Ltd*,[116] concerning noise and glare from a factory, it was held that the alleged nuisances could not be regarded as significant given that noise levels were already high due to the proximity of a major road and other commercial activity.

It is now well established that a planning consent can instantly alter the character of the neighbourhood.[117] The assertion that the reasonableness of activities could be judged by reference to 'the aspirations of planners'[118] rather than the 'situation on the ground'[119] represented a radical departure from previous authority[120] and was met with a degree of consternation in the academic literature.[121] These concerns were allayed somewhat by refinements in the case law which established that only strategic planning decisions would have such an effect.[122] In *Watson v. Croft Promo-Sport Ltd*[123] a planning consent allowing the use of a disused aerodrome for motor racing was found not to fall into this 'strategic' category. Thus local residents were entitled to pursue their claim in respect of noise nuisance. The significance of these cases, in terms of the relationship between private law and regulation, will be examined in Chapter 4 in the context of the role of tort.

The major problem with the locality doctrine is that it has been interpreted as drawing a rigid distinction between tangible and intangible harms. The harshness of this distinction is exposed by the facts of *Allen v. Gulf Oil Refining Ltd* in which an oil refinery was built overshadowing the village of Waterston near Milford-Haven in Pemrokeshire, Wales. The level of discomfort endured by the residents of Waterston was extremely high and the fumes, noise and smoke caused by the refinery severely interfered with the use and enjoyment of their properties. Yet, as Cumming-Bruce LJ observed *obiter* in the Court of Appeal judgment,[124] the harms failed to cross the material damage threshold. Thus, the harms would have to be judged by reference to the locality of the neighbourhood which, his Lordship argued, had been rendered industrial by the planning powers used to authorize the plant. In this respect the locality doctrine trivializes harms which are far from trivial.[125] Simpson has questioned whether Lord Westbury intended to draw a rigid distinction between physical and non-physical loss when he used the terms 'material harm' and 'sensible personal discomfort'. An alternative explanation is that his Lordship was concerned to draw a

---

116. [1998] Env. L.R. 732.
117. *Gillingham Borough Council v. Medway (Chatam) Dock Co Ltd* [1992] 3 All E.R. 923.
118. A. Waite, *The Gillingham Case: The Abolition of Nuisance by Planning Controls?*, 4 Land Mgt. Envtl. L. Rev. 119 (1992).
119. *Ibid*. See also T. Jewell and J. Steele, *Nuisance and Planning*, 56 The Modern L. Rev. 568 (1993).
120. *R. v. Exeter City Council ex parte J.L. Thomas & Co Ltd* [1990] 1 All E.R. 413.
121. *Ibid*.
122. *Wheeler v. JJ Saunders Ltd* [1996] Ch 19 (CA); *Hunter v. Canary Wharf* [1997] A.C. 655, Lord Cooke at 722F-G.
123. [2009] EWCA Civ 15; [2009] 3 All E.R. 249.
124. [1980] QB 156 (CA), 171F–172F.
125. See Noga Morag-Levine, *Chasing the Wind: Regulating Air Pollution in the Common Law State*, 55–56 (Princeton 2003), who argues that the locality doctrine was a judicial sleight of hand which enabled the illusion of absolute liability to be maintained by not regarding many nuisance type harms as actionable.

distinction between serious harm and trifling inconveniences.[126] The harms suffered by the residents of Waterston were certainly not trivial. However, there is authority for the proposition that, even where the character of the neighbourhood has been altered by industrial development, it does not render all intangible harm trivial and hence in actionable. In *Halsey v. Esso Petroleum*, Veale J. held that the 'nauseating' and 'pungent' oily smell and excessive night time noise was clearly unacceptable notwith-standing the mixed residential and industrial character of the neighbourhood. As Cozens- Hardy LJ stated in *Rushmer v. Polsue & Alfieri, Ltd*:

> It does not follow that because I live, say, in the manufacturing part of Sheffield I cannot complain if a steam-hammer is introduced next door, and so worked as to render sleep at night almost impossible.[127]

A more recent example of a technology which gives rise to significant difficulties regarding the boundaries of 'material damage' and 'sensible personal discomfort' concerns Genetically Modified Organisms (GMOs). The growing of Genetically Modified (GM) crops has been a source of conflict with conventional or organic farmers, who fear cross-pollination and the undermining of GM free status,[128] although no common law nuisance action has yet to reach a conclusive outcome. It is at least arguable that the mere presence of GM material in an organic field could constitute 'material damage'. However, if the courts were to find that limited cross-pollination did not cross the material damage threshold[129] then the issue would have to be judged according to the character of the neighbourhood. In a mixed agricultural area it might be difficult to argue that a GM crop test site was out of keeping with the predominant land use.[130]

It is also important to note that the mere presence of alien matter in the land does not necessarily constitute material damage. The substance must interfere in some way with the use of that property. This is clearly demonstrated by the recent Canadian case of *Smith v. Inco Ltd*[131] concerning nickel deposits in the soil stemming from the defendant's smelter. Residents sought damages on the basis that the presence of the nickel deposits in the soil had had a deleterious effect on the market value of their properties. The first point to note is that the residents' claims specified material damage

---

126. A.W.B. Simpson, *Victorian Judges and the Problem of Social Cost: Tipping v. St Helen's Smelting Company (1865)* in *Leading Cases in the Common Law*, 190 (Clarendon Press 1995): "'Material" here is quite ambiguous between meaning either "physical", or alternatively "non-trivial"'.
127. [1906] 1 Ch. 234, 250.
128. This situation was the subject of a judicial review application in *R. v. Secretary of the State for the Environment, ex parte Watson* [1999] Env L.R. 310 in which an organic farmer challenged the Secretary of State's decision to aurthorize a GM crop field trial.
129. Campbell argues that in the *Watson* case (above), the Court of Appeal did not appear to fully appreciate that even a very limited degree of cross-pollination between GM and non-GM crops could be harmful due to the rate at which 'contaminated' plants could reproduce. In the respect the Court was wrong to downplay the magnitude of the potential harm by accepting evidence to the effect that only one in 40,000 sweet corn kernels would be pollinated by GM pollen. See D. Campbell, *Of Coase and Corn: A (Sort of) Defence of Private Nuisance*, 63 The Modern L. Rev. 197, 211 (2000).
130. For a fuller account of these issues see C.P. Rodgers, *Liability for the release of GMOs into the environment: exploring the boundaries of nuisance*, 62(2) Cambridge L.J. 371 (2003).
131. (2011) ONCA 628.

rather than interference with the use and enjoyment of property. It is likely that this was an attempt to prevent the court from indulging in a balance of convenience test of the type demanded by the locality doctrine. However, the Court of Appeal for Ontario accepted scientific evidence to the effect that there was no health risk associated with the deposits and no impact on plants growing in the soil. As a result the court concluded that there had been no material change in the soil sufficient to constitute material damage:

> In our view, a mere chemical alteration in the content of soil, without more, does not amount to physical harm or damage to the property. For instance, many farmers add fertilizer to their soil each year for the purpose of changing, and enhancing, the chemical composition of the soil. To constitute physical harm or damage, a change in the chemical composition must be shown to have had some detrimental effect on the land itself or rights associated with the use of the land.[132]

This raises the interesting possibility that it is the nature of the claimant's interest in his property which may determine whether or not damage is material. For example, to return to the GMO example, it is clear that an organic farmer may suffer material damage as a result of GM contamination because a fundamental characteristic of his crops, their GM free status, is lost. Crops grown by an conventional farmer would not be damaged in the same way, unless he was still reliant upon GM free status for marketing purposes.

[C]   Nuisance and Fault

One of the most complex issues in nuisance concerns the extent to which it is necessary to establish culpability on the part of the defendant. At one time there was no doubt that private nuisance was of strict liability in that it was concerned with the protection of an interest in land, namely, the right to the undisturbed use and enjoyment of one's property. The matter is now less certain;[133] the reasons for this state of affairs were examined by Professor Newark in his well known article on 'the Boundaries of Nuisance'.[134]

Public nuisance was created by analogy with private nuisance in that the blocking of a public highway was seen as analogous to the blocking of an easement across a private tenement. As the matter affected a class of His Majesty's subjects the act was criminalized, nevertheless, it was accepted that private and public nuisance were unrelated. However, in an anonymous decision of 1535[135] Baldwin C.J. linked the

---

132. *Ibid.*, [55].
133. The uncertainty which emerged is demonstrated by two cases which were decided at a similar time. In *Hole v. Barlow* (1858) 4 CB (NS) 334; 140 ER 1113, Willes J. appeared to equate nuisance with negligence where he stated that, apart from consideration of nature of the locality, it was legitimate to ask whether the plant had been *operated* in a reasonable manner. However in *Stockport Waterworks v. Potter* (1861) 7 H & N 160; 158 ER 433, Martin B. doubted whether reasonable conduct could have any bearing on liability. See Mclaren (n. 108), at 174–175.
134. Newark (n. 86).
135. *Anon*, Y.B. 27 Hen. 6, Trin. pl. 10.

two, mistakenly according to Professor Newark, by stating that the only reason why a private individual could not bring a private action in respect of a public nuisance was that to do so would result in a 'multitude of claims'. Nevertheless, he went on to state that any individual who suffered individual loss in excess of the general inconvenience suffered by the population as a whole would be able to recover damages by reason of that 'special hurt'. This assertion eventually led to a proliferation of private nuisance claims in respect of loss caused by obstructions on the highway. Consequently, a clear overlap between private nuisance actions (brought in respect of public nuisances) and negligence emerged[136] with the result that the courts introduced the need to establish fault in respect of private nuisance claims brought pursuant to public nuisances.[137] Henceforth, defendants were only expected to guard against nuisances which were reasonably foreseeable.

Despite the assimilation of private and public nuisance in clear cases of overlap, private nuisance (or 'nuisance proper' as Professor Newark termed it) remained untainted by notions of fault based liability in its traditional sphere of operation. This was until the judgment of the Privy Council in the *Wagon Mound (No. 2)*[138] the facts of which are too well known to require repetition here. Lord Reid cited the highways cases in which public nuisance had been assimilated with negligence as authority for the proposition that fault was an established component of nuisance.[139] However, he went on to state that, although nuisance had grown to encompass a wide range of activities, it could not be right to discriminate between different types of nuisance so as to make fault an issue in certain cases but not in others.[140] Lord Reid's reasoning can be criticized on this point in that it is in fact logical to draw such a distinction if one accepts the differing origins of public and private nuisance. Instead, his Lordship attempted to maintain some distinction between nuisance and negligence by stating that fault in nuisance has a broader meaning than the specific and narrower meaning of the tort of negligence.[141] This left the way open for applying a stricter standard of liability in other cases since negligence entails establishing more than foreseeability. Although a risk of a certain type of damage may be foreseeable, in negligence, it is still necessary to show that all reasonable steps were taken to reduce the risk of the damage occurring to acceptable levels. In Lord Reid's formulation of fault in nuisance he stated:

---

136. In more recent times this has given rise to difficult moot points. For, example, the courts have been faced with the issue of whether a poorly parked car should result in an action in nuisance, on the grounds that it is an obstruction, or negligence on the grounds that it has been parked carelessly. See *Ware v. Garston Haulage Co.* [1944] K.B. 30 and *Maitland v. Raisbek* [1944] 1 K.B. 689.

137. See, for example, *Sharp v. Powell* (1872) L.R. 7 C.P. 253, where the defendant had caused water to be deposited on the highway which later froze and formed sheet ice; it was held, 'the defendant could not reasonably have been expected to foresee that the water would accumulate and freeze at the spot where the accident happened.' per Bovill C.J.

138. *Overseas Tankship (U.K.) Ltd. v. The Miller Steamship Co. Pty. (The Wagon Mound) (No.2)* [1967] A.C. 617.

139. *Ibid.*, 637D-E.

140. *Ibid.*, 640B-D.

141. *Ibid.*, 639C-D.

the fault is in failing to abate the nuisance the existence of which the defendant is or ought to be aware as likely to cause damage to his neighbour.[142]

This suggests that, where the harm is foreseeable, liability will automatically follow if the nuisance is not abated. No mention is made of a need to establish that the defendant did not take reasonable steps to abate the nuisance.

The *Wagon Mound (No. 2)* decision is particularly important from an environmental perspective in that the House of Lords chose to apply it in *Cambridge Water v. Eastern Counties Leather*.[143] This is still one of the most important decisions as regards the relationship between common law rights and environmental protection.

The plaintiff water company began abstracting drinking water from a bore-hole at Sawston Mill in 1976. In 1980 the Council of the European Community issued a Directive on water quality (80/778/EEC) which required Member States to ensure that levels of perchloroethene (PCE) were reduced by 1985. As a result, water undertakers were required to commence monitoring for this substance. Cambridge Water discovered that levels of PCE in drinking water abstracted from its bore-hole at Sawston Mill were far in excess of both the guide limit set by the EC and the actual limit set by the department of the Environment. As a result Cambridge Water was unable to continue abstracting water at Sawston Mill and was required to relocate its pumping station at a cost of EUR 1 million. The source of the contamination was traced to a tannery operated by Eastern Counties Leather where PCE had been used in the de-greasing of pelts. Over time, spillages of the substance permeated the porous layers of chalk beneath the works and contaminated the subterranean water source; it was then carried downstream to the plaintiff's bore-hole.

The Court of Appeal did not feel bound by Lord Reid's judgment in the *Wagon Mound* to find that foreseeability was an essential ingredient of nuisance. Mann L.J., citing Lord Wilberforce in *Goldman v. Hargreaves*,[144] emphasized the point that the tort of nuisance is 'uncertain in its boundaries'[145] and that negligence only plays a part in some cases. On basis of the decision in *Ballard v. Tomlinson*,[146] which also concerned contamination of an underground water source, Mann L.J. concluded that the present case was one in which liability was strict.[147]

On appeal to the House of Lords, Lord Goff rejected the claim in nuisance and, contrary to the Court of Appeal, considered that Lord Reid's judgment in the *Wagon Mound* was decisive on the issue of foreseeability in nuisance:

> It is widely accepted that this conclusion, although not essential to the decision of the particular case, has nevertheless settled the law, to the effect that foreseeability of harm is indeed a pre-requisite of the recovery of damages in private nuisance, as in the case of public nuisance.[148]

---

142. *Ibid.*, 639F.
143. [1994] 2 A.C. 264.
144. [1967] 1 A.C. 645, 657.
145. *Ibid.*
146. (1885) 29 Ch. D. 115.
147. [1994] 2 A.C. 264, 275F-G.
148. *Ibid.*, 301C.

In reaching this conclusion the House of Lords was heavily influenced by policy considerations. Lord Goff noted that pools of PCE were still present under Eastern Counties Leather's works and were continuing to cause contamination.[149] Thus, now the hazardous nature of PCE has been established, applying strict liability without any foreseeability requirement would render ECL liable for pollution which was now beyond their control and was caused prior to the identification of PCE as a hazardous substance. This would amount to retroactive liability for 'historic pollution'. It seems that, had his Lordship been unable to find authority for holding that foreseeability is a prerequisite of liability, he would have declined to hold ECL liable on policy grounds. This is confirmed by his Lordship's closing comments on the issue of fault in nuisance:

> I wish to add that the present case may be regarded as one of what is nowadays called historic pollution, in the sense that the relevant occurrence (the seepage of PCE through the floor of ECL's premises) took place before the relevant legislation came into force; and it appears that, under the current philosophy, it is not envisaged that statutory liability should be imposed for historic pollution (see, e.g. the Council of Europe's Draft Convention on Civil Liability for Damage resulting from Activities Dangerous to the environment (Strasbourg 26 January 1993) article 5.1, and paragraph 48 of the Explanatory Report). If so, it would be strange if liability for such pollution were to arise under a principle of common law.[150]

The issue of whether the courts and the legislature are right to exercise such caution regarding the issue of civil liability for historic pollution will be returned to in later chapters.

Nevertheless, Lord Goff emphasized the fact that the standard of liability in nuisance still differs from the standard of liability in negligence:

> It is still the law that the fact that the defendant has taken all reasonable care will not of itself exonerate him from liability, the relevant control mechanism being found in the concept of reasonable user.[151]

This suggests that, once it has been established that it was foreseeable that an activity would give rise to a nuisance, it is no defence to show that all reasonable steps were taken to abate the nuisance. This appears to be the interpretation adopted by the High Court in *Graham and Graham v. Re-Chem International*.[152] The case concerned an allegation by the owners of a dairy farm that their cattle had been poisoned as a result of grazing on land contaminated by emissions containing dioxins and furans stemming from the defendant's hazardous waste incinerator at Roughmute.

Although the decision ultimately turned on the issue of causation[153] the court also had the opportunity to consider the meaning of foreseeability in nuisance in the light of the *Cambridge Water* decision. The defendant argued that, at the time the incinerator was in operation, between 1974 and 1984, it was unknown that such a facility could give rise to the emission of dioxins and furans. It was not until 1985 that a scientific

---

149. *Ibid.*, 306H-307A-B.
150. *Ibid.*, 307C-D.
151. *Ibid.*, 300E-F.
152. [1996] Env. L.R. 158.
153. See Chapter 3.

paper was presented at a conference which demonstrated that the offending chemicals could be produced by a hitherto unknown chemical reaction (referred to as a *de novo* synthesis) which occurs whilst the exhaust gases are cooling in the post combustion zone, after, having passed through the gas cleaning scrubbers. However, Forbes J. found ample scientific evidence to show that, although there had been considerable uncertainty regarding how these compounds were formed, at the material time it was known that such facilities produced dioxins and furans. Thus, given the state of scientific knowledge at the time the incinerator was in operation, the judge was satisfied that:

> [A]t all material times, Re-Chem would have been aware that the operation of a commercial incinerator, such as Roughmute could result in the emission of dioxins and furans in fly ash and flue gases and that some of these compounds were very toxic.[154]

He went on to state that, once it has been established that it was foreseeable that an activity gives rise to a nuisance, it is unnecessary to show that the defendant was aware of precisely how his activity caused the nuisance:

> For the purposes of liability in nuisance in cases such as the present, it does not seem to me that actual knowledge of the precise chemical processes, whereby the toxic compounds in question are created, is a necessary ingredient.[155]

This illustrates how fault in nuisance now differs from fault in negligence. As Forbes J. went on to point out, knowledge of the means by which the activity gave rise to the harm would be relevant in deciding whether there had been any breach of the common law duty of care thereby giving rise to a cause of action in negligence:

> Of course, Re-Chem's knowledge at the relevant time as to how, when and where dioxins and furans might be formed in a waste incinerator during its operation would be clearly material to any determination as to what Re-Chem then knew and understood about the full nature of the chemical processes involved in the activity being carried out on the Roughmute site. In certain circumstances, such a determination might be of considerable importance in deciding whether the emission of such substances constituted a breach of a common law duty of care. However, in my opinion, Re-Chem's state of knowledge as to the fine detail of such matters is irrelevant in deciding whether the activity in question was potentially a nuisance, i.e. a nuisance, subject to proof of foreseeable damage to a neighbouring occupier of land [however] ... such a consideration might have been material in deciding whether a breach of duty had occurred in negligence.[156]

Thus, in negligence, it might have been possible for the defendant to argue that, given the state of scientific knowledge at the material time, there were no reasonable steps which he could have taken in order to prevent the harm. However, even where there is no great mystery regarding how a particular activity might adversely affect neighbouring interests, it seems that the conduct of the defendant may have some bearing on

---

154. [1996] Env. L.R. 158, 167.
155. *Ibid.*, 168.
156. *Ibid.*, at p. 169.

whether the harm was foreseeable. In *Savage v. Fairclough*,[157] the claimant brought an action in nuisance regarding the contamination of his underground spring by nitrate pollution from a pig farm. The Court of Appeal held that, given that the defendant had followed best agricultural practice, it was unforeseeable that the manner in which the farm was operated would lead to the harm in question. This sets the bar too high in terms of foreseeability and brings nuisance perilously close to negligence. It is well known that use of inorganic fertilizers contaminates groundwaters and this has led to specific legislation.[158] The approach adopted by the Court of Appeal exonerated the defendant on the basis of his non-negligent conduct rather than any objective analysis of whether groundwater contamination was foreseeable according to the state of scientific knowledge at the time.

It should also be noted that the problem of historic pollution, which forms part of the context of the *Cambridge Water* decision, is germane to another aspect of fault in private nuisance. In some circumstances a person may find himself liable in respect of a nuisance started by a third party,[159] which could include a predecessor in title, or arising from a natural phenomenon.[160] The claimant must show, however, that the defendant failed to take adequate steps to discontinue, or abate, the nuisance.[161] A clear recent example arises from the High Court decision in *Anthony v. The Coal Authority*.[162] This concerned the spontaneous combustion of a landscaped spoil tip which served the National Coal Board's (NCB) Brynlliw colliery. Spoil tips are one of the enduring legacies of industrialization. Waste material from mining operations was simply dumped on site and often assumed mountainous proportions over many years. The tip in question took spoil from the colliery between 1957 and 1971. Some years later the site was landscaped and conveyed to a group of commoners in 1995. The following year a fire erupted in the heart of the spoil tip which was not brought under control until 2000. Smoke and noxious sulphurous gases escaped to the surface causing considerable discomfort to local residents. On occasion the smoke was so dense that the nearby M4 motorway had to be closed. The expert evidence indicated that the most likely cause of the fire was the spontaneous combustion of volatile waste materials in the spoil.

Actions in private nuisance were commenced against the Coal Authority which manages the remnants of the UK coal industry and is responsible for the assets and liabilities of the now defunct NCB. The defendant argued that the spoil tip contained a high proportion of 'high rank' coal which is generally less volatile and thus less susceptible to spontaneous combustion. Although the problem of spontaneous combustion had been well known in the coal industry at the material time, the defendants

---

157. [2000] Env. L.R. 183.
158. Council Directive (EC) 91/676/EEC concerning the protection of waters against pollution caused by nitrates from agricultural sources [1991] OJ L375/1.
159. *Sedleigh-Denfield v. O'Callaghan* [1940] A.C. 880
160. *Leakey v. National Trust* [1980] 1 Q.B. 485; see also the Privy Council decision in *Goldman v. Hargrave* [1967] 1 A.C. 645.
161. In this respect some question whether such cases should be regarded as apects of nuisance at all and argue that they should be regarded as a species of negligence; see C. Gearty, *The Place of Private Nuisance in a Modern Law of Torts*, Cambridge L.J. 214 (1989).
162. [2006] Env L.R. 17.

argued that it was not foreseeable that material of this nature would ignite. Pitchford J. accepted that this may have been true at the time the spoil was dumped. However, shortly after the NCB ceased using the spoil tip compelling scientific evidence emerged which indicated that spoil tips containing a high proportion of high rank coal were also prone to spontaneous combustion.

At this point the spoil tip became a nuisance and the harm which later ensued was clearly foreseeable. In this respect the Coal Authority were in the position of an occupier who continues a nuisance started by a third party; in this case the Authority's predecessor, the NCB.[163] According to the established common law principles noted above, this introduces an element of fault into the equation in terms of whether reasonable steps were taken to abate the nuisance. On the evidence the judge concluded that sufficient steps had not been taken to mitigate the risk of spontaneous combustion at the time the site was landscaped.[164]

In the US there is some variation between states on this issue although as a general rule it seems that liability is strict in the sense that a polluter will be liable once he becomes aware of the nuisance. This will be the case notwithstanding the fact that he may have complied with the common law duty of care. Thus, as Dobbs explains, the Second Restatement of Torts:

> does impose liability upon reasonable and careful defendants who repeatedly or continuously discharge substances that deprive the plaintiff of her rights or use and enjoyment ... In such cases, the fact that the defendant exercises care or uses the best technology available does not relieve it of responsibility for activity that unreasonably invades the plaintiffs rights to use and enjoy her land.[165]

In this respect it seems that the US common law position is broadly in accordance with English Common Law post *Cambridge Water*.

[D]   General Restrictions on Liability in Nuisance

The foregoing indicates that a cause of action in nuisance will now only be available in respect of foreseeable harm; furthermore, it seems that liability may be excluded on policy grounds in the case of historic pollution. In addition, there are certain other restrictions which may preclude the use of the tort in certain circumstances including a number of defences which are specific to the tort.

---

163. *Ibid.*, [129].
164. *Ibid.*, [156]–[162].
165. Dobbs (n. 102), 1325.

[1]   The Defence of Prescription

Although the fact that the claimant has 'come to the nuisance' is generally no defence,[166] the defence of prescription provides that no cause of action will lie in respect of an activity which has been continued for at least twenty years.[167] However, it is necessary to show that the activity was exercised lawfully, openly, continuously and was not dependent upon express grant or the permission of a neighbour.[168]

In the United States there is a change of emphasis in that the courts start from the general presumption that a person who voluntarily comes to a nuisance has no basis for a claim. Thus, 'when a plaintiff moves her residence to a neighbourhood of non-residential uses such as a neighbourhood of small factories, the non-residential uses are not often a nuisance.'[169] However, the same result could be achieved through a simple application of the character of the neighbourhood test as 'prior use in that case has stamped the neighbourhood with its character, so the residents must reasonably expect the kind of factory operations that were present when the residents chose to move in.' However, it seems that, even where there may be a prima facie case for raising a defence of coming to the nuisance it seems that the US courts are not prepared to apply it in a rigid and inflexible manner. In *Spur Industries Inc. v. Del E. Webb Development Co*, which is dealt with in more depth in Chapter 4, an expanding residential development had begun to encroach upon an agricultural area where there was a cattle feeding station. This caused nuisance to the new residents in the form of smells and flies attracted by the manure. On the face of it the case seemed to be a clear case of 'coming to the nuisance', however, the court found in favour of the residential developers and required the cattle feeding station to move. Dobbs explains the rationale for this decision as follows:

> [T]he first landowner to arrive upon the scene should not be permitted to rule out all other uses, in effect unilaterally zoning his neighbor's land for the uses he has adopted by his own. In a dynamic country, a certain amount of change must be expected in many communities and neighborhoods.[170]

However, there were other important aspects to the case concerning the inequitable conduct of the property developer. This necessitated an unusual remedy whereby the cattle feed station owners were required to move their operation, but at the developer's

---

166. See for example *Bliss v. Hall* (1839) 4 Bing. N.C. 183, 186 in which the defendant had established a tallow-chandlery which emitted: 'divers noisome, noxious, and offensive vapours, fumes, smells and stenches' to the discomfort of the plaintiff. It was no defence that the business had been established for three years by the time the plaintiff arrived since he 'came to the house ... with all the rights which the common law affords, and one of them is a right to wholesome air.' per Tindal C.J.
167. *Sturges v. Bridgman* (1879) 11 Ch.D. 852.
168. For the purposes of private nuisance, a neighbour is a person who has suffered an interference with an interest in land as a result of another's use of their land. See *Read v. Lyons & Co. Ltd.* [1947] A.C. 156, 183 (Lord Simmonds): 'He alone has a lawful claim who has suffered an invasion of some proprietary or other interest in land'. Standing requirements in tort are dealt with more fully in chapter 3, below.
169. Dobbs (n. 102) 1327–1328.
170. Dobbs (n. 102) 1328.

expense. This aspect of the case shall be dealt with in Chapter 4. Nevertheless, for present purposes the case illustrates the difficulties faced by the court in balancing competing land uses and finding solutions which are fair to both parties whilst serving the wider economic interests of the community. This theme shall be returned to in due course as it is an issue which permeates the entire debate regarding the role of tort in an environmental context.

[2]   The Defence of Statutory Authority

The defence of statutory authority may defeat an action against a body which has statutory authority to pursue the activity of which complaint is made. In fact the defence encompasses two different types of situation. Certain statutes impose duties, usually on public authorities, which may inevitably cause some discomfort to neighbours; if the duties are particularly onerous, the authority may be powerless to suspend the activity in order to abate the nuisance. For example, in *Smeaton v. Ilford Corporation*[171] sewers became overloaded due to the fact that many new houses were being connected to the existing system. Upjohn J. held that the Corporation could rely on the defence of statutory authority in that the local authority had no power to refuse the connection of more houses to the sewer system and had no means of restricting the flow. The reasons for this approach were explored more fully in the case of *Marcic v. Thames Water Utilities Ltd*[172] which again concerned nuisance caused by overflowing sewers. Lord Nicholls[173] explained that allowing actions in common law risked undermining carefully thought out regulatory regimes, many of which contain alternative dispute resolution mechanisms. Nevertheless, it is important to note that the harm must be an inevitable result of the use of those powers. In the High Court decision in *Dobson v. Thames Water Utilities Ltd*[174] it was held that the flies, mosquitoes and stench caused by a sewerage treatment works arose from poor decisions regarding the management of the facility and were not a necessary consequence of the statutory duties per se. This introduces an element of fault into the equation.

The other area in which the statutory authority defence operates concerns the construction and operation of major infrastructure projects authorized by Act of Parliament or other statutory powers. The operators of the facility will be entitled to rely upon the defence if the nuisance, of which complaint is made, is the inevitable consequence of the authorized activity. This expressly reverses the general proposition that permissions granted by administrative bodies to pursue an activity operate without prejudice to existing common law rights. The concept was almost entirely developed in the context of nuisance caused by steam locomotives in the early days of the railways.[175] The leading authority is the case of

---

171. [1954] 1 Ch. 450.
172. [2004] 2 A.C. 42.
173. *Ibid.*, at [34]–[35].
174. [2008] Env. L.R. 21
175. See *R v. Pease* (1832) 4 B. & Ad. 30, 110 E.R. 366; *Aldridge v. The Great Western Railway Company*; (1841) 3 Man. & G. 514, 133 E.R. 1246; *Piggot v. The Eastern Counties Railway*

Allen v. Gulf Oil Refining Ltd[176] in which the defendants were empowered to acquire land for the purpose of constructing an oil refinery by a private Act of Parliament (the Gulf Oil Refining Act 1965). Neighbours later complained of smells, noxious emissions, noise, glare and vibration emanating from the facility and argued that, as the 1965 Act merely empowered Gulf Oil to acquire the land and, as it was silent on the issue of how the main refinery should be operated, there could be no statutory authority for the nuisances. This argument was accepted by Denning MR in the Court of Appeal[177] but rejected on appeal. The House of Lords held that, the fact that the statute had authorized the activity to be pursued at the location in question, meant that it must have conferred an implicit immunity in respect of disturbances inevitably flowing from the construction of the refinery. As Lord Diplock put it, 'Parliament can hardly be supposed to have intended the refinery to be nothing more than a visual adornment to the landscape in an area of natural beauty'.[178]

Once again it is important to note that the harm must have been an *inevitable* result of the use of the powers. Furthermore, it would not suffice to show that the nuisances were the inevitable result of building the plant in question. Rather, for the defence to operate the defendant would have to show that no plant of whatever design could have been built and operated without causing that type of harm.[179] In this respect the House of Lords did not deliver a 'knock out' blow to the plaintiffs' case. Had the matter proceeded to a full trial of the facts it would have been open to them to argue that the plant could have been better designed or operated so as to reduce the nuisances. However, this may have been an uphill task in evidential terms. Although a similar argument was successful in the earlier case of *Manchester Corporation v. Farnworth*,[180] which concerned crop damage caused by sulphur dioxide emissions from a coal-fired power station. Here it was held that the plant should have been built with taller chimneys with a faster draft so as to disperse the emissions.

The statutory authority defence marks a crucial point of tension between the common law and statute. The defence rests upon the justification that Parliament is in a much better position than a court as regards assessing the merits of the scheme and weighing them against losses to individuals. There is much evidence to the effect that this has not always been a safe assumption to make. In *Allen v. Gulf Oil Refining Ltd* there was little, if any, consideration of the impact of the scheme on the villagers of

---

Company; (1846) 3 C.B. 228, 136 E.R. 92; *Vaughan v. The Taff Vale Railway Company* (1860) 5 H. & N. 678, 157 E.R. 1351; *Jones v. Festiniog Railway Company* (1867–68) L.R. 3 Q.B. 733.
176. [1981] A.C. 1001 (HL); [1980] 1 Q.B. 156 (CA).
177. Denning MR was heavily influenced by the railway nuisance cases which appeared to draw a distinction between powers to build a railway and powers to both build and operate a railway. See *Allen v. Gulf Oil Refining* [1980] 1 Q.B. 156 at 164(F)–166(F).
178. [1981] A.C. 1001, 1014.
179. *Ibid*. See Lord Edmund-Davies at 1015. His Lordship noted that, although this introduced an element of fault, the standard of liability would still differ from that in negligence. The statutory authority defence would not admit considerations of expense whereas it was legitimate to take account of expenses when determining whether the defendant had taken reasonable care in the context of negligence.
180. [1930] A.C. 171.

Waterston.[181] This is still of concern inasmuch as the statutory authority defence has been preserved by the Planning Act 2008.[182] The object of the Act is to replace the private Bill procedure with a unified planning mechanism for major infrastructure projects under the auspices of the Infrastructure Planning Commission (IPC).[183] However, one major change which has been brought about since Gulf built its oil refinery at Waterston in the mid-1960s is the need to conduct an environmental impact assessment.[184] Today it would not only be unthinkable, but unlawful, to build such a facility without taking full account of the impact on public health and the wider environment. Indeed, one of the key functions of the IPC is to ensure that such requirements are fully complied with.[185] In this respect one can now have a higher degree of confidence that environmental issues, such as the harms suffered by the villagers of Waterston, would be foreseen and ameliorated in the planning process.

The statutory authority defence occurs in other common law world jurisdictions although its scope varies greatly depending upon how narrowly, or otherwise, the statutory powers are construed. For example, in the Canadian case of *Barrett v. Ciment du St Laurent inc*[186] private nuisance claims were brought in respect of dust and noise from a cement plant which had been built in 1952 pursuant to statutory powers (the St Lawrence Cement inc Special Act). The Supreme Court held that, in the absence of express words, the mere fact that the Act authorized the construction and operation of the plant could not lead to the conclusion that there had been an attempt to oust common law remedies.[187] This appears to adopt a stricter approach than that applied by the House of Lords in the *Allen* case. In the *Allen* case it was held that it would suffice to show that the nuisances were inevitable in order to make out the defence. The decision in *Barrett* suggests that the defence cannot operate in respect of any harms, irrespective of whether they are inevitable, in the absence of express words. The Canadian Supreme Court was not prepared to make an assumption that there had been an intention to authorize any harms, irrespective of whether they could be described as inevitable. In many respects this approach is to be preferred to that adopted by the House of Lords in *Allen*. In *Allen* there was no consideration of what constitutes an inevitable nuisance and the merits of regarding inevitably as the key trigger of liability. It would be surprising if their Lordships regarded any inevitable

---

181. This issue is discussed more fully at §4.03[C], below, in the context of the role of the common law as a means of correcting regulatory failure.
182. See s. 158.
183. It should be noted that the IPC ceased to exist on 1 April 2012 and its functions were passed to the Planning Inspectorate. For details of the Planning Inspectorate's role in relation to major infrastructure projects see its main planning portal website at http://infrastructure. planningportal.gov.uk/ (accessed Nov. 15, 2012).
184. An EU requirement to conduct an environmental impact assessment is set out in the following legislation: Council Directive (EEC) 85/33 on the assessment of the effects of certain public and private projects on the environment [1985] OJ L 175/40, as amended by Council Directive (EC) 97/11 [1997] OJ L 73/5. The Directive is implemented in a myriad of specialist regulations pertaining to different industries and forms of development.
185. Pursuant to the Infrastructure Planning Commission (Environmental Impact Assessment Regulations 2009/2263.
186. [2008] 3 S.C.R. 392.
187. *Ibid.*, [97]–[98].

nuisance as acceptable, no matter how serious the harm. Moreover, it is most unlikely that the legislature would have intended to authorize harm above a certain threshold of seriousness.

[3]   The Hypersensitive Claimant

Provided an activity is reasonable according to the locality doctrine, a person who is pursuing an exceptionally delicate trade or activity may be unable to sustain an action in nuisance against his neighbour. Thus, the courts are reluctant to curtail an ordinary, lawful use of a person's property in the interests of an activity which may be unusual and unduly susceptible to everyday occurrences.

In *Robinson v. Kilvert*[188] Lopes L.J. stated:

> A man who carries on an exceptionally delicate trade cannot complain because it is injured by his neighbour doing something lawful on his property, if it is something which would not injure anything but an exceptionally delicate trade.

The law clearly places the onus on the person conducting the activity to move himself out of harm's way or take preventative measures, otherwise, he must endure the consequences of pursuing an activity which is out of keeping with the character of the neighbourhood. However, if the activity of which complaint is made is unreasonable, the defence cannot be used on the grounds that the sensitive nature of the claimant's activity meant that he incurred a greater loss than that which would have been incurred by a person not engaged in that particular activity. For example, in the Canadian case of *McKinnon Industries Ltd v. Walker*[189] the plaintiff grew orchids on a commercial basis; his stock was killed by poisonous gas emissions emanating from the defendants motor car production plant. The plaintiff brought an action in nuisance; it was argued on behalf of the defence that the plaintiff's activity was hypersensitive and that accordingly the emissions did not constitute an unreasonable use of land. It was held that the issue of reasonableness was entirely separate from the issue of hypersensitivity; once it has been established that an activity is unreasonable, the defendant will be liable for the consequences of his activity notwithstanding the fact that the nature of the claimant's activity renders him particularly sensitive to the consequences of the activity. This is clearly in accordance with the 'egg-shell' skull principle by which the defendant must take his victim as he finds him.[190] The point is neatly illustrated by the decision of the Tennessee Court of Appeals in *Jenkins v. CSX Transportation Inc.*[191] Here the claimant suffered an extremely rare allergic reaction to creosote fumes emanating from railway ties (or sleepers as they are termed in the UK) which were frequently stored in, or transported through, the defendant's railway yard. It was held

---

188. (1889) 41 Ch. D. 88, 97.
189. [1951] 3 D.L.R. 577.
190. See *Dulieu v. White* [1901] 2 K.B. 669, 679, 'if a man is negligently run over or otherwise negligently injured in his body, it is no defence to the sufferer's claim for damages that he would have suffered less injury ... if he had not had an unusually thin skull or an unusually weak heart.', per Kennedy J.
191. 906 S.W.2d 460 (1995).

that the claimant was affected 'only because of her peculiar susceptibility to that chemical'.[192] Had others been affected by the fumes, the fact that the claimant's symptoms were exacerbated by her allergic reaction would not have negated the defendant's liability. However, in this case the harm was solely due to her abnormal sensitivity.

More recently the UK Court of Appeal has questioned whether the hypersensitivity defence still has a useful role to play in the light of the decision of the House of Lords in *Cambridge Water v. Eastern Counties Leather*.[193] When the standard of liability in nuisance was stricter, there was a greater need for specific defences. However, the hypersensitivity of the claimant can equally well be dealt with as an aspect of foreseeability of harm which, it will be recalled, is now an essential ingredient of the tort following the *Cambridge Water* decision. Thus in *National Rail Infrastructure Ltd v. Morris (t/a Soundstar Studio)*,[194] in which new electronic railway signalling equipment interfered with the claimant's sound studio recording equipment, it was held that the harm was unforeseeable. There was no need to consider issues of abnormal sensitivity in respect of the claimant's land use. This approach is certainly less arbitrary than a defence based upon hypersensitivity which could bestow blanket immunity on the polluter in respect of an entire class of claims. The point is clearly illustrated by the issue of GM crops; which has already been referred to in the context of material harm. As previously noted, disputes have arisen regarding the contamination of organic and conventional crops by GM crops. The consequences of such cross-pollination for an organic farmer are potentially disastrous as it could jeopardize the organic status of his produce.[195] It is at least arguable that organic farming could be construed as a hypersensitive activity.[196] Yet, one could also argue that it is highly foreseeable that a neighbouring organic farm could be damaged by cross-pollination, notwithstanding issues of hypersensitivity.

[4]   Environmental Permits

Certain industrial activities cannot be undertaken unless an environmental permit has been obtained from the appropriate regulator. This may stipulate how the activity is to be carried out, what technology should be used, days and hours of operation and so forth. There has long been an intuitive belief that an authorization of this type must operate without prejudice to existing common law rights.[197] Thus, a permit should not offer the holder any protection from liability in respect of nuisances caused by the authorized activity. Surprisingly, the English Courts have not had the opportunity to consider the effect of permits on liability in nuisance until recently. In *Barr v. Biffa*

---

192. *Ibid.*, per Farmer J., at [2].
193. [1994] 2 A.C. 264.
194. [2004] Env L.R. 41.
195. See *R. v. Secretary of the State for the Environment, ex parte Watson* [1999] Env L.R. 310 (above).
196. *Ibid.*, at 323. Buxton L.J. made obiter comments regarding the effect of framing the action as a private nuisance claim in which he noted the hypersensitivity issue.
197. See, for example, Peter Cane, *Tort Law and Economic Interests*, 392 (Clarendon Press 1992).

Waste Services Ltd the defendant was granted a waste management permit to operate a landfill site. Local residents brought claims in nuisance in respect of flies and noxious odours associated with the site. The case turned upon the status of environmental permits and whether they could effectively limit tortious liabilities. The High Court[198] accepted that an environmental permit could not be equated with a statutory authority. Nevertheless, it was held that such a permit could operate as conclusive evidence regarding the 'reasonableness' of an activity. As has been explained above, liability in nuisance hinges on the concept of 'reasonable user'; thus one cannot be liable in respect of harm flowing from a reasonable use of one's property. The Court of Appeal overturned the High Court's decision[199] holding that a permit has no special status which enables it to render an otherwise unreasonable activity reasonable. The term 'reasonable user' merely encapsulates a number of existing nineteenth century principles relating to the circumstances which render an activity unacceptable. There was no authority for the proposition that the grant of a permit could, at a stroke, remove the tortious quality of a particular land use. The Court of Appeal also appeared to reject the notion that the approach adopted by the High Court stopped short of conferring a form of statutory authority on the holders of permits. The assertion that a permit renders an otherwise unreasonable activity reasonable is tantamount to saying that the permit authorizes the holder to conduct activities in a manner which would normally be actionable. It was clear that a permit was incapable of conferring such an authority. Moreover, it could not be equated with a strategic planning decision capable of altering the character of the neighbourhood.

The *Biffa* case is of crucial importance in terms of re-establishing the independence of nuisance and preventing any further encroachments on the scope of liability by statute. As will be argued below,[200] tort fulfils a vital role in protecting private interests which may have been neglected by the legislature or the regulator. It cannot perform this role effectively unless it remains focused upon those private interests and maintains some distance from the regulatory response.

§2.04   THE RULE IN *RYLANDS V. FLETCHER*

The rule in *Rylands v. Fletcher*, which has already been touched on above, stems from the judgment of Blackburn J. in the eponymous case. In short, the rule establishes strict liability for any escapes resulting from an unnatural use of land:

> We think that the rule of law is, that the person who for his own purposes brings on his lands and collects and keeps there anything likely to do mischief if it escapes, must keep it in at his peril, and, if he does not do so, is prima facie answerable for all the damage which is the natural consequence of its escape.[201]

---

198. [2011] EWHC 1003 (TCC), [2011] 4 All E.R. 1065.
199. [2012] EWCA Civ 312, [2012] All ER (D) 141 (Mar).
200. See §4.03[C], below.
201. *Fletcher v. Rylands* (1866) L.R. 1 Ex. 265, 279–280.

This assertion was upheld by the House of Lords where Lord Cairns emphasized that the 'non-natural' use of land was the key factor establishing liability.[202]

The genesis of the rule is one of the great mysteries of the common law. In his seminal paper on 'The Boundaries of Nuisance'[203] Newark argued that the rule arose as an offshoot of nuisance and was intended to establish liability in respect of a sudden and accidental escape as opposed to an on-going state of affairs. This theory is not uncontested[204] and Nolan[205] argues that Blackburn J. was in fact evoking the Medieval default position on liability, namely, that a 'man acts at his peril.'[206] Although fault based liability was in the ascendency by the 1860s, the courts in *Rylands* may have been of the view that strict liability should be preserved in respect of certain perilous activities.[207] Notwithstanding these reservations, Newark's theory has become part of the established orthodoxy and was wholeheartedly endorsed by the House of Lords in *Cambridge Water v. Eastern Counties Leather.*[208] The assimilation of *Rylands v. Fletcher* with private nuisance limits the scope of the rule in some respects. Given that private nuisance is concerned with the protection of interests in land, an action in *Rylands* would only be open to an individual in respect of damage to real property in which he has a sufficient interest. This casts doubt on the use of the rule in respect of personal injuries unconnected with the protection of such property rights.[209] Furthermore, given that foreseeability of harm is an ingredient of private nuisance it must also be established in order to make out liability under *Rylands v. Fletcher.* More recently the distinction between nuisance and *Rylands* has been further eroded by the emerging

---

202. (1868) L.R. 3 H.L. 330.
203. Newark (n. 86).
204. See W.C. Porter, *The Role of Private Nuisance Law in the Control of Air Pollution*, 10 Ariz. L. Rev. 107, 109–110 (1968–69); who points out that the judgment made no mention of nuisance.
205. D. Nolan, *The distinctiveness of Rylands v. Fletcher*, 121 L.Q.R. 421 (2005).
206. *Ibid.*, 430–431. Nolan points out that the claim was framed as an 'action on the case'. Action on the case was used as the vehicle for developing the idea of fault based liability which evolved into negligence. However, Nolan argues that by the 1860s fault based liability was still the exception rather than the rule and did not apply in respect of cases concerning interference with real property. However, it is also interesting to note Pollock's analysis of the case, written much closer in time to the judgment. In his view certain hazardous activities removed the need to distinguish between the activity itself and the manner in which it was carried out: or as he put it 'to consolidate the judgment of fact into an unbending rule of law.' Thus culpability would flow from merely carrying out the activity, irresopective of how carefully the activity had been conducted. In this respect one could argue that a rule of strict liability was not entirely out of place in an action on the case. See F. Pollock, *Duties of Insuring Safety: The Rule in Rylands v. Fletcher*, 2 L.Q.R. 52, 2 (1886).
207. In this respect it is useful to bear in mind the historical context of the case whereby there had been many resevoir collapses and the activity was regarded as inherently dangerous. For the definitive historical account of the case see A.W.B. Simpson, *Bursting Reservoirs and Victorian Tort Law: Rylands and Horrocks v. Fletcher, (1868)*, in *Leading Cases in the Common Law* (OUP 1995). See also A.J. Waite, *De-constructing the Rule in Rylands v. Fletcher*, 18(3) J. Envtl. L. 423 (2006).
208. [1994] 2 A.C. 264, esp Lord Goff at 298–299.
209. From time to time in its history *Rylands v. Fletcher* has been applied in personal injuries cases not remotely connected with the protection of interests in land. See *Read v. Lyons* [1947] A.C. 167 (the majority overlooked the fact that the harm was not connected with interests in land and the case turned upon whether there had been an 'escape'; only Lord MacMillan made the point that the action should not be entertained at all due to the lack of a property dimension to the case) and *Perry v. Kendricks Transport Ltd.* [1956] 1 W.L.R. 85.

view that private nuisance is not necessarily confined to an on-going state of affairs. Recall that in *Colour Quest Ltd v. Total Downstream UK plc*,[210] a case which resulted from the conflagration at the Buncefield petroleum depot, the High Court held that there was no fixed minimum duration for a nuisance. Thus actions in nuisance could be entertained in respect of the explosion without recourse to *Rylands v. Fletcher*.[211]

The convergence (or reunification as Newark would no doubt have argued) of private nuisance and *Rylands* calls into question whether the rule still has any useful role to play. Indeed, in *Transco plc v. Stockport Metropolitan Borough Council*[212] the House of Lords was invited to follow the Australian courts[213] and consign the rule to history. Although their Lordships accepted that the instances in which the rule could be invoked may become increasingly narrow, they declined to kill-off the rule altogether. In fact, there may yet be circumstances in which the rule could plug gaps left by other causes of action. For example, it could be argued that liability under *Rylands v. Fletcher* demands a lesser degree of foreseeability than in private nuisance. In *Rylands* foreseeability is confined to knowledge that the substance will cause harm if it escapes; it is not necessary to show that the escape itself was foreseeable.[214] Whereas, in circumstances where private nuisance is applied in respect of harm which has already occurred, it is necessary to show that both the invasion of noxious substances and the consequent harm were foreseeable. It could also be argued that the 'non-natural use of land', which, as noted above, is the lynchpin of liability under the rule, results in stricter liability than in private nuisance. This is because the non-natural use criterion is entirely distinct from the concept of 'reasonable user' in nuisance. A non-natural land use cannot be rendered 'reasonable' by virtue of the fact that there are many potentially hazardous industrial concerns in the area.[215] However, this must be set against the fact that the list of uses deemed 'unnatural' has been continually eroded as once novel activities become well established.[216] A topical example concerns GMOs. In the UK the technology is still regarded as relatively novel and unusual. Therefore, if

---

210. [2009] 2 Lloyd's Rep. 1 at [407]–[421].
211. The distinction between *Rylands* and nuisance in respect of this type of harm appears to be instinctive and intuitive and no clear guidance can be discerned from the *Colour Quest* judgment, above. However, one would have thought that there is a qualitative difference between an accidental escape of the type which gave rise to *Rylands* in the first place and harm resulting from the routine manner in which a plant was operated. According to this analysis *Rylands* should have no application to the chronic pollution which occurrred in *Cambridge Water*.
212. [2004] 2 A.C. 1.
213. In *Burnie Port Authority v. General Jones Pty Ltd* (1994) 179 C.L.R. 520 the High Court of Australia held that *Rylands v. Fletcher* had been subsumed by the law of negligence in that the hazardous land use was an aspect of determining the appropriate duty of care.
214. In fact the very essence of the rule is that the escape was unintentional, unexpected and unforeseeable. See comments of Lord Hoffmann in *Transco* (above) at [27].
215. [1994] 2 A.C. 264, 309B-F, per Lord Goff.
216. See, for example, *British Celanese Ltd. v. A.H. Hunt* [1969] 1 W.L.R. 959, 963: 'The manufacturing of electrical and electronic components in the year 1964 ... cannot be judged to be a special use nor can the bringing and storing on the premises of metal foil be a special use in itself ... The metal foil was there for use in the manufacture of goods of a common type which at all material times were needed for the general benefit of the community', (Lawton J).

pollen from a GM crop test site were to contaminate neighbouring organic or conventional crops, there is a possibility that liability could arise under *Rylands v. Fletcher*.[217] Although, some doubt whether the gradual spread of GM pollen over a period of time would be regarded as a sudden and accidental escape for the purposes of liability under the rule.[218]

The rule has been adopted by the US courts on frequent occasions although there has often been much debate regarding the scope of the principle. Nevertheless, the rule has played an important part in apportioning liability for environmental liability. *In State v. Ventron Corp.*[219] the State of New Jersey sought to recover clean-up and removal costs from several chemical companies in respect of the contamination of a tidal estuary by mercury emanating from land upon which the companies had carried on operations. The land beneath the site was described as being 'saturated' by 268 tons of toxic waste the bulk of which consisted of mercury. The interaction of the mercury with other elements created a highly toxic compound know as ethyl mercury which had wiped out all fish in the creek and deoxygenated the water. Pollock J, in the Supreme Court of New Jersey had no doubt that the defendants could be held strictly liable for the clean-up costs under the rule in *Rylands v. Fletcher*:

> We believe it is time to recognize expressly that the law of liability has evolved so that a landowner is strictly liable to others for harm caused by toxic wastes that are stored on his property and flow onto the property of others. Therefore ... we adopt the principle of liability originally declared in *Rylands v. Fletcher*. The net result is that those who use, or permit others to use, land for the conduct of abnormally dangerous activities are strictly liable for resultant damages.

Furthermore, as Pollock J noted, it seems that the rule has largely been absorbed into the Second Restatement of Torts whereby a landholder may be held strictly liable in respect of 'ultrahazardous' activities. In determining whether an activity should attract such liability the Restatement sets out the following criteria for consideration by the court, namely:

(a) the existence of a high degree of risk of some harm to the person, land, chattels or others;
(b) likelihood that the harm that results from it will be great;
(c) inability to eliminate the risk by the exercise of reasonable care;
(d) extent to which the activity is not a matter of common usage;

---

217. See D. Howarth, *Civil Liability for GM Farming: GM Crops and the Existing Law: Pt 2*, 12(5) Env. Liability 185 (2004).
218. See C.P. Rodgers, *Liability for the Release of GMOs into the Environment: Exploring the Boundaries of Nuisance*, 62(2) C.L.J. 371, 377 (2003). This conclusion was reached by the Saaskatchewan Court of Queen's Bench in *Hoffmann v. Monsanto Canada Inc* [2005] S.K.Q.B. 225 (see Smith J. at 97).
219. Supreme Court of New Jersey, 1983, 94 N.J. 473, 468 A. 2d 150.

> (e) inappropriateness of the activity to the place where it is carried on; and
>
> (f) extent to which its value to the community is outweighed by its dangerous attributes.[220]

These criteria are far more specific and exacting than the vague and ill-defined concept of 'non-natural' usage. To return to the topical example of GM crops, given the fact that the widespread cultivation of GM crops in the US is now routine and largely uncontroversial, it would be difficult to show that the activity was sufficiently unusual and hazardous as to attract strict liability.[221]

Although the rule has certainly been watered down in the UK, the principle enunciated in *Rylands v. Fletcher* is significant in that it provides an example of the courts having taken a policy decision to impose the costs of an activity on the person who conducts it irrespective of fault. In other words, where a hazardous activity is involved, the party who creates the risk and gains some economic benefit from that activity, should also bear the risk. As will be seen in subsequent chapters, the development of a specialist environmental liability regime requires legislators to make such policy decisions in respect of polluting activities.

§2.05 PUBLIC NUISANCE

[A] The Nature of Public Nuisance

As has been explained above, the creation of the crime of public nuisance resulted from a misleading analogy made between obstruction of the public highway and obstruction of an easement such as a right of access.[222] It was then established that a person who has suffered harm in excess of the general inconvenience suffered by the population as a whole would be able to pursue a civil claim by reason of that 'special hurt'. Hence a private action in respect of a public nuisance has never been a proprietary remedy. However, the association of public nuisance with private nuisance has resulted in its expanding to encompass those activities which have normally been the preserve of private nuisance, namely, interferences emanating from a neighbouring land use. This has resulted in a distinction being made between nuisances affecting a limited number of persons and those which affect enough landholders to constitute a class of Her Majesty's subjects.[223] In *Attorney General v. PYA Quarries*[224] which concerned noise and vibration caused by blasting at the defendant's quarry, Denning L.J. formulated the following test for determining whether an activity constituted a public or private nuisance:

---

220. Restatement (Second) of Torts § 520 (1977).
221. See M.R. Grossman, *Genetically Modifed Crops in the United States: Federal regulation and State Tort Liability*, 5(2) Env. L. Rev. 86, 105–107 (2003).
222. See §2.03[C], above.
223. Courts are reluctant to specify how many persons constitute a class. In *R. v. Lloyd* (1802) 4 Esp. 200 it was held that three guests at an inn was clearly insufficient to constitute a class.
224. [1957] 2 Q.B. 169.

> I prefer to look to the reason of the thing and to say that a public nuisance is a nuisance which is so widespread in its range or so indiscriminate in its effect that it would not be reasonable to expect one person to take proceedings on his own responsibility to put a stop to it, but that it should be taken on the responsibility of the community at large.[225]

Notwithstanding the public nature of the harm, an individual or individuals within that class may be able to point to special harm which exceeds that suffered by the class as a whole. In which case a related civil action for damages or injunctive relief may be possible.

[B]   Public Nuisance and Individual Harms

Thus, public nuisance is of interest in an environmental context in that many pollutants can disperse quickly and affect large numbers of people living some distance from the source of the escape.[226] Those who suffer special or particular loss, over and above the general inconvenience suffered by the public at large, may pursue private claims in respect of that loss. It is important to note that there can be a considerable overlap between public and private nuisance where the use and enjoyment of the claimant's property has been adversely affected. This is neatly illustrated by the case of *Halsey v. Esso Petroleum*[227] which concerned noise, emissions and vibration from the defendant's oil storage and distribution depot. The noise and vibration was caused by boilers on the site (comprising part of the facility's own power plant) and tanker lorries coming and going throughout the night. Acid smuts from the boilers sullied laundry on the washing line and damaged the paint-work of the plaintiff's car which was parked on the street outside his house.[228] Furthermore, the acidic emissions were accompanied by a pungent smell which pervaded the neighbourhood. It was held that the plaintiff could maintain an action in private nuisance in respect of these harms as they clearly constituted interferences with the use and enjoyment of his property. However, it was held that the noise and emissions also constituted public nuisances and that certain harms endured by the plaintiff could be construed as special damages arising therefrom. For example, the deposition of acid smuts could be regarded as an interference with the public use of the highway, which included the right to park one's car without it being damaged. Similarly, the noisy nocturnal vehicle movements interfered with the comfort and convenience of local residents and the plaintiff's loss of sleep could be regarded as special damage. Thus, although the nature of the harm may have to be reframed in order to engage the rights protected by public nuisance, the outcome is essentially the same. Nevertheless, despite the large areas of overlap, the facts of

---

225. *Ibid.*, 190.
226. For an overview of the modern role of public nuisance in an environmental context see N. Parpworth, *Public Nuisance in the Environmental Context*, 11 J. Plan. Envtl. L. 1526 (2008).
227. [1961] 1 W.L.R. 683.
228. Although Veale J. expressed some doubt as to whether private nuisance was the appropriate cause of action here given that the car was parked on the highway rather than on the plaintiff's land. In any event, and as has been noted above, he was of the opinion that the damage would still be caught by liability under *Rylands v. Fletcher*: see *Halsey* (n. 227), 692.

Halsey serve to highlight the outer boundaries of private nuisance and the point at which public nuisance takes over. At one point it was argued that a private nuisance must emanate from neighbouring land use and that vehicle movements on the highway clearly did not constitute such land use. However, Veale J. concluded that they could be regarded as part and parcel of the defendant's operations on the site. This can be contrasted with the case of *Esso Petroleum v. Southport Corporation*,[229] in which the plaintiff's beaches were contaminated by oil discharged by a tanker at sea stricken by steering failure. Denning L.J. (as he then was) held that private nuisance had no application here in that the harm was in no way connected with neighbouring land use. He continued that the harm could properly be regarded as public nuisance although, for reasons which are outlined below, the public nuisance theme was not pursued.[230]

The relationship between public and private nuisance was examined more recently in the afore-mentioned case of *Colour Quest Ltd v. Total Downstream UK plc*[231] which arose from the explosion at the Buncefield oil storage and distribution depot near Hemel Hempstead in Hertfordshire. This raised the issue of whether public nuisance should oust private nuisance where there are a multitude of similar claims. Early on the morning of 11 December 2005 much of South-East England was rocked by what was reported to be the largest explosion in peacetime Europe. A number of human and technical failures had led to the overfilling of a petroleum storage tank at the Buncefield depot causing the escape of petroleum vapours. The vapours were ignited by electrical equipment or car engines and the spectacular conflagration ensued. Miraculously, there were no fatalities or serious injuries; however, there was widespread damage to property and a degree of environmental impact.[232] The media carried images of the huge pall of black some which could clearly be seen from as far afield as London and appeared to turn day into night in certain areas. The property damage resulted in a multiplicity of similar claims in respect of which damages were sought in private nuisance. The widespread nature of the harm and the number of parties affected also brought public nuisance into play. However, the High Court held that there was abundant authority to the effect that private and public nuisance were not mutually exclusive. In other words, the claims in private nuisance were not subsumed by public nuisance.[233] This conclusion is certainly logical if one accepts the fact that the rights engaged by private nuisance, namely, the use and enjoyment of property, differ somewhat from the public interests engaged by public nuisance.

---

229. [1954] 2 Q.B. 182.
230. *Ibid.*, 196 et seq.
231. [2009] 1 C.L.C. 186.
232. Much of the property damage was sustained by businesses on a neighbouring industrial estate. As regards the wider environmental impact the river Colne was contaminated by 800,000 litres of contaminated water used in fighting the fire and a drinking water pumping station had to be closed for a considerable time at a cost of EUR 2.2 million. Despite its dramatic appearance the atmospheric pollution did not lead to major public health or ground contamination issues. The damage is fully outlined in the official enquiry report: Buncefield Major Incident Investigation Board, *The Buncefield Incident 11 December 2005* (Report) (2008).
233. [2009] 1 C.L.C 186, per Steel J., at [432]–[434].

Another important legal clarification to emerge from the *Colour Quest* case was that pure economic loss was recoverable in public nuisance.[234] This finding was of crucial importance in that a significant proportion of the claims focused on loss of trade sustained by businesses on the neighbouring industrial estate. In this respect public nuisance may offer significant advantages over negligence where the common law severely restricts the recoverability of economic loss. This theme is pursued in more depth in Chapter 3 in the context of recoverable loss.[235]

However, as noted above, where the entire class suffers the same, or at least a similar type of loss, an individual member of that class shall not be deemed to have sustained a distinct loss actionable in a private nuisance claim. In an environmental context, this limitation is clearly demonstrated by one of the actions stemming from the *Exxon Valdez* disaster in which there was a massive oil spill in Prince William Sound Alaska following the grounding of a super-tanker. Native Americans claimed that they had suffered particular loss, over and above that suffered by the local Alaskan population as a whole.[236] In short they argued that Native Americans had a special relationship with the local environment due to its ancient cultural and spiritual significance and their dependence upon it for sustenance. However, the court came to the view that their interest could not be sufficiently differentiated from that enjoyed by the local population as a whole and that accordingly their separate claims for damages in private nuisance should not be entertained:

> the right to obtain and share wild food, enjoy uncontaminated nature, and cultivate traditional, cultural, spiritual, and psychological benefits in pristine natural surroundings is shared by all Alaskans.[237]

Of course, had the Native Americans enjoyed a direct proprietary interest in the resources affected, there can be no doubt that they could have brought individual actions in private nuisance. However, as shall be explained in subsequent chapters, the common law has traditionally taken a very narrow view of what constitutes a sufficient proprietary interest in natural resources to found an action in private nuisance. One of the issues which current developments are addressing is the extent to which this should be extended into some form of public equitable beneficial interest in the environment.

[C]   Public Nuisance and Personal Injuries

Clearly, there is a pronounced overlap between public and private nuisance where the activity interferes with the use and enjoyment of land. However, public nuisance is extremely broad in its scope and encompasses harms which are in no way connected with interference with rights in property. This is especially the case where an activity has public health implications. For example, in Camelford in 1988, a contractor

---

234. *Ibid.*, [435]–[465].
235. See §3.05[A][2].
236. re the *Exxon Valdez*, 104 F.3d 1196 (9th Cir. 1997).
237. *Ibid.*, 1198.

delivering aluminium sulphate to a water treatment works operated by South West Water Services Ltd deposited 20 tonnes of the chemical into the wrong tank with the result that it was released into the public water supply. South West Water services were convicted of creating a public nuisance and 180 residents, who had suffered ill-health effects as a result of drinking or washing with contaminated water, pursued private claims in respect of their particular losses.[238]

At no point in the Camelford litigation was it questioned whether damages should be recoverable at all in public nuisance for personal injuries. However, a few years later in *Hunter v. Canary Wharf* Lord Hoffmann made a strong assertion to the effect that personal injury claims had no place in *private* nuisance.[239] Whilst adverse effects may be a symptom of interference with the use and enjoyment of property they should not be actionable in their own right under private nuisance. This was at odds with the property based notion of private nuisance and could lead to the invidious consequence that individuals suffering exactly the same injury would be subject to differing standards of liability. Those with a property interest in the area would be in a position to benefit from the stricter standard of liability offered by nuisance whereas as those without such an interest would have to establish negligence. As noted above, the doctrinal and historical basis for this assertion has been the subject of some criticism although there is strength in the argument that for jurisprudential reasons the time may have come to shift such claims into negligence.[240]

Lord Hoffmann did not address the issue of whether this rationale should also be applied to public nuisance. Given that public nuisance only has somewhat tenuous connections with private nuisance and given that it is not exclusively concerned with the protection of property rights, there could be no assumption that Lord Hoffmann also intended to exclude personal injuries from the realms of public nuisance. Indeed, the Court of Appeal reached this conclusion in the recent case of *re Corby Group Litigation*.[241] This on-going litigation arose from the redevelopment of the former British Steel works in Corby, Northamptonshire.[242] The plant was closed in the early 1980s and the site and liabilities were acquired lock, stock and barrel by Corby Borough Council. The Council set about decontaminating and redeveloping the site and the work lasted a number of years. The claimants alleged that during the course of the earth moving works toxic chemicals (collectively known as teratogens) were released. When ingested by pregnant women in the locality, who were exposed to the emissions, it was argued that the toxins resulted in upper limb deformities in their offspring. The children allegedly afflicted by the condition sought damages for these personal injuries under a number of heads including public nuisance. The defendants unsuccessfully applied to have the public nuisance claim struck out and appealed against the decision

---

238. South West Water admitted liability; reported litigation focused on the issue of the quantum of damages (*AB v. South West Water Services Ltd* [1993] Q.B. 507). See Chapter 3 below.
239. [1997] A.C. 655, 707–708.
240. See Palmer (n. 97) and the discussion of this issue at §2.03[A][2].
241. [2009] Q.B. 335.
242. For an extensive overview of the litigation and the legal issues raised see, D. Hart, J. Jolliffe, J & R. Marcus, *Contaminated Land in Corby and Sandridge: Historic Liabilities: Part 1: Corby*, 17(3) Env. Liability 102 (2009).

to the Court of Appeal. Dyson L.J., delivering the judgment of the court, stated that there was nothing in Lord Hoffmann's judgment in *Hunter v. Canary Wharf* to suggest that he intended to exclude personal injuries from public nuisance and that this part of the judgment was obiter in any case. Having undertaken an extensive review of the academic authorities, Dyson L.J. also emphasized the distinct nature of public nuisance and the fact that, historically, it has never been concerned with the protection of interests in land. Thus, a restriction on recoverability for personal injuries in private nuisance could not be automatically extended to public nuisance. Nevertheless, he was aware of the strength of the argument that in this case there was a strong overlap with harm which typically falls within the province of negligence.[243] However, it would be for the Supreme Court (as successor to the House of Lords) to decide in future litigation whether personal injuries should be excluded from the province of public nuisance.

From an environmental perspective this issue is highly significant. Although public health is often treated as a distinct issue from environmental protection, in truth there are inextricable links between the two. Humans are part of the environment and personal injuries may constitute a key symptom of environmental harm. The ability to pursue public nuisance claims in respect of widespread harm provides a strong civil remedy against polluters.[244] The advantage of public nuisance, as opposed to negligence, is that generally speaking the standard of liability in public nuisance is stricter than in negligence. However, this is a complex issue which needs to be addressed in some detail.

[D]   Public Nuisance: A Tort of Strict Liability?

The standard of liability in public nuisance can be difficult to determine due to the eclectic nature of the tort; there is no single answer to the question of whether the tort is based on strict or fault based liability. In some cases there is a strong overlap with matters which are typically the province of negligence. Here, the courts have often been reluctant to allow public nuisance to circumvent the need to establish fault.[245] However, where there is a strong overlap between private and public nuisance it seems that a stricter form of liability may be appropriate. Thus, in the *Wagonmound (No 2)* Lord Reid held that it was necessary for the claimant to show foreseeability of harm; although, it would be no answer for the defendant to say that he had taken reasonable steps to prevent the damage once he had become aware of it.[246] As we have already seen in the context of private nuisance, in this respect we can say that nuisance may impose stricter liability than in negligence. The distinction between public nuisance

---

243. Corby Group Litigation (n. 241). In this respect the much quoted seminal paper of Professor Newark on *The Boundaries of Nuisance* (n. 86) was referred to at many points in the judgment.
244. For an analysis of the environmental implications of the judgment see, M. Lee, *Personal Injury, Public Nuisance and Environmental Regulation*, 20(1) K.L.J. 129 (2009).
245. Obstructions or hazards on the public highway constitute one such example. Thus in *Dollman v. Hillman Ltd* [1941] 1 All E.R. 355 the Court of Appeal seemed preoccupied with the question of whether a butcher's shop was at fault in allowing slippery fat to be deposited on the pavement outside the premises.
246. *Overseas Tankship U.K. Ltd. v. The Miller Steamship Co. Pty.* [1967] 1 A.C. 717, 639–640.

and negligence was explored by Denning L.J. in *Esso Petroleum v. Southport Corporation*.[247] He argued that in most cases public nuisance was a tort of strict liability although it was subject to the defence of necessity. The necessity defence placed the onus on the defendant to show that his actions were justified to save life and limb. Thus, as we have already seen in respect of the arguments pertaining to trespass to land in this case, it would have been for the defendant to show that discharging the oil was necessary to save the lives of the crew by preventing the break-up of the vessel. If, however, the tanker had become stranded as a result of the defendant's negligence the defence could not have operated. To some extent this brings the issue back to negligence, although, whereas negligence places the evidential burden on the claimant, arguing necessity in public nuisance places the evidential burden on the defendant. Interestingly, the way in which the Court of Appeal dealt with this point removed this crucial distinction between negligence and public nuisance. As regards negligence it was held that res ipsa loquitur could apply, the effect of which was to shift the burden onto the defendant in any case.[248] In this respect the public nuisance arguments seemed superfluous and were not pursued. When the case reached the House of Lords on appeal the public nuisance argument was barely addressed and the issue turned solely upon whether the defendant had been negligent. On this issue the Court of Appeal was reversed and it was held that there had not been any breach of the duty of care on the part of the defendant.[249]

As noted in the context of the *Corby* litigation, ultimately, it may be another personal injuries case which causes the new Supreme Court to reflect upon whether strict liability should be maintained in respect of harms which overlap with negligence. The Court would have to determine whether there is something special about such harms which merits strict liability and make a policy decision to ring-fence them from the ever expanding scope of negligence. This is an issue which is explored more thoroughly in Chapter 6 on strict liability.

[E]   Pushing at the Boundaries of Public Nuisance: Climate Change Liability

Until recently the notion that one could contemplate pursing a civil action against, for example, a power company in respect of damage attributable to climate change would have seemed far-fetched in the extreme. Yet, in recent years, public nuisance has been the chosen vehicle for pursuing a number of speculative claims in respect of this type of harm, especially in North America; although, at the time of writing, the courts still seem a long way from holding a defendant liable on this basis.[250]

---

247. [1954] 2 Q.B. 182., 197–200.
248. The nature of *res ipsa loquitur* is discussed in more detail below in the context of negligence.
249. [1956] A.C. 218.
250. For an overview and some analysis of the North American cases see J.A. Smith, *A Climate Change Trilogy – Connecticut v. AEP, Comer v. Murphy Oil and Kivalina v. ExxonMobil Corp. – Just the Beginning, or the Beginning of the End?* 4 Envtl. Liability 119 (2009); J.A. Schatz, Climate Change Litigation in Canada and the USA 18(2) R.E.C.I.E.L 129 (2009). As regards the

Initial attempts were not promising as lower courts adopted a very conservative approach and doubted whether climate change raised justiciable issues. In *California v. General Motors et al.*[251] the State pursued a public nuisance case against a number of motor manufacturers on the grounds that they had failed to reduce tailpipe emissions of CO2. California alleged that this made a significant contribution to global warming placing undue strain on the State's infrastructure and resources. The US Federal Court for the Northern District ruled that the case raised political issues which it was not competent to address and that:

> injecting itself into the global warming thicket at this juncture would require an initial policy determination of the type reserved for the political branch of government.[252]

This statement is particularly revealing because it tells us something of the legal and political landscape which prevailed at the time the proceedings were initiated. The Federal District Court in this case was clearly reluctant to leap into an area which was virgin territory in terms of policy making and legislative intervention. The court was simply not prepared to set about tackling the 'global warming thicket' without at least some guidance from the policy makers regarding how they should go about it. It is important to note that the case originated under the Bush administration[253] at a time when the legislature was opposed to engaging with the global warming issue and CO2 was not even recognized as a pollutant under the Clean Air Act 1970. In this respect there was a regulatory vacuum which the court was not prepared to fill.[254]

The approach adopted in *California v. General Motors* was also followed at first instance in the case of *Connecticut et al. v. American Electric Power Inc (AEP)*[255] in which a number of States, the City of New York and a number of land trusts initiated proceedings against America's largest power company. The Federal District Court again dismissed the claims on the grounds that they did not raise justiciable issues. However, on this occasion the litigants were not deterred and, as the lengthy appeals procedure progressed, the political and legal landscape began to change. On the political front the new Obama administration brought with it a commitment to engage with the global warming issue.[256] As regards legal developments the Supreme Court

---

likelihood of such actions being brought in the UK see, J. Burton, M. Edwards & S. Tromans, *Climate change: what chance a damages action in tort?*, 55 Envtl. Law 22 (2010).

251. 2007 WL 2726871 (N.D. Cal. 2006).
252. *Ibid.*, 14.
253. The United States famously withdrew from the Kyoto Protocol under the Presidency of George W Bush; see J. Brunnee, *The United States and International Environmental Law: Living with an Elephant in the Room*, 15(4) Eur. J. Intl. L. 617 (2004). Although, towards the end of the Bush Administration there were some signs of a shift in policy which commenced with acknowledgement of global warming as a real issue; see ENDS, *Bush inches towards a new UN climate deal*, [2007] 389 ENDS Report 4.
254. See Smith (n. 250) 120.
255. 406 F. Supp. 2d 265 (SDNY 2005).
256. See Environmental Data Services (ENDS), *Obama sets a course for a low-carbon economy*, [2009] 409 ENDS Report 48.

handed down a vitally important judgment in *Massachusetts v. Environmental Protection Agency*[257] where it declared that CO_2 could properly be regarded as a pollutant for the purposes of the Clean Air Act. Against this background the Court of Appeals for the Second Circuit ruled in *AEP* that the lower courts had been far too diffident. In such a case the duty of the court was to assess whether there were issues upon which it could adjudicate rather than seeking to second guess what the legislature may, or may not do, about the problem. Much constitutional case law was considered which suggested that the mere fact that an issue has a political dimension does not preclude the court from intervening.[258] Indeed, one might question what the role of the court is if it is not to attempt to resolve disputes which have yet to be tackled by the legislature. In this respect we can see a strong argument in favour of using the common law as a form of judicial legislation to compensate for legislative inactivity.[259]

A similar conclusion was reached by the Court of Appeals for the Fifth Circuit in *Comer v. Murphy Oil*[260] which concerned losses caused by Hurricane Katrina. It was alleged that greenhouse gas emissions increased, in a measurable way, the intensity and frequency of extreme weather events such as hurricanes. Once again the Court reached the view that the lower courts had shown undue deference to the legislative and executive branches of government in dismissing the case on the grounds that it raised political issues and was thereby non-justiciable. The courts are not precluded from dealing with issues which have 'political implications or ramifications'[261] unless the matter has been specifically removed from the judicial arena by Constitutional or Congressional means. No such steps had been taken in respect of climate change, thus the courts were at liberty to adjudicate upon such matters. Furthermore, the issue of justiciability is concerned with the separation of powers, or other Constitutional issues, and has nothing to do with, 'judges' capability, intellect, knowledge, expertise or training, nor upon the inherent difficulty, complexity, novelty or esotery of the matter to be resolved.'[262]

Thus, in the US at least, it now seems clear that climate change raises justiciable issues for the purposes of public nuisance. Although this has been an important legal and conceptual hurdle to cross it only marks the start of a very long battle. In this respect it is important to note that not all North American courts have sought to reject jurisdiction on grounds of justiciability. Even before the rulings of the higher courts on justiciability were handed down, at least one court was prepared to look beyond this issue and to examine the substance of the claims in more depth. Its findings do not bode well for others seeking to hold polluters liable for damage allegedly caused by climate change. In the *Native Village of Kivalina v. ExxonMobil Corp.*[263] the villagers, many of whom were indigenous Inupiat Eskimos, commenced proceedings against a number of US energy companies in respect of their activities in Alaska. It was alleged

---

257. 127 S. Ct. 1438 (2007).
258. For analysis of this aspect of the judgment see Smith (n. 250) 121–122.
259. In this respect see §4.03[C] on the role of the common law as a response to regulatory failure.
260. 585 F.3d 855 (5th Cir. 2009).
261. *Ibid.*, 869–870.
262. *Ibid.*
263. 663 F.Supp.2d 863 (N.D.Cal. 2009).

that their contribution to climate change had caused ice to melt and sea levels to rise threatening the plaintiffs' way of life. They sought damages in respect of the cost of relocating the village. Rather than dismissing the claim out of hand on the basis that it was a political issue the court attempted to see whether the existing common law framework was capable of addressing such issues. The court noted that the Restatement (Second) of Torts requires the court to determine the reasonableness of the defendant's activities in the light of several factors including the gravity of the harm and the utility of the conduct. This exercise could only be undertaken if the climate change issue disclosed 'judicially discoverable or manageable standards'.[264] In this respect the court derived little assistance from other cases on complex environmental issues. Whereas most cases involved definable geographic areas and an ascertainable number of sources, climate change stems from 'innumerable sources located throughout the world...affecting the entire planet and its atmosphere'.[265] Furthermore, the court could not determine what levels of emissions were harmful and thus unreasonable. The court concluded that the courts and the common law simply do not have the tools to resolve the issue and for this reason the matter should be diverted to the legislative arena.[266]

Most of the problems identified in *Kivalina* are essentially causation difficulties and these were also readily acknowledged by the appeal courts in *Connecticut* and *Comer*. The difference is that in *Kivalina* the court could be regarded as 'putting the cart before the horse.' It looked ahead to the difficulties which the court would face if a case was allowed to proceed; it then concluded that they were insurmountable and thus a matter for the legislature. The appeal courts in *Connecticut* and *Comer* were equally aware of the huge causation difficulties which would be faced by plaintiffs but were of the opinion that that alone was not a reason to throw the case out. Having removed the policy bar to advancing such claims it would be for future proceedings to determine whether causation difficulties and the like could be resolved. These causation difficulties shall be examined in more depth in the next chapter.

§2.06   NEGLIGENCE

[A]   Key Elements of the Tort

The tort of negligence arose from the *form of action* known as *action on the case* (or simply *case*) and was designed to provide redress for harm resulting from a careless as opposed to a deliberate and forceful act.[267] This type of claim could not be brought

---

264. *Ibid.*, 873.
265. *Ibid.*, 875.
266. *Ibid.*, 877.
267. One of the earliest successful applications of the writ, found by Fifoot, concerns the case of *Waldon v. Marshall* (1367) Y.B. 43 Ed. 3, f. 33, pl. 38, in which a horse died at the hands of a negligent veterinary surgeon. See Fifoot (n. 53), 75.

under trespass since it concerned indirect and consequential harm.[268] The earliest writs could only be used in cases where the defendant had made some 'prior undertaking' to carry out a service for the plaintiff.[269] The 'prior undertaking' test was eventually expanded into an implied undertaking to conduct activities in a manner which would not cause loss to neighbours, meaning all those who are foreseeable victims of carelessness.[270] At first, the term 'negligence' was merely one of a series of adverbs used to describe the concept of fault. As negligence hardened into a specific cause of action with its own principles other terms fell into disuse.

Negligence is now dominant in the field of personal injuries and damage to personal property and has arguably ousted trespass where liability hinges on fault.[271] It is important to note that in negligence fault is the essence of the tort whereas in nuisance and trespass to land fault may, to a greater or lesser extent, be a factor in determining liability depending upon the circumstances.

The basic elements of the tort were identified as early as the eighteenth century where Buller[272] offered a definition which subsists in essence to this day. Since Buller, the definition has been refined through case law and can now be said to consist of three elements, namely a duty to take care, a breach of that duty, and loss sustained by another person as a result of the breach of duty. A duty of care is owed to those persons who are at potential risk from an activity; in other words they must be foreseeable victims of any misfeasance. In *Donoghue v. Stevenson*, Lord Atkin formulated his famous proximity test to assist with determining foreseeable victims:

> You must take reasonable care to avoid acts or omissions which you can reasonably foresee would be likely to injure your neighbour. Who, then, in law is my neighbour? The answer seems to be – persons who are so closely and directly affected by my act that I ought reasonably to have them in contemplation as being so affected when I am directing my mind to the acts or omissions which are called in question.[273]

As regards conduct which gives rise to a breach of the duty, Alderson B. proposed an objective test in *Blyth v. Birmingham Waterworks Co.* which is still followed today:

---

268. *Ibid.* Thus in *Waldon v. Marshall* the defendant's argument that the plaintiff should have brought the action under common trespass was rejected on the grounds that 'the horse was not killed by force, but by default if his cure.'
269. See Fifoot (n. 53), 156.
270. This development appears to have occurred during the course of a series of seventeenth century cases concerning running down on the highway and collisions at sea: these include *Mitchil v. Alestree* (1676) 1 Vent. 295 and *Mustart v. Harden* (1680) T. Raym. 390. See Prichard (n. 71); Fifoot (n. 53), 164–166.
271. Hence it is now doubtful whether an action in 'negligent trespass' could still be maintained; see *Letang v. Cooper* [1965] Q.B. 232.
272. Francis Buller, *Trials at Nisi Prius*, 25 (6th ed., Phèney & Sweet 1817): 'Every man ought to take reasonable care that he does not injure his neighbour; therefore, where-ever a man receives any hurt through the default of another, though the same were not wilful, yet it be so occasioned by negligence or folly, the law gives him an action to recover damages for the injury so sustained.'
273. [1932] A.C. 562, 580.

> Negligence is the omission to do something which a reasonable man, guided upon those considerations which ordinarily regulate the conduct of human affairs, would do, or doing something which a prudent and reasonable man would not do.[274]

Whether the defendant's conduct was reasonable has to be judged by reference to the circumstances of the case including, for example, industry standards,[275] the magnitude of the risk[276] and generally 'what the reasonable man would have in contemplation'.[277] This latter requirement means that the reasonable man should be in a position to foresee that damage would be caused by his failure to act with due care. The rationale for this is that one cannot conduct activities with a view to avoiding unforeseeable harm.[278]

[B]   Negligence and the Environment

[1]   Property Damage

Trespass and nuisance have featured most prominently in litigation arising from pollution. This is because most recognized forms of pollution have interfered with neighbouring property. It has been usual to plead negligence in addition to the torts to land, however, a land owner generally has a far greater chance of success under the latter. The main reason for this is that, despite the decision in *Cambridge Water*, it seems that liability in trespass and nuisance is still stricter than in negligence.

It is often extremely difficult to establish fault on the part of the defendant. Negligence was alleged in *Esso Petroleum v. Southport Corporation*,[279] in addition to the claims in trespass and nuisance. The House of Lords rejected the Court of Appeal's finding that the case was one in which res ipsa loquitur could apply. In other words, the facts call for an explanation and in the absence of an explanation the mere occurrence of the accident is sufficient proof of fault.[280] The mere fact that the steering mechanism had developed a fault was not in itself sufficient to raise res ipsa loquitur. It would be necessary to adduce evidence of faulty maintenance or installation and this the plaintiff had failed to do.[281] The allegation that the master of the vessel should not have proceeded to navigate a narrow channel knowing that the steering mechanism had developed a fault was also rejected by their Lordships. Weather conditions were worsening and any attempt to turn or weigh anchor would have been hazardous. The master had weighed up the risks before opting to head for sheltered water. In reaching

---

274. (1856) 11 Ex. 781, 784.
275. *Wither v. Wessex Area Health Authority* [1987] Q.B. 730.
276. *Bolton v. Stone* [1951] A.C. 850; *Paris v. Stepney Borough Council* [1951] A.C. 367.
277. *Glasgow Corporation v. Muir* [1943] A.C. 448, at 457, per Lord Macmillan.
278. *Roe v. Minister of Health* [1954] 2 Q.B. 66.
279. [1956] A.C. 218, 240.
280. Much controversy surrounds the concept of res ipsa loquitur and whether it constitutes a real legal concept at all. Certainly, modern courts are very hostile to the notion that it actually reverses the burden of proof on causation. See *Carroll and Others v. Fearon and Others*; *Barclay v. Dunlop Ltd* [1999] E.C.C. 73, [15] (Judge L.J.).
281. [1956] A.C. 218, 237 (Earl Jowitt).

this decision he had not shown any want of care or skill. It is significant that this case concerned maritime-oil-pollution damage. This continues to be one of the most significant environmental issues as recent events in the Gulf of Mexico illustrate.[282] It is interesting to note that just a few years after this litigation an international consensus emerged to the effect that the need to establish fault was an unacceptable obstacle to establishing liability given the scale of the problem. This gave rise to a new international oil pollution compensation scheme which shall be addressed in subsequent chapters.[283]

The issue of negligence was quickly dispensed with by the High Court in *Cambridge Water v. Eastern Counties Leather*[284] and did not feature as a significant issue on appeal (or at least only insofar as whether negligence is an ingredient or not of nuisance). Since PCE in relatively small concentrations was not recognized as being harmful at the material time, Eastern Counties Leather was not expected to have taken steps to prevent any spillages from occurring.[285]

There was also an attempt to establish negligence on the part of the defendants in *Graham and Graham v. Re-Chem International.* It was alleged that the incinerator was operated in a manner which failed to sustain the temperature, recommended by Environmental Protection Agency (EPA) and Her Majesty's Inspectorate of Pollution (HMIP) regulations, needed for destroying polychlorinated biphenyls (PCBs) (1050–1100iC). The main argument put forward on behalf of the plaintiffs on this point was that the doors to the furnaces were frequently left open thereby allowing the temperature to fall. Evidence produced by the manufacturers of the incineration equipment referred to the fact that the waste materials were in fact passed through five separate chambers (termed 'cells') each of which contained burners. The temperature in the final cell was crucial in that it operated as the 'safety net' and was designed to destroy any PCB molecules not already destroyed by the burners in the other four cells. Forbes J. found, as a matter of fact, that the doors to the first cell were only open for relatively short periods for loading or ashing out and, although the door was often left slightly ajar, this would not be sufficient to affect the temperature in the fifth cell.[286] In any event, further scientific evidence, produced by the United States EPA, was accepted which showed that PCBs were destroyed at temperatures falling considerably below these levels and that the recommended temperature included a considerable built in safety margin.[287] In addition the Roughmute incinerator subjected the waste materials to a longer than usual burn time which would offset slight drops in the recommended temperature.

The issue of negligence was not of crucial importance in this case in that, as stated above, the matter was settled on the basis of causation. However, it provides further evidence to suggest that, despite the *Cambridge Water* decision, it is still more

---

282. The massive oil polution incident arising from the explosion of the Deepwater Horizon oil rig, owned and operated by Transocean on contract to BP, on 20 April 2010. The incident is now probably the most widely reported and notorious oil pollution incident in the history of the industry. The liability issues arising therefrom are dealt with at §3.05[A][2], below.
283. See §5.05[A], below.
284. [1993] Env. L.R. 116.
285. *Ibid.*, 142 (Kennedy J).
286. [1996] Env. L.R. 158, 186–189.
287. *Ibid.*, 180–181.

difficult to establish liability in negligence than in nuisance due to the need to establish breach of the duty of care in addition to foreseeability of damage. As noted above, as regards the claim in nuisance, there was no need to examine the manner in which the plant was operated, the sole issue concerned whether it was known that the facility was emitting pollutants which had in fact caused damage.

Nevertheless, on occasion successful actions have been brought in negligence in respect of environmentally harmful activities. A clear example is provided by the case of *Tutton v. A.D. Walter Ltd.*[288] The defendant was a farmer who grew rape seed in West Sussex. One summers day, he sprayed his crop with an insecticide called Hostathion which was known to be harmful to bees. As a result, a large number of the plaintiff's bees, which had been foraging in the field, were killed. The plaintiffs brought an action in negligence on the grounds that the chemical had been used in a manner which contravened advice issued by the Agricultural and Advisory Service (ADAS) and the manufacturer's instructions issued with the product. The advice and instructions recommended that in order to reduce the risk of harming bees, the chemical should be used on cool days or at dusk and never when the crop was in bloom.

In the High Court, Denis Henry Q.C. applied Lord Reid's proximity test in order to determine whether the plaintiffs were foreseeable victims of the misuse of the chemical. The presence of the bee-keepers was well known to the defendant due to the fact that they had exchanged correspondence regarding a spraying incident the previous year. The harmful nature of the chemical was also well-known to the defendant who had the benefit of the ADAS advice and the instructions on the drums which contained the chemical. Given these facts it was held that the defendant ought reasonably to have had the plaintiffs in contemplation whilst spraying his crops. The judge then turned to the issue of whether this duty had been broken. The advice and instructions pertaining to the use of the chemical could not be said to have imposed onerous requirements when balanced against the potential threat to the bees, thus a failure to observe the instructions was clearly a breach of the duty of care owed to the bee-keepers. The tort of negligence operates in a similar manner in the US as regards the issue of proximity. Thus in *Shockley v. Hoechst Celenese Corporation*[289] the court had no difficulty in finding that there was sufficient proximity between the defendant, who knowingly delivered leaking drums of hazardous waste to a site, and a neighbour who owned property adjoining that site.

[2]   Personal Injuries

Negligence is the only available cause of action where loss is unrelated to any interference with interests in land. In this respect the tort is becoming of increasing importance in an environmental context. Scientific advances have begun to establish links between illnesses and certain pollutants, hence, there is likely to be an increase in personal injury litigation arising from pollution. For example, in *Margereson v. J.W.*

---

288. [1985] 3 W.L.R. 797.
289. 793 F. Supp. 670 (D.S.C. 1992), *aff'd in relevant part*, 996 F. 2d 1212 (4th Cir. 1993).

Roberts Ltd.,[290] the plaintiffs had developed mesothelioma as a result of exposure to asbestos dust from the defendant's factory during childhood when they used to play in the factory loading bay. JWR was found liable on the grounds that the risks of asbestos had been known since 1925 and, since the children were allowed to play in the immediate vicinity of the factory, it was foreseeable that they would be exposed to the risk of pulmonary disease. The case is significant in that it was the first such claim in which the duty of care has been extended, beyond factory employees, so as to encompass those immediately outside the factory walls.

Once pollutants escape into the wider environment, affecting local inhabitants and passers-by, the issue becomes one of environmental exposure and the class of potential litigants may increase dramatically. Environmental exposure to toxic compounds, allegedly causing personal injuries, is at the heart of the long running Corby litigation. As noted above, the litigation stems from the redevelopment of the former British Steel works site in Corby. It is alleged that the land decontamination works released various toxic compounds (known collectively as teratogens) into the atmosphere which were ingested by pregnant women and that this led to upper limb deformities in their offspring. In the High Court judgment in *Corby Group Litigation v. Corby District Council*[291] Ackenhead J. found numerous examples of negligence both in terms of identifying the level of risk and in taking steps to reduce the risk. As regards the initial assessment of risk the claimants argued that res ipsa loquitur could apply as there had been no assessment of the dangers posed to the unborn child; this was said to be 'self evidently negligent'.[292] Ackenhead J. did not pass comment on the applicability of res ipsa, which, as noted above, is of debateable legal consequence. The fact that the judge felt it necessary to examine the state of scientific knowledge at the material time suggests that he was not convinced that such an assumption could be made. If such risks were not foreseeable then there could be no assumption that the failure to conduct such an assessment amounted to negligence. In this respect it is all too easy to look at the issue with the benefit scientific knowledge which may not have been available to the defendant at the material time.[293] However, even allowing for the more limited state of scientific knowledge at the time, the judge was still able to find that the defendant should have known that toxic dust would pose a hazard to the unborn child. Moreover, in this respect foreseeability of harm should not be too narrowly defined and it would not be necessary to show that the defendant could have anticipated the *precise* type of harm.[294] As regards other failures, survey reports and soil sampling techniques were deemed inadequate and sufficient means were not taken to reduce the level of dust. For example, soil was carried in uncovered lorries and there were no wheel washing facilities for a significant proportion of the works. The judge

---

290. Joined cases: *Hancock v. J.W. Roberts Ltd*; *Hancock v. T.&.N. Plc* [1996] Env. L.R. (4)304. See J. Steele and N. Wikely, *Margereson v. J.W. Roberts Ltd*, 60(2) M.L.R. 265 (1997).
291. [2009] EWHC 1944 (TCC); [2010] Env. L.R. D2.
292. *Ibid.*, [702].
293. As Lord Denning put it in *Roe v. Minister of Health* [1954] 2 Q.B. 66, at 84, 'we must not look at the 1947 accident with 1954 spectacles'. Similarly, in the *Corby* case the court had to be careful not to look at the 1980s redevelopment works through 2010 spectacles.
294. *Corby* (n. 291) [683].

also quickly dispensed with any argument to the effect that the main fault lay with the independent contractors engaged by the Corby D.C. and that the local authority could not be held vicariously liable. Although one is generally not vicariously liable for the torts of independent contractors, an exception is made in respect of activities which cause 'special danger' to another.[295] Activities which fall into this category have never been adequately defined although Ackenhead J. had no hesitation in finding that the redevelopment works fell into this category.[296]

The claimants won a significant victory in the High Court judgment in *Corby* and the case received widespread media attention.[297] In truth, however, the victory could easily have turned out to be a hollow one as the judgment left open the vital issue of causation.[298] On the basis of epidemiological evidence the judge was prepared to find that there was prima facie evidence of a causal link between the birth defects and the exposure to toxic dust.[299] However, this evidence would have to be tested in subsequent proceedings and each individual claimant would have to prove causation in his or her individual case. In the event the defendant has agreed to settle out of court and negotiations were still in progress at the time of writing.[300] Had the claimants been faced with establishing causation they may well have found it to be an uphill task.

In fact, it is often extremely difficult to establish causation where the pollutant is dispersed into the wider environment and adverse health effects resulting from toxicological effects are alleged. For example, in the US case of *Sterling v. Velsicol Chemical Corporation*,[301] the plaintiffs could not prove to the satisfaction of the court that certain illnesses had been caused by drinking water contaminated by pollutants leaching from a waste burial site. This issue shall be returned to in more detail in the next chapter.

---

295. See *Salsbury v. Woodland* [1970] 1 Q.B. 324.
296. *Corby* (n. 291) [684]. In fact, the correctness of this finding is debatable in that the authorities require a much greater risk than the term 'special danger' suggests in order to make an exception to the rule against no vicarious liability. In *Honeywell & Stein v. Larkin Bros* [1934] 1 KB 102 it was proposed that the activity would have to be 'extra-hazardous or dangerous.' Although the case has been heavily criticized (see, for example, G. Williams, Liability for Independent Contractors, 14(2) CLJ 180 (1956)) in that the standard is not well defined it certainly suggests a greater risk than 'special danger.' In *Biffa Waste Services v. Maschinenfabrik Ernst Hese GmbH* [2008] EWCA Civ 1257, [2009] 3 WLR 324; the Court of Appeal set the bar very high in terms of what types of activity can be regarded as falling within this classification. Indeed, in the light of this judgment it is difficult to conceive of any lawful activity which would be sufficiently dangerous to fall within the 'ultra-hazardous' exception to the principle of no vicarious liability for independent contractors.
297. See, for example, Frances Gibb, *'Toxic soup' Families Win Right to Sue Council over Birth Defects; High Court says Corby Liable after Waste Removal*, The Times, News 25 (London July 30, 2009).
298. *Corby* (n. 291) [867]. The Group Litigation Order (GLO) was confined to the question of whether any relevant breach of duty 'had the ability to cause upper and/or lower limb defects of the type complained of' rather than making findings of fact on this issue in each case.
299. *Ibid.*, [885].
300. See ENDS, *Corby Agrees Steelworks Compensation* [2010] 423 ENDS Report 8; ENDS, *Birth Defect Children to Receive Payouts*, The Times, News 34 (London Apr. 17, 2010).
301. 855 F2d 1188 (6th Cir. 1988).

§2.07   BREACH OF STATUTORY DUTY

Many industries and authorities are regulated by statutes which set out duties and impose criminal or regulatory sanctions for breach of those duties. Although the primary purpose of these statutes is not to provide redress for an individual who has suffered loss, as a result of any breach of the duties imposed, certain statutes give rise to a private cause of action. This is known as the tort of breach of statutory duty; it is important to note that it is an independent tort which has given rise to its own body of case law.[302] Thus, issues such as the applicable standard of liability must be determined by reference to the Act creating the duty rather than comparison with other torts such as negligence.[303]

A limited number of statutes make specific provision for private tort claims following a breach of duty, conversely certain statutes expressly preclude private compensation claims for breach of duty. In such circumstances the breach of duty may nevertheless provide evidence of a breach of the common law duty of care in a separate action in negligence.[304] Where a private right of action is neither expressly included nor excluded the courts have developed a number of tests for determining whether an intention to facilitate private actions can be implied.[305] As regards those statutes which do make express provision for civil liability, it is important to note that such duties may either oust existing common law duties altogether or operate without prejudice to existing common law rights depending upon the nature of the provision.

As the tort is governed, to a large extent, by the statute under which it arises there are few common principles. However, from the case law it is possible to discern certain key elements which the claimant must establish. In short, the duty must be owed to the claimant;[306] the injury must be of the kind which the statute is intended to prevent;[307] the defendant must be in breach of an obligation which falls within the scope of the Act;[308] and, the breach of duty must have caused the damage.[309]

---

302. This differs from the situation in certain States of the US and Canada where it merely serves as compelling evidence of a breach of the duty of care or 'concretises' the duty of care.

303. See *L. P. T. B v. Upson* [1949] A.C. 155, 168–169 (Lord Wright), 'A claim for damages for breach of a statutory duty intended to protect a person in the position of the particular plaintiff is a specific common law right which is not to be confused in essence with a claim in negligence ... I have desired before I deal specifically with the regulations to make it clear how in my judgment they should be approached, and also to make it clear that a claim for their breach may stand or fall independently of negligence. There is always a danger if the claim is not sufficiently specific that the due consideration of the claim for breach of statutory duty may be prejudiced if it is confused with the claim in negligence.'

304. See, for example, *Lochgelly Iron & Coal Co. v. M'Mullan* [1934] A.C. 1.

305. There is little consistency in the case law regarding the circumstances in which the tort should be implied. In general, it has been stated that Acts which are designed to protect a class of individuals are capable of giving rise to a private cause of action: *Lonrho Ltd v. Shell Petroleum Co. Ltd. (No. 2)* [1982] A.C. 173. In such circumstances, the existence of separate enforcement measures in the Act such as criminal penalties does not necessarily preclude the existence of a private cause of action: *Groves v. Wimborne* [1898] 2 Q.B. 402.

306. *Hartley v. Mayoh & Co.* [1954] 1 Q.B. 383.

307. *Gorris v. Scott* (1874) L.R. 9 Exch. 125.

308. *Chipchase v. Titan Products* Co. [1956] 1 Q.B. 545.

309. *Ginty v. Belmont Building Supplies Ltd.* [1959] 1 All E.R. 414.

In an environmental context, an important example of a statutory provision which gives rise to a cause of action for breach of statutory duty concerns section 12 of the Nuclear Installations Act 1965. This provides that any person who suffers injury or damage, as a result of a breach of any of the duties set out in sections 7 to 10 of the Act, shall have a right to compensation. Section 7 of the Act simply imposes a duty on the licensees of nuclear installations to prevent occurrences at the site causing property damage or injury to any persons, other than the licensee, by the release of any substances having radioactive, toxic, explosive or other hazardous properties. Sections 8 to 10 impose similar duties to prevent occurrences leading to the above results on the Regulatory Authority, the Crown and certain foreign operators respectively. As will be seen in the next chapter, there have been various attempts to found civil claims on section 12 in respect of alleged releases of ionizing radiation from nuclear installations.[310] It will also be seen that these cases expose the limited scope of the section 12 liability; this is a cause for concern in that the provision is an example of a duty which entirely precludes the operation of the common law. Any statutory duty which is drawn too narrowly and excludes alternative causes of action risks denying remedies to deserving parties.

Another key example of relevance in an environmental context concerns section 73(6) of the Environmental Protection Act 1990. This provides that anyone who deposits controlled waste in contravention of the licensing requirements imposed by the regime shall be liable to pay damages in respect of any personal injury or damage to property arising therefrom. The key duties are set out in sections 33(1) and 34(1) which also establish criminal liability. Section 33(1) is principally aimed at those engaged in waste management, such as waste disposal or recycling companies, and makes it an offence to cause or knowingly permit the deposit of waste otherwise than in accordance with the requirements of the regime. Section 34 imposes an overarching duty of care on any person who has control of waste or who transfers waste to another. This could include any individual who stores waste upon his property with a view to transferring it to a waste operator. A typical example would be a factory which has to store its waste products until such time as they can be removed by a waste management company. The section 34 duty requires a person holding waste to take reasonable measures to ensure that the waste does not escape from his control whilst it is in his possession. Furthermore, the duty does not end when the waste has been transferred to a waste operator in that the transferor must take reasonable measures to ensure that the waste is not disposed of in a manner which constitutes a breach of section 33(1). Thus a breach of section 34 could occur if the factory carelessly transferred the waste to a disreputable waste handler, without checking his credentials, who subsequently fly-tips the waste. However, it is important to note that section 73(6) only refers to section 33(1) offences which means that the regime only establishes a specific tort of breach of statutory duty in respect those directly engaged in the unlawful deposit or disposal of the waste (the errant waste contractor in our example).

---

310. *Merlin v. British Nuclear Fuels plc* [1990] 2 Q.B. 557; *Blue Circle Industries v. Ministry of Defence* [1999] Ch. 289; *Magnohard v. United Kingdom Atomic Energy Authority* [2004] Env. L.R. 19.

Nevertheless, section 34 may be invoked as evidence of the nature of the duty of care owed by others (such as the factory which transferred the waste to said errant waste management contractor) for the purposes of a separate claim in negligence. In *C (A Child) v. Imperial Design Ltd*[311] a servant or agent of the defendant kitchen unit manufacturing company left a drum of waste solvent on an area of open ground near the factory pending its removal by the defendant's waste management contractors. The claimant happened upon the drum whilst playing and set fire to it causing an explosion in which he was badly burned. The defendant was found to be in breach of the duty of care established by section 34 in that the hazardous nature of the waste meant that it should have been more securely stored pending its removal. The Court of Appeal found that the High Court was wrong to regard a breach of section 34 as constituting a breach of statutory duty under section 73(6) in that the latter provision does not refer to the general duty of care. However, the provision was treated as defining the extent and nature of the duty of care for the purposes of liability under the common law of negligence.[312] In any event, given that the child was old enough to know the risk and given that his friends had cautioned against his foolish actions his damages were reduced by 50% on account of contributory negligence. The waste management duty was also invoked in the afore-mentioned *Corby* litigation in which the High Court had little hesitation in finding that the local authority had not taken sufficient care to ensure that the waste was safely disposed of.[313] In this respect there were found to be breaches of both the 'direct duties' imposed by section 33(1) and the 'general duty' of care under section 34(1). As regards section 34 it seems that the High Court once again made the mistake of treating a breach of section 34 as giving rise to an independent tort of breach of statutory duty.[314] However, given the widespread findings of negligence under common law this would not have had any effect on the outcome of the case.

In both the *Imperial Design* and *Corby* cases the statutory duties bolstered, or 'buttressed' as Potter L.J. put it in *Imperial Design*,[315] the common law causes of action. However, given that the statutory duties were also based upon fault they added little to the existing common law cause of action in negligence; thus the claimant was still faced with establishing want of care on the part of the defendant. In such cases one might ask whether there is any 'added value' arising from the tort of breach of statutory duty. The answer is that the statute serves to clarify the nature and extent of the duty which is owed. For example, section 33(1) of the EPA appears to impose a somewhat more stringent standard of care than that which would be applied under negligence. Furthermore, although section 34 does not in itself give rise to a separate tort of breach of statutory duty, it provides a clear guide as to the nature and extent of the duty of care. Thus, the regime makes it clear that the duty of care does not end when the waste has been transferred to a waste disposal operator. It is not entirely clear what position the

---

311. [2001] Env. L.R. 33.
312. *Ibid.*, see Arden L.J. at [48–53].
313. *Corby Group Litigation v. Corby D.C.* [2010] Env. L.R. D2; see [692–697] regarding the applicability of the duties imposed by the Environmental Protection Act 1990.
314. See R. Lee, *Old iron: birth defects litigation and the Corby steelworks reclamation,* 25(4) J. of Prof. Negl. 174, 182–184 (2009).
315. *Imperial Design* (n. 311) [31].

courts would have adopted if the matter had to be determined through the application of negligence. In any case, certain statutory duties may replace the fault based notion of harm with a stricter duty; this is the case in respect of section 12 of the Nuclear Installations Act 1965. In this case a major barrier to establishing liability may be removed, although, as we shall see below, there may be other significant obstacles in the path of the claimant.

§2.08   CONCLUSIONS

It is a measure of the versatility of the common law that ancient principles, which initially evolved as a response to prosaic problems such as smells from pigsties and tallow makers, are still at the forefront of disputes arising from many of the great environmental issues of the age. Most notably the common law has featured in the climate change debate and public anxiety arising from the proliferation of GMOs. The earliest torts, namely trespass and nuisance, arose in the context of the protection of private interests in land. Thus, tort is engaged when environmental harm coincides with the invasion of a private interest which is protected by such private rights. This is perhaps the greatest limitation of traditional tort-based remedies; it is difficult to engage those rights unless the damage happens to affect an individual with the wherewithal to pursue an action against the polluter. However, the US public nuisance actions on climate change indicate one means of harnessing tort based principles in pursuit of broader public interests objectives; although, the litigants still face formidable difficulties which are outlined below. Other problems arising from the property based torts concern the narrow range of interests which are protected; although, as we have seen, some of the longstanding doctrinal arguments against recoverability of damages for personal injuries are now being challenged.

Negligence evolved much later than trespass and nuisance as an implied obligation to conduct activities with due care. Due to the fact that it is free of the shackles of property law, negligence provides a much more versatile remedy than the property based torts. Negligence has continued to grow in importance and has succeeded in infiltrating other areas of tort where there is a clear overlap in terms of subject matter. The most pronounced overlap between the torts occurs where there has been tangible damage. Thus, whereas a householder, who suffers health effects as a result of noxious emissions, may have a cause of action in negligence and nuisance, a family member living in the same property, with no proprietary interest in the house,[316] would be confined to negligence.[317] As a result of such anomalies, it has been argued that, where there has been tangible damage, the time has come to establish a uniform negligence based standard of liability.[318] This would limit nuisance, based upon strict liability, to

---

316. Standing requirements for actions in tort are discussed in chapter 3.
317. See Newark (n. 86) 489, 'A sulphurous chimney in a residential area is not a nuisance because it makes householders cough and splutter but because it prevents them from taking their ease in their gardens.'
318. See C. Gearty, *The Place of Private Nuisance in a Modern Law of Torts*, 48(2) Cambridge L.J. 214 (1989).

circumstances in which there has been no physical loss and the dispute is purely proprietary in nature.[319] Such an approach has long since been adopted in Germany.[320] However, the effect of this is to limit the range of situations in which the stricter standard of liability applicable in the property torts can apply. This has implications for the efficacy of tort as a means of environmental protection.

Overall, it is difficult to secure public interest objectives, such as environmental protection, by means of a system which focuses on the private rights and the conduct of the individuals in a dispute. Although, as shall be argued in subsequent chapters, the two objectives are not necessarily antipathetic. In addition there are a range of other difficulties which serve to limit the role of tort as a means of environmental protection including causation and a host of other factors. These difficulties and limitations shall be discussed in depth in the next chapter.

---

319. See Law Commission, *Civil Liability for Dangerous Things and Activities*, 25 Law Commn. No 32 (1970). In cases where the defendant is seeking an injunction to prevent an on-going nuisance, 'consideration of the strictness of the duty is than out of place – all the court is concerned with is the question, "should the plaintiff be told to stop this interference with the plaintiff's rights?" Whether or not the defendant knew of the smell or noise or the like when it first began to annoy the plaintiff does not matter; he becomes aware of it at the latest when the plaintiff brings his claim before the court.'

320. Under paragraph 906 of the Civil Code (Das Bürgerliches Gesetzbuch: BGB), nuisance actions may only be brought in respect of interferences from 'unweighable particles'. These include gases, vapours, smells, smoke, soot, heat, noises and shocks. According to the decision in the 'Smelting Oven' (*Kupolofen*) case, BGHZ 92, 143 (1985), any actions in respect of physical damage to property or personal injury must be brought under the all embracing duty to take care, set out in paragraph 823 BGB. See B.S.Markesinis, *The German Law of Torts*, 880–881 (3d ed., Clarendon Press 1994).

CHAPTER 3

Establishing Liability for Environmental Damage: Main Issues

§3.01 INTRODUCTION

Establishing civil liability for environmental damage in an environmental context is subject to certain difficulties which currently limit its role in environmental protection. In many cases concerning pollution the claimant faces exceedingly high procedural costs, known as 'transaction costs', which represent legal costs associated with establishing liability on the part of the defendant. Transaction costs are increased by factors such as the need to establish fault and causation; as will be seen below, these costs may be particularly acute in many cases concerning environmental damage.

The use of civil liability in an environmental context is also limited by the fact that, as stated towards the end of the previous chapter, torts are concerned with the protection of private interests. This creates two problems, first, the loss suffered by an individual may not reflect the full costs of the damage caused to the environment; thus compensation awarded to a claimant may not be sufficient to fund, for example, clean-up costs. Second, as torts are closely tied to the protection of individual rights and interests, there is a limited notion of standing. As a result, in the absence of an individual victim, organizations concerned with environmental protection are generally not in a position to pursue civil claims on behalf of the environment in its own right.

§3.02 THE NEED TO ESTABLISH FAULT

The extent to which it is necessary to establish fault on the part of the defendant has already been explored in some detail in the previous Chapter. To reiterate, negligence is the only tort in which fault forms the actual basis of the cause of action. However, as a result of cross-contamination between the old forms of action, aspects of fault based liability have now entered other torts such as nuisance. Towards the end of the previous chapter it was noted that there is increasing support for the view that, in cases of personal injury or tangible damage to real or personal property, negligence should be adopted as a uniform basis of liability; this is already the position in Germany.[321]

Taking this step would certainly clarify the law and remove anomalies. However, from an environmental perspective, the need to establish fault in all cases would place a heavy burden on the claimant. To recap, in nuisance, it suffices to show that the defendant knew that his activity was causing, for example, the emission of noxious substances. However, it is not necessary for the claimant to establish that the defendant was at fault in failing to abate the pollution. Thus, in *Graham and Graham v. Re-Chem International*,[322] had the Grahams been able to establish causation, they would have succeeded in their nuisance claim in that there was ample evidence that Re-Chem knew that polycyclic aromatic hydrocarbons (PAHs) were being released from their facility. Thus, the fact that, at the material time, science had yet to isolate the chemical processes which led to the harmful emissions had no bearing on the issue of nuisance; knowledge of the emissions would have been sufficient to establish liability. However, in negligence, in addition to establishing that the defendant knew of the emissions, it is necessary to show that he failed to take adequate steps to abate them. For example, in *Graham and Graham*, in order to succeed in negligence, it would have been necessary to demonstrate that Re-Chem was in a position to prevent the emissions and failed to do so. This would entail establishing that Re-Chem was aware of the chemical processes which led to the pollution; clearly, it is impossible to introduce abatement technology without knowing how the pollution is caused.

Due to the scientific complexity of many processes which cause pollution, it may be extremely difficult for the claimant to establish that, given the current state of scientific knowledge, the pollution was preventable.

§3.03   CAUSATION

[A]   Difficulties in Establishing Causation for Environmental Damage

Damage arising from nuisances or negligent acts constitutes a form of indirect consequential harm. Thus the causal link between the act complained of and the alleged consequential damage is susceptible to being broken, or at least cast into doubt, by intervening factors or other possible causes. The industrial revolution led to a rapid increase in development with the result that it became increasingly difficult for a land holder to determine which of his neighbours was responsible for a nuisance. Whereas before, there would probably only have been one possible candidate for the source of the pollution, post-industrial revolution, a landholder would have found himself surrounded by belching chimneys. In giving testimony to a Select Committee on Noxious Vapours, Robert Gerard stated:

---

321. See ch. 2 (n. 320), above.
322. [1996] Env. L.R. 158.

> I might explain that the reason why I have not myself brought actions against the alkali manufacturers at St. Helens has been simply this: I am assured by my solicitor that it is impossible to bring an action with any chance of success unless I can put my finger upon the right man. I cannot put my finger upon the right man, with all the assistance I can get, when there are a dozen or 20 works all emitting vapours at the same time.[323]

The problem was compounded when there were a number of different industries in the area, each producing different substances which mixed together. Scientific knowledge was not usually capable of isolating the individual elements and tracing them to their respective sources. In giving evidence to the same committee Michael Garvey, a barrister, stated that it was almost impossible to establish liability on the grounds of:

> The difficulty of selecting any one of those effluvia and tracing it up to its source, so as to bring it home to the manufacturer by legal evidence. We have always been defeated on this point.[324]

Scientific techniques for tracing pollutants to source have undoubtedly improved, however, it is still often extremely difficult to establish causation. In the nineteenth and early twentieth centuries, claims were usually only brought in respect of self-evident pollution such as smoke, fumes and waste products. As scientific knowledge has progressed, increasingly complex links between latent toxins and various types of harm have been discovered. However, it is one thing to discover a potential link, it is quite another to provide sufficient proof of the link for the purposes of establishing liability. Negligence claims for personal injuries are likely to increase as advances in scientific knowledge begin to establish possible links between health problems and environmentally harmful activities. This creates difficult causation problems in that a toxin is often only one of a number of possible causes for a particular illness. Nevertheless, even a small dose of a certain toxin may increase the incidence of certain illnesses; this is referred to as the 'stochastic effect'. As will be seen below, such developments are already beginning to strain existing legal tests for establishing causation.

[B] Establishing Causation for Environmental Damage

In common law jurisdictions, following the Anglo-American tradition, it is incumbent upon the claimant to demonstrate, on a balance of probabilities, that the defendant caused or made a 'material contribution' to the loss.[325] In one case, the House of Lords appeared to establish that there could be a presumption of causation where the defendant's activity materially 'increased the risk' of the harm occurring.[326] However, this was subsequently limited to cases where there is no doubt regarding the nature or source of the causal agent and the only issue is which of the defendant's failures caused

---

323. Report from the Select Committee on Noxious Vapours (HL 1862, 486 – IX), Minutes of Evidence 17 [161].
324. *Ibid.*, 189 [2027].
325. See *Bonnington Castings v. Wardlaw* [1956] A.C. 613.
326. See *McGhee v. National Coal Board* [1972] 3 All E.R. 1008.

the exposure leading to loss or injury. Thus, there can be no presumption of causation where there are alternative candidates for the loss unrelated to the defendant's activities.[327] In fact, the material increase in risk approach has been pushed somewhat further in cases involving asbestos related diseases attributable to workplace exposure.[328] Thus, where an employee has worked for a number of different employers, each of whom negligently exposed him to asbestos fibres, each employer may be held jointly and severally liable on the basis that they each enhanced a common risk.[329] However, it is doubtful whether these cases amount to any more than a limited exception to general principles based upon the unique characteristics of asbestos. Mesothelioma and asbestosis can only be caused by asbestos; thus, although there may be doubt regarding where the 'guilty fibre' was inhaled there is no doubt regarding the identity of the causal agent. Moreover, where consecutive employers, through their failings, expose the claimant to this common hazard one might argue that some form of collective responsibility is reasonable. However, as we shall see in the following analysis, in most cases of environmental exposure there are usually far more uncertainties regarding the nature and source of the harmful element. For example, in the asbestos cases one can argue that there is a linkage between the employers, who exposed the claimant to harm, and the type of risk which they created. In environmental exposure cases there may be no linkage between the potential sources and the harm may not be uniquely associated with the substance in question.

To date most cases in tort, which have raised the issue of causation, have concerned medical negligence or industrial diseases, it is only in recent years that a number of cases concerning environmental damage have been decided which address the issue of causation. From these cases, which are discussed below, it is clear that if the pollution occurs in high concentrations in the immediate vicinity of a plant, the claimant should not be presented with major difficulties in establishing causation. However, once in the environment, a pollutant may merge with other substances already present in the environment with the result that the damage pathways become obscured; it may not be possible to disentangle the effects of the pollutant from the effects of other possible causal agents. In such circumstances it may be impossible to establish causation to the satisfaction of the court due to the need to establish that the activity of which complaint is made actually contributed, as a matter of fact, to the harm in a particular case. This problem is particularly acute in cases where personal injury is alleged to have been caused by environmental damage. This is due to the

---

327. See *Wilsher v. Essex Area Health Authority* [1986] 3 All E.R. 801.
328. See *Fairchild v. Glenhaven Funeral Services Ltd* [2003] 1 A.C. 32; *Barker v. Corus UK plc* [2006] 2 A.C. 572.
329. *Ibid.*, although in *Barker v. Corus* the House of Lords took a step back from its earlier decision in *Fairchild* and held that damages would be adjusted so as to reflect the amount of time which an employee had worked for a particular employer. In other words, employers would be *severally* as opposed to *jointly and severally* liable. This approach risked leaving a claimant undercompensated with the result that Parliament stepped in and enacted section 3 Compensation Act 2006. This effectively reinstated joint and several liability in asbestos cases and indicates a clear policy decision to hold employers collectively liable for losses associated with the mishandling of asbestos over many decades.

complexity of the human body and the numerous explanations which can lie behind a certain condition.

[1]   Cases Where There Is Only One Known Cause

As noted above, where the identity and source of the polluting substance is not in doubt, the claimant is not presented with major difficulties in establishing causation. The afore-mentioned asbestos issue provides a useful case study in this respect. As we have seen, much progress has been made in terms of establishing causation in *occupational* exposure cases. The outcome in respect of *environmental* exposure, that is, where the noxious substance is encountered in places other than the workplace, is less certain. A recent asbestos case which links the issues of occupational and environmental exposure is *Sienkiewicz v. Greif (UK) Ltd.*[330] In this case the claimant was required to show that the occupational exposure materially increased the risk of contracting mesothelioma beyond the risk created by the environmental exposure which affected all those in the locality. The Court of Appeal found that section 3 Compensation Act 2006[331] preserved the common law rules on causation and that an 18% increase in risk would suffice to establish liability. This judgment begs the question of whether the environmental exposure in the locality could have been regarded as an independent cause irrespective of occupational exposure. If this was the case, other local residents could have claimed in respect of asbestos related illnesses irrespective of whether they had worked with the material.

In fact such a claim was brought in the earlier case of *Margereson v. J.W. Roberts Ltd.*[332] in which two women, who had lived in the vicinity of an asbestos plant, successfully claimed damages in negligence having developed the cancer mesothelioma. Residents in the immediate vicinity of the plant had been exposed to extremely high concentrations of asbestos dust during the 1930s. In winter, children used to gather for warmth outside the extraction ducts and were coated with dust. Furniture in houses in the area was described as having been coated with dust to the extent that it was possible to write in it. The trial judge commented that, 'I cannot sensibly distinguish the conditions at thirteen Aviary Road from those in the factory ... the defendants knew or ought to have known that their dust emissions created such conditions'.[333] However, the judge also stated that:

> ...what I reject is the proposition that all exposure outside this category could be categorised as 'environmental', something contrasting with, and markedly less potentially hazardous than, exposure within the factory. I have no doubt but that, in the immediate vicinity of the defendants' premises, factory conditions in terms of dust emission were at various points effectively replicated so as to give rise to like foresight of potential injury to those exposed for prolonged periods.[334]

---

330. [2010] W.L.R. 951.
331. See (n. 415), below.
332. [1996] P.I.Q.R. P154.
333. *Ibid.*, 183 (Holland J).
334. *Ibid.*

However, difficulties in establishing causation increase significantly where the pollution can in fact be referred to as 'environmental'. As stated above, once a pollutant has been dispersed into the environment over a wide area, the number of alternative causes is multiplied. In the afore-mentioned *Sienkiewicz* case the background environmental levels of asbestos appear to have been somewhat lower and arose from multiple sources, not all of which could be identified. In this respect there are far fewer 'common denominators' than the occupational exposure asbestos cases with the result that it may not be possible to stretch the material increase in risk approach to cover that type of exposure. These difficulties are compounded still further where the identity of the causal agent is also in doubt and are especially acute in the context of toxicological exposure of both animals and humans.

[2]   The Agricultural Cases

In *Graham and Graham v. Re-Chem International*[335] the plaintiffs faced additional difficulties in establishing causation in that there was more than one possible explanation for their loss. It will be recalled that the case concerned an allegation by the Grahams that their dairy cattle had been poisoned by emissions emanating from the defendant's toxic waste incinerator at Roughmute. It was the plaintiffs' contention that the symptoms displayed by the cattle were consistent with a condition known as Polyhalogenated Aromatic Hydro-carbons (PHAH) toxicosis which could have been caused by ingestion of grass contaminated with dioxins and furans. Re-Chem argued that the symptoms in fact bore a closer resemblance to those displayed by cattle suffering from an entirely unrelated condition known by the inelegant title of Fat Cow Syndrome (FCS) and certain other ancillary causes.

Forbes J. stated that, where there was more than one possible cause for the harm, it would suffice to show that the defendant's conduct caused or materially contributed to the plaintiff's loss.[336] The judge also referred to the judgment of Lord Reid in *McGhee* where his Lordship stated that it would suffice to show that the activity materially increased the risk of the harm occurring.[337] As regards the effect of the House of Lords decision in *Wilsher*, Forbes J. concluded that Lord Reid's risk formulation of the material contribution test was reaffirmed.[338] The only part of the decision which was rejected, in his view, concerned comments made by Lord Wilberforce which appeared to suggest that, in certain circumstances, the effect of the material contribution test as formulated by Lord Reid would be to reverse the burden of proof. Thus, it seems that Forbes J. would have been content for the plaintiff to establish that the emissions from the incinerator materially increased the risk of damaging the health of the cattle. It is respectfully suggested that the judge erred on this point of law in that he did not refer to the distinction made by Lord Bridge in *Wilsher* between the facts of that case and *McGhee*. The facts in the *Graham and Graham* case are more closely related to *Wilsher*

---

335. [1996] Env. L.R. 158.
336. *Ibid.*, 171–172.
337. *Ibid.*
338. *Ibid.*

than *McGhee* in that the alternative cause was unrelated to the operation of the incinerator. However, in the event this issue had no effect on the outcome of the case as the plaintiffs could not satisfy even this liberal interpretation of the material contribution test.

Having reviewed the evidence, Forbes J. was satisfied that the symptoms were more typical of FCS than PHAH toxicosis. In particular, he referred to the existence of intercellular fat deposits which are indicative of the onset of FCS and are in no way associated with PHAH toxicosis. Furthermore, many symptoms were closely associated with a reduction in the immune response of the cattle which is also indicative of FCS. Especially damning to the Grahams' case was the fact that FCS had been diagnosed by veterinary surgeons when the cattle first began to fall ill in 1984. A course of treatment was prescribed, involving a change of diet, to which the cattle responded. The Grahams failed to continue the treatment as they were convinced that the toxic waste incinerator was the true cause of the harm. It was stated that Mr Graham was 'blind to any signs of improvement and quickly gave up any hope of saving his herd'.[339] This led Forbes J. to conclude that 'the proper welfare of the Grahams' cattle was sacrificed on the altar of Mr Graham's obsessive belief in Re-Chem's responsibility for his problems'.[340] In addition, the FCS symptoms could have been compounded by a number of ancillary causes also unrelated to the operation of the incinerator. For example, it was found that the cattle suffered from copper and selenium deficiency; this was probably due to the fact that the land upon which the cattle grazed was naturally deficient in these elements. Furthermore, it was found that the cattle suffered from vitamin A and E deficiency, a condition which was also entirely inconsistent with PHAH toxicosis.

This judgment can be neatly contrasted with the Canadian case of *Jones v. Mobil Oil Canada Ltd*,[341] (Alberta Court of Queen's Bench) which also concerned harm suffered by cattle grazing in proximity to a source of pollution. However, in this case the circumstantial evidence against the defendant was far greater. The claimant's herd grazed in close proximity to the defendant's oil and gas operations and fell victim to a number of ailments over a ten-year period resulting in illness, failure to breed or death. It was the claimant's contention that the cattle had ingested large quantities of polluted grass and drunk contaminated water due to the defendant's failure to properly fence their operations or to contain the spread of pollutants. There were numerous sources of pollution at the site including a filled in flare pit near which the cattle had grazed until it was discovered and the contaminated soil removed.[342] On other occasions the claimant had discovered his cattle drinking from pools of run-off fluid leaking from well heads and licking fence posts which had been sprayed by emissions from a ventilator stack. Furthermore the cattle had been allowed to wonder into highly contaminated areas through the defendants' failure to properly fence their facilities. As a result of this

---

339. *Ibid.*, 176.
340. *Ibid.*, 177.
341. 72 Alta. L.R. (3d) 369, [2000] 1 W.W.R. 479, 248 A.R. 1, 1 W.W.R. 479.
342. Mr Jones gave evidence that a bulldozer operator, involved in the operation to remove the contaminated soil from the flair pit, had become disorientated and dizzy as a result of the fumes released during the excavation process; see *Jones* (n. 341) [32].

long term exposure the cattle had been exposed to all manner of noxious substances including hydrocarbons, sodium, chlorides, iron, lead, boron and chromium. Following years of fruitless negotiation with Mobil, Mr Jones sued Mobil in negligence and nuisance in respect of the harm suffered by the cattle. Mobil defended the action on causation grounds arguing that the symptoms displayed by the cattle were also consistent with bowel virus diarrhoea (BVD) and selenium deficiency.

In the light of the overwhelming evidence of poor environmental management on the part of Mobil, the Romaine J, in the Alberta Court of Queen's Bench, adopted a robust common sense approach to the issue of causation stating that, although the onus was on the plaintiff to established that the negligence and nuisance caused or materially contributed to the harm: 'causation need not be determined with scientific precision, and it is essentially a question of fact that can be answered by the application of ordinary common sense'.[343] Thus:

> Mr Jones does not have to prove conclusively that exposure to contaminants or ingestion of them led to the symptoms suffered by the herd: the test is the balance of probabilities. There must be more than conjecture for an inference to be drawn in the absence of exact proof. Such inference must be reasonable. However, the inability of the experts to give a firm diagnosis, or to agree a diagnosis, is not fatal to such an inference. All the evidence must be considered in considering whether such an inference is reasonable.[344]

The well documented instances of cattle being exposed to high levels of pollutants[345] and the various failures on the part of Mobil were found to justify such an inference on the facts of the case and the court quickly dispensed with Mobil's alternate cause arguments. As regards the BVD virus it was found that the testing instigated on Mobil's behalf had been 'sporadic' and that those results which had been obtained did not show evidence of BVD in any case. In the absence of such supporting evidence the BVD alternate-cause argument appeared little more than conjecture and was certainly insufficient to refute the inference of causation: 'I find that the evidence of this BVD is weak and speculative at best.'[346] The selenium deficiency argument was stronger as it was established that the cattle also had this condition, however, the argument was refuted as, once the contaminants had been removed, the cattle enjoyed reasonably good health notwithstanding the fact that they still had the condition.[347]

Thus although the toxicologists could not say with scientific certainly whether the traces of chemicals found in dead animals caused the harm, the circumstantial evidence of exposure to oilfield contaminants and the breaches of duty on the part of Mobil tipped the scales firmly in the plaintiff's favour.[348]

---

343. *Ibid.*, [161].
344. *Ibid.*, [168].
345. Mr Jones had kept meticulous records of each incident during the dispute, this greatly helped his case at court: see Jones (n. 341) [169].
346. *Ibid.*, [170].
347. *Ibid.*, [175].
348. *Ibid.*, [166].

Similarly, circumstantial evidence was important in the UK High Court judgment in *Clifton v. Powergen*[349] concerning crop damage caused by emissions from a power station. In this case the plaintiffs alleged that scorch marks on their crops of Iceberg lettuces, spring greens and Brussels sprouts were consistent with the effects of emissions from the neighbouring Richborough power station. Significance was attached to the fact that the damage began when the power station was brought out of reserve and converted to burning a different type of fuel known as Orimulsion, 'a finely-dispersed emulsion of bitumen droplets in water'.[350] The plaintiffs case was that the burning of this fuel had resulted in the emission of fine particles, referred to as 'Orimulsion dust', and that when this was deposited on crops it caused an acidic reaction causing the burn marks. Experts acting on behalf of the plaintiffs carried out experiments both in the laboratory and in field trials whereby they were able to replicate the crop damage through the application of Orimulsion dust to the crops. The defendants attempted to refute this evidence with an alternate cause argument based on the contention that the damage was also consistent with a bacterial disease known as vanish spot. However, the court accepted the plaintiff's expert witness testimony that the pattern of damage was far more consistent with exposure to a toxic compound than vanish spot. Nevertheless, the court accepted that the onus was on the plaintiff to establish a causal link and that an inference could not be made simply on the basis that the defendant could not adduce compelling evidence of an alternate cause:

> The defendants correctly submitted that no burden lay on them to establish some cause alternative to that contended for by the plaintiffs: the cause may be unknown or unproven: the plaintiffs fail unless they establish on a balance of probabilities causation as alleged by them, and it is insufficient for them to establish that the cause they allege is more probable than any other stated cause.[351]

Thus, as in *Jones v. Mobil*, the court proceeded to a consideration of whether there was circumstantial evidence pointing to Richborough as the source of the pollution. In fact there were several well documented incidents where oily sooty deposits had been detected in the vicinity causing damage to the paint-work of vehicles in the power station car park and in a neighbouring compound owned by a car dealership. Further deposits were found on vegetation some 2 km from the power station stack. Engineers' logs reported specific equipment failures leading to emissions, however, there was also evidence to the effect that the entire manner in which the power station was operated was prone to cause emissions of the dust. In short, it was found that exhaust gases were allowed to cool causing condensation on the exhaust ducting; this trapped particles forming sticky concentrated deposits which became detached and escaped through the stack.[352] However, the simplest, yet perhaps most compelling piece of evidence, is briefly dealt with at the end of the judgment where it appears almost as an afterthought. This is simply that the period during which the damage occurred corresponded exactly with the burning of Orimulsion at the power station:

---

349. (QB (T & CC), Aug. 1, 1997).
350. *Ibid.*, [5].
351. *Ibid.*, [54].
352. *Ibid.*, [143].

The damage started when Orimulsion started to be burnt at Richborough power station in substantial quantities and continued thereafter until the last season, 1995, when Orimulsion was burnt there; the damage then ceased ... in my judgment that coincidence adds weight to the evidence that the damage to the plaintiffs' lettuces, Brussels sprouts and spring greens sustained between 1991 and 1995 was caused by the emission of acid agglomerates from Richborough power station. On the totality of the evidence, I find that that was the cause of the damage.[353]

Thus it seems that, where there is compelling circumstantial evidence pointing towards a particular facility, the courts are not prepared to allow a mere theoretical possibility of an alternate cause to defeat the plaintiff's case, simply on the basis that it is not possible to refute the alternative explanation with scientific certainty.

This point was made forcefully in the Irish case of *Hanrahan v. Merck Sharp and Dohme*[354] in which the plaintiffs alleged that a chemical factory, built just one mile from their farm, had injured the health of their cattle and had caused crop damage. It was not possible to establish a scientific causal link between the chemical plant and the loss sustained by the plaintiffs. However, given the fact that the loss occurred within a relatively short time of the plant opening and given the fact that there was no other plausible explanation, the court was prepared to infer that the harm was due to emissions emanating from the plant. Henchy J. stated that to insist upon scientific certainty in establishing causation:

> ... would be to allow scientific theorising to dethrone fact to dispose of this claim by saying ... that there was 'virtually no evidence in this case of injury to human beings or animals which has been scientifically linked to any chemicals emanating from the defendant's factory' ... the most credible explanation offered for the ailments and abnormalities in the cattle was the toxic emissions from the factory.[355]

However, a common feature of the cases discussed so far is that the courts had concrete facts upon which to base their judgments. There was no dispute that the pollutants in question were, as a matter of scientific fact, *capable* of causing the harm. The issue for the courts was whether the defendant's conduct was, in the particular circumstances of the case, and on a balance of possibilities, the most *likely* explanation for the harm. This determination could be made by reference to circumstantial evidence. Thus in *Jones v. Mobil Oil* the claimant was able to cite the documented instances of cattle drinking from contaminated pools, licking contaminated fence posts and straying into highly polluted areas through poorly maintained fencing. The evidential task facing the Grahams in *Re-chem* was much more difficult as the concentrations of pollutants involved were much lower. Nevertheless, the circumstances clearly pointed away from Roughmute as the source of the harm. The fact that the cattle actually responded to treatment for FCS and that certain symptoms were far more consistent with FCS than PHAH toxicosis cannot have left the court in any doubt.

---

353. *Ibid.*, [392–393].
354. [1988] I.R. 629.
355. *Ibid.*, 645.

[3]   The Public Health and Toxic Micro-Pollutant Cases

A still greater challenge for established legal reasoning is presented by toxic micro-pollutants and the risk they pose for human health. The effects of these elements are extremely difficult to quantify due to the fact that they interact with the receiving media in a complex manner. As a result it may be impossible to disentangle the effects of the pollutant from other elements in the environment for the purposes of estimating the extent to which they contributed to the loss suffered by the claimant. Thus it is extremely difficult, if not impossible, to establish a definite biological link between the pollutant and the harm in an individual case. An illustration of the difficulties associated with establishing causation in these circumstances is provided by litigation arising out of claims for loss alleged to have been caused by radiation from nuclear facilities.

The case of *Merlin v. British Nuclear Fuels* PLC[356] concerned an alleged breach of statutory duty under the Nuclear Installations Act 1965, The plaintiffs lived in the vicinity of the Sellafield Nuclear Waste reprocessing plant. They were led to believe that their house may have been contaminated by radionuclides emanating from the defendant's plant. The likely source of the contamination was traced to a waste pipe discharging effluent into the sea. Samples of house dust were sent to various experts for analysis. The plaintiffs were greatly concerned by the findings of Professor Radford in the United States who claimed to have discovered levels of the alpha emitting substances plutonium and americium which were greatly in excess of the national average. On the basis of this information the plaintiffs decided to move house in order to avoid potential health risks to their children. However, as a result of publicity caused by a television documentary, the plaintiffs were unable to sell their property and were eventually compelled to sell it for an undervalue at auction. They claimed for the difference between the original asking price and the price obtained at auction.

Following a great deal of scientific debate, the High Court came to the conclusion that the plutonium and americium detected in the property did not add significantly to radiation caused by naturally occurring radon gas. It was accepted that levels of these substances in excess of the national average is not necessarily harmful. This is because plutonium and americium are manmade substances and average levels have only been introduced since nuclear weapons testing; this level is in fact exceedingly low and is not as significant as naturally occurring radiation which provides a more reliable bench mark for monitoring increases in radiation. Gatehouse J. stated:

> The radionuclides with which this case is concerned – plutonium isotopes and americium – are alpha emitters. These cannot do any significant damage to persons or property externally, but when inhaled, ingested or otherwise enabled to enter the body they may induce cancers, but, of course, will not necessarily do so. The presence of alpha emitting radionuclides in the human airways or digestive tracts or even in the blood stream merely increases the risk of cancer to which

---

356. [1990] 3 W.L.R. 383.

everyone is exposed from both natural and artificial radioactive sources. They do not per se amount to injury.[357]

In order to overcome the difficulties associated with establishing a biological link in an individual case an attempt was made to rely upon epidemiological evidence in the joined cases of *Reay and Hope v. British Nuclear Fuels Plc.*[358] The first plaintiff, Elizabeth Reay, claimed that the death of her baby daughter in 1962 from leukaemia was attributable to her husband's exposure to radiation whilst employed as a fitter by BNFL at Sellafield in the 1950s and early 1960s. She claimed damages under the Fatal Accidents Acts 1956–1970 and the Law Reform (Miscellaneous Provisions) Acts 1934–1970 in respect of the death of her daughter. In addition, she claimed damages for injury to herself and on behalf of the estate of her late husband for injury caused by the trauma of the loss of their daughter. The second plaintiff, Vivien Hope, also claimed that her cancer, in this case lymphoma, had been caused by her father's exposure to unacceptably high doses of radiation whilst employed by BNFL. Although she had largely recovered, she had been left partially disabled and infertile as a result of her treatment; damages were claimed in respect of these disabilities plus the pain and suffering which she had endured. BNFL accepted that they had breached their statutory duty under the Atomic Energy Authority Act 1954 which required the operator:

> ... to secure that no ionising radiations from anything on any premises occupied by them, or from any waste discharged (in whatever form) on or from any premises occupied by them, cause any hurt to any person or any damage to any property, whether he or it is on any such premises or elsewhere.[359]

The case turned solely on the issue of whether there was a causal link between this breach of duty and the losses claimed by the plaintiffs. In both cases the causal mechanism, by which the plaintiffs claimed that the fathers' exposure to radiation at Sellafield led to their children developing cancer, was extremely complex. The evidence was based on a hypothesis proposed by Professor Gardner termed paternal pre-conception irradiation (PPI). This proposed that exposure to radiation could lead to genetic mutation in fathers' sperm which would result in their offspring being genetically pre-disposed to developing cancer. The exact causal mechanism by which this process could take place was unknown although it was argued that a genetic pre-disposition to cancer could be passed to children through the germline. The main evidence for this assertion was that other syndromes by which a person may become genetically pre-disposed to leukaemia such as Down's Syndrome and Bloom's syndrome may also be passed to children through the germline.

---

357. *Ibid.*, 396 E-G.
358. *Elizabeth Reay v. British Nuclear Fuels Plc* and *Vivien Jane Hope v. British Nuclear Fuels Plc* [1994] Env. L.R. 320.
359. The facilities in question, known as 'Piles', were opened in 1950 and were designed to produce plutonium. It is now widely accepted that their construction was poor; indeed, in giving evidence, one of the engineers who was largely responsible for their construction referred to them as 'monuments to our initial ignorance'. See *Reay* (n. 358), 328.

In order to overcome the difficulties associated with establishing the exact causal mechanism by which this process took place, the Gardner study adduced epidemiological evidence to suggest that there was a strong association between PPI and cancer in the children of Sellafield workers.[360] Epidemiology is a statistical exercise which relies upon the study of a large number of cases with a view to determining whether there is a correlation between the symptoms displayed by a class of people and possible causes.[361] If a large percentage of the class were exposed to a common element, there is a statistical probability that their symptoms are attributable to the same cause.[362] The Gardner study established an association between workers at Sellafield and the incidence of cancer in their children.

However, the plaintiffs did not rely entirely upon the Gardner study, this is possibly due to the fact that they were aware of certain shortcomings in the report which were in fact later identified by the judge. Oncologists believe that cancers, including leukaemia and lymphoma, are multifactorial and are triggered by two separate events or 'hits'. It was argued on behalf of the plaintiffs that the babies were born genetically pre-disposed to cancer and that the second 'hit', which actually triggered the cancer, may have been caused by exposure to background radiation in the environment. The plaintiffs contended that levels of background radiation in the vicinity of Sellafield had been enhanced by emissions of uranium oxide into the environment emanating from the Sellafield installation. It was alleged that this increased background radiation to levels over and above that which was due to other causes for which the defendant was not responsible such as atomic weapons testing, Chernobyl and naturally occurring radon gas.

In order to test the reliability of the epidemiological study, French J. applied the Bradford-Hill criteria which were drawn up by an eminent professor in the field in 1965.[363] Two of these criteria proved to be particularly significant in the outcome of the case, namely, consistency and biological plausibility.

---

360. M.J. Gardner et al., *Results of a Case-Control Study of Leukaemia and Lymphoma among Young People near Sellafield Nuclear Plant in West Cumbria*, 300 Brit. Med. J. 423 (1990); J.A. Morris, *Leukaemia and Lymphoma among Young People near Sellafield*, 300 Brit. Med. J 676 (1990).
361. The House of Lords accepted that such evidence could be used to establish causation in *Hotson v. East Berkshire Health Authority* [1987] 2 All E.R. 909, 913: 'In some cases, perhaps particularly medical negligence cases, causation may be so shrouded in mystery that the court can only measure statistical chances' (Lord Bridge).
362. A succinct explanation of the subject was provided by one of the expert witnesses, Professor MacMahon, and was cited by French J. in his judgment: 'In the end it must be recognised that the idea of cause is a probabilistic one. Rarely can we be certain that a causal relationship exists, but by assembling evidence from many different angles we may build a body of support sufficient to convince most reasonable people that it is more prudent to act as though the association were causal than to assume that it is not. The point in the accumulation of evidence at which this decision is reached depends in considerable part on the consequences of the alternative actions to be taken as a result of the judgment.' [1994] Env. L.R. 320, 336. The use of epidemiological evidence alone has been accepted by the courts in some cases. See, for example, *Loveday v. Renton, The Times*, (Mar. 31, 1988).
363. The head note of the judgment usefully summarises the criteria as follows: '(i) *The strength of the association found by the study*; (ii) *biological gradient* – that is, the consistency of dose with response in a dose response relationship; (iii) *Temporal Relationships* – that is, cause must always precede effect; (iv) *The consistency of the result of the study with other similar studies concerned with the same subject matter*; (v) *Biological plausibility* – that is, the existence of a

French J. considered the study failed the consistency test on the grounds that the findings did not accord with other leading epidemiological studies on the children of radiation victims. Of particular interest was a detailed study of the offspring of the victims of the A-bombs dropped on Nagasaki and Hiroshima. The survey was carried out over many years and was described by the judge as, 'the largest and most thoroughly executed epidemiological study ever carried out'.[364] The study followed 30,000 offspring of over 70,000 parents over a forty-five year period. The results of this study proved to be entirely inconsistent with the Gardner study in that the genetic mutation rate alleged to have been caused by exposure to radiation at Sellafield was 'off the scale' in comparison with the genetic mutation rates detected in the A-bomb studies[365] and smaller scale animal tests.[366] Furthermore other epidemiological studies into PPI did not discover any link between exposure to radiation and cancer in offspring.[367]

These inconsistencies cast doubt on whether the association identified by the Gardner Report between Sellafield and the incidence of cancer in children was in fact attributable to Sellafield. As a result, attention was focused on the biological plausibility test. The reason for this can be explained as follows. If there was a scientifically well established and highly plausible damage pathway between Sellafield and the victims by way of PPI, it would suggest that, although out of keeping with other studies, there was a probability that radiation emanating from Sellafield caused or contributed to the high incidence of cancers in the area. In such circumstances, the fact that rates of genetic mutation were out of keeping with the other studies would be of less significance and it would be reasonable to explain the discrepancies on the basis that there was some unique circumstance at Sellafield of which science was not yet aware. However, in this case, although it was accepted that the PPI hypothesis was not impossible, science had yet to establish a plausible causal mechanism by which this process could take place. Although French J. accepted that a causal relationship could not be excluded on mechanistic grounds, given the fact that the results of the Gardner study were entirely inconsistent with other studies, it would be necessary to show that a causal relationship was more than a theoretical possibility:

---

plausible or reasonable biological pathway by which radiation could cause or contribute to a disease; (vi) *Coherence*; this criterion looks to the compatibility of a postulated cause with the known facts; (vii) *Experimental evidence* – a criterion which did not assist in this case because there have been no relevant laboratory experiments on live humans; (viii) *Analogy* – for example, if chemicals were shown to produce a similar result, that would be an example of analogy; and (ix) *Specificity of the alleged link between the disease of interest and the exposure of interest* – not very useful in this case because radiation is known to cause a variety of diseases.' See *Reay* (n. 358), 323.

364. See *Reay* (358) 351.
365. *Ibid.*, 365.
366. *Ibid.* The Drosophila studies exposed mice to radiation with a view to determining the effect on offspring.
367. *Ibid.*, 361–363. These included studies into the children of Canadian uranium miners (McLaughlin); Dounreay employees (COMARE, 1988, and Urquhart, 1991); Sellafield employees in Gateshead and North Humberside (McKinney, 1991); patients exposed to diagnostic radiation i.e., X-rays (Graham, 1966 and Shu, 1988).

> These witnesses command great respect. In my judgment they do indeed show that a causal relationship between PPI and leukaemia in F.1 [immediate offspring] should not be excluded on purely mechanistic grounds, though, clearly, a great deal more research is necessary. What they do not do in my judgment, is to show that, in the light of current knowledge, the Seascale cluster is capable of being explained numerically by the biological mechanisms which are the subject matter of their research.[368]

The plaintiffs argued that the discrepancies between the findings of the Gardner study and the various other studies, in particular the Japanese A-bomb studies, were attributable to unique environmental circumstances in the Sellafield area which were not replicated elsewhere. In particular, they referred to the fact that the PPI may have synergized with radiation from other sources. This would provide the 'second hit' necessary to trigger the cancer. At an early stage in his judgment, French J. dismissed the argument that radiation in the vicinity of Sellafield was augmented significantly by emissions of uranium oxide into the atmosphere. The plaintiffs had originally claimed that some 400 kilograms of uranium oxide had been released into the atmosphere whereas the defendants claimed that only 15–20 kilograms had in fact been released. Weighty scientific reports were adduced in support of this conclusion. In the event, the plaintiffs elected not to challenge the evidence on scientific grounds in the interests of saving time and money. Instead, they sought to cast doubt on the reliability of the witnesses produced to support BNFL's estimates regarding uranium dioxide emissions. For example, counsel for the plaintiffs suggested that the National Radiological Protection Board (NRPB), which had produced a report which supported BNFL's figures, had not acted with impartiality. Based on the impression he had gained of the witnesses whilst they were under cross examination, French J. stated that he could find no reason to doubt their reliability.[369]

The plaintiffs appeared to concede this point. However, they argued that it was irrelevant whether the 'second hit' was caused by uranium oxide or background radiation from other sources. The fact that rates of genetic mutation in the sperm were much higher than those detected in other studies indicated that it was reasonable to assume that PPI had synergized with some other element which was not present in, for example, the A-bomb studies. If this was the case, the material contribution test would be satisfied in that it would have been shown that the PPI was instrumental in creating the conditions necessary for cancer to develop. However, French J. also rejected this argument on the grounds that it was highly speculative and presupposed the phenomena which it sought to explain, namely, why the genetic mutation rates indicated by the Gardner study were so much higher than those indicated by other studies.[370]

In summary, although French J. accepted that the Gardner study fulfilled the first Bradford-Hill criterion (strength of the association found by the study) in that it indicated 'an arithmetically strong prima facie association'[371] this was not in itself sufficient to discharge the burden of proof. The judge was persuaded by various studies

---

368. *Ibid.*, 367.
369. *Ibid.*, 334.
370. *Ibid.*, 366.
371. *Ibid.*, 361.

which demonstrated that the existence of a cancer cluster was not in itself evidence of a common cause.[372] As a result, it would be necessary to fulfil other Bradford-Hill criteria in order to establish causation on a balance of probabilities. In this case, the criteria of consistency and biological plausibility proved to be decisive; for the reasons set out above the Gardner study was found to fail both these tests.

Thus, as Wilkinson[373] noted, according to the law as it stood, and indeed as it still stands, it would not have been appropriate for the judge in *Reay* and *Hope* to infer that there must have been a causal link between PPI and cancer on the basis of the Sellafield clusters. However, French J. was criticized in this case for placing too much emphasis on the need to establish a plausible biological explanation for the harm.[374] The common sense approach would suggest that, once it has been established that there is a strong association between the incidence of a disease and the potential source of the harm, it is not necessary to identify the precise scientific chain of events between the source of the harm and its impact. Holder argued that there was established authority for such a common sense approach:

> A review of the case law suggests that the higher courts have not found an absence of a scientific *explanation* of the causal mechanism underlying an association fatal to a plaintiff's claim once the association has been prima facie proven. Pugh and Day[375] describe this as 'the use of common sense to fill gaps where scientific understanding is incomplete' and consider that the approach 'has a perfectly respectable legal pedigree.'[376]

Support for this contention is drawn from obiter comments made by Lord Bridge in *Wilsher* where he accepted that it is not necessary to prove causation scientifically:

> ... where the layman is told by the doctors that the longer the brick dust remains on the body, the greater the risk of dermatitis, although the doctors cannot identify the process of causation scientifically, there seems to be nothing irrational in drawing the inference as a matter of common sense, that the consecutive periods when brick dust remained on the body probably contributed cumulatively to the causation of the dermatitis. I believe that a process of inferential reasoning on these general lines underlies the decision of the majority in *McGhee*.[377]

Furthermore, Holder argued that it is possible to distinguish *Reay* and *Hope* from *Wilsher* on the basis that the alternative causes in *Wilsher* were capable of causing the harm independently whereas in *Reay* and *Hope* it was likely that the alternative causes

---

372. *Ibid.*, 356–359. Cancer clusters can be produced by unusual demographic circumstances and population mixing, particularly where a rural community is subject to an influx of people as a result of the establishment of an industry in the vicinity. The judge was particularly persuaded by the Kinlen study which suggested that a leukaemia cluster in the vicinity of the Dounreay nuclear reprocessing plant was attributable to this phenomena rather than PPI.
373. See D. Wilkinson, *Reay and Hope v. British Nuclear Fuels Plc*, 5 W.L. 22 (1994).
374. *Ibid.*
375. Charles Pugh & Martyn Day, *Toxic Torts*, 52 (Cameron May 1992).
376. J. Holder, *Causation in Environmental Law*, 47(2) Current Leg. Probs. 287, 299 (1994).
377. [1988] W.L.R. 557, 567.

would act cumulatively or synergistically.[378] Thus, it would be reasonable to infer that the defendant's activity must have contributed in some way to the harm.

The problem with this argument is that substances which are capable of acting in synergy with other substances may also be capable of acting independently. In *Reay* and *Hope* French J. could not see any reason why the cancers may not have been entirely due to the alternative causes which the plaintiffs postulated synergized with PPI in a manner which triggered the development of the cancers:

> It [the synergy theory] does not demonstrate the *necessity* for an underlying radiation induced mutation transmitted by fathers with which 'factor X' can synergise or co-operate to induce leukaemia in children; why should factor X not operate on its own?[379]

Although this comment was buried deep in the judgment it actually dealt a devastating blow to the claimant's case. The action was predicated on the notion that a statistical correlation could be regarded as sufficient evidence that the synergistic effect must have occurred. In this respect the Sellafield radiation could be regarded as having made a material contribution to the harm and thereby satisfy the standard 'but for' test; i.e., but for the parental exposure to Sellafield radiation the cancers would not have developed in the offspring. However, the afore-mentioned comment made by French J. clearly shows that the court rejected this assertion. The cancers may have been caused by independent causes notwithstanding the pre-natal exposure. In this case the epidemiological evidence could do no more than show that the pre-natal exposure had materially increased the risk of the harm. However, the material increase in risk argument was not advanced by the claimants. This is not surprising given the fact that, as we have seen in respect of the asbestos cases, the material increase in risk approach has been confined to cases where the identity of the causal agent is not in doubt.

Causation issues were also raised in the *Corby* group litigation[380] which, it will be recalled, also concerned environmental exposure to toxic elements, namely, teratogens.[381] In fact the reported cases focused on preliminary points of law including the applicability of public nuisance and whether there were breaches of the common law duty of care and statutory duties. As regards causation the High Court confined itself to determining whether the toxic elements were capable of causing the birth abnormalities and whether it was arguable that the type of exposure arising from the defendant's failings could have caused this harm. It would be for future proceedings to determine whether the toxic exposure actually had caused the harm in each individual case. As noted in the previous chapter the claimants were spared this arduous process by the offer of an out of court settlement. Nevertheless, from the comments of the judge on the issue it is possible to gain clues as to what the causation arguments would have centred on had such proceedings been necessary. The High Court accepted that the chemicals

---

378. Holder (n. 376) 302.
379. *Reay* (n. 358) 366.
380. *Corby Group Litigation v. Corby District Council* [2009] E.W.H.C. 1944 (TCC).
381. *Ibid.*, [753]. Teratogens is a collective term for chemicals known to induce birth defects in children as a result of pre-natal exposure. The tertogens present at the Corby steelworks site included PAHs, dioxins, furans and heavy metals.

in question could, as a matter of scientific fact, cause the injuries;[382] the uncertainties arose from whether the types of environmental exposure, arising from the defendant's failings, would have been sufficient to cause the onset of the injuries. Interestingly, Akenhead J referred to the fact that the claimants had made much reference to the asbestos cases including *Fairchild* and *Barker v. Corus*.[383] This was to support the argument that the material-increase-in-risk approach could be applied where the identity of the causal agent was not in doubt, but it was not clear which specific breach of duty had triggered the loss. The judge noted that the defendants had not challenged the assertion that the decontamination works were the only source of exposure to the toxic elements. In this respect it might have been open to the claimants to argue that they were relieved of the burden of having to show which specific breaches of duty caused the loss; it would suffice to show that each breach materially increased the risk of the injury occurring.

Nevertheless, the judge's comments on causation tend to raise more questions than they answer. Had the defendants gone to town on the issue of causation, as they surely would have done had the litigation proceeded, the claimants would have faced an uphill struggle. First, it would have been necessary to establish a dose-response relationship between the quantities of teratogens released and the incidence of birth defects. If the general background levels of chemicals released into the environment were not sufficient to cause the harm it would have been necessary to show whether the mothers of affected offspring were exposed to exceptionally high levels.[384] At one point in the judgment reference is made to the fact that one of the mothers worked as a security guard at the site for a period of time.[385] Another worked in a bar which was frequented by workers from the site.[386] These cases are reminiscent of the *Sienkiewicz v. Greif (UK) Ltd*[387] judgment where environmental exposure to asbestos was augmented by occupational exposure. Another lived very close to the site which is reminiscent of the *Margereson v. J.W. Roberts Ltd*[388] case where conditions in the immediate vicinity of the factory were deemed to replicate those within the factory walls. Most importantly, although the defendants did not refer to any other possible causes of the birth defects, this is not to say that they would not have done so had there been a full trial of the facts on causation.[389] The existence of causal agents other than the teratogens released in the decontamination works would have precluded the claimants from adopting the *Fairchild* approach. To recap, the courts are only prepared to determine liability on the basis of a material increase in risk where there is no doubt regarding the substance which caused the harm and where it could only have been

---

382. *Ibid.* See the review of the toxicological evidence at [743]–[770].
383. *Ibid.*, [690].
384. *Ibid.*, [769]; reference is made to the general background levels of such chemicals in the environment.
385. *Ibid.*, [867].
386. *Ibid.*
387. n. 330, above.
388. n. 332, above.
389. See *Corby Group Litigation* (n. 380), [768] where it was noted that such deformities could also be caused by certain diseases and infection. Aside from these they can be caused by certain drugs and chemicals or genetic factors.

encountered at specific locations as a result of failures on the part of those handling the substance. If the court had been faced with the task of showing that the teratogens released during decontamination works were the most likely cause of the deformities it would have been necessary to examine the epidemiological evidence. Akenhead J reached the view that there was a statistically significant cluster of cases in and around Corby between 1989 and 1999;[390] although the correlation was not sufficiently strong in itself to rule out other causes.[391] Furthermore, there was evidence of biological plausibility in that laboratory experiments had demonstrated that limb deformities in mice and other animals could be induced through exposure to teratogens. Of the various teratogens cadmium was found to produce symptoms which were especially redolent of the Corby cases.[392] Nevertheless, it is clear from the judgment that this evidence was not unequivocal in that there is always doubt regarding the extent to which laboratory conditions involving small mammals replicate environmental exposure affecting humans.[393]

This is not to say that the claimants would not have surmounted these evidential difficulties had they been required to do so. Nevertheless, there can be no doubt that the evidence left much scope for protracted scientific arguments.[394] In due course it will be considered whether there are good reasons, in an environmental context, for easing the burden of proof faced by the claimants. In other words, where there have been clear breaches of duty and where the harm is consistent with those breaches; to what extent should the defendant be in a position to escape liability by introducing alternate explanations which can neither be proved nor disproved?

[4] Climate Change Litigation: Pushing Causation to Breaking Point?

As we have seen in the context of the debate on the use of public nuisance as a means of apportioning liability for climate change, the need to establish causation is one of the major stumbling blocks facing litigants. Tromans et al., have concluded that, according

---

390. *Ibid.*, [884].
391. *Ibid.*, [715].
392. *Ibid.*, [764].
393. *Ibid.*, [758]. Akenhead J. acknowledged that there is uncertainty regarding the extent to which the results of such laboratory experiments can be scaled up to humans. Due to the fact that it is of course impossible to conduct experiments on human foetuses the only large scale study of the effect of teratogens on humans has focused on the effects of Agent Orange used by the US Army during to defoliate the jungle during the Vietnam War; see [761]. However, given the very different way in which exposure occurred in this case it is difficult to see how such studies may be of assistance.
394. See F. Dominic et al., *The Role of Epidemiology in the Law: A Toxic Tort Litigation Case*, 7(1) L., Prob. & Ris. 15 (2007). Dominic et al., analysed the use of epidemiological evidence in a toxic tort case concerning the prevalence of neuroblastoma in children borne near an explosive waste disposal facility near Los Angeles. It was noted that the heavy evidential burden meant that the court adopted a particularly inflexible approach in respect of matters such as the Bradford-Hill criteria. They argue that the Bradford-Hill criteria are supposed to operate as a 'sensible or reasonable standard for imputing causation in practice or for policy reasons where knowledge of a disease may be incomplete.' This common sense approach which does not necessarily entail satisfying each criterion in every case; some may carry more significance than others depending on the circumstances. See Dominic et al., 30.

to existing common law principles, the causation difficulties confronting a claimant are seemingly insurmountable.[395] It is difficult to contest this assertion given the narrow circumstances in which the English and Scottish courts are prepared to relax causality tests. There are 6 billion anthropogenic sources of greenhouse gases worldwide and innumerable non-anthropogenic sources; even the largest polluters are unlikely to account for more than 1% of total emissions. As Tromans et al., put it, it would take an 'optimistic' lawyer to argue that a 1% contribution to greenhouse gases makes a material contribution to the harm or materially increases the risk of rising sea levels or extreme weather events.[396] The asbestos cases currently mark the outer limits of the extent to which the courts are prepared to stretch causality tests. One can safely argue that climate change cases could not be accommodated by the new 'pocket' of liability created by the asbestos cases. In these cases it is clear that the material increase in risk test was applied in a very particular manner in order to overcome the specific causation difficulties associated with asbestos exposure. There was no doubt what substance caused the harm and the defendants formed part of a well defined and select group which had a close connection with the claimants by virtue of being their successive employers. The only evidential gap concerned which specific employer had exposed a claimant to the 'guilty fibre'. Given that each employer had been negligent and given that each employer had exposed the claimants to the same type of risk it appeared reasonable to bridge this evidential gap by making an assumption that each had materially increased the risk. This reasoning was underpinned by a barely disguised policy argument that industry should be held collectively responsible for the negligent way in which it had handled asbestos over many decades.[397]

Thus it seems uncontroversial to assert that a climate change case could not be brought within the exception established by the asbestos cases. However, Tromans et al., argue that dismissing the prospects for climate change litigation on this basis alone rather misses the point. They argue that the House of Lords in Fairchild 'turned causation on its head in order to achieve a result consistent with justice'.[398] The effect of this has been to create a pocket of industrial disease cases where exceptions have been made to the orthodox application of causality principles. Indeed, this is not the only area in which the House of Lords has been prepared to 'turn causation on its head' in order to serve the interests of justice. In *Chester v. Afshar*[399] causation was applied in a highly unorthodox manner as this was deemed to be the only way to give effect to a surgeon's duty to warn his patient about all risks associated with a proposed operation. Tromans et al., argue that, although climate change cases could not be

---

395. S. Tromans, J. Burton & M. Edwards, *Climate Change: What Chance a Damages Action in Tort*, 55 Env. L. 22 (2010).
396. *Ibid.*,[46].
397. *Ibid.*, [48].
398. *Ibid.*, [55].
399. [2005] 1 A.C. 134. The evidential difficulty here was that the patient would have gone ahead with the operation in any case, albeit after a delay. In no way did the failure to warn affect the outcome of the operation; nevertheless, a bare majority of the House of Lords found that causation had been established. Thus, an assumption of causation was made on the basis that the harm might not have occurred had the operation been conducted on another day although in fact the risk would have been exactly the same.

accommodated within the modified causation principles created by the industrial disease cases; this is not to say that at some point in the future the courts would not consider establishing a new exception so as to accommodate such actions. However, very strong policy reasons, of equal force to those which justified the findings in the asbestos cases, would have to emerge in order to modify causation principles in order to give effect to a duty to prevent or mitigate the effects of climate change; this, they argue, is conceivable:

> If the consequences of climate change do begin to manifest in ever more devas-tating form, might their Lordships now sitting in the new Supreme Court be prepared to reach a similar conclusion regarding climate change, and hold that justice demands that those whose activities have led to substantial emissions of greenhouse gas pick up a share of the bill for the damage brought about? The tentative suggestion is made that whilst such a result is unthinkable at present, the position could easily change over the coming years.[400]

Tromans et al., do not expand upon how such a change may come about. Given that the common law evolves in an incremental manner the courts generally have to find some means of building upon existing approaches. In this respect it must be considered whether there is any conceptual means of bridging the gap between the current restrictive approach to causality and the novel methodology which would have to be employed in respect of climate change. Scientists are currently working on the issue of 'attribution' which entails establishing a mathematical correlation between climate change and its causes and effects. For example, the extent to which a power station contributes to climate change and the extent to which this enhances the risk of extreme weather events such as floods and hurricanes. These calculations rely purely on mathematical models and computer simulations; there is no physical means of testing the hypotheses. In the context of medical negligence the courts have acknowledged that 'in some cases…causation may be so shrouded in mystery that the court can only measure statistical chances.'[401] Thus, there is no conceptual bar to the use of purely mathematical probabilities which are uncorroborated by physical experimentation. However, any methodologies would have to gain widespread acceptance in the scientific community and be capable of producing compelling results.

Assuming that such models are developed,[402] there would be major difficulties associated with presenting the data in a manner which is acceptable to the court. Any such model could do no more that establish a probability, expressed in percentage terms, regarding the extent to which a certain operator contributed to an extreme weather event or sea level rises. Anything less than 50% would fail to show that the defendant's activities were the cause on a balance of probabilities. It is most unlikely that such results would be produced. The contribution of a power company to the harm would have to be expressed as materially increasing the risk of harm. However,

---

400. Tromans et al. (n. 395) [55].
401. *Hotson v. East Berkshire Area Health Authority* [1987] 2 All E.R. 909, 913 (Lord Bridge).
402. For a detailed overview of the science of climate change attribution and the challenges associated with presenting the evidence in a manner which could be used in the courtroom see, M. Allen, et al., *Scientific Challenges in the Attribution of Harm to Human Influence on Climate*, 155(6) U. Pa. L. Rev. 1353 (2007).

according to existing doctrinal principles, this is where we would meet an evidential roadblock. As we have seen, the asbestos cases currently mark the outer limits of the extent to which the courts are prepared to push the material increase in risk approach. The courts show no sign of extending the approach to cases where there is any doubt regarding the identity of the causal agent. This begs the question of whether it is conceptually possible to bridge the evidential gap in climate change cases using statistical evidence.

The material increase in risk test is now a firmly entrenched part of English and Scots law and it is easy to forget that it is itself the product of a major paradigm shift in the treatment of causation. It was brought about by the necessity to do justice in industrial disease cases so as to prevent errant employers from shirking their respon-sibilities. In this respect there is a precedent for taking a sudden leap across conceptual barriers in a manner which marks a break with the incremental approach. Asserting that an activity materially increased the risk of harm is not the same as asserting that the activity actually caused the harm. In *Sienkiewicz v. Greif (UK) Ltd*[403] it was held that the occupational exposure to asbestos increased the risk of contracting mesothelioma by 18%. This is tantamount to saying that it was more likely than not that the harm was caused by general environmental exposure as opposed to the workplace exposure. However, the increase in risk brought about by the workplace exposure was deemed unacceptable. In effect, the material increase in risk approach reframes the employer's duty not to injure his employee as a duty not to materially increase an existing risk of injury. This raises the issue of whether it would be possible to frame a claim arising from climate change in terms of the extent to which a polluter enhanced the risk of flooding etc. through contribution to global warming. The issue for the court would be the extent to which the risk was enhanced rather than whether the activity actually did cause the harm. However, a substantial difference remains between the asbestos cases and climate change litigation. In the asbestos cases the damage could only have been caused by a particular substance released into the workplace or the wider environment by specified industries. The problem with climate change is that a particular event could have been caused by a range of factors entirely unconnected with anthropogenic emissions. Nevertheless, there is no scientific rationale for excluding any approach based upon material increase in risk in such circumstances. This is because the enhancement of an existing risk will be the same whether or not alternate causes stem from other industries or natural phenomena. Thus, the decision to confine material increase in risk to a certain type of industrial disease case is based upon policy rather than any clear scientific rationale.[404] Having said that, policy based limitations in tort

---

403. [2009] EWCA Civ 1159, [2010] Q.B. 370.
404. Similar arguments have been made in respect of the grounds upon which the courts have sought to distinguish the medical negligence from the industrial disease cases with a view to preventing the material increase in risk approach from being extended to the former. In the industrial disease cases there is a 'single agent' whereas in the medical negligence cases there is usually an alternate natural cause. However, from a scientific point of view, the manner in which the tortious cause affects risk is the same irrespective of whether the alternate causes stem from other tortious or non-tortious causes such as natural phenomena: see C. Miller, *Causation in Personal Injury: Legal or Epidemiological Common Sense?*, 26(4) Leg. Stud. 544

are often of equal force to any arguments based upon sound scientific principle or logic. Whether the UK courts would be prepared to increase the scope of the material increase in risk approach so as to accommodate claims based upon climate change without statutory intervention is open to question. In due course it shall be considered whether some form of alternative compensation regime may be necessary.

As regards other common law world jurisdictions it should be noted that not all have followed the material increase in risk approach adopted in the UK. In Australia, for example, the courts have not moved beyond the material contribution approach, and then only in 'exceptional circumstances'.[405] The general view in the Australian judiciary is that an increase in risk is merely a possibility and meaningless unless one can prove that the risk made a material contribution. The courts in the UK have tended to merge material increase in risk with material contribution by making an assumption that the increased risk must have made a material contribution.[406] There is a distinction between material increase in risk and material contribution in that the former denotes a mere possibility whereas the latter denotes a proven actual cause. In other words, the enhanced risk must be shown to be the catalyst which actually triggered the events causing the harm. The Australian courts have not been prepared to blur these tests and have asserted that there can be no assumption that an increase in risk will have made a material contribution in a particular case.[407] This may be an impossible evidential bar to cross in the context of climate change. As noted above, in conceptual terms the main difficulty is uncoupling risk from the need to show actual cause on a balance of probabilities. This can only be achieved if the claim is formulated in terms of a duty not to enhance an existing risk. Durrant argues that the Australian courts are still very far from accepting material increase in risk, let alone a formulation which separates it from material contribution and an actual cause.[408]

As previously noted, a number of climate change cases are underway in the US although, at the time of writing none had reached the stage where the causation issues could be confronted directly. Similar difficulties arise in that current causality tests are not attuned to the formidable evidential difficulties caused by climate change.[409] In common with the position in the UK, a number of special rules have developed to deal with very particular types of causation difficulty. For example, in certain types of product liability claim a market share analysis has been adopted in order to overcome difficulties arising from the fungibility of a product such as medicines licensed to several manufacturers. In medical negligence cases certain courts have accepted the 'lost chance' approach. The lost chance approach reformulates the claim in terms of the

---

(2006). As regards the policy reasons for making such distinctions see J.R. Spencer, *Damages for Lost Chances: Lost for Good?*, 64(2) Cambridge L.J. 282 (2005).

405. See N. Durrant, *Tortious Liability for Greenhouse Gas Emissions? Climate Change, Causation and Public Policy Considerations*, 7 Queensland U. Tech. L. & J. 403, 418–419 (2007).

406. See S.H. Bailey, *Causation in Negligence: What is Material Contribution?*, 30(2) Leg. Stud. 167 (2010).

407. See Durrant (n. 405) 418. The relationship between material contribution and material increase in risk was considered in *Seltsam Pty Ltd v. McGuiness* (2000) 49 N.S.W.L.R. 262.

408. Durrant (n. 405) 419.

409. See M. Duffy, *Climate Change Causation: Harmonizing Tort Law and Scientific Probability*, 28 Temp. J. Sci. Tech. & Envtl. L. 185 (2009).

extent to which the defendant reduced the plaintiff's prospects of avoiding the harm. The English courts have also considered the use of 'lost chance' in medical negligence cases although it was ultimately rejected.[410] Nevertheless, it is interesting to note that in *Hotson v. East Berkshire Area Health Authority* Lord MacKay asserted that the lost chance approach merely turns material increase in risk on its head.[411] An argument that the defendant's actions reduced the claimant's chance of avoiding the harm by 25% is equivalent to saying that the risk of harm was increased by 25%. Indeed, in the US the lost chance approach has been justified on the basis of section 323 of the Second Restatement of Torts which focuses on the increase of risk. A failure to reduce risk clearly equates with increasing a risk. However, Duffy argues that there is much muddled thinking in this area and the courts have not disentangled the concept of risk, or 'probabilistic causation' as he terms it, from the standard 'but for' approach to causation. The 'but for' test can only be applied to the issue of whether the defendant actually caused the harm. This entails crossing the magic 50% threshold of certainty in order to satisfy the balance of probabilities. As has already been noted in respect of the UK position, any evidence based upon an analysis of risk is most unlikely to cross this high threshold; this is especially the case in respect of climate change where a multitude of factors are at work. Conflating probabilistic evidence with the 'but for' approach in a 'collapsed' causality test[412] is bound to lead to the conclusion that the plaintiff has failed to make out his case. In this respect Duffy's argument is redolent of those expressed above in respect of the UK case law, namely, that in some cases a standalone duty not to increase risk must be recognized.

Duffy acknowledges that none of these approaches in isolation could provide a solution to the problem of causation in climate change cases. However, the fact that a number of special rules have evolved as a means of dealing with particular problems indicates that causation is not entirely hidebound by an immutable set of principles.[413] In short, he advocates the application of a new causality test in respect of climate change comprising elements of existing tests.[414] In many respects the approach is similar to the material increase in risk approach adopted in the UK, although, as we have seen, in the UK the test has been closely pegged to industrial disease cases. Crucially, Duffy's suggested model also incorporates the market share approach which hitherto has been confined to products liability cases. This would result in several liability as opposed to joint and several liability which raises the possibility that a claimant could not recover damages in respect of all the loss caused by industrial activities.[415] Nevertheless, such an approach would be vital in order to avoid overburdening a single polluter with unsustainable and potentially open-ended liability. In

---

410. See *Gregg v. Scott* [2005] 2 A.C. 176.
411. [1987] A.C. 750, 786B-C.
412. See Duffy (n. 409) 219–223.
413. *Ibid.*, 216.
414. *Ibid.*, 216–230.
415. In the asbestos case of *Barker v. Corus* [2006] 2 A.C. 572 the House of Lords backtracked somewhat from its position in *Fairchild* by holding that the extent of each employer's liability would be commensurate with the length of time for which the claimant had been in his employ. This form of several liability raised the possibility of under compensation in that some employers were no longer extant. For this reason Parliament immediately reversed this part of

certain US-product-liability cases involving fungible products such as medicines licensed to several manufacturers, liability has been apportioned according to the market share of the manufacturer. The market share approach could be adapted for use in a climate change context by assessing the extent of an operator's contribution to greenhouse gas emissions.[416] It is conceded that such an approach would be controversial and would entail the use of complex calculations.[417] For example, there are difficult issues associated with the extent to which historic emissions should be taken into account. Furthermore, there is evidence that a 'tipping point' may have been reached whereby the environmental impact of a certain quantity of greenhouse gases is magnified by certain 'feedback effects'. For example, the melting of the icecaps exposes more areas of 'black' open water which absorb more radiation and thus accelerate the rate of heating in a vicious circle. Furthermore, greenhouse gases are emitted at a far faster rate than the planet can absorb them. Thus industrial emissions linger far longer in the atmosphere in ever increasing concentrations. This is commonly referred to as the 'bathtub' effect in that a bathtub will overflow if the rate at which more water is added exceeds the capacity of the overflow to get rid of existing water. Arguments pertaining to how such effects should be modelled and accounted for are certain to be complex and protracted should litigation ever reach this stage.[418]

In conclusion, litigants endeavouring to establish liability for damage caused by events allegedly connected to climate change resulting from industrial activities face formidable evidential difficulties. However, a conceptual Rubicon has been crossed inasmuch as such actions are now regarded as difficult rather than unthinkable or impossible.

§3.04   STANDING REQUIREMENTS IN TORT

Locus standi to pursue an action in tort is limited to those who have suffered some form of loss such as property damage and personal injury, or, an interference with the rights and benefits which flow from an interest in land. Thus, in negligence, damages may only be recovered by the individual or legal person who has sustained the loss or, in the case of fatal accidents, dependants.

As regards nuisance, it is well established that a person must have an interest in land;[419] whilst this encompasses freehold estates and tenancies it does not encompass bare licenses or a mere permission to reside in a certain property. The usual case cited in support of this proposition is *Malone v. Lasky* in which the plaintiffs occupied a

---

the Lords' decision by enacting section 3 of the Compensation Act 2006 which expressly holds employers jointly and severally liable in respect of workplace asbestos claims. The Parliament took a policy decision to hold industry collectively responsible for the losses caused by asbestos due to industry wide failings. Given the much wider nature of climate change cases such an approach would lead to unsustainable liability.

416. Duffy (n. 409) 225–230.
417. *Ibid.*
418. *Ibid.*
419. See, for example, *Read v. Lyons & Co. Ltd* [1947] A.C. 156, 183, 'He alone has a lawful claim who has suffered an invasion of some proprietary or other interest in land' (Lord Simonds).

house as licensees of the husband's employers who owned the property. The wife was injured when vibrations emanating from an engine operated in the defendant's property dislodged a bracket which struck her on the head. Sir Gorell Barnes stated that:

> Many cases were cited in the course of the argument in which it had been held that actions for nuisance could be maintained where a person's rights of property had been affected by the nuisance, but no authority was cited, nor in my opinion can any principle of law be formulated, to the effect that a person who has no interest in property, no right of occupation in the proper sense of the term, can maintain an action for nuisance arising from the vibration caused by the working of an engine in an adjoining house. On that point, therefore, I think that the plaintiff fails, and that she has no cause of action in respect of the alleged nuisance.[420]

The only known exceptions to this general principle concern certain cases in which the plaintiff enjoys exclusive possession of the property although he may not be able to prove title to the land.[421] The House of Lords reaffirmed this interpretation of the law in the recent case of *Hunter v. Canary Wharf Ltd*[422] which concerned actions in nuisance relating to interferences with television signals and dust and noise caused by the construction of the Canary Wharf building. As many of the plaintiffs had no interest in the houses affected other than the householders' permission to reside in the properties, one of the issues which fell to be determined concerned whether their interest in the matter would suffice to sustain an action in nuisance. Lord Goff[423] was impressed by Professor Newark's seminal article on the origins of nuisance[424] in which it was emphasized that nuisance arose as a means of protecting certain rights flowing from *proprietary* interests in land. Professor Newark's historical analysis led him to the conclusion that, in order to find an action in nuisance, it is necessary to establish an interference with a right which flows from a legal interest in the property:

> In true cases of nuisance the interest of the plaintiff which is invaded is not the interest of bodily security but the interest of liberty to exercise rights over land in the amplest manner. A sulphurous chimney in a residential area is not a nuisance because it makes householders cough and splutter but because it prevents them taking their ease in their gardens. It is for this reason that the plaintiff in an action for nuisance must show some title to realty.[425]

Lord Goff noted that various courts, both in the UK and the Commonwealth, had attempted at various times to relax this standing requirement in order to allow those with lesser interests in property to pursue actions in nuisance.[426] These authorities led

---

420. [1907] 2 K.B. 141, 151.
421. This is because *jus tertii* is no defence to an action in nuisance. See *Foster v. Warblington Urban District Council* [1906] 1 K.B. 648.
422. [1997] 2 W.L.R. 684, at 693B-C, per Lord Goff.
423. *Ibid.*, 691D-H.
424. F.H. Newark, *The Boundaries of Nuisance*, 65 L.Q. Rev. 480 (1949). See §2.03[A][1], above.
425. *Ibid.*, 488–489.
426. See *Motherwell v. Motherwell* (1976) 73 D.L.R (3d) 62 and *Khorasandjian v. Bush* [1993] Q.B. 727. In both these cases family members sought injunctions in order to prohibit the continuance of harassing telephone calls. The judgments cited the case of *Foster v. Warblington Urban*

the Court of Appeal, below,[427] to conclude that it would suffice to show that an individual enjoyed a 'substantial interest' in property. However, his Lordship emphatically rejected this approach on the grounds that it would effectively sever nuisance from the law of property and could conceivably lead to a situation in which, for example, employees could sustain actions in nuisance in respect of discomforts endured at their place of work. This would eviscerate the rationale of the tort and would:

> [T]ransform it from a tort to land into a tort to the person, in which damages could be recovered in respect of something less serious than personal injury and the criteria for liability were founded not upon negligence but upon striking a balance between the interests of neighbours in the use of their land.[428]

In his dissenting judgment, however, Lord Cooke asserted that this restrictive approach would be out of step with developments in human rights jurisprudence where a more liberal approach is adopted in the interests of access to justice. His Lordship proposed a new test based upon whether the claimant occupied the premises as the family home.[429] In fact the judgment was delivered in the same years that the Human Rights Act was passed in the UK which enshrined the European Convention on Human Rights in domestic law. Although the Human Rights Act operates in the public sphere, whereas tort operates in the private sphere, there is a degree of overlap between the two. Thus, Article 8 of the ECHR, on the right to the protection of private and family life, has been invoked as a vehicle for pursuing claims against the state, or an emanation of the state, which are strongly redolent of nuisance type actions.[430] Given that such claims are not subject to a 'property qualification' and given that the courts must interpret the common law in a manner which is commensurate with human rights jurisprudence, insofar as this is possible, it has been argued that the matter needs to be revisited. On this basis Neuberger J. refused to strike out a nuisance claim brought by children living in proximity to the British Aluminium plant on Anglesey, North Wales, in *McKenna v. British Aluminium Ltd.*[431] Various nuisances were alleged relating to noise, noxious emissions and adverse health effects. In the light of the above developments in human rights law Neuberger J. held:

> There is a real possibility of the court concluding that in the light of the different landscape, namely Article 8.1 now being effectively part of our law, it is necessary

---

District Council, above, which provided that it would suffice to show 'occupancy of a substantial nature' as authority for the proposition that close family members with no title to the realty would be in a position to obtain injunctive relief. Lord Goff dismissed this approach on the grounds that it misconstrued the Foster decision (presumably on the grounds that the case was solely concerned with the issue of *jus tertii* and should not be treated as a general proposition) and constituted an attempt to establish a tort of harassment 'via the back door'. There was no need to develop the law in this way following the enactment of the Harassment Act 1997. See Lord Goff, [1997] 2 W.L.R. 684, 693–695.

427. *Hunter v. Canary Wharf Ltd.* [1996] 1 All E.R. 482 (C.A.), 494–498.
428. [1997] 2 W.L.R. 684, 696F-G.
429. *Ibid.*, 712.
430. See, for example, *Lopez Ostra v. Spain* (1995) 20 E.H.R.R. (1) 277 discussed below, at §4.03[B], in the context of the public interest in the environment.
431. [2002] Env. L. R. 30.

to extend or change the law, even though, in circumstances where the Convention was no part of English Law, the majority of the House of Lords thought otherwise.[432]

The House of Lords never had the opportunity to revisit the issue in the context of the *McKenna* litigation. In 2009 the plant was closed due to economic factors unrelated to the case.[433] This has solved the problem from the residents' perspective although it leaves somewhat of a question mark over the *Hunter v. Canary Wharf* decision. Nevertheless, as a House of Lords decision with a strong majority, the orthodox approach adopted in *Hunter* will continue to constitute an inescapable authority until such time as the new Supreme Court has the opportunity to look at the matter afresh. Given that the Supreme Court has no control of what cases are brought before it there is no telling how long this will take, if ever.

A similarly restrictive approach has been adopted in other common law jurisdictions. A serious attempt to loosen the strictures of the orthodox approach was made in the Canadian case of *Devon Lumber Co. v. MacNeill*[434] concerning nuisance caused by sawdust from a neighbouring sawmill which adversely affected a neighbouring family. Stratton C.J.N.B. held that precluding the children from bringing claims in respect of the adverse impact upon their health would amount to 'senseless discrimination'.[435] However, later decisions have not adopted this more liberal view and the decision only received scant attention in *Hunter* due its limited appreciation of the property basis of nuisance. In the US case of *Re the Exxon Valdez*,[436] which concerned damage caused by the *Exxon Valdez* oil spill, a number of indigenous Alaskan tribes attempted to bring civil claims in respect of damage to the so-called 'un-owned environment'. In short, they argued that their ancient cultural and historical connection with the landscape set them apart from later European settlers. The US Court of Appeals (Ninth Circuit) rejected this argument on the grounds that the right to hunt, fish and enjoy the landscape was common to all Alaskans. In this respect there was nothing distinctive about the loss suffered by the native Alaskans.[437] This case raises interesting issues regarding the nature of property rights and the extent to which there is, or should be, an equitable interest to enjoy the 'un-owned environment'. This is an issue which shall be returned to in more depth in due course.[438]

Trespass to land also constitutes a tort which is concerned with the protection of rights in property, namely exclusive possession. Generally speaking, the person who enjoys exclusive possession of a parcel of land may rely upon the tort in order to exclude others.[439] This is not necessarily the owner of the property, where there is a

---

432. *Ibid.*, [52]. For an analysis of the human rights implications see M. Wilde, *Locus Standi in Environmental Torts and the Potential Influence of Human Rights Jurisprudence*, 12(3) Rev. Eur. Community Intl. Envtl. L. 284 (2003).
433. BBC News, *Final Shift at Anglesey Aluminium* (Sept. 30, 2009), http://news.bbc.co.uk/1/hi/wales/north_west/8281699.stm (Mar. 8, 2011).
434. (1987) 45 D.L.R. (4th) 300. See Wilde (n. 432), 287.
435. *MacNeill* (n. 434) [14].
436. (1997) 104 F.3d 1196. See Wilde (n. 432) 289.
437. *Re the Exxon Valdez* (n. 436) 1198.
438. See below at §4.03[B].
439. See, for example, *Radaich v. Smith* (1959) 101 C.L.R. 209, 222, (Windeyer J.).

tenancy agreement (as opposed to a license) the right to exclusive possession will vest in the tenant for the duration of the agreement.[440] In common with nuisance, a person who cannot prove that he has title to the property may nevertheless rely upon the tort until another person can establish a better title.[441]

Thus, from an environmental perspective, a major draw-back of tort is that it cannot be used in order to protect the environment in its own right, liability is contingent upon damage coinciding with loss suffered by an individual. Of course, even where environmental damage does coincide with such loss, there is no guarantee that the individual concerned would choose to pursue the matter. For example, where an area of waste land is owned by a distant property developer, he may have no interest in the property until the time comes to develop it; this could be a matter of years. In the mean time the site could become an unofficial waste dump which would render it vulnerable to contamination by all manner of polluting substances; in order to deal with situations such as this it has been necessary to develop regulatory responses.[442] Alternatively, the individual concerned may be willing to institute civil proceedings but may lack the necessary resources.

Thus standing requirements in tort raise major issues relating to access to justice. In some extreme cases pollution may result in a multitude of similar personal injury claims. The GLO[443] provides one means of aggregating such claims and reducing costs. In an environmental context the GLO was put to good effect in the *Corby* litigation.[444] However, there is seldom a direct connection between environmental degradation and widespread personal injuries. Most pollution is of an on-going and chronic nature which damages the environment in an insidious manner. As we have seen, damage of this nature typically engages the 'property torts' comprising trespass, nuisance and *Rylands v. Fletcher*. However, in common law there is no mechanism for allowing environmental interest groups, such as environmental Non-governmental Organizations (NGOs), to step in and pursue claims where the damage does not coincide with interference with property rights or where the individual concerned lacks the desire or wherewithal to pursue litigation.

This contrasts with developments in the field of public law where NGOs have made significant progress in establishing *locus standi* in judicial review proceedings. The High Court decision in *R v. Pollution Inspectorate ex parte Greenpeace (No. 2)*,[445] in which Greenpeace successfully argued that it should be in a position to challenge a decision to vary consents relating to the Thorp nuclear reprocessing plant, was instrumental in this respect. In a more recent significant development it was held that

---

440. The issue of whether an agreement constitutes a license or a tenancy must be determined by reference to the substance of the agreement, not merely the label attached to it. See *Street v. Mountford* [1985] A.C. 809.
441. *Jones v. Chapman* (1849) 2 Exch. 803.
442. Local authorities are granted certain powers to carry out remediation works in default and to recover costs from the polluter or owner or occupier of the site. See, for example, Environmental Protection Act ss. 79–80; Town and Country Planning Act s. 215; Water Resources Act s. 161.
443. Part 19.11 Civil Procedure Rules 1998 S.I. 1998/3132.
444. *Corby Group Litigation v. Corby D.C.* [2009] EWHC 1944 (TCC); [2009] N.P.C. 100.
445. [1994] 4 All E.R. 329.

a limited company, formed by residents opposed to a new landfill scheme, should be afforded standing in its own right.[446]

From the above it is clear that, as regards issues of standing, the law draws a major distinction between private damages claims and claims for judicial review. To date, this distinction between standing requirements in the respective realms of public and private law has been explicable on the basis that, in judicial review proceedings, there is usually a clear public interest issue at stake. Thus it is logical to afford standing to those groups which are concerned with the protection of such interests. The law of tort, on the other hand, is preoccupied with the protection of private interests. However, in an environmental context, this distinction between the realms of public and private law is somewhat of a fiction, as Betlem explained in his analysis of the Dutch system in the mid 1990s:

> [M]ost legal systems purport to allocate general interests to the field of public law and limit private law to concrete, individual interests. However, this distinction breaks down in environmental law in that diffuse environmental damage is closely related to individual health interests, which are, of course, typical concrete private interests. Accordingly, private law remedies should be available alongside public law remedies such as judicial review.[447]

As will be seen in Chapter 4 there has been an attempt to blend public and private interests in this manner in the Netherlands where standing has in fact been extended to NGOs in respect of private actions in tort arising out of pollution. Although, it will also be seen that lately there has been some retrenchment on this issue.[448]

§3.05   REMEDIES IN TORT FOR ENVIRONMENTAL DAMAGE

A claimant will only go to the trouble of establishing a cause of action if he considers that an appropriate remedy is available. Common law remedies seek to compensate for any loss sustained, prevent future infringements of proprietary interests or rectify damage which has already occurred as a result of such infringements. This is achieved by means of the award of damages, the granting of various types of injunction, or the award of damages in lieu of an injunction. From an environmental perspective it is necessary to consider the extent to which these remedies coincide with environmental protection.

[A]   Damages

The guiding principle for the measure of damages is *restitutio integrum* which means that:

---

446. *Residents Against Waste Site Ltd. v. Lancashire County Council* [2007] EWHC 2557; [2008] Env. L.R. 27.
447. G. Betlem, *Standing for Ecosystems – Going Dutch*, 54(1) Cambridge L.J. 153, 154 (1995).
448. See H. Tolsma, R. De Graaf & J. Jans, *The Rise and Fall of Access to Justice in the Netherlands*, 21(2) J. Envtl. L. 309 (2009).

> Where an injury is to be compensated by damages, in settling the sum of money to be given for reparation of damages you should nearly as possible get at that sum of money which will put the party who has been injured, or who has suffered, in the same position as he would have been in if he had not sustained the wrong for which he is now getting his compensation or reparation.[449]

Thus, in *Marquis of Granby v. Bakewell U.D.C.*,[450] where the operator of a gas works had discharged poisonous effluent into a river over which the plaintiff had fishing rights, the compensation received equalled the cost of restocking the river in addition to an amount for the loss of food supply for other stocks.

However, in many cases concerning damage to land or buildings, the cost of restoring the property to its exact former state may be out of all proportion to the diminution in market value of the property caused by the harm. In this case damages will be calculated on the basis of the diminution in market value.[451] In an environmental context this means that whilst damages may compensate for the financial loss suffered by the claimant, they may not reflect the full costs of cleaning up pollution. This problem is examined in more detail below.

A further complication regarding the measure of damages arises from the overlap between private nuisance and Article 8 of the European Convention on Human Rights, the nature of which has been addressed elsewhere.[452] One of the arguments which the House of Lords put forward against increasing *locus standi* in private nuisance was that it could result in multiple claims in respect of the same harm. Thus, it would be conceivable for each member of the household to make a similar claim in damages. In *Hunter v. Canary Wharf* The House of Lords held that such multiple claims would be inconsistent with the fact that nuisance concerns injury to the land with the result that there can be only one claim for damages.[453] Any other solution would result in over-compensation and undermine the principle of restitutio in integrum. However, this did not deal with the problem of what would happen if other members of the household brought separate parallel claims under Article 8 ECHR on the protection of the home and family life. Such claims are entirely separate from nuisance claims and relate to the personal harm suffered by the claimants rather than the land itself. Thus, there is no reason in principle why other members of the household should not bring such claims in addition to any claim brought by the homeowner in respect of injury to the land. Nevertheless, it could be argued that, despite these technical distinctions, the gist of the action is still the same in many cases with the result that multiple claims could give rise to over-compensation.

This is precisely the problem which faced the Court of Appeal in the afore-mentioned case of *Dobson v. Thames Water Utilities Ltd.*[454] In this case, which concerned nuisance caused by odours and mosquitoes from a sewerage treatment works, those who lacked the requisite *locus standi* for an action in nuisance pursued

---

449. *Livingstone v. Rawyards Coal Co.* (1880) 5 App. Cas. 25, 39 (Lord Blackburn).
450. (1923) 87 J.P. 105.
451. *Jones v. Gooday* (1841) 8 M. & W.
452. See §4.03[B], below.
453. [1997] A.C. 655, 706H-707C, (Lord Hoffmann).
454. [2009] EWCA Civ 28; [2009] 3 All E.R. 319.

separate claims under Article 8 ECHR. In some cases this was in addition to nuisance claims brought by the landowner in respect of the same property. The Court of Appeal acknowledged that the human rights claims were distinct from the claims in nuisance. However, it was also acknowledged that in reality most of the claims stemmed from a single harm. It was held that in most cases of this nature a single damages award in private nuisance to the householder would suffice to afford the claimants 'just satisfaction' pursuant to Article 8(3) of the Human Rights Act 1998. This is because such an award would reflect the loss of amenity suffered by all those in the household. It could be said that the householder's right to use and enjoy his property is indistinguishable from the ability of other family members to enjoy the home in a similar way. Nevertheless, it is important to point out that the Court of Appeal stated that the issue depends very much upon the facts. It is conceivable that there could be situations in which others who occupy the land could maintain separate damages claims. One example could be where the loss suffered by a claimant, without the requisite legal interest in the property to maintain an action in nuisance, is of a fundamentally different nature to that suffered by the landowner. Thus, it is conceivable that a person who suffers a distinct injury, because of an existing allergy for example, could obtain damages in his or her own right under human rights law. This assertion has yet to be tested, however, if it is correct it means that in such cases an individual could use human rights law to circumvent the limited notion of standing under common law private nuisance.

[1]   Exemplary or Punitive Damages

These are an exception to the restitutio in integrum maxim and allow for an award over and above the normal quantum of damages where the defendant's conduct was calculated to make a profit which would exceed any damages payable, or, where there has been oppressive, arbitrary or unconstitutional action by servants of the government.[455]

In *Gibbons v. South West Water Services Ltd*[456] the plaintiffs had successfully brought an action in public nuisance, negligence, *Rylands v. Fletcher* and breach of statutory duty following an incident where the plaintiff's contractor deposited 20 tonnes of aluminium sulphate into the public water supply. The plaintiffs sought exemplary damages on the grounds that the defendants had attempted to conceal the incident. However, the Court of Appeal did not consider that this was part of a calculated attempt to gain some financial advantage by deliberately perpetuating the nuisance. The plaintiffs also attempted to justify the award of exemplary damages under the second limb of the exception, namely oppressive conduct by a government

---

455. *Rookes v. Barnard* [1964] A.C. 1129.
456. [1992] 4 All E.R. 574.

servant. This argument was also rejected on the grounds that a statutory undertaker is not part of the government.[457]

It seems that the courts intend to take a restrictive view of the grounds on which exemplary damages can be awarded. In the *Gibbons* case the Court of Appeal accepted that the defendant's conduct had been high handed but were not prepared to extend the restitutio exception so as to penalize this type of behaviour.

Generally speaking the US courts have been more receptive to the notion of punitive damages although there is variation between states regarding the extent of the egregiousness which must be shown in order to justify such an award. In the Exxon Valdez litigation, concerning the notorious oil spill in Prince William Sound Alaska, the US District Court for the District of Alaska initially awarded punitive damages amounting to USD 4.5 billion which was subsequently reduced to USD 2.5 billion by the US Court of Appeals for the Ninth Circuit.[458] Exxon then appealed to the US Supreme Court regarding its liability for punitive damages.[459] On the issue of the circumstances in which exemplary or punitive damages can be awarded the Supreme Court acknowledged that they were more readily available in the US than under the common law as applied in England and Wales. Furthermore, the laws in different states varied greatly on the issue although by and large such damages were reserved for the most egregious conduct whether wilful or amounting to gross negligence. However, the Supreme Court failed to resolve the issue of whether it was appropriate to award punitive damages against the employer in cases of vicarious liability. The act of gross recklessness in this case had been committed by the master of the vessel who was an employee of Exxon. It is clear that the employer must be vicariously liable to the extent of the actual losses caused but less clear whether this should extend to punitive damages. Exxon argued that punitive damages should be reserved for cases where there is a breach of the employer's personal duty amounting to gross negligence. A curious feature of the US Supreme Court is that it is constituted in manner which allows for even splits in which case it may fail to reach a decision. In such circumstances the finding of the court below must be allowed to stand although no precedent is set. This phenomenon occurred in this case with the result that Exxon was unable to overturn the finding that it was liable for punitive damages in respect of the egregious conduct of its servant who, as we shall see below, was drunk on duty. Nevertheless, Exxon met with rather more success in terms of challenging the level of damages awarded. In this respect the Supreme Court held that, in the interests of certainty, a ratio of compensatory to punitive damages of 1:1 should be applied which effectively doubles any compensatory award made by the jury. This ratio was not arrived at through any scientific enquiry, rather, it was merely a median average based upon an analysis of the awards typically made in various states. In this case the compensatory damages amounted to USD 507.5 million with the result that the Court of Appeals award was

457. See R. Macrory, *Damages in Nuisance*, 214 ENDS Report 43 (1992). Macrory pointed out that the European Court of Justice would undoubtedly have classed the defendant as an emanation of the state as the incident occurred prior to privatization.
458. *Baker v. Exxon Mobil Corp.* 490 F.3d 1066 (9th Cir. 2007).
459. *Exxon Shipping Co. v. Baker* 128 S.Ct. 2605 (2008).

effectively five times over the going rate and thus clearly excessive. This may greatly reduce the deterrent effective of damages although, as will be seen in the next chapter, such overtly utilitarian objectives are not the main purpose of tort in any case.

[2]   Pure Economic Loss

As a general rule, damages may only be recovered in respect of loss which flows directly from physical harm.[460] In the absence of a special relationship between the parties, pure economic loss is not recoverable.[461] Thus it is necessary to establish a high degree of proximity, usually brought about by some prior undertaking between the parties,[462] before damages for pure economic loss can be recovered. However, if this relationship is established by contract, the courts will not usually interfere with the apportionment of liability agreed between the parties as this would undermine the freedom to contract.[463]

The issue of economic loss is important in an environmental context in that the market value of property may be adversely affected by contamination, or even the possibility of contamination, by a pollutant. Diminution in market value will be classed as economic loss and hence irrecoverable unless it flows from actual physical damage to the property. This distinction is illustrated by two cases concerning claims for diminution in the market value of land alleged to have been caused by radioactive contamination.

It will be recalled that in the aforementioned-mentioned case of *Merlin v. BNFL* the market value of the plaintiffs' property was dramatically reduced following publicity concerning levels of radiation in the immediate vicinity of the defendant's nuclear installation at Sellafield. It was alleged that there had been an escape of radionuclides from the installation in breach of the absolute duty imposed by section 7(1) of the Nuclear Installations Act 1965. Even if the plaintiffs had succeeded in establishing that emissions from Sellafield had increased levels of radiation in their property, it seems that the damages claimed would have been classed as economic and thus irrecoverable. The loss in market value claimed did not flow from any physical damage to the property itself; it had been the plaintiffs' contention that the alleged increased levels of radiation in the property constituted a health risk. Gatehouse J. was of the opinion that this did not constitute physical damage:

> Personal injury or damage to property is a familiar enough phrase and in my judgment it means, as it does in other contexts, physical (or mental) injury or physical damage to tangible property ... The plaintiff's argument that 'property' included the air space within the walls, ceilings and floors of (the house); that this

---

460. *Sparton Steels and & Alloys Ltd. v. Martin & Co. (Contractors) Ltd.* [1973] Q.B. 27.
461. *Hedley, Byrne v. Heller* [1964] A.C. 465; *Muirhead v. Industrial Tank Specialists* [1986] Q.B. 507.
462. Somewhat analogous to the prior undertaking which had to be established before a negligence based action in case could be brought in Medieval times.
463. *Simaan General Contracting Co. v. Pilkington Glass Ltd. (No. 2)* [1988] Q.B. 758; *Greater Nottingham Cooperative Ltd. v. Cementation Piling and Foundations Ltd.* [1989] Q.B. 71.

has been damaged by the presence of radionuclides and the house rendered less valuable as the family's home, seems to me too far-fetched.[464]

As the 1965 Act did not define 'property damage' Gatehouse J. decided to apply the common law approach. This led him to the conclusion that, as the loss claimed was purely economic and as there was no special relationship or prior undertaking between the parties, damages would not have been recoverable in respect of the diminution in market value of the property:

> I can see no reason why compensation under the Act of 1965 should extend to pure economic loss when such loss would not be recoverable at common law ... No special relationship existed between the defendants and the plaintiffs, who were merely part of the general public living in the Sellafield area, such as would give rise to a duty of the *Hedly Byrne & Co. Ltd. v. Heller & Partners Ltd.* [1964] A.C. 465 type, so it seems to me that any such claim at common law must have failed: see, for example, the judgments of the Court of Appeal and particularly Bingham L.J. in *Simaan General Contracting Co. v. Pilkington Glass Ltd.* (No. 2) [1988] Q.B. 758.[465]

The *Merlin* decision was distinguished in *Blue Circle Industries Plc v. Ministry of Defence.*[466] The plaintiffs owned a large estate which adjoined the Aldermaston Atomic Weapons Establishment (AWE). As a result of heavy rainfall ponds on the AWE site overflowed onto the plaintiffs property thereby contaminating a small area with radioactive material. The contamination did not come to light until the plaintiffs were in negotiation for the sale of the site at a cost of approximately EUR 10m. Following disclosure of the information the prospective purchaser withdrew from negotiations. The defendants accepted liability for the escape of radioactive materials and paid for the costs of removing the contaminated soil which amounted to EUR 350,000. However, they refused to pay further costs in recognition of the diminution in market value of the land and the reduction of its saleability; the plaintiffs sought to recover these costs under section 12 of the Nuclear Installations Act 1965 and the rule in *Rylands v. Fletcher.* The Court of Appeal reaffirmed that damage both for the purposes of the 1965 Act and the common law denotes physical damage to tangible property. Although the levels of radiation did not constitute a health risk the contamination nevertheless amounted to a physical change which impaired the use and hence value of the property. As radiation levels exceeded those permitted by regulation (Radioactive Substances Act 1960) the contaminated soil could not be left *in situ*; thus the land was damaged in the sense that it could not be used for its original purpose until remediation measures had been taken.[467] Thus damages in respect of the diminution in market value of the property were not purely economic in that they flowed from physical damage. Accordingly, the plaintiffs were awarded damages amounting to the full clean-up cost plus the income lost as a result of the failure to sell the property

---

464. [1990] 3 W.L.R. 383, 394E-F.
465. *Ibid.,* 395G-H.
466. [1998] 3 All E.R. 385 (CA).
467. There was authority for the proposition that property which has been contaminated without physical alteration of its structure will be regarded as damaged in the sense that it cannot be used to its full extent until it has been cleaned; part of the value of property resides in its usability. See The *Orjula* [1995] 2 Ll.L.R. 395 and *Hunter v. LDDC* [1996] 2 W.L.R. 348.

(subject to a 25% discount to reflect the possibility that the property might not have been sold in any case); this amounted to EUR 5m.

A similar conclusion was reached in the Scottish case of *Magnohard v. United Kingdom Atomic Energy Authority*[468] which concerned escapes of radioactive particles from the Dounreay nuclear facility. A handful of particles had been detected on a beach owned by the claimant company which had an adverse impact upon its leisure business. The defendant advanced a *de minimus* argument on the basis that the risk posed by such a limited number of particles was vanishingly small with the result that there was no real damage. The court disagreed with this argument on the basis that the escape of the particles and their turning up on the beach was an 'occurrence' within the meaning of section 7 of the Nuclear Installations Act 1965, no matter how insignificant the risk to health and the environment. In any case, from the perspective of the claimant, the harm was real and significant because it had necessitated the introduction of an extensive monitoring and clean-up programme requiring the use of intrusive lorries and detection equipment.

These cases are significant in that they demonstrate that the ability of the claimant to recover damages in respect of contamination may depend upon how damage is defined. In the *Blue Circle* case physical damage was determined by reference to whether radiation levels exceeded regulatory standards. In *Magnohard* less emphasis was placed on regulatory standards as the threshold of harm, nevertheless, the fact that the harm was sufficient to justify remediation measures was the decisive factor. In the absence of this physical dimension the loss would have been deemed as purely economic and thus irrecoverable. In fact Tromans exposes the fine line between physical and non-physical harm in this small group of nuclear contamination cases. In particular, he has argued that the distinction drawn between contamination of the airspace within the walls of a property and contamination of the fabric itself is nonsensical:

> [T]he distinction seems to leave the law in a difficult state. How is removal of dust which is dissipated throughout a house substantially different to the removal of a layer of contaminated top soil? If anything, it might be more difficult to remove dust which was in the interstices of roof spaces, floorboards, etc.[469]

The damage at issue in the cases discussed so far was localized in nature in that it occurred between neighbouring properties and was not widespread. However, where there has been a major environmental disaster, economic repercussions may be felt far from the site of the original accident. In these circumstances the problem of economic loss, and how the courts should endeavour to establish a logical cut off point, is particularly acute. In recent times these problems have been exemplified by certain maritime oil tanker disasters and the extensive civil litigation which has stemmed from them. Notable cases include the *Braer* litigation in the UK and the *Exxon Valdez* litigation in the United States.

---

468. [2004] Env. L.R. 19. For a detailed analysis of the case see M.L. Wilde, *Magnohard the United Kingdom Atomic Energy Authority: Paying for the Economic and Psychological 'Legacy' of Nuclear and Maritime Pollution*, 12(6) Env. Liability 243 (2004).
469. S. Tromans, *Nuclear Liabilities and Environmental Damages*, 1(1) Env. L. Rev. 59, 61 (1999).

On 5 January 1993 the tanker *Braer* grounded off Shetland and deposited 84,700 tonnes of crude oil and 1600 tonnes of bulk fuel oil into the sea. Suffice it to say, the consequences for fisheries, the coastline of the islands, wildlife, tourism and the local economy in general were devastating. The economic consequences went far beyond those whose property had been contaminated by oil and included fishermen, fish-farms, and all manner of related industries which served the fishing and tourist industries. A number of civil actions were commenced before the Scottish courts which required consideration of the extent to which economic loss should be recoverable.

A significant case stemming from the disaster is *Landcatch Ltd v. International Oil Pollution Compensation Fund*[470] concerning economic losses suffered by a supplier of smolt to the Shetland salmon farm industry. Following the disaster a number of emergency regulations were introduced which prohibited the preparation, processing or supply of fish obtained from a designated exclusion zone in the contaminated area.[471] Consequently salmon farmers were forced to suspend operations pending the completion of clean-up operations. As a result, Landcatch suffered a serious loss of orders for smolt and had to destroy the surplus stock for which there was no market. Further damages were sought in respect of the long term 'tainting' of their produce, in other words, once restrictions had been lifted the market value of the smolt was reduced due to its association with Shetland and the *Braer* disaster. Clearly, all these losses were purely economic in nature in that the business was carried on in locations far from the site of the spillage,[472] the smolt itself was not contaminated and the pursuers did not own any heritable property damaged by the oil pollution. Thus the pursuers faced the difficult task of establishing grounds for the recovery of economic loss in the absence of any form of physical damage. Had the incident been governed entirely by common law principles it is doubtful whether proceedings would have been brought in the first place. However, maritime oil pollution is governed by an international agreement on civil liability and an oil pollution compensation fund, namely, the International Convention on Civil Liability for Oil Pollution Damage (ICCOP), 1969 and the International Convention on the Establishment of an International Fund for Compensation for Oil Pollution Damage, 1971. The pursuers hoped to persuade the courts that the claim should be viewed in the light of the objectives of these international compensation systems and that recovery of economic loss in these circumstances should not be unduly fettered by strict adherence to common law principles.

Landcatch brought simultaneous actions against Braer and its insurers under the Civil Liability Convention, as implemented in the UK under the Merchant Shipping (Oil Pollution) Act 1971 and the Compensation Fund, as implemented in the UK under the Merchant Shipping Act 1974.[473] Lord Gill, in the Outer House of the Court of Session, dealt with both claims concurrently as the conventions were similar in terms of the

---

470. [1998] 2 Lloyd's Rep 552.
471. Food Protection (Emergency Prohibitions) (Oil and Chemical Pollution of Fish) Order, 1993 (SI 1993 No 143).
472. In fact the pursuer's place of business was in Ormsary, Argyll, some 500 kilometres from Shetland.
473. The nature of the international regimes governing maritime oil pollution is dealt with in more detail below at §5.05[A].

types of claim which could be met.[474] In short, the Conventions and implementing legislation in the UK provide that where, as a result of an occurrence, persistent oil escapes from a ship, compensation may be sought in respect of pollution damage or contamination resulting from the escape. Specific allowance for compensation is also made in respect of costs incurred through preventing further damage and remediation costs. The issue which fell to be determined was whether this definition could be interpreted as encompassing pure economic loss.

The first, and perhaps most unrealistic, argument put forward on behalf of the pursuer was that the fact that the legislation did not qualify the terms 'loss' and 'damage' demonstrated that the intention was to create unlimited liability. In other words, once a causal link had been established through a simple application of the 'but for' test, the defendants would be liable for all losses flowing from the incident. As Lord Gill succinctly put it, the essence of such an approach is that 'on a "but for test" the repercussions of the causative test continue until its force is eventually spent.'[475] Lord Gill quickly dispensed with this argument on the grounds that Parliament could not have intended to establish such a far-reaching and open-ended system of liability. Any intention to do so would have been expressly set out in the Acts.[476] He was also dismissive of arguments that national legislation had to be read in the light of the overall aims and objectives of the Conventions which were to provide a comprehensive system of compensation for oil pollution damage. His Lordship was of the firm opinion that the implementing legislation was clear and unambiguous and that in such circumstances there was no need to have recourse to the conventions as an aid to construction.[477] In any case, whilst it was true that in principle the Conventions could be construed as allowing recovery for economic loss, Lord Gill could not accept the implication that 'that of itself removes any further limitation on the ambit of liability other than causation itself.'[478]

The next argument put forward by the pursuers was that the Court should have regard to the decisions of the Fund itself in which the Executive Committee of the Fund had, on occasion, appeared to have made payments in respect of similar claims. These reported decisions are sometimes referred to as 'fund jurisprudence'. However, his Lordship did not consider that the decisions of the Executive Committee of the Fund could be regarded as establishing any form of cohesive precedent and certainly not binding precedent. Whilst the Executive Committee endeavoured to attain a certain

---

474. There was some discussion in the judgment as to whether the action against the Fund was premature and should have been held in abeyance pending a determination of whether the tanker owners and insurers could be held accountable for the entire losses under the civil liability system. This is because it is clearly stated that recourse should only be had to the fund where liability has been established under the Liability Convention but compensation cannot be obtained in full from the tanker owners or their insurers: see Article 2 Fund Convention and sections 1, 4(1) and 4(5) Merchant Shipping Act 1974. However, Lord Gill was of the opinion that both actions raised identical issues on economic loss with the result that both actions could be dealt with in a single judgment: [1998] 2 Lloyd's Rep. 552, 563.

475. *Landcatch* (n. 470)565.

476. *Ibid.*, 567.

477. *Ibid.* See also *Saloman v. CEC* [1967] 2 QB 116, 143–144 (Diplock LJ).

478. *Landcatch* (n. 470) 567.

degree of consistency, decisions were reached on an ad hoc basis according to the merits of the individual claim. In any case, the minutes of the decisions upon which the pursuers sought to rely did not contain any detailed reasoning.[479] In fact the decisions worked more in the defendant's favour as they established the fact that the Executive Committee did not make payments on the basis of an application of a simple 'but for' test, rather, it was necessary to adduce additional factors establishing proximity.[480]

Thus, in order to establish proximity it was necessary to fall back upon established common law principles. As discussed above, at common law it is necessary to establish a proprietary interest in the resource affected in order to recover damages. Where the loss is purely economic the claimant must establish an additional factor 'beyond the mere occurrence of the loss and the fact that its occurrence could have been foreseen.'[481] This presented a substantial obstacle for the pursuers in that their place of business was not even in the Shetland Islands. Furthermore, they did not have on-going contractual relationships with the salmon farmers as smolt was supplied on request.[482] Instead, they sought to rely on the claim that their business activities were 'bound with' and 'closely integrated' with the Shetland salmon industry, however, Lord Gill determined that this would not suffice to establish the requisite degree of proximity:

> When one examines the primary facts averred by the pursuers, it is plain that the pursuers were no more than potential trade suppliers to salmon farmers carrying on business in the area of the contamination.[483]

The pursuer's final and perhaps weakest argument was that the Court should follow the decision of *Junior Brookes v. Veitchi Co*[484] in which economic loss was recoverable despite the fact that there did not appear to be an additional factor linking the parties such as a contract. However, whilst the decision has not been expressly overruled the House of Lords has, in subsequent cases, consistently distinguished the decision and has endeavoured to confine it to its particular facts.[485] Although there was no direct contract between the parties in that particular case, the fact that the defendant sub-contractor had been nominated by the pursuer meant that 'the relationship between the parties was seen to be as close as it could be short of actual privity of contract'.[486]

---

479. *Ibid.*, 569.
480. *Ibid.* His Lordship referred to the Report of Seventh Inter-Sessional Working Group (1994), paras. 7.2.25–7.2.30.
481. *Ibid.*, 570.
482. In fact Lord Gill stated, at 569, that the pursuer's case would not have been any stronger even if they had been in a contractual relationship with the salmon farmers. Persons other than the owner of damaged property, such as those who have some contractual interest related to the property, cannot claim on the basis that the economic expectations under that contract have become less profitable as a result of the damage. See *Candlewood Navigation Corporation Ltd v. Mitsui OSK Lines* [1986] AC 785.
483. *Ibid.*
484. [1983] 1 A.C. 520.
485. See, for example, *D and F Estates Ltd v. Church Commissioners for England* [1989] AC 177, 202 (Lord Bridge).
486. *Landcatch* [1998] (n. 470) 571 (Lord Gill).

The decision was upheld on appeal to the Second Division Inner House Court of Session,[487] however, it was acknowledged, *obiter*, that a rigid adherence to the notion that economic loss must be anchored in physical damage in order to be recoverable would have excluded the claims of fishermen. This would have seemed an unduly harsh outcome. Lord McCluskey was of the opinion that in these circumstances, the loss of opportunity to fish could be regarded as being as immediate and direct as physical damage:

> For the fishermen I am considering, the pollution of the waters in which he regularly fishes does no physical harm to his person or his property; the oil does not touch him or anything belonging to him; there is no contamination of him or of his vessel or equipment. Nevertheless, it appears to me that the loss of his livelihood is properly described as damage that is caused directly and immediately by contamination resulting from the discharge or escape of oil from the ship. The contamination does not set in train a chain of events that eventually results in his suffering loss or damage. On the contrary, the contamination is both the immediate, direct and, in such a case, the only cause of his loss.[488]

This is because the fishermen could be described as having a 'direct economic interest' in the damaged resource. Thus damage to that resource can be regarded as having a direct impact on this 'economic interest'. Lord McClusky distinguished fishermen from the position of those who, for example, supply the fishing industry with equipment and diesel. Their loss is one step removed in that their economic interests lie in the fishing industry itself rather than the resource which the industry harvests, thus:

> [T]he wholesaler who supplies the diesel in bulk to the trader, or the netmaker who sells the trader nets for onward sale to fishermen may be economically prejudiced by the disruption of his market; but his economic prejudice, or loss, is not caused directly by oil pollution, or contamination. It is directly caused by the trader's decision not to buy what he has to sell.[489]

By this device, Lord McCluskey sought to keep the floodgates firmly shut.

On the basis of the *Landcatch* decision other economic loss claims brought by other industries affected by the spillage were also dismissed. This included a claim brought by P&O Scottish Ferries in respect of loss of custom.[490] The English Court of Appeal followed its Scottish counterpart in *Algrete Shipping Co. Ltd. v. International Oil Pollution Compensation Fund*[491] which stemmed from the other major oil tanker spillage off the British Isles in recent times, namely, the grounding of the *Sea Empress* off Milford-Haven. In this case the claimants, who operated a whelk processing business which mainly exported to the Far East, claimed several hundred thousand pounds in lost profits. The claimant attempted to distinguish *Landcatch* on the basis that the pursuer in that case was a mere supplier of produce to the fish industry,

---

487. [1999] 2 Lloyd's Rep 316.
488. *Ibid.*, 332.
489. *Ibid.*
490. *P&O Scottish Ferries v. The Braer Corporation and another and International Oil Pollution Compensation Fund* [1999] 2 Lloyd's Rep. 316.
491. [2003] 1 Lloyd's Rep. 327.

whereas, in the present case the claimant was a prospective recipient of contaminated produce in which they had a direct economic interest. In this respect their loss was more akin to that suffered by the fishing industry, which, as noted above, is deemed to be in a special position by virtue of its reliance on the sea. The Court of Appeal rejected the claim on the basis that the distinction between a frustrated purchaser and a frustrated supplier was too fine to draw.[492] Furthermore, that there is a qualitative difference between fish as a natural resource and fish as a product once it has been abstracted from the natural environment. All manner of parties, including wholesalers and restaurateurs, may have an interest in the product but this purely economic interest is of an entirely different nature to the unique connection between the fishing industry and the sea as a natural resource.[493]

The comments on the nature of the fishing arising from these judgments raise an interesting issue. They show that an economic interest in a polluted natural resource, which falls short of actual ownership, can still be regarded as establishing a link with the damaged resource which is sufficiently strong to justify a claim for economic loss. This is not to say that these comments can be regarded as a major departure from the common law in that they relate specifically to the rather special circumstances of fishermen and their unique relationship with the sea.[494] Nevertheless, the comments are significant in that the Courts appear to acknowledge that a rigid application of the dogmatic common law physical damage test can, in certain circumstances, lead to unjust, if not to say absurd results. It also demonstrates that in the context of a specialist environmental liability regime, of the type which is discussed in subsequent chapters, it may be necessary to consider a rather more flexible approach to the issue of the recoverability of economic loss.

Nevertheless, as matters stand it is clear that the UK courts will always adopt a cautious approach to the recovery of economic loss. In the absence of express provision for the recovery of economic loss in a statutory liability and compensation system, the courts will not be prepared to depart from existing restrictive common law principles.

In the United States the issue of economic loss was also brought to the fore by an oil tanker disaster, albeit on an even larger scale.

Shortly after midnight on 23 March 1989 the super-tanker *Exxon Valdez* was negotiating a difficult channel in Prince William Sound, Alaska. The vessel was under the command of Captain Joseph Hazelwood, who had a long history of alcohol abuse, which was known to his employers. By his own admission on the night in question he had been drinking and had left the bridge two minutes before the tanker was due to commence a difficult turn leaving an inexperienced third mate to execute the manoeuvre. Shortly after midnight the ship struck Bligh Reef and was holed causing the release of 10.8 million US gallons of oil thereby unleashing an environmental disaster of epic proportions. Apart from the impact on flora, fauna and the ecosystem in general,

---

492. *Ibid.*, [26] (Mance LJ).
493. *Ibid.*, [27].
494. As will be seen below, in the United States an express exception from the general prohibition on the recovery of economic loss resulting from maritime torts has been made in respect of fishermen.

discussed below, the disaster had a devastating impact on the local economy. As in *Braer* it was the fishing industry which bore the brunt of the losses. Apart from the fishermen themselves, losses were incurred by supply industries and fish processing plants. A further similarity with *Braer* was that most of these losses were economic in nature as many of these businesses were far removed from the zone of contamination.

The disaster triggered a lengthy and complex legal battle involving both individual and class actions.[495] Parties suffering economic loss launched concurrent civil suits in the State and Federal Courts.[496] One of the preliminary issues, which fell to be determined, was whether State common law or maritime law should apply. This issue was crucial in that economic loss is far more difficult to recover in respect of maritime torts.[497] Judge Holland, sitting in the Federal District Court, determined that the matter should be dealt with under maritime law as the circumstances satisfied the 'locality' and 'maritime nexus' tests. Accordingly the Federal Court ruled that the matters should be dealt with as a maritime tort. Furthermore, it was ruled that maritime law pre-empted state common law torts such as negligence, trespass and nuisance. This immediately reduced the scope for economic loss claims before the Federal Court as, under maritime law, claims for pure economic loss are strictly limited by the *Robins Dry Dock* rule.[498] This precludes all claims for pure economic loss caused by a maritime tort. Thus, generally speaking, US law on maritime torts mirrors the UK common law position on this issue as only those touched by the oil are in a position to claim. However, an exception was made in respect of economic losses suffered by fishermen as a result of a 1974 ruling of the Court of Appeals for the Ninth Circuit.[499] However, even this exception was applied very narrowly by Judge Holland in the Federal Court with the result that fishermen were only permitted to claim in respect of lost harvests. Claims in respect of devaluation of boats and fishing permits were not entertained.[500]

In the State Court, however, Judge Shortell reached a somewhat different conclusion and stated that claims under maritime law could be brought in addition to state common law claims. However, as the litigation progressed Exxon was able to move an increasing number of claims into the Federal Court where the stricter rules on the recovery of economic loss were applied.[501]

---

495. The main trial took place in the United States District Court for the District of Alaska between 2 May and 16 September 1994: *re, The Exxon Valdez*, A89-0595-CV(HRH).
496. A peculiarity of the United States legal system is that Federal Courts and State Courts may enjoy concurrent jurisdiction in the same matter and may reach different conclusions. This overlapping jurisidction contributed to the complexity and protracted nature of the Exxon Valdez litigation.
497. Generally speaking, under the US common law system of tort, economic loss is not strictly limited to those who have suffered physical damage. Rather, the courts apply a 'proximate cause' analysis which does not preclude claims for pure economic loss.
498. *Robins Dry Dock & Repair Co. v. Flint*, 275 U.S. 303 (1927).
499. *Union Oil Co. v. Oppen*. 501 F. 2d 588 (9th Cir. 1974).
500. The Federal Court drew a distinction between 'economic loss' and 'lost profits'; the *Oppen* ruling was interpreted as applying an exception in respect of loss of profits only.
501. Although, as noted above, State and Federal Court enjoy concurrent jurisdiction, where certain aspects of Federal Law are concerned, the matter must be moved to a Federal Court; see *Cippollone v. Liggett Group*, Inc. 505 US 504 (1992). Exxon's lawyers skillfully identified Federal issues and were thus able to move a large proportion of the claims to the Federal Court.

The *Exxon Valdez* litigation highlighted many complexities and uncertainties in terms of the recoverability of economic loss flowing from environmental catastrophes of epic proportions. The incident provoked an immediate legislative response in the shape of the Oil Pollution Act 1990 (OPA) which has sought to tidy up the patchwork quilt of legislation and common law rules governing such incidents. However, the OPA was not cast as a retrospective measure which meant that it played no part in resolving the Exxon Valdez dispute. It would be another twenty years before the legislation was faced with its greatest test; a worst case scenario greater than anyone could have predicted.

Until recently the name *Exxon Valdez* was synonymous with the worst environmental disaster in US history. However, in 2010 this most unwelcome of accolades was passed to *Deepwater Horizon*, an oil spill which eclipses *Exxon Valdez* in scale several times over. The *Deepwater Horizon* was a moveable offshore drilling rig at the forefront of efforts to open up ever more deeply deposited and inaccessible oil reserves. It had been leased to BP which had won exploration rights for deepwater reserves in the Gulf of Mexico. On 20 April 2010 the rig was drilling at the Macondo Prospect in the Gulf of Mexico, some 41 miles off the coast of Louisiana. On that fateful day a 'gas-kick' caused an explosion leading to the loss of eleven lives and the total destruction of the rig. A device known such as a Blow Out Preventer (BOP) should have automatically sealed the well in such circumstances thereby preventing the leakage of oil. The mechanism failed for a variety of technical reasons relating to the design and maintenance of the device. So began one of the worst oil spillages in the history of oil exploration. For more than three months wall to wall media coverage showed pictures of oil flowing unabated from the well, save for the relatively small amount which salvage operators were able to siphon off.[502] The leak was not plugged until early August following the intersection of the well with a relief shaft drilled at an angle in an astonishing feat of engineering. This was used to pump heavy drilling mud and cement into the shaft thereby plugging the well for good. By this stage, however, the leak had already had a devastating impact on wildlife, fishing, tourism and other industries in the area.[503]

As lessee of the rig and holder of the drilling rights BP inevitably drew much of the fire aimed by furious politicians and the world's media. However, a number of other parties were involved including Transocean, which owned and operated the rig under contract to BP, and the civil engineering companies which had supplied and fitted the BOP and associated infrastructure including Cameron International and Halliburton. In addition BP shared the exploration rights with a number of partners

---

At an early stage in the proceedings they had established that the Federal Judge, Judge Holland, was rather more sympathetic to the defendant's case than the Alaskan State Judge, His Honour, Judge Brian Shortell.

502. It is estimated that an astonishing 4.9 million barrels of oil (200 million gallons) were released into the Gulf whilst only 800,000 barrels were captured. See *BP Oil Spill: Disaster by Numbers*, The Independant (London, Sept. 14, 2010), http://www.independent.co.uk/environment/bp-oil-spill-disaster-by-numbers-2078396.html# (accessed Mar. 31, 2011).

503. Material on the background to the disaster, its causes and effects has assumed mountainous proportions. A useful summary is provided by the BBC, *What do we Know about the Deepwater Horizon Disaaster?*, (*BBC News*, Sept. 8, 2010), http://www.bbc.co.uk/news/10370479 (accessed Mar. 22, 2011).

with more limited stakes in the venture including Anadarko Petroleum (25%) and Mitsui (10%). For the purposes of the OPA liability is focused in the owner(s) of the drilling rights and the operator of the rig – the 'responsible parties'; this would include BP and its partners and Transocean. Suppliers of services and equipment are normally protected by indemnity clauses in service contracts whereby the operator of the site effectively underwrites any losses irrespective of cause. For example, it has been alleged that the cement supplied by Halliburton was defective and contributed to the failure of the BOP. An indemnity clause would protect Halliburton from liability arising from environmental damage, economic loss and so forth. However, such clauses may also contain a provision which removes the protection if gross negligence or wilful conduct is found. In this case suppliers may find themselves exposed to full liability in respect of their contribution to the accident. For this reason Halliburton and any other suppliers criticized in the initial reports into the disaster will vigorously defend any accusations of such conduct.[504]

Such was the scale of the disaster and its immediate environmental and economic impact it would have been unthinkable to delay questions of liability until matters started grinding their way through the courts. Under the full glare of the world's media BP executives were summoned to Washington for a face to face meeting with President Obama.[505] Irrespective of any legal liability, BP agreed to set up a USD 20 billion dollar escrow account (or trust fund) with a view to making immediate out of court settlements and to underwrite eventual legal liabilities.[506] Whilst some claims may be straightforward, including those brought by fishermen under the *Oppen* exception to the non-recoverability of economic loss, other claims are likely to be more complex with the result that we can look forward to many years of litigation. As noted above, *Exxon Valdez* produced some twenty years of litigation culminating in the US Supreme Court decision on punitive damages.

The OPA is broad in scope and encompasses off shore drilling in addition to the transport and distribution of oil. It will play a crucial role in terms of clarifying what types of economic loss claim may be brought in respect of the *Deepwater Horizon*

---

504. The Commission of Enquiry into the cause of the accident made a number of criticisms pertaining to the composition of the cement supplied by Halliburton although Halliburton has vigorously refuted the findings and will continue to do so in the impending enquiry. As regards the report see National Commission on the BP Deepwater Horizon Oil Spill, *Deep Water: The Gulf Oil Disaster and the Future of Offshore Drilling*, (Report to the President (final), January 2011), http://www.oilspillcommission.gov/final-report (accessed Mar. 23, 2011). As regards Halliburton's respnse to the Commission's initial findings see Halliburton, *Halliburton Comments on National Commission Cement Testing*, (Press Release, Oct. 28, 2010), http://www.halliburton.com/public/news/pubsdata/press_release/2010/corpnws_102810.html

505. See T. Webb and T. Hill, *BP to Pay Out USD 20bn after Meeting with Obama*, The Guardian (London, June 16, 2010), http://www.guardian.co.uk/environment/2010/jun/16/bp-20bn-trust-oil-spill

506. US Department of Justice, *Statement of Associate Attorney General Tom Perrelli on Deepwater Horizon Escrow Fund* (Press Release, Aug. 9, 2010), http://www.justice.gov/opa/pr/2010/August/10-asg-910.html (accessed Mar. 22, 2010); BP, *BP forms Gulf of Mexico Oil Spill Escrow Fund* (Press Release, Aug.9, 2010), http://www.bp.com/genericarticle.do?categoryId=2012968&contentId=7064316 (accessed Mar. 22, 2011).

disaster.[507] § 2702 sets out the types of damage which may be recoverable under the legislation which includes 'loss of profits or impairment of earning capacity due to an injury to property or natural resources.'[508] Loss of this nature is clearly economic in nature and many had hoped that it would clarify what types of economic loss claim can be brought. The guidance offered by the House of Representatives Conference Report was not helpful, however, in that it chose to use fishermen as an example of the type of economic loss claim which could be brought.[509] Given that such claims had already been well established under common law this hardly constituted much of an advance. Nevertheless, there remains a consensus that the legislation is intended to expand the type of economic loss claim which can be brought.[510] This raises the issue of what type of control mechanism could be used to ensure that the floodgates are not thrown open so wide that the industry is brought down by crippling costs. Perry is of the opinion that a remoteness test will be applied to differentiate between different types of economic loss claim. Indeed, in the *Exxon Valdez* litigation such an approach was applied in respect of those economic loss claims which were allowed under various state laws.[511] Furthermore, the liability of offshore drilling operators is capped at USD 75 million unless there is a finding of gross negligence.[512] At the time of writing this issue had yet to be resolved and is of crucial importance regarding the extent of BP's liability. If the cap on BP's liability is removed, as a result of a finding of gross negligence, BP's liability could be unlimited although this possibility would have been factored into the USD 20 billion escrow account.

Such is the scale and the notoriety of the *Deepwater Horizon* disaster, it is not surprising to find that the application of the OPA to the incident has already been the subject of much academic speculation. One of the most interesting issues has been addressed by Perry.[513] Perry is critical of how the law distributed damages in the wake of the *Exxon Valdez* disaster. Of particular note is the fact that, whereas a fairly strict approach was taken in respect of economic loss claims, much was made of the need for punitive damages. According to Perry, restricting economic loss whilst simultaneously expanding punitive damages leads to anomalous results. The main justification for limiting the recovery of economic loss is that it avoids opening the floodgates and keeps liability within reasonable bounds. However, punitive damages pull in the opposite

---

507. For an analysis of the extent to which the OPA is likely to extend the scope of economic loss claims in the context of the Deepwater Horizon disaster see, R. Perry, *The Deepwater Horizon Oil Spill and the Limits of Civil Liability*, 86 Wash. L. Rev. 1 (2011).
508. Section 1002(E).
509. H.R. Conf. Rep. No. 101-653 (1990), at 103.
510. See Perry (n. 507) 43 who cites a number of earlier cases brought under the Act where such assertions have been made.
511. *Ibid.*, at p. 44.
512. Mobile drilling rigs are classified as vessels and the liability of the operator is capped according to the same formula: see OLA § 2704, section 1004 1(a)(1)(A). This is calcualted as USD 1,900 per gross ton of the vessel or USD 16 million, whichever is the greater. Thus Transocean's liabity for removal costs may amount to USD 65 million dollars according to some initial estimates. The operator of the offshore facility as a whole, which will be the holder of the exploration rights etc., is capped at USD 75 million dollars unless gross negigence or wilful conduct is established: see OLA § 2704, section 1004 (a)(3)
513. Perry (n. 507).

direction and expand liability thereby cancelling out any moderation achieved by a cautious approach to economic loss. Furthermore, it has major implications in terms of distributive justice. The effect of awarding punitive damages whilst precluding economic loss claims results in some parties gaining a windfall, by gaining damages which exceed their actual losses, while others gain nothing at all.

Perry argues that the OPA goes some way towards redressing this imbalance. The fact that liability caps are removed if gross negligence can be shown increases the funds which must be made available for the settlement of claims. However, the underlying policy of the Act appears to make clear that these funds should be made available for settling a more diverse range of claims and should not be delivered in a concentrated form as punitive damages for the benefit of a limited number of parties. Perry's main reservation regarding the OPA is the use of 'gross negligence' as the key test for determining whether the liability caps should be removed. In his view it would have been better to make this determination according to the 'gravity of the harm'. Indeed, if there is a finding that BP had not been grossly negligent the liability caps would severely restrict the extent of BP's liability and total damages payable would in no way reflect the true aggregated damage costs. In fact, due to the political and economic implications of the case, BP has indicated that it will not seek to limit its liability under the terms of the Act.[514] However, such payments would be *ex gratia* and would not reflect BP's actual legal liability. Nevertheless, a delicate balance has to be struck in terms of ensuring that liability schemes are sufficiently comprehensive whilst avoiding the introduction of unsustainable liability which could cripple an entire industry. As noted above, in the *Exxon Valdez* litigation it was possible to bring some economic loss claims under certain Alaskan state laws. In these cases the courts applied a foreseeability approach which filtered out some of the more tenuous and derivative economic loss claims.[515] It must be acknowledged that foreseeability of harm masks a multitude of policy considerations and inevitably leads to the drawing of an arbitrary cut off point somewhere. However, it does at least offer a more flexible approach than the current inflexible 'bright line' policy bar to economic loss claims.[516] As regards the OPA, Perry envisages a system whereby economic loss claims would be categorized according to type with the most directly affected victims at the core such as fishermen. The categories would then be expanded outwards so as to encompass less directly affected groups including suppliers of equipment to the fishing industry, tourism and leisure and so on. In this respect liability can be visualized as a series of concentric circles with fishermen in the middle and other groups in the outer circles.[517] Of course, the main objection to this approach is that it lacks certainty. Whether or not damages are payable

---

514. According to papers filed with the Federal District Court in Houston. See *BP turns down Legal Right for $75m cap on Gulf of Mexico Liabilities*, The Telegraph (London, Oct. 19, 2010) http://www.telegraph.co.UK/finance/newsbysector/energy/oilandgas/8074593/BP-turns-down-legal-right-for-75m-cap-on-Gulf-of-Mexico-liabilities.html# (accessed Mar. 22, 2010).
515. See Perry (507) 44. One example of a claim which failed this test concerns California drivers who complained about the additional cost of gasoline!
516. For these reasons Edmund-Davies L.J., in his dissenting judgment in *Sparton Steels and Alloys v. Martin* [1972] 3 All ER 557, 569–571, was oppposed to an inflexible policy exclusion for economic loss claims and preferred an approach based upon foreseeability of harm.
517. In class actions claimants are grouped into categories.

to, for example, a diving school, would depend upon the scale of the disaster or whatever other criterion is chosen. This is entirely alien to a common law approach where one either owes a duty not to inflict economic loss on a diving school by depositing oil in coastal waters or one does not. From the point of view of the diving school the loss would be the same whether or not it was caused by gross negligence or was part of a major disaster as opposed to a more minor incident. Perry would no doubt counter that this loss of certainty is an acceptable price to pay for a more flexible compensation system which more accurately reflects true damage costs and achieves greater distributive justice. He would also argue that the approach would be a great deal more certain that the use of punitive damages. Although, this argument would not apply in the UK where, as we have seen above, punitive damages are now virtually unknown.

It remains to be seen how the OPA will be interpreted over the coming years in the context of the *Deepwater Horizon* litigation. No doubt many parties will hope that it will be used to facilitate an expansion in economic loss claims beyond the narrow exception currently afforded to fishermen. Indeed, in the absence of statutory inter-vention there is little prospect for recoverability of economic loss being expanded at common law. Even where the common law has been pre-empted by statute, the case law in the UK demonstrates that, in the absence of clear terminology in the statute, the courts are prone to fall back on common law notions of recoverable loss. There is some doubt as to whether the OPA is sufficiently unequivocal on the issue of economic loss to expand recoverability in the manner envisaged above. The floodgates implications of economic loss are always at the forefront of the issue and explain why the courts adopt a cautious approach. Nevertheless, there is no reason why a more flexible approach should not be adopted in respect of this type of harm, although, alternate control mechanisms such as liability caps or foreseeabilty tests would be required.

[3]   Intangible Environmental Values

The methods of assessing environmental damage above focus on tangible costs such as the value of restoring a resource or the economic impact of an environmental incident. However, these heads of damage take a narrow view of the value of environmental media in that they focus on its direct value to humans. However, it can be argued that the value of the environment goes beyond these immediate considerations and encompasses intangible elements relating to the pleasure derived from wildlife and unspoilt landscapes. These are sometimes referred to as 'passive use values' as they do not involve activities which have any physical impact on the environment. For many years there has been an economic debate, largely taking place in the United States, regarding whether these values are capable of being quantified in monetary terms and whether they should form a component in damages settlements.

The most widely used technique is known as the contingent valuation method (CVM) although it remains highly controversial. In short the method seeks to ascertain what people would be willing to pay (WTP) for an increase in environmental quality, or, what they would accept as compensation in order to forgo such an increase

(WTAC).[518] The method relies upon survey techniques and involves a number of distinct stages. The first stage entails the setting up of a 'hypothetical market'. For example, researchers could invent a scenario whereby survey participants are informed of plans to clean-up an area of contaminated land and establish a nature reserve. However, they are also told that this will entail expenditure and a possible increase in local taxes. In stage two survey techniques are used in order to ascertain participants WTA or WTAC values. In other words how much would they pay in order to establish the reserve, or, how much compensation would they accept in order to leave the site as it is or establish another polluting activity there. Once this data has been collected it is simply a matter of calculating the mean or median average sums which the survey participants would be WTP for the environmental improvements or how much they would be WTP to forego such improvements.[519] The final stage involves extrapolating these results into a wider context by calculating what the population as a whole would be WTP for improvements or accept as compensation for degradation.

Despite continuing controversy surrounding the reliability of the method,[520] it gained legal recognition in the *Exxon Valdez* litigation as a legitimate means of determining intangible environmental values.[521] On the run up to the trial Exxon's lawyers sought to discredit the technique and exclude it from consideration as a component in any damages settlement. An independent panel of distinguished economists was convened in order to assess the reliability of the technique. In their final report they afforded the technique a cautious approval although a number of guidelines were proposed. However, in terms of the overall settlement, the CVM element was insignificant in that the bulk of the damages consisted of a punitive element calculated on the basis of Exxon's turnover. CVM derived elements were also dwarfed by calculations relating to loss of profit on fishing harvests and long term economic consequences caused by tainting of the industry in that area.

[B]   Injunctions

These are discretionary remedies originating from the equitable jurisdiction of Chancery. They are most frequently granted in respect of continuing trespasses or nuisances

---

518. See N. Hanley, J.F. Shogren & B. White, *Environmental Economics in Theory and Practice*, 384–401 (MacMillan 1997).

519. *Ibid*. Although this is very much an over simplification as the economic theory involved is beyond the scope of this book. In short, the data is filtered through various economic algebraic formulas designed to correct certain errors and biases which typically occur in survey data of this nature.

520. *Ibid*. The main difficulties associated with the technique focus on overcoming problems of bias. For example, it has been found that many people consistently overstate what they would be WTP as they know that the exercise is hypothetical in nature. Various methods have been used in both the manner in which the surveys are conducted and the analysis of the data in order to correct bias. However, these methods may themselves be the subject of academic disagreement.

521. *Ibid*. In fact the method had gained earlier acceptance as a means of assessing passive use values regarding the clean up of contaminated land under CERCLA. See *State of Ohio v. Department of the Interior* 880 F.2d432 (D.C.Cir. 1989).

although there is no theoretical reason why they should not be issued to restrain the continuation of any tort of any kind. As a discretionary remedy the courts are free to take into account a range of factors including the seriousness of the harm and the effect the granting of the injunction would have on the plaintiff. Turner L.J. summed up the manner in which courts should approach the use of injunctions in *Goldsmith v. Tunbridge Wells Improvement Commissioners*:

> It is not in every case of nuisance that this Court should interfere. I think that it ought not to do so in cases in which the injury is merely temporary or trifling; but I think that it ought to do so in cases in which the injury is permanent and serious: and in determining whether the injury is serious or not, regard must be had to all the consequences which may flow from it.[522]

[1] Prohibitory Injunctions

These orders require the cessation of a continuing tortious activity and are thereby closely associated with the restoration of proprietary interests; namely, the rights to use and enjoyment and exclusive possession. Hence it is not necessary to establish physical damage before such relief is granted. As the remedy is discretionary and requires the courts to consider all the consequences flowing from its use, it is inextricably linked with the land use conflict aspects of nuisance. This is because the courts must balance the harm suffered by the plaintiff against the consequences of requiring the defendant to cease the offending activity. It may often be the case that the nuisance can be abated without significant loss to the defendant.[523] However, where prohibition of the activity would result in substantial loss to the defendant or even the closure of the defendant's plant, the court may be tempted to balance the utility of the defendant's activity against the usually conservatory land use interests of the plaintiff. In the past there has been strong judicial disapproval of this approach, for example, in *Shelfer v. City of London Electric Lighting Co.*, Lindley L.J. stated:

> The circumstance the wrongdoer is in some sense a public benefactor ... [has never] been considered a sufficient reason for refusing to protect by injunction an individual whose rights are being persistently infringed. Expropriation, even for a monetary consideration, is only justifiable if Parliament has sanctioned it.[524]

Thus, on occasion, the courts have been prepared to grant prohibitory injunctions at the expense of the defendant's business. Not least of these few examples is the case of *St. Helens Smelting v. Tipping*. The availability of damages in lieu of an injunction means that it is rare for courts to take this step with the result that the remedy is more readily available where the consequences are less drastic for the defendant.

---

522. (1866) 1 Ch. App. 349.
523. As in the New Zealand case of *Bank of New Zealand v. Greenwood* [1984] 1 N.Z.L.R. 525 where it was held that the nuisance caused by the glare of the defendant's windows could be abated by the installation of blinds in the plaintiff's premises at the defendants' expense.
524. [1895] 1 Ch. 287, at 315–316.

As will be seen below, in the context of damages awarded in lieu of an injunction, the courts are faced with a dilemma when an injunction could result in the closure of a large and successful industrial plant with consequent loss of jobs and damage to the economy. In *St. Helens Smelting v. Tipping* the defendant actually moved the plant, albeit a relatively short distance, in response to the injunction granted to Tipping. This may not always be a practicable solution. The courts were faced with this dilemma in the case of *Farnworth v. Manchester Corporation*[525] concerning crop damage caused by sulphur dioxide emissions from a newly completed coal-fired power station. The novel solution was to suspend the injunction pending further investigations into methods of pollution abatement. The law reports do not tell us what the final outcome was of this approach; however, historical sources reveal that the plant was actually fitted with taller chimneys so as to disperse the emissions.[526] This solved the immediate crop damage problem although, unbeknown to all, it may have contributed to transboundary pollution and the acidification of Scandinavian lakes and forests.[527]

[2]   Quia Timet Injunctions

In exceptional cases, this type of injunction may be obtained, where, if allowed to continue, the defendant's conduct would inevitably result in harm to the claimant. To give a hypothetical example, if leaking barrels of chemicals were brought onto land adjacent to a waterway, a down catchment riparian landholder may be able to obtain an injunction requiring removal of the barrels before any of the chemicals seep into the waterway. In practice, claimants have rarely been able to satisfy the court that the apprehended harm is imminent[528] with the result that the remedy has been little used. In any case, in the hypothetical example given above, it is unlikely that the down catchment owner would be aware of the potential harm until it was too late. The test is even more difficult to satisfy where there is scientific uncertainty regarding the link between an activity and possible harm.

For example, an unsuccessful attempt was made to obtain a *quia timet* injunction in the Irish case of *Szabo v. Esat Digifone Ltd.*[529] The defendants in this case wished to install and operate a cellular mobile phone base station. This was to be mounted on the roof of the Garda station in Easkey, County Sligo. An action was brought on behalf of the plaintiffs, who were five minors at a neighbouring school, seeking *quia timet* relief on the grounds of possible adverse health effects, which could result from the installation of the mast. The plaintiffs' expert witness, Dr Firstenberg, stated that resulting health problems could include attention deficit disorder, insomnia, bronchitis, sinusitis and vision problems. In addition he forecast that a minority of the children could become 'electrically sensitive'; this could lead to neuralgic and cardiac reaction.

---

525. [1930] A.C. 171.
526. Roy Frost, *Electricity in Manchester*, 41–43 (Neil Richardson 1993).
527. Transboundary pollution is dealt with in more depth at §5.02[A], below.
528. *Att. Gen. v. Nottingham Corporation* [1904] 1 Ch. 673; *Redland Bricks Ltd. v. Morris* [1970] A.C. 652.
529. Unreported, 6th February 1998. Case note in 5(1) I.P.E.L.J. 35 (1998).

The defendant's expert witness, Professor Walton, countered that the type of radiation in question was non-ionizing. In short, this means that it does not possess enough energy to disrupt molecules in the body in a manner that can lead to cancer. He also pointed out that there were several existing sources of non-ionizing radiation in the vicinity of the school which were far more powerful than the proposed base station.

The authorities on the subject[530] left the judge in no doubt that the onus is on the plaintiff to establish a strong probability that the activity will lead to the predicted consequences. In particular he referred to the judgment of the Irish Court of Appeal in *Attorney General (Boswell) v. Rathmines and Pembroke Joint Hospital Board*[531] in which the Vice Chancellor stated:

> It is a quia timet action: the projected hospital has not been built, but we are not altogether without experimental evidence of its probable effects ... To sustain the injunction the law requires proof by the plaintiff of a well founded apprehension of injury, proof of actual and real danger – a strong probability, almost amounting to a moral certainty, that if the hospital be established, it would be an actionable nuisance.

In considering the conflicting scientific evidence on the effects of electromagnetic radiation Geoghegan J. stated that a judge could not form his own expert opinion. In *quia timet* actions, if the result of the conflict was to leave the judge in doubt as to the inevitability of the harm, he could not conclude that the case for the plaintiff had been made out. The judge was conscious of the fact that the plaintiffs' evidence was inconsistent with the main body of scientific evidence amassed during the past fifty years.[532] Hence, as regards the present case he was led to the conclusion that:

> Having regard to the stringent requirement of probability before a *quia timet* injunction would be granted on a permanent basis, I am very doubtful that there is a serious issue to be tried here.

It is also possible to obtain injunctive relief in respect of prospective harm in the United States although the term *quia timet* is not used to describe this form of relief. According to the Second Restatement of Torts, a plaintiff is entitled to an injunction in respect of prospective harm where there is a 'dangerous probability' that such harm will occur.[533] This would appear to be a slightly less onerous test than a 'moral certainty' in that it suggests that the risk need not be immediate.

For example, in *Village of Wilsonville v. SCA Services, Inc.*,[534] the plaintiffs sought injunctive relief in respect of the threat to public health caused by a chemical waste landfill site. Substances disposed of at the site were extremely toxic and included PCBs, solid cyanide, paint sludge, asbestos, pesticides, mercury and arsenic. The chemicals, normally contained in steel drums or reinforced paper sacks, were placed in large

---

530. Such as *Attorney General v. Manchester Corporation* [1893] 2 Ch. 87 in which a *quia timet* injunction was sought to prevent the establishment of a smallpox hospital.
531. [1904] I.R. 161.
532. This mirrors the consistency test applied by French J. In *Reay v. Hope* (n. 358).
533. Restatement (Second) of Torts s. 933(1), at 561.
534. Supreme Court of Illinois, 1981. 86 Ill.2d 1, 55 Ill.Dec. 499, 426 N.E.2d 824.

trenches and then packed with clay. A further layer of clay was laid over the top of the chemicals to a thickness of one foot before the trench was in-filled with soil.

Although harm had yet to occur, local villagers and farmers feared that it was only a matter of time before the waste leached into a subterranean water source which was abstracted for a variety of purposes including drinking. A series of abandoned mine workings were discovered directly underneath the landfill site. Coal had been abstracted using the 'room-and-panel' method by which coal is left in pillars as a means of support. If the pillars were to collapse, as they surely would in time, subsidence would occur under the landfill, which could lead to contamination of the water supply.

The Supreme Court of Illinois was persuaded that the facts established that there was a 'dangerous probability' that harm would occur unless the site was closed and cleaned up. The defendant's contention that the risk was not sufficiently great to satisfy the test was rejected. Referring to a leading work on US Tort Law Clark J stated:

> We agree with the defendant's statement of the law, but not with its urged application to the facts of this case. Again, Professor Prosser has offered a concise commentary. He has stated that '[o]ne distinguishing feature of equitable relief is that it may be granted upon the threat of harm which has not yet occurred. The defendant may be restrained from entering upon an activity where it is highly probable that it will lead to a nuisance, although if the possibility is merely uncertain or contingent he may be left to his remedy after the nuisance has occurred.' (Prosser, Torts sec. 90, at 603 (4th ed. 1971).) This view is in accord with Illinois law.

Nevertheless, the 'dangerous probability' test could still prove difficult to satisfy in the majority of situations. Whilst concurring with Clark J, Ryan J expressed the view that the standard should not be fixed. He argued that if the damage, which would result from contamination, was likely to be severe the Court should be able to grant relief on the basis of a lesser degree of probability:

> Although the 'dangerous probability' test has certainly been met in this case, I would be willing to enjoin the activity on a showing of probability of occurrence substantially less than that which the facts presented to this court reveal, due to the potentially hazardous nature of the chemicals being dumped and the potentially catastrophic results.[535]

[3]   Mandatory Injunctions

This type of injunction can be used to require the rectification of physical damage which has already occurred. In *Redland Bricks Ltd. v. Morris* Lord Upjohn set out the circumstances where the remedy should be used. First, where damages would be an inadequate remedy; this may include situations in which the defendant is best placed to rectify the damage himself. For example, where a contractor has caused damage to

---

535. Ryan J drew support for this conclusion from comments in the Second Statement of Torts relating to preventative injunctions in general: 'The more serious the impending harm, the less justification there is for taking the chances that are involved in pronouncing the harm too remote.' (Restatement (Second) of Torts s. 933, at 561, comment *b* (1979).)

neighbouring property during the course of operations and is still on site. In the *Redland Bricks* case there was an immediate threat of subsidence occurring on the plaintiff's land unless the defendant took preventative action. The second instance his Lord Upjohn gave of where the remedy should be used was in cases in which the defendant had attempted to steal a march on the plaintiff or the court. This would include cases in which the defendant has hastened to complete an activity with a view to presenting the court with a *fait accompli*. As a final point, his Lordship stated that the injunction should specify the remedial works to be carried out as precisely as possible.

Prima facie, this remedy would appear to provide the ideal means of requiring the defendant to rectify any lasting damage caused by pollution or to clean-up types of pollution which accumulates without dispersing. This latter category would encompass contaminated land. However, it is necessary to take account of the decision in *Jordon v. Norfolk County Council and another*.[536] In this case, the defendants had purchased land for the purposes of development. They mistakenly believed that the parcel of land they had purchased included part of a disused railway embankment belonging to the plaintiff. Their contractors trespassed upon the land and chopped down all the trees which grew on it and dug a drain. The plaintiff obtained a mandatory injunction requiring the removal of the drain and the replacement of trees so far as was reasonably practicable and to the reasonable satisfaction of the plaintiff's experts. The plaintiff's expert devised a scheme of works which took no account of cost and was designed to restore the land to the exact state it had been in before the trespass. This entailed obtaining fully mature trees with a girth of 60–70 centimetres and transporting them to the site at huge expense and the installation of complex irrigation equipment whilst the trees became established. The estimated cost of the works came to EUR 231,000; the diminution in the value of the land caused by the trespass had only been estimated at EUR 25,000. The defendants sought to have the order set aside and replaced with a less ambitious scheme requiring replacement of the trees with younger trees at a cost of EUR 12,000. It was argued that the phrase 'reasonably practicable' embraced financial viability and not just that which was physically possible.

It was held by Sir Donald Nicholls V.C. that the term 'Reasonably practicable' embraced cost considerations and in determining costs regard should be had to the value of the land:

> In determining what should be the extent of the tree, hedge and shrub replacement, the landscape architect should prescribe items in so far, but only in so far, as their cost would be reasonable, having regard to the nature and value of the site.[537]

In this case the scheme, proposed by the plaintiff, cost several times the market value of the land even before taking into account the diminution in value brought about by the removal of the trees. Hence the scheme could not be regarded as meeting the 'reasonably practicable criteria'. Thus, the approach adopted in this case mirrors the

---

536. [1994] 1 W.L.R. 1353.
537. *Ibid.*, 1358B.

assessment of damages, whereby, the costs of remediation will not be awarded if they are out of proportion to the diminution in market value of the land.

[4]   Damages in Lieu of an Injunction

The power to grant damages in lieu of an injunction was first conferred on Chancery by Lord Cairn's Act of 1858 (the Chancery Amendment Act) and is now vested in the High Court by virtue of section 50 of the Senior Courts Act 1981. They differ from ordinary damages in that they may be granted in respect of future damage which may occur in the absence of an injunction.

The issue of when damages should be awarded in place of an injunction has given rise to much debate. The main problem is that the award of damages in lieu of an injunction amounts to a compulsory purchase of the claimant's rights to the undisturbed use and enjoyment or exclusive possession of his property. This is because the sum is regarded as being in full and final settlement of the dispute with the result that the claimant may not return to court on future occasions if the nuisance continues.[538] Thus, unless the remedy is used with care, it can give rise to an extreme unfettered market philosophy which takes no account of externalities. The courts have been aware of this problem for some considerable time. In *Shelfer v. City of London Electric Lighting Co.*, Lindley L.J. stated that, in granting Chancery the power to award damages in lieu of an injunction, the legislature had not:

> Intended to turn the Court into a tribunal for legalising wrongful acts; or in other words, the Court has always protested against the notion that it ought to allow a wrong to continue simply because the wrongdoer is able and willing to pay for the injury he may inflict.[539]

Despite this assertion, the courts sometimes calculate the quantum of damages on the basis of what the defendant would have had to pay the claimant for the right to

---

538. In fact this point has caused the courts some conceptual difficulties in the past. In *Anchor Brewhouse Developments Ltd. v. Berkley House (Docklands Developments) Ltd.* (1987) 38 B.L.R. 87 Scott J. considered that damages could not put the defendant in the same position as someone who enjoys an easement over the neighbouring property. Hence, in theory the plaintiff would be in a position to claim further damages on limitless future occasions for as long as the trespass (as it was in this case) continued. However, this view was firmly rejected by the Court of Appeal in *Jaggard v. Sawyer* [1995] 1 W.L.R. 269, 285H-286B. Millet L.J. dismissed Scott J.s argument as 'fallacious' on the grounds that, ' ... it is not the award of damages which has the practical effect of licensing the defendant to commit the wrong, but the refusal of injunctive relief. Thereafter the defendant may have no right to act in the manner complained of, but he cannot be prevented from doing so. The court can in my judgment properly award damages 'once and for all' in respect of future wrongs which an injunction would have prevented. The doctrine of res judicata operates to prevent the plaintiff and his successors in title from bringing proceedings thereafter to recover even nominal damages in respect of further wrongs for which the plaintiff has been fully compensated.'
539. [1895] 1 Ch. 287, 315–316.

continue the activity.[540] In view of Lindley L.J.'s caution, A.L. Smith L.J. (also in *Shelfer*) set out a number of guidelines for determining whether the court should exercise its discretion to grant damages in lieu:

> (1) If the injury to the plaintiff's legal rights is small, (2) And is one which is capable of being estimated in money, (3) And is one which can be adequately compensated by a small money payment, (4) And the case is one in which it would be oppressive to the defendant to grant an injunction:- then damages in substitution for an injunction may be given.[541]

The court must take particular care when applying the 'oppression' criteria; in *Jaggard v. Sawyer* Sir Thomas Bingham M.R. noted:

> It is important to bear in mind that the test is one of oppression, and the court should not slide into application of a general balance of convenience test.[542]

This refers to the fact that, in deciding whether an injunction would be oppressive to the defendant, courts should not be drawn into consideration of the merits of the defendant's activity. In his dissenting judgment in *Miller v. Jackson*,[543] which concerned whether injunctive relief should be available in order to protect the plaintiff from cricket balls hit for six, Lord Denning M.R. was in favour of such a 'public interest' approach:

> In this case it is our task to balance the right of the cricket club to continue playing cricket on their cricket ground – as against the right of the householder not to be interfered with ... The *public* interest lies in protecting the environment by preserving our playing fields in the face of mounting development, and by enabling our youth to enjoy all the benefits of outdoor games, such as cricket and football. The *private* interest lies in securing the privacy of his [the plaintiff's] home and garden without intrusion or interference by anyone ... In a new situation like this, we have to think afresh as to how discretion should be exercised ... Either the cricket club has to move: but goodness knows where. I do not suppose for a moment there is any field in Lintz to which they could move. Or Mrs Miller must move elsewhere. As between their conflicting interests, I am of [the] opinion that the public interest should prevail over the private interest. The cricket club should not be driven out.[544]

Cumming-Bruce L.J. found academic support for this view and quoted from *Spry on Equitable Remedies* (1971), p. 365:

> Regard must be had 'not only to the dry strict rights of the plaintiff and the defendant, but also the surrounding circumstances, to the rights of interests of other persons which may be more or less involved.' So it is that where the plaintiff

---

540. See, for example, *Bracewell v. Appleby* [1975] 1 Ch. 406, 419G-H: ' ... I think that for the purpose of estimating damages they and the other servient owners in Hill Road, albeit reluctant, must be treated as being willing to accept a fair price for the right of way in question ... ' (Graham J).
541. [1895] 1 Ch. 287, 322–323.
542. [1995] 1 W.L.R. 269, 283B.
543. [1977] 1 Q.B. 966.
544. *Ibid.*, 981D-982C.

has prima facie a right to specific relief, a court of equity will, if occasion should arise, weigh the disadvantage or hardship which he will suffer if relief were refused against any hardship or disadvantage which would be caused to third persons or to the public generally if relief were granted.

This reasoning was applied at first instance in *Kennaway v. Thompson*[545] in which the plaintiff sought injunctive relief against a noise nuisance created by a power boat club which used a nearby lake:

> The question remains as to whether I should grant an injunction. I have considered the question most carefully and as to whether damages in this case would meet the position – and substantial damages. I have come to the conclusion from what I have heard there is considerable public interest in this club, that the public do attend in large numbers and that it would be oppressive in all the circumstances to grant an injunction other than the injunction I have indicated which would merely cause further litigation.[546]

On appeal the public interest approach was firmly rejected and the Court of Appeal reaffirmed Lindley L.J.'s rejection, in *Shelfer*, of the view that the utility of the defendant's conduct should be taken into account:

> Lord Denning M.R.'s statement that the public interest should prevail over the private interest runs counter to the principles enunciated in Shelfer's case and does not accord with Cumming-Bruce L.J.'s reason for refusing an injunction. We are of the opinion that there is nothing in *Miller v. Jackson* [1977] Q.B. 966 binding on us, which qualifies what was decided in *Shelfer's* case ... which give support for the proposition that the public interest should prevail over the private interest must be read subject to the decision in *Shelfer's* case.[547]

At present the conduct of the defendant appears to be the most important factor when deciding whether to exercise the discretion; in *Jaggard v. Sawyer*, Sir Thomas Bingham M.R. was of the opinion that:

> It would weigh against a finding of oppression if the defendants had acted in blatant and calculated disregard of the plaintiff's rights, of which they were aware.[548]

This would be case where the defendant had deliberately set out to present the court with a *fait accompli* by, for example, hurrying to complete a building in breach of covenant. In such circumstances the court may decide to grant an injunction;[549] however, it seems that an honest yet mistaken belief that an activity was lawful will not count against the defendant.[550]

---

545. [1981] 1 Q.B. 88.
546. *Ibid.*, 92C.
547. *Ibid.*, 93F-G.
548. [1995] 1 W.L.R. 269, 283D.
549. *Harrow London Borough Council v. Donohue* [1993] N.P.C. 49.
550. See the judgment of Millett L.J. in *Jaggard v. Sawyer* [1995] 1 W.L.R. 269, 289A: 'In considering whether the grant of an injunction would be oppressive to the defendant, all the circumstances of the case have to be considered. At one extreme, the defendant may have acted openly and in good faith and in ignorance of the plaintiff's rights, and thereby inadvertently placed himself

Above it was noted that the courts are faced with a dilemma where the defendant is a large and profitable enterprise providing jobs and wider economic benefits. One notable instance where the courts were prepared to grant an injunction, despite the economic damage which would ensue, concerns the Irish case of *Bellew v. Cement Co. Ltd.*[551] In *Bellew* an injunction was granted which had the effect of closing the defendant's works for three months despite the fact that it was the only cement factory in Ireland and building was a national priority at the time. This raises the issue of whether the discretion to award damages in lieu of an injunction could be used as a compromise solution which recognizes the wrong suffered by the claimant whilst relieving him of the burden of having to determine which land use should predominate. Recent Court of Appeal judgments have reasserted the narrow nature of the *Shelfer* criteria and have strongly rejected the notion that economic hardship to the defendant or public utility can be accommodated by the *Shelfer* criteria. In *Watson v. Croft-Promo Sport Ltd,*[552] concerning noise nuisance from a motor racing circuit built on a disused airfield,[553] the Court of Appeal brushed aside any arguments to the effect that an injunction would be oppressive because of the amount already spent on developing the circuit or the public benefits associated with the facility.[554] However, a motor racing circuit, and a small one at that, is small beer when compared with a power station or an oil refinery. One cannot help wondering whether the Court would still be willing to paint itself into a corner with the *Shelfer* criteria when faced with the possible closure of a plant on this scale. In fact, there is one major case in which the possibility of using the equitable discretion to award damages in lieu was contemplated as a compromise solution to avoid such an eventuality. However, as we shall see, the matter was finally settled on other grounds which leaves the law in an uncertain state.

In the Court of Appeal decision in *Allen v. Gulf Oil Refining Ltd*, concerning various nuisances from an oil refinery,[555] Lord Denning was faced with just such a dilemma; his solution was as follows:

> I realise that there is a difficulty about an injunction. No court would wish to grant an injunction to stop a great enterprise and render it useless. But that difficulty is easily overcome. By means of Lord Cairn's Act, the Chancery Amendment Act 1858, the court can award damages to cover past or future injury in lieu of an injunction.[556]

On appeal the argument received scant attention and the case turned on whether a statutory authority defence was applicable. The House of Lords did not offer any

---

in a position where the grant of an injunction would either force him to yield to the plaintiff's extortionate demands or expose him to substantial loss'.
551. [1948] Ir. R. 61.
552. [2009] EWCA Civ 15; [2009] 3 All E.R. 249. See also *Regan v. Paul Properties Ltd* [2006] EWCA Civ 1391; [2007] Ch. 135. For analysis see W. Hanbury, *Shelfer Stands the Test of Time Again: when a Final Injunction will be Considered 'Oppressive'*, 15(3) Env. Liability 149 (2007).
553. The case is discussed elsewhere in the context of the character of the neighbourhood test; see Ch. 2, p. [...] above.
554. [2009] EWCA Civ 15; [2009] 3 All E.R. 249, esp. [49]–[51].
555. For full facts and discussion of the circumstances surrounding the case see §2.03[D][2], above.
556. [1979] 3 W.L.R. 523, at 532F.

opinion on whether the *Shelfer* criteria should be broadened so as to accommodate such considerations. As we have seen in Chapter 2, their Lordships decided that the enabling Act (the Gulf Oil Refining Act 1965) was capable of establishing a statutory authority defence notwithstanding the fact that such nuisances were not expressly authorized; it was held that an implicit authorization would suffice. The problem with this approach is that it left the residents with no remedy despite the fact that the nuisances were real and serious.[557] In the Court of Appeal Lord Denning was acutely aware of this fact and he was also concerned that the legislation failed to make any provision for compensation in respect of this type of harm. His proposed solution of allowing damages in lieu of an injunction would have allowed the claimants to move to a new development whilst enabling the refinery to continue operating. Tromans criticized their Lordships for adopting an overly generous interpretation of the statutory authority defence.[558] The House of Lords may have been of the opinion that, if the nuisances were found to be actionable, the court would be bound to grant an injunction possibly leading to the closure of the plant subject only to a 'precarious appeal to Lord Cairns Act'.[559] This eventuality may well have coloured the judgment and led to a cautious approach. Their Lordships were clearly not convinced that the economic argument advanced by Lord Denning would be sufficient to enable the court to exercise its discretion in favour of granting damages in lieu of an injunction.

On one level a strict adherence to a narrow interpretation of the *Shelfer* criteria may appear to be a good thing from an environmental perspective. Damages are clearly not as effective as injunctive relief in terms of remediating damage or preventing future damage. However, without the availability of this compromise solution the courts may find reasons to find against the claimant so as not to have to deploy the 'nuclear option' of an injunction. This is clearly demonstrated by *Allen* where, despite the lack of specific words in the Act authorizing nuisances and despite the lack of provision for compensation, the statutory authority defence was found to be available. Furthermore, even if the statutory authority argument had failed, the courts could well have found that the refinery had changed the character of the neighbourhood so as to neutralize any claims in nuisance.[560] As argued in Chapter 2, the problem with the character of the neighbourhood test is that it draws an arbitrary and unrealistic distinction between tangible and intangible harms.[561] The mere fact that harm fails to cross the tangibility threshold does not mean that it is not serious or socially unacceptable.

This is not to say that the discretion to award damages should be taken lightly and there should remain a rebuttable presumption in favour of the entitlement to an injunction once the case is made out. Furthermore, the court should treat with caution arguments to the effect that the grant of an injunction would inevitably result in closure of the business. We have seen that injunctions need not have such ruinous consequences. For example, mandatory injunctions may enable the defendant to continue

---

557. See §2.03[D][2], above.
558. S. Tromans, *Nuisance – Prevention or Payment?*, 41(1) Cambridge L.J. 87 (1982).
559. [1981] A.C. 1001, 1013B, (Lord Wilberforce).
560. See §2.03[B], above.
561. *Ibid.*

operating whilst requiring the adoption of certain improvements. Alternatively, the injunction may be suspended pending the investigation of pollution abatement techniques as occurred in *Farnworth*. Nevertheless, there may be cases where damages may prove the best practicable solution and this option should not be closed down by a dogmatic adherence to the narrowest possible interpretation of the *Shelfer* criteria. In the *Allen* case the residents of Waterston actually wanted a financial settlement which would enable them to move. However, uncertainties regarding whether the court would be able to use its discretion to bring about such a settlement contributed to the outcome of the case and a finding that the nuisances were not actionable at all. As Tromans succinctly put it in his contemporaneous account of the House of Lords judgment in *Allen*, 'the Allens of this world pay dearly for the judicial insistence that the plaintiff get nothing but the best by getting nothing at all.'[562]

Similar disagreements, regarding the factors which the court should take into account when exercising its discretion to award damages in lieu of an injunction, have occurred in US case law. The dichotomy of views is most clearly demonstrated by the case of *Boomer v. Atlantic Cement Co*[563] the facts of which mirror those of *Bellew*. This case also concerned nuisance caused by smoke, dust and noise emanating from the defendant's cement works and once again local residents sought injunctive relief to prevent the continuance of the nuisance.

In the Court of Appeals of New York Bergan J. accepted the fact that residents had suffered as a result of the defendant's activities, however, he felt unable to grant the relief sought on the grounds that:

> The total damage to plaintiffs' properties is, however, relatively small in comparison with the value of the defendant's operation and with the consequences of the injunction which the plaintiffs seek. The ground for the denial of injunction, notwithstanding the finding both that there is a nuisance and that plaintiffs have been damaged substantially, is the large disparity in economic consequences of the nuisance and of the injunction.

It was calculated that the costs of relocating the plant would amount to USD 45m whereas the total loss incurred by the residents was calculated as amounting to a mere USD 185,000. On this basis the court was inevitably led to the conclusion that damages should be awarded in lieu of an injunction.[564] In this respect the decision broke new ground in that existing New York case law suggested that, once a nuisance had been established, the plaintiff would be entitled to injunctive relief notwithstanding any disparity in economic consequences. There was no equivalent of Lord Cairn's Act empowering the Court to award damages in lieu. Nevertheless Bergen J. considered that it was appropriate for the Court to depart from existing precedent on this issue as:

> [T]o follow the rule literally in these cases would be to close down the plant at once. This court is fully agreed to avoid that immediately drastic remedy; the difference in view is how best to avoid it.

---

562. Tromans (n. 558) 108.
563. 26 N.Y. 2d 219, 309 N.Y.S. 2d 312, 257 N.E. 2d 870 (Court of Appeals New York, 1970).
564. This decision broke new ground in that there was no equivalent of Lord Cairn's Act in American law which allowed for the award of damages in lieu of an injunction.

He concluded that, in a case such as this, it would be within the equitable jurisdiction of the Court to award permanent damages in lieu of an injunction.

As noted above in respect of the UK position, in some cases the imposition of a financial settlement by the court may be the best solution. However, it was also noted that the discretion to award damages in lieu should be used as a matter of last resort in that the solution may not deal with the core of the problem. In *Boomer* Bergen J. appeared to use the discretion as a matter of first resort. The judge clearly viewed injunctions in absolutist terms with the result that he feared that the grant of an injunction would inevitably lead to the closure of the business. This led him to weigh the value of the competing land uses according to narrow financial criteria. The problem with making direct cost comparisons of this type, whereby the value of a land use is measured in monetary terms, is that it takes a very narrow view of value. As the *Boomer* case demonstrates, in most cases this approach will lead to the inevitable conclusion that an industrial land use should prevail. This is simply because the benefits of industrial activities, such as contribution to the economy, are easier to quantify in monetary terms than the need for environmental protection. Economists have attempted to devise means of pricing conservatory land uses so as to redress the balance.[565] However, these values are still likely to be outweighed by the economic benefits of industrial activities.[566] There is also a fundamental objection to such an approach which goes to the core of the purpose of tort in an environmental context. Pricing natural resources converts them into tradable commodities which can be bought at the right price. Such an approach invites the economic analysis of tort; for reasons which are discussed in the next chapter this is not always conducive to environmental protection. It is for this reason that the courts should be slow to exercise

---

565. It is relatively easy to quantify certain environmental costs such as the loss in market value of damaged crops or the costs of removing contaminated soil. However, intangible environmental benefits, such as the pleasure one derives from a landscape, are extremely difficult to cost. Economists have experimented with a number of different valuation techniques over the past thirty years. Hedonic pricing methods examine the differences in property prices and rents payable in areas subject to differing degrees of pollution. Thus, environmental harm in the vicinity of the property is regarded as causing a loss in market value of the property. CVM relies upon detailed surveys designed to ascertain how much a person would be WTP for a change in the quality of the environment. For a review of these methods see S. Navrud & G.J. Pruckner, *Environmental Valuation – To Use or Not to Use? A Comparative Study of the United States and Europe*, 10
Envir. Resour. Econ. 1 (1997); I.J. Bateman R.K. & *Turner, Valuation of the Environment, Methods and Techniques*, in, *Sustainable Environmental Economics and Management* (R.K. Turner ed., Belhaven Press 1993); M.H. Clayton & N.J. Radcliffe, *Sustainability: A Systems Approach*, 109–111 (Earthscan Publications 1996).

566. Various CVM studies have been conducted in the US to determine the extent to which people value conservatory uses of natural resources. Results have been compiled by ERM Economics (1996), (*Economic Aspects of Liability and Joint Compensation Systems: Valuation of Environmental Damage*, European Commission DGXI). One study (Brookshire et al., 1982) indicated that a resident would be prepared to pay between USD 14.54 to USD 20.31 per month to have air quality restored from poor to good. Thus if such a calculation had been made in the *Boomer* case, in order to price the value of the plaintiffs' land use, this figure would have been multiplied by the number of residents involved in the dispute. Clearly, as the number of residents involved was low, this amount would not have approached the value of the defendant's activity.

the discretion in favour of awarding damage in lieu, although to reiterate, in some cases this result may prove inevitable if not desirable.

The *Farnworth* case shows that injunctions need not be viewed in absolutist terms and can be uses as a coercive means of persuading polluters to solve the problem. Elements of the *Farnworth* approach are apparent in the dissenting judgment of Jasen J. in the *Boomer* case. It is clear that Jasen J. did not regard the injunction as an absolutist measure inevitably leading to the closure of a valuable business. As a result he avoided being drawn into a cost – benefit analysis based upon narrow financial criteria. This freed him to take a much broader view of the merits of the competing land uses and the wider issues at stake. Rather than focusing purely on the private loss of the plaintiffs and balancing this with the potential loss to the defendant, Jasen J, considered the wider environmental impact of the cement works:

> It is interesting to note that cement production has recently been identified as a significant source of particulate contamination in the Hudson Valley. This type of pollution, wherein very small particles escape and stay in the atmosphere, has been denominated as the type of air pollution which produces the greatest hazard to human health. *We have thus a type of nuisance which not only is damaging to the plaintiffs, but also is decidedly harmful to the general public.* [emphasis added]

Thus, in his view, the private rights of the parties could not be viewed in isolation from the wider public interest objective of environmental protection. In an exact parallel of the *Farnworth* approach Jasen J considered that the best solution would be to grant the injunction but suspend its operation for eighteen months to enable the defendants to improve pollution abatement measures. Although the judge accepted that the best available equipment had already been installed, he submitted that 'this does not mean that better and more effective dust control devices could not be developed within the time allowed to abate the pollution'.

Overall the issue of in what circumstances the court should exercise its discretion to award damages in lieu of an injunction raises fundamental issues regarding the role of tort in an environmental context. Some useful comparisons can be drawn between the Irish case of *Bellew* and the US case of *Boomer* which both conveniently concerned pollution from cement works. In different ways each case illustrates the difficulties associated with focusing on the narrow interests of one or other of the parties in isolation from the wider issues. In *Bellew* the court could be criticized for not paying sufficient attention to the wider economic impact of the decision to grant an injunction. And in Boomer the majority decision could be criticized for an overly utilitarian approach which allowed industry to ride roughshod over the private interests of aggrieved residents. As we have seen, Jasen J. adopted an approach which allowed him more latitude to consider public interest issues going beyond the narrow financial interests at stake. However, this raises important questions regarding the extent to which tort, which is primarily concerned with the resolution of private disputes, can be used to solve wider problems such as environmental degradation. These issues shall be addressed in more detail in the next chapter.

§3.06   CONCLUSIONS

The difficulties associated with establishing liability in tort for environmental damage, described above, severely limit the role of civil liability in an environmental context. In some cases it is necessary to establish fault on the part of the defendant; in negligence, this entails demonstrating that, not only was the defendant aware of the hazard created by his activity, but that he also failed to take adequate steps to negate the hazard. The complexity of many industrial processes, which are capable of causing pollution, renders it extremely difficult for the claimant to establish that the defendant failed to take these steps. Furthermore, whether or not it is necessary to establish fault in a particular case, the claimant must establish a causal link between the defendant's activity and the harm. Once pollution is dispersed into the environment it becomes increasingly difficult to trace the damage pathways from source to impact. These difficulties are multiplied in the case of toxic micro-pollutants where the harmful substances are invisible and their effects insidious. It seems that existing common law tests for establishing causation have failed to keep pace with modern scientific techniques for identifying links between, for example, radiation and various forms of cancer. Thus, the need to establish factors such as fault and causation places high costs on the claimant, often referred to as 'transaction costs'. The obvious effect of these costs is that a potential claimant may be dissuaded from pursuing litigation.

The other major limitation of tort is that it focuses on the loss suffered by the individual rather than the loss suffered by the environment. As a result, although the level of damages awarded may reflect the personal financial loss of the claimant, they may not provide sufficient funds to effect a full environmental clean-up. Furthermore, the fact that liability is contingent upon personal loss means that, in the absence of such loss, no one may be in a position to instigate proceedings. At present, environmental pressure groups, at least in the UK, are not afforded standing to seek civil remedies on behalf of the environment. Hence, in such circumstances it is necessary to rely entirely upon regulatory responses.

Thus, it seems that the use of tort as a means of environmental protection will continue to be extremely limited, unless, there is a fundamental change of emphasis from the interests of the parties to the interests of the environment. In the next chapter it will be considered whether this is possible in conceptual terms and, furthermore, whether such a development would be desirable.

Part III: The Role of Tort as a Means of Environmental Protection: Theoretical Perspectives and Legislative Initiatives

CHAPTER 4
The Role of Tort in an Environmental Context

§4.01 INTRODUCTION

The procedural difficulties associated with establishing liability in tort and the fact that it focuses on personal loss, as opposed to environmental damage, must inevitably lead to consideration of whether there remains a role for civil liability in this context. The occasional assertion of private rights, which may or may not produce any collateral environmental benefit, is unlikely to have a significant impact on industry. Due to the limitations of the common law, environmental protection has largely been perceived as a matter for regulation. In the US case of *Boomer v. Atlantic Cement*, Bergan J. stated that it is pointless to attempt to settle matters of public interest as a by-product of resolving private disputes.[567] Thus, he argued, it was entirely inappropriate to impute public policy considerations into the consideration of the case. This assumes that private law and public law operate in entirely different spheres and that private law

---

567. 26 N.Y. 2d 219, 309 N.Y.S. 2d 312, 257 N.E. 2d 870 (Court of Appeals New York, 1970). 'Effective control of air pollution is a problem presently far from solution even with the full public and financial powers of government. In large measure adequate technical procedures are yet to be developed and some that appear possible may be economically impracticable. It seems apparent that the amelioration of air pollution will depend on technical research in great depth; on a carefully balanced consideration of the economic impact of close regulation; and of the actual effect on public health. It is likely to require massive public expenditure and to demand more than any local community can accomplish and to depend on regional and interstate controls. A court should not try to do this on its own as a by-product of private litigation and it seems manifest that then judicial establishment is neither equipped in the limited nature of any judgment it can pronounce nor prepared to lay down and implement an effective policy for the elimination of air pollution. This is an area beyond the circumference of one private law suit. It is a direct responsibility for government and should not thus be undertaken as an incident to solving a dispute between property owners and a single cement plant – one of many in the Hudson River valley.'

should in no way encroach upon the territory of public law. Bergan J. clearly perceived matters of environmental policy as falling within the realm of public law, whereas, interference with private rights was perceived as falling squarely within the realm of private law. Hence, it seems that Bergan J. was of the opinion that one's private interests in, for example, land are divisible from the public interest in environmental protection. However, as will be seen below, the objectives of public and private law are not necessarily mutually exclusive and there is a role for both in the implementation of environmental policy.

The purpose of this Chapter is, therefore, to identify a role for the use of tort in a system of environmental regulation which is dominated by public law responses. This entails consideration of two main issues. First, it is important to have regard to theoretical perspectives on the role of tort with a view to determining whether it is conceptually possible to harness private mechanisms in pursuit of public interest objectives. Assuming that this is the case, it is then necessary whether there is a practical need to develop a specific environmental role for civil liability.

§4.02   THEORETICAL PERSPECTIVES ON THE ROLE OF TORT

Various attempts have been made to establish a unifying (monistic) theory of the purpose of tort; it is possible to identify two monistic schools of thought.[568] The proponents of the economic analysis of tort argue that the purpose of the law should be to ensure an efficient allocation of resources. The more traditional view is that the law of tort is founded on principles of 'corrective' justice in that it reflects the moral obligation of one individual to compensate another for the loss he has caused. In contrast to the monists, the pluralists have abandoned the quest for theoretical purity and argue that tort is multi-faceted and cannot be explained by reference to a single overriding principle.

It is necessary to explore these ideas in more depth in order to determine whether it is possible to identify a sound conceptual basis for an environmental application of tort.

[A]   The Economic Analysis of Tort

Economists and lawyers have differing views regarding the proper function of tort in that, whereas most lawyers are concerned with rectification of harm suffered by an individual, the proponents of the economic approach are of the opinion that the courts should strive to ensure that the solutions at which they arrive are efficient in economic terms. As will be explained in more detail below, the effect of this is that, whilst lawyers consider that the role of tort should be to protect certain rights from harm, certain economists consider that the role of tort should be to provide a framework in which the market is left to determine whether such rights are worthy of protection.

---

568. See Izhak Englard, *The Philosophy of Tort Law*, 30 (Dartmouth Publishing 1993).

According to the more extreme proponents of the economic analysis of tort, one of society's main objectives is to achieve 'wealth maximization'. This is achieved through allocating resources to their most highly valued uses as determined by voluntary transactions between individuals. Since wealth maximization is central to the economic approach it is worth quoting Posner's definition in its entirety:

> By 'wealth maximization' I mean the policy of trying to maximize the aggregate value of all goods and services, whether they are traded in formal markets (the usual 'economic' goods and services) or (in the case of 'non-economic' goods and services, such as life, leisure, family and freedom from pain and suffering) not traded in such markets. 'Value' is determined by what the owner of the good or service would demand to part with it or what a non-owner would be willing to pay to obtain it – whichever is the greater. 'Wealth' is the total value of all 'economic' and 'non-economic' goods and services and is maximized when all goods and services are, so far as is feasible, allocated to their most valuable uses.[569]

Posner argues that the law of tort should reflect this objective.[570] Of course, the problem with this approach is that buyers and sellers are normally motivated by self-interest and do not, as a rule, consider the effect of a transaction on third parties. This gives rise to a phenomenon known by economists as 'externalities' which constitute unwanted by-products caused by the operation of the free market; pollution is a classic example of an externality.[571] Thus, an agreement reached between a property developer and an industrial concern to build a new facility may be mutually beneficial as far as the parties to the agreement are concerned, however, it may impose costs on neighbours in the form of pollution.

Economists have long recognized this problem. However, they have proposed radically different solutions. One school of thought was of the opinion that the market should be regulated in a manner which punished those who failed to take externalities into account. For example, Pigou[572] proposed the introduction of a punitive tax on pollution; to this day such taxes are often referred to as 'Pigouvian'. However, another group of more radical economists, from the opposing 'Chicago school', were in favour of a less interventionist approach which would allow the market to find its own solutions to such problems. Their cause was greatly advanced by the publication of Coase's famous paper on social cost the underlying thesis of which is now commonly referred to as the 'Coase theorem'.[573] This appeared to provide a theoretical framework for a market solution to the problem of externalities with minimal intervention from the

---

569. R.A. Posner, *Wealth Maximization and Tort Law: A Philosophical Inquiry*, in *Philosophical Foundations of Tort Law*, (Clarendon Press 1995).
570. *Ibid.*
571. See R.A. Posner, *Economic Analysis of Law*, 343 (Little Brown & Co. 1986): 'Monopoly, pollution, fraud, mistake, mismanagement, and other unhappy by-products of the market are conventionally viewed as failure's of the market's self-regulatory mechanisms and therefore as appropriate occasions for public regulation'.
572. Arthur Cecil Pigou, *The Economics of Welfare* (first published 1920, Transaction Publishers 2009).
573. R.H. Coase, *The Problem Social Cost*, 3 J. L. & Econ. 1 (1960).

law. In short, the so-called 'theorem'[574] states that, provided there are no obstacles to bargaining (or transaction costs), the parties will reach their own agreement as to the most efficient allocation of the resource irrespective of any solution imposed by the court.

When viewed at face value the theorem appears utterly unrealistic in that it relies upon the existence of a state of affairs, namely zero transaction costs, which cannot exist in reality;[575] as a result the theorem has been repeatedly attacked over the years.[576] However, as Coase himself was at pains to point out, the theorem should not be taken literally,[577] rather, by illustrating the irrelevance of the law in a world of zero transaction costs, Coase hoped to illustrate the vital role which the law plays in a world of high transaction costs:

> The world of zero transaction costs has been described as a Coasian world. Nothing could be further from the truth. It is the world ... I was hoping to persuade economists to leave... ...
> ... The same approach which with zero transaction costs, demonstrates that the allocation of resources remains the same whatever the legal position, also shows that, with positive transaction costs, the law plays a crucial role in determining how resources are used.[578]

In practice, the economic approach is crystallized by the issue of the purpose of injunctive relief. According to the economic view, the function of the law of tort is to improve the bargaining position of, for example, neighbours affected by noise or fumes so as to enable them to reach a settlement with the polluter. Thus the remedy of injunctive relief is regarded as an instruction to the parties to bargain rather than a once and for all prohibition on the continuance of the activity. In other words, it merely serves to prevent a polluter from expunging a neighbour's right to the undisturbed enjoyment of his property without first offering compensation. The assumption is that the price at which the neighbour is prepared to settle will reflect the value of his use of

---

574. The term 'theorem' must be applied to Coase's paper with a high degree of equivocation. Coase pointed out on several occasions that he never actually used the term 'theorem'; it was actually the economist George Stigler, a fellow economist of the Chicago School who would also go on to win the Nobel Prize for Economics, who coined the term 'Coase theorem' and presented it to a wider audience in George Stigler, *The Theory of Price* (Collier MacMillan 1966). See S. Medema, *A Case of Mistaken Identity: George Stigler, 'The Problem of Social Cost,' and the Coase theorem*, 31(1) Eur. J. L. & Econ. 11 (2011); R. H. Coase, *Law and Economics at Chicago*, 36(1) J. L. & Econ. 239, 249 (1993).
575. The theorem makes certain assumptions; for example, it assumes that there are no information costs. As the discussion in the previous chapter demonstrates, in many cases involving environmental damage, the claimant must undertake expensive investigations in order to establish causation. Thus, the production of this *information* gives rise to high information costs.
576. See, for example, D. Q. Posin, *The Coase Theorem: If Pigs Could Fly*, Wayne L. Rev. 89 (1990–91).
577. See Antony W. Dnes, *The Economics of Law*, 180 (International Thomson Business Press 1996).
578. R.H. Coase, *Notes on the Problem of Social Cost*, in *The Firm, the Market and the Law* (University of Chicago Press 1988).

the resource. In the words of Landes and Posner the effect of injunctive relief is, therefore, to channel transactions to the market.[579]

Veljanowski has applied this analysis to the case of *Bellew v. Cement Co. Ltd.*[580] in which, it will be recalled, the court granted injunctive relief in order to enjoin the emission of dust and noise from a cement works despite the fact that building was a national priority at the time:

> [T]he critical literature on the law of nuisance has often claimed that the injunction is a blunt instrument because it freezes land use, and that the doctrinal framework does not take sufficient account of the benefits of the defendant's activities. The most extreme case of this kind is *Bellew v. Cement Co. Ltd.*, where the court awarded the plaintiff an injunction that would have halted the operations of the only cement-producer in the Irish Republic at a time when building was an urgent public necessity. The courts seem in these rights-based torts often not to 'balance the equities' in a way that would be implied by economic consideration. This, however, overlooks the fact that in many of these situations the parties are in a position to bargain both before and after litigation. *The judges determine, not a final solution which imposes on the parties some immutable set of consequences, but the starting points for negotiations between the disputing parties. A great deal of the law of nuisance can be viewed as a framework for bargaining, either preventatively if the law is clear, or after the injunction has been granted.* It is naive to assume, as does much legal discussion, that when the stakes at hand are so disproportionate and the defendant stands to lose so much, as in *Bellew*, he would not be driven to bargain with the plaintiff.[581] [emphasis added]

However, it is also recognized that the parties may not bargain *around* an injunction in which case the court should impose its own settlement by making an award of damages. This may occur in circumstances where the pollution is diffuse and the number of victims is large. In such circumstances it may be impractical to expect the polluter to reach an individual settlement with each victim.[582] Obstacles to bargaining may also occur where there are relatively few parties involved as a result of the 'hold out' phenomenon which simply means that, where the stakes for the polluter are high, one of the victims may 'hold out' for a settlement which is in excess of offers which have already been made to other victims.[583] Even where there are only two parties to a transaction, namely one victim and one polluter, there is still no guarantee that the parties will bargain as a result of the 'bilateral monopoly' problem which occurs where the victim refuses to settle at any price.[584]

The US case of *Boomer v. Atlantic Cement*[585] is often used as a case study for demonstrating how the courts should apply this approach in practice. It will be recalled that this action also concerned an application for injunctive relief brought by the

---

579. William M. Landes & Richard A. Posner, *The Economic Structure of Tort Law*, 31 (University of Chicago Press 1988).
580. [1948] I.R. 62.
581. C. Veljanowski, *Legal Theory, Economic Analysis and Tort*, in *Legal Theory and Common Law*, 229–230 (W.L. Twining ed., Basil Blackwell 1986).
582. See Robert D. Cooter and Thomas Ulen, *Law and Economics*, 171 (Addison-Wesley 1997).
583. See Landes and Posner (n. 579) 45.
584. *Ibid.*, 34.
585. 26 N.Y. 2d 219, 309 N.Y.S. 2d 312, 257 N.E. 2d 870 (Court of Appeals of New York, 1970).

neighbours of a cement works in respect of noise and dust emanating from the facility. Bergan J. conducted a cost/benefit analysis between the cost to the cement works of having to relocate and the costs incurred by the plaintiffs. This inevitably led to the conclusion that injunctive relief should be denied as the costs to the defendant would far outweigh the costs incurred by the plaintiffs. The authorities on the economic analysis of law agree with the outcome in this case although they disagree with the reasoning used to arrive at the decision.[586] The consensus is that, given the fact that courts are not very good at conducting a cost-benefit analysis between competing land uses, the decision should have been based on whether there was any likelihood of the parties negotiating a settlement between themselves. This decision should have been reached on the basis of whether the level of transaction costs (which it will be recalled constitute obstacles to bargaining) were high or low. In this case Landes and Posner were of the opinion that transaction costs were high in that, as the stakes were high, there was a risk of the 'hold out' phenomenon coming in to play. It was, therefore, appropriate to award damages in lieu of an injunction:

> Each party would have tried to acquire as much of the bargaining profit as possible, and given the large stakes to each of a successful outcome of the negotiation, both might have invested large amounts of time and money in hard bargaining. These transaction costs were avoided by the Court's manner of deciding the case.[587]

The practical result of this approach, as the proponents of the economic analysis admit, is that the courts would end up substituting an award of damages in almost all cases.[588] A neighbour who values the undisturbed use of his property beyond any price which the polluter is prepared to pay would, according to this analysis, be regarded as an unscrupulous individual who is attempting to extort an exorbitant offer from the polluter in return for releasing him from the threat of an injunction. Thus, the court would be led to award damages in lieu of an injunction on the grounds that he was exploiting a 'bilateral monopoly' situation. This outcome is justified by Landes and Posner on the grounds that a solution which results in an operator having to close or move his plant at great expense is an inefficient solution.[589] In the previous chapter it was acknowledged that there may well be circumstances in which an award of damages in place of an injunction may prove to be the best solution.[590] However, the hold out phenomenon should not be used as the main criterion in this respect and it should certainly not be used as an argument for establishing damages in lieu as the default position. If damages are awarded too readily there is little incentive for the polluter to attempt to reach a bargain. No doubt the operators of the power station in *Manchester Corporation v. Farnworth*[591] would sooner have paid the farmer off than spend money on trying to reduce the harm. However, the suspended injunction hung

---

586. Cooter and Ulen (n. 582) 176; Landes and Posner (n. 579) 45.
587. Landes and Posner (n. 579) 45.
588. *Ibid.*, 45–47.
589. *Ibid.*
590. See §3.05[B][4], above.
591. [1930] A.C. 171.

over the defendant Corporation like the Sword of Damocles and brought about an engineering solution to the problem.

Where an engineering solution cannot be found the court may be faced with the stark choice of awarding damages and allowing the pollution to continue, or making an order which could lead to the closure of the plant or moving it at huge cost. Calabresi and Melamed[592] suggested a novel way of reducing the inefficiencies resulting from such an outcome. In short, they argued that the plant operator could be paid compensation in return for closing or moving the plant. This approach 'turns the tables' in that the conservatory land users would be effectively purchasing the right to an unpolluted environment, rather than the operator purchasing the right to pollute. However, it is not readily apparent how a court could make such an order in practical terms in that it apportions liability between the parties in a manner which is not usually associated with injunctive relief. The grant of an injunction normally serves to vindicate the claimant's rights. An order to the effect that the claimant has suffered wrongful harm whilst simultaneously saddling him with the defendant's compliance costs seems incompatible with such a finding. Nevertheless, there is in fact one highly unusual case, often cited in US literature on the economics of law, where the court adopted a solution which appeared to follow such an approach. In *Spur Industries, Inc. v. Del E. Webb Development Co.*,[593] Del Webb was the developer of a retirement community to the west of Phoenix, Arizona. Some years after the development began, it had spread towards a cattle feeding station; formerly, this had been set some distance from the town. The judgment provides the charming statistic that 30,000 head of cattle were fed at the station per day each producing 35–40 pounds of wet manure. This caused odours, attracted swarms of flies and posed a potential threat to the health of local residents. Not surprisingly, Del Webb suffered a serious loss of sales and sought injunctive relief in order to have the feeding station moved. In the United States the common law differs somewhat from the position in the UK in that, if a new resident knowingly 'comes to the nuisance', the creator of the nuisance will generally have a defence. As the feeding station had been established for several years prior to the commencement of the development one would have assumed that relief would have been refused on these grounds. In the Supreme Court of Arizona, Cameron VCJ accepted that this would normally be the case:

> In the so called 'coming to the nuisance' cases, the courts have held that the residential landowner may not have relief if he knowingly came into a neighbourhood reserved for agricultural endeavours and has been damaged thereby ... Were Webb the only party injured, we would feel justified in holding that the doctrine of 'coming to the nuisance' would have been a bar to the relief asked by Webb, and, on the other hand, had Spur located the feedlot near the outskirts of a city and had the city grown towards the feedlot, Spur would have to suffer the cost of abating the nuisance as to those people locating within the growth pattern of the expanding city.'

---

592. G. Calabresi & A. D. Melamed, *Property Rules, Liability Rules and Inalienability: One View of the Cathedral*, 85 Harv. L. Rev. 1089 (1972).
593. Supreme Court of Arizona, In Banc. 1972. 108 Ariz. 178, 494 P.2d 700.

However, the Court took the unusual step of granting injunctive relief in the interests of the local residents who had purchased the properties; even though they were not party to the proceedings:

> There was no indication in the instant case at the time Spur and its predecessors located in western Maricopa County that a new city would spring up, full-blown, alongside the feeding operation and that the developer of that city would ask the court to order Spur to move because of the new city. *Spur is required to move not because of any wrongdoing on the part of Spur, but because of a proper and legitimate regard of the courts for the rights and interests of the public.* [emphasis added]

Thus Cameron VCJ appeared to have balance the competing interests and reached the conclusion that the wider public interest should prevail over the commercial interests of the feeding station. Recall that this was the approach suggested by Jasen J in his dissenting judgment in *Boomer v. Atlantic Cement.* However, the novel part of the judgment, which accords with Calabresi and Melamed's solution to the efficiency problem in these circumstances, was that Del Webb should compensate Spur in respect of its relocation costs. Thus Del Webb was required to 'buy out' Spur's interest in the land. This is the reverse of cases in which damages are awarded in lieu of an injunction in that in these circumstances it is normally the polluter who is thereby permitted to purchase residents' interests.

However, due to the special facts of this case it is difficult to extrapolate a principle of general application. It is perhaps the inequitable conduct of Del Webb which prompted the Court to adopt this solution;[594] as Cameron VCJ stated:

> It does not seem harsh to require a developer, who has taken advantage of the lesser land values in a rural area as well as the availability of large tracts of land on which to build and develop a new town or city in the area, to indemnify those who are forced to leave as a result.

---

594. Commentators have struggled to find a solid doctrinal bases for the decision and have only been able to find the slimmest of authorities in the case law; see Osborne M., Jnr Reynolds, *Of Time and Feedlots: The Effect of Spur Industries on Nuisance Law,* 41 Wash. U. J. Urb. & Comtemp. L. 76 (1992). Theories which have been put forward to justify the court's approach range from unjust enrichment to the doctrine of indemnity. The latter is the most convincing and relies on the idea that one who discharges a duty, which is owed to another, has an equitable right to recover those costs from the party who is actually responsible. Thus, Spur discharged its duties to the residents by moving the feed station and was entitled to recoup these costs from Del Webb who were primarily responsible for bringing about the situation. In effect, the law was interpreted in a manner which enabled Spur to counterclaim against Del Webb on the basis that it was not solely to blame for the harm. Such an approach jars with modern notions of civil procedure whereby the defendant can seek to avoid liability but has limited capacity to 'counter attack' within the confines of the process relating to claim brought against him. However, historically equity has a long heritage as a means of 'counter attack' due to the rigid doctrinal and procedural distinction between common law and equity. Thus the party on the receiving end of common law proceedings could invoke a separate action in equity with a view to defeating the common law claim on equitable grounds. See, for example, *Williams and others v. the Earl of Jersey* (1841) 41 E.R. 424; Cr. & Ph. 91 in which Lord Jersey's claim for damages against a copper smelter at common law was scuppered by equitable proceedings commenced in chancery. It was found that Lord Jersey had acted unconscionably by delaying the action.

Had it fallen to the residents themselves to seek injunctive relief the outcome would have been different. It is most unlikely that the residents would have been in a position to compensate Spur. This would have made it far more difficult for the Court to grant an injunction as there would have been no means of offsetting the costs to Spur. The Court would have been confronted with the familiar dilemma highlighted in *Boomer*: to what extent should the public interest in a clean environment prevail over the more readily quantifiable economic benefits of a polluting activity? However, as will be explained in due course, there is far more scope for balancing these interests than might first appear; it is only in the most extreme circumstances that an injunction need result in the total closure of a business. Before considering these issues it is worth considering the extent to which this North American economic analysis of tort has permeated other common law jurisdictions.

From time to time the economic rationale for the granting of injunctive relief has surfaced in English judgments. For example, in *Jaggard v. Sawyer* Millett L.J. described the effect of injunctive relief as follows:

> The grant of an injunction would merely restore the parties to the same position, with each of them enjoying the same bargaining strength, that they had enjoyed before the trespass began.[595]

This is all well and good unless negotiations fail and the courts have to step in once more with a view to imposing a settlement, such as an award of damages in lieu of an injunction. In making this determination the court should avoid adopting an overly market-orientated analysis in that there are dangers with this approach. The market analysis of tort gives rise to a situation in which the rights which persons enjoy in property are priced and converted into tradable interests which they can be forced to sell by the court. As Penner argues in his analyses of the decision in *Gillingham Borough Council v. Medway (Chatham) Dock Co. Ltd*:

> [T]he economic analysis of law has been in the forefront of characterizing the law of nuisance as the law of competing land use rights; to the extent that use rights can be isolated from the general right to property courts can determine conflicts between them on any number of basis: public benefit, overall economic efficiency, etc., and the concept of harm is jettisoned. Buckley J.'s decision seems to implicitly accept that the case in Gillingham was a conflict between the rights of the dock company and the shippers to cause a serious noise disturbance and the right of the residents to make use of their property in ways which required a lesser degree of noise, and because of the planning permission given to the dock company the neighbourhood standard was to be regarded as one which favoured the dock company's and the shipper's use.[596]

The major problem with the economic approaches described above is that they assume that efficiency is the sole objective of law, this is clearly not the case. Most economists would accept that the operation of the market should be restricted in certain areas in pursuit of some higher objective. The eminent economist C.A.E. Goodhart is critical of

---

595. [1995] 1 W.L.R. 269, 288E.
596. J.E. Penner, *Nuisance and the Character of the Neighbourhood*, 5 J. Envtl. L. 1, 22 (1993).

the work of Posner in that there is little reference to concepts such as justice and fairness:

> I find Posner's arguments unconvincing ... [in] that they often seem contrary to our personal beliefs in fairness, and in our beliefs in rights and wrongs ... [597]

Similarly, in respect of Posner's assertion that the primary function of law is wealth maximization,[598] Goodhart notes:

> What I notice about that definition is that there is no reference there to the law being perceived as fair and just by those to whom it is addressed. Wealth maximisation is, indeed, a proper goal both for society and for the legal system within it, but can and should that objective be pursued without due recognition of what that same society regards as just and fair outcomes? I doubt it.[599]

Furthermore, in *The Economic Analysis of Tort*, Landes and Posner only make passing reference in the introduction to those who have criticized the economic analysis of tort on similar grounds;[600] there is no attempt to answer these criticisms.

Goodhart concludes that economists must accept that they cannot extend their efficiency approach into all areas of human activity in that such an approach is not always in the best interests of society. Certain objectives, such as morality, cannot be priced and included in a cost/benefit analysis. As an extreme example Goodhart refers to the issue of corporal punishment. According to an economic analysis, corporal punishment is more cost effective than prison which is extremely expensive, however, as Goodhart states:

> Flogging and cutting off peripheral bits of people's bodies would, by standard economic criteria, be far more wealth maximising for society than prison sentences. And yet a society that flogged and amputated is not one that I would want to embrace. When it comes to the questions of who should be allowed to do what to our bodies, *we economists will just have to accept a boundary to our imperial grasp.*[601] [emphasis added]

Dworkin[602] goes even further in his criticism of the wealth maximization approach and doubts whether the concept can provide any useful guide as to the value of a resource. One obvious flaw in the approach is that the seller may value a resource more highly than the purchaser yet may be forced to part with it out of necessity. To use Dworkin's example, an impoverished person may feel bound to sell a book, which has sentimental value, to a wealthier person who decides to purchase it on a whim on the off chance that he 'might someday read it'.[603] In this case it would be absurd to argue that the

597. C.A.E. Goodhart, *Economics and the Law: Too Much One-Way Traffic?*, 60 The Modern L. Rev. 1, 13 (1997).
598. R.A. Posner, *Essay on Utilitarianism, Economics and Social Theor*, in *The Economics of Justice* 74–75 (Harvard University Press 1983): 'Wealth maximization provides a foundation not only for a theory of rights and of remedies, but for the concepts of law itself ... '
599. Goodhart (n. 597) 16.
600. Landes and Posner (n. 579) 9.
601. Goodhart (n. 597) 17.
602. R.N. Dworkin, *Is Wealth a Value?*, 9 J. Leg. Stud. 191 (1980).
603. *Ibid.*, 200.

transaction has resulted in the transfer of the resource to the person who values it most highly. This highlights the fact that the wealth maximization approach has no facility for attaching anything other than a monetary value to resources. Indeed, it leaves the legal/economic analysis open to the criticism that, rather than being objective as it purports to be, it is motivated by political free market ideology which seeks to exclude considerations other than the financial interests of the parties to a transaction. Dworkin argues that it is a mistake to equate individual wealth with the overall well being of society.[604] Any gains achieved through the reallocation of resources, pursuant to private transactions, may be outweighed by the damage caused to other societal interests.[605] It will be recalled that this is why the economist Pigou was in favour of punishing those who failed to take into account the environmental implications of their transaction by means of taxation.

The environment concerns an area in which the operation of the market should be limited on the grounds that wealth maximization cannot be equated with the public interest. For example, the quality of life may be impaired and natural resources may be exhausted; as Steele argues, the economic analysis is flawed in that:

> No attention is given to the fact that, in some instances, improvements in the quality of environmental media such as air may actually be feasible; or, indeed, that they may be essential in order to sustain human welfare. In some instances, true 'sustainability' might therefore involve a decision not to allocate a 'resource' between different claims, particularly in those instances where 'use' takes the form of 'contamination', or where there is a risk of extinction or exhaustion. A preference based view of costs and benefits, where allocative solutions are generated through disputes over ownership or entitlement, does not leave sufficient scope for consideration of such issues. Such an approach, therefore, appears unconvincing where sound environmental policy requires positive improvements in quality, rather than different rates of contamination, or where the relevant issue is one of conservation.[606]

Posner eventually conceded the fact that an approach based upon resource allocation, according to market criteria, may be to the detriment of the environment. He accepted that 'the non-pecuniary dimension of wealth is important to emphasize.'[607] However, he also accepted that, as the wealth maximization approach relies upon the assignment of property rights, transactions must be governed by the monetary value attached to those rights.[608] He then echoed Dworkin's argument that there is a difference between what a person may be WTP for a resource and the price at which he may be prepared to sell the resource.[609] Furthermore, these prices may in no way reflect the value placed on the resource by the parties to the transaction:

---

604. *Ibid.*, 194.
605. *Ibid.*, 201.
606. J. Steele, *Remedies and Remediation: Foundation Issues in Environmental Liability*, 58(5) M.L.R. 615, 633–634 (1995).
607. R.A. Posner, *Wealth Maximization and Tort Law: A Philosophical Inquiry*, in *Philosophical Foundations of Tort* 99 (D.G. Owen ed., Clarendon Press 1995).
608. *Ibid.*
609. *Ibid.*, 100.

> An indigent may not be able to pay anything for freedom from pollution, while a
> wealthy person may demand an astronomical price to surrender his right (if it is his
> right) to clean air and water.[610]

Rather than propose a solution to this issue, Posner elected to 'prescind from these
baseline problems and examine wealth maximization in the more common tort
situations in which such problems are not acute.'[611] In this admission it seems that
Posner may also have come to the conclusion that the environment is an area in which,
in the words of Goodhart, economists must accept a limit to their imperial grasp.

Nevertheless, as has already been acknowledged, on occasion an award of
damages may provide the best overall solution; the case of *Allen v. Gulf Oil Refining
Ltd*,[612] dealt with at length in the previous chapter,[613] provides the best evidence for
this. However, the law should not lightly deprive an individual of his or her property
rights. To reiterate a point which has already been made, an award of damages in lieu
of in injunction should be a matter of last, as opposed to first resort.

[B]   Corrective Versus Distributive Justice

Given the limitations of the economic approach, it is necessary to consider whether the
use of tort, in an environmental context, should be founded on some idea of justice.
However, at this point we encounter a complication in the form of the Aristotelian
distinction between corrective and distributive justice.

[1]   *Corrective Justice*

Corrective justice, of which one of the main proponents in recent times has been
Weinrib,[614] focuses on the relationship between individuals and the moral obligation of
one party to compensate another for the loss which he has caused.[615] Hence, according
to this view, the sole purpose of the law of tort is to restore the *status quo ante* between
the parties. The early development of the common law was clearly firmly rooted in the
corrective principle in that the *forms of action* were designed to restore some interest of
which the plaintiff had been wrongfully disseised.[616]

From an environmental perspective, this narrow view of corrective justice cannot
provide a satisfactory theoretical basis. The main reason for this is that it precludes
consideration of public interest objectives, of which environmental protection is an

---

610. *Ibid.*
611. *Ibid.*
612. [1981] A.C. 1001 (HL).
613. See §3.05[B][4], above.
614. E.J. Weinrib, *Understanding Tort Law*, 23 Val. U. Rec. 485 (1989).
615. Weinrib, in common with most proponents of the corrective approach, bases this moral
    obligation on Kantian premises. In short, this provides that it is wrong for one person to use the
    other as a means to the first person's ends. See E.J. Weinrib, *Law as a Kantian Idea of Reason*,
    87 Colum. L. Rev. 472 (1987).
616. See Chapter 2, above.

example. The distributional objectives of society are deemed to fall within the realm of public law. Thus, as Englard points out, according to Weinrib's corrective approach:

> The plaintiff sues in order to have the wrong done to him set right. He or she is not a private enforcer of a public interest.[617]

In the previous chapter it was argued that one of the main limitations of tort in the field of environmental protection is that it focuses on the loss suffered by the individual; this may not correlate with the environmental damage caused. Thus, in order to be effective in this context, it is necessary to identify a theoretical basis which allows the law of tort to accommodate public interest considerations. To this end it is necessary to consider the extent to which tort may accommodate distributional considerations.

[2]   Distributive Justice

The industrialization of the nineteenth century and the resultant increase in industrial accidents, pollution and nuisance caused many to doubt whether society could afford a system of tort which was based purely on high moral principles.[618] Thus attention shifted from the theoretical to the practical and the extent to which tort could be harnessed in pursuit of social objectives.[619] In more recent times Josef Esser argued that the Aristotelian distinction between corrective and distributive justice could be used as a philosophical basis for a public interest model of tort.[620] Esser noted that the law of tort involves distributional issues in that it determines the circumstances in which a loss should be borne by the defendant as opposed to the plaintiff. As tort does not exist in a vacuum, it must inevitably absorb societal preferences regarding the distribution of such losses. These preferences are reflected in the criteria applied by the decision maker:[621]

> Thus, in respect of distributive justice, which is directed at distributing a given object among persons according to a criterion of merit, the substance of that criterion will depend, among other things, on the deciding authority's moral and political philosophy.[622]

For example, the development of strict liability, in certain areas, represents a move towards a distributional approach in that it invites consideration of 'at whose risk' should an activity be conducted as opposed to 'whose fault' was the accident.[623]

---

617. Izhak Englard, *The Philosophy of Tort Law*, 46 (Dartmouth Publishing 1993).
618. *Ibid.*, 98.
619. *Ibid.*, 97. Englard notes that as early as 1889 The German jurist Otto von Gierke (1841–1921) delivered a paper at a lecture in Vienna entitled, *The Social Function of Private Law (Die soziale Aufgabe des Privaterechts)* (Julius Springer 1889) in which he derided the tendency to isolate pure, abstract, dogmatic and individualistic private law from the social needs of the people.
620. Josef Esser, *Grundlagen und Entwicklung der Gefährdungshaftung* (2d ed., C.H. Beck 1961).
621. This would include the court when deciding the outcome of a dispute or the legislature when deciding whether to modify existing common law rules.
622. Englard (n. 617) 11.
623. See J.A. Jolowicz, *Liability for Accidents*, 26(1) Cambridge L.J. 50 (1968).

The rapid growth in insurance markets, since the last century, has also increased the distributive role of tort. Given the fact that tort is concerned with loss allocation, the issue of which party is best placed to bear the loss is an important issue. In this respect the availability of insurance is clearly a material consideration. At one time, the courts were firmly of the opinion that the issue of whether or not the defendant was insured should have no bearing on the outcome of the case.[624] However, the courts have become more ambivalent in their attitude towards the existence of insurance. On a number of occasions, Lord Denning overtly based certain decisions, at least in part, on the fact that the insured party would be better able to bear the loss.[625] Most judges have not gone as far as Lord Denning, nevertheless, it seems that the availability of insurance may add 'a little extra tensile strength'[626] to the chain which binds a tortfeasor to his responsibilities.

It has been argued that the existence of insurance is incompatible with the corrective function of tort and represents a move towards an alternative system of compensation such as a social security scheme.[627] Such an approach, based entirely upon distributive principles, severs the bilateral relationship between the parties and 'violate[s] the moral foundations of personal responsibility'.[628] For reasons which shall be discussed in due course, a system which relies entirely upon compensation funds is unsatisfactory in that it reduces incentives for risk management. However, the relationship between insurance and tort does not necessarily dispense with all notions of corrective justice in that it retains a degree of individual accountability. For example, a careless person is likely to incur higher premiums and in extreme cases may be denied cover altogether. Furthermore, the insurance policy may only meet part of the costs incurred by the insured; in certain cases there is an agreed upper limit or ceiling.[629]

---

624. See Viscount Simmonds in *Lister v. Romford Ice and Cold Storage Ltd* [1957] A.C. 555, 576-577: 'In determining the rights inter se of A and B, the fact that one of them is insured is to be disregarded.'

625. See *Nettleship v. Weston* [1971] 3 All E.R. 581 which concerned whether a learner driver should be expected to display the same degree of competence as a qualified driver. Lord Denning stated that judges would impose a high standard of skill, even on learner drivers, because every driver was required to be insured against third party risks; the reason being 'that a person injured by a motor car should not be left to bear the loss on his own, but should be compensated out of the insurance fund. The fund is better able to bear it than he can.' Thus, Lord Denning concluded that, 'we are, in this branch of the law, moving away from the concept: 'no liability without fault.' We are beginning to apply the test 'On whom should the risk fall?' Morally the learner driver is not at fault: but legally she is liable to be because she is insured and the risk should fall on her.' Other decisions in which Lord Denning made similar determinations include *Lamb v. Camden LBC* [1981] Q.B. 625; *Spartan Steel v. Martin* [1973] Q.B. 27; and *R.H. Willis and Son v. British Car Auctions Ltd* [1978] 2 All E.R. 392.

626. *Executor Trustee and Agency Co. Ltd v. Hearse* [1961] S.A.S.R. 51, 54 (Chamberlain J.).

627. See R.V.F. Heuston & R.A. Buckley, *Salmond and Heuston on the Law of Torts*, 28 (20th ed., Sweet & Maxwell 1992): 'Once it is conceded that insurance renders compensation the sole purpose of damages, then the tort action itself becomes more vulnerable to attack, for there are many ways – some perhaps fairer and administratively cheaper than tort – of compensating a victim for a loss he has suffered'.

628. England (617) 13.

629. See Peter Cane, *Tort Law and Economic Interests*, 479–81 (Clarendon Press 1996).

[C]   The Pluralistic View of Tort

Given that tort cannot function purely as a corrective or distributive mechanism, it is necessary to consider whether there is a theoretical basis which can accommodate both distributive and corrective objectives. There is increasing recognition of the fact that the objectives of tort are multi-faceted and cannot be encapsulated by monistic theories such as economic efficiency or corrective justice. Epstein argues:

> It is unwise, indeed futile, to attempt to account for the complete structure of a complicated legal system by reference to any single value or principle – be it liberty or efficiency.[630]

Nevertheless, certain proponents of the corrective theory remain of the opinion that the distributional objectives of society should be met by entirely separate mechanisms.[631] However, to remain firmly entrenched in the corrective view of tort is to ignore the existence of strict liability and insurance. As Englard argues, these factors introduce issues of efficient loss allocation:

> Weinrib's insistence on complete theoretical purity, on the rigorous pursuit of one single value is ... unsatisfactory. Areas of strict liability have become deeply entrenched in tort law, and the reality of insurance cannot be isolated from tort adjudication. The idea of efficient loss allocation should not be totally excluded from tort law, even if it does not accord with the Kantian premises of autonomy and moral responsibility.[632]

In theoretical terms, this 'pluralistic' approach may appear unsatisfactory in that it lacks the purity of the monistic approaches. In order to overcome this objection, Englard has suggested grounding the pluralistic view of tort law in the theory of 'complementarity'.[633] This derives from the physicist Neils Bohr's philosophical explanation for the anomalies produced by quantum mechanics. In short, the theory provides that conflicting principles may appear irreconcilable when viewed in isolation, yet, when viewed collectively, they may constitute a unified whole:[634]

---

630. R.A. Epstein, *Causation and Corrective Justice: A Reply*, 8 J. Leg. Stud. 477, 503 (1979).
631. According to Weinrib, damage costs must be met either by the injurer according to tort rules founded upon corrective principles, or, from a compensation fund operated according to distributive principles. Thus, in his view there is no middle ground where both principles may be combined. See E.J. Weinrib, *Aristotle's Forms of Justice*, 2 Ratio Juris 211, 214 (1989).
632. Itzhak Englard, *The Idea of Complementarity as a Philosophical Basis for Pluralism in Tort Law*, in *Philosophical Foundations of Tort*, 185 (D.G. Owen ed., Clarendon Press 1995).
633. *Ibid.* See also R.G. Wright, *Should the Law Reflect the World?: Lessons for Legal Theory from Quantum Mechanics*, 18 Fla. St. U.L. Rev. 855 (1991).
634. See Dugald Murdoch, *Neils Bohr's Philosophy of Physics* (CUP 1987). In quantum mechanics it is possible to explain matter and radiation either as particles or waves (wave-particle duality). Despite the fact that the two concepts are incompatible, experimental findings may point to the existence of one or the other. In isolation the two concepts provide an explanation for some findings: together they provide an explanation for all findings.

Two or more descriptions of a thing are complementary if each alone is incapable of providing a complete description or explanation of the thing in question and both or all together provide a complete description.[635]

Thus, in certain cases, 'opposing principles constitute a harmonious totality'.[636] As England notes, this is an idea that occurs throughout philosophy and religion.[637] Indeed, Bohr contended that the theory could be extended into many areas other than physics including culture, art and music.[638] Englard argues that complementarity is also consistent with a pluralistic view of tort.

Such an approach may confer some degree of theoretical elegance on the pluralistic approach. However, the issue of whether it is possible to embody competing objectives in a single concrete legal rule or court decision in practice is another matter. Englard argues that such an approach is possible and refers to the fact that the solutions adopted by the court, in many cases, represent compromise solutions which embody competing objectives. He uses the example of criminal penalties, thus, in a case where a theory of retribution requires a term of imprisonment of two years whilst a theory of deterrence demands a term of ten years, the court may decide to impose a term of five years.[639]

England's analysis appears to provide a viable explanation for the use of tort in an environmental context where the difficulties of reconciling distributive and corrective issues are acute. It is possible to detect the application of a pluralistic approach in some of the substantive common law rules which have been encountered in the previous chapter. For example, the development of the 'character of the neighbourhood' test[640] in nuisance, as a threshold of damage, can be interpreted as an example of a pluralistic approach. The test clearly introduced distributional considerations in that it allowed activities to continue which would previously have been deemed unacceptable. However, it also retained the harm principle in that damage which exceeded the threshold remained actionable; this preserved an element of corrective justice.

In *Rylands v. Fletcher* Blackburn J. explicitly addressed the issue of where the loss should fall where one land owner made an unnatural use of his property.[641] A conscience decision was made to hold the land owner liable, in such circumstances, by the establishment of a rule of strict liability. However, strict liability retains elements of corrective justice in that defences are normally available in respect of events which are entirely beyond the control of the land owner; these include acts of a stranger[642] and Acts of God (or Nature).[643]

---

635. England (n. 632) 188.
636. *Ibid.*, 190.
637. *Ibid.*, 190.
638. See, for example, N. Bohr, *Natural Philosophy and Human Culture,* 143 Nature 268 (1939) and N. Bohr, *Unity of Knowledge* (1958) in *Atomic Physics and Human Knowledge* (First published 1961, Dover Publications 2010).
639. England (n. 632) 194.
640. *St. Helen's Smelting v. Tipping* (1865) 11 H.L.C. 462.
641. (1866) L.R. 1 Ex. 265, 279–280.
642. See, for example, *Northwestern Utilities Ltd. v. London Guarantee and Accident Co. Ltd* [1936] A.C. 108; *Rickards v. Lothian* [1913] A.C. 263.
643. See, for example, *Nichols v. Marsland* (1876) 2 Ex. D. 1.

The use of injunctive relief also provides a clear example of an area in which the courts may adopt a pluralistic approach. On the face of it, the decision to grant injunctive relief may appear to represent a purely corrective approach which excludes consideration of distributional issues. However, this is based on the view that injunctions inevitably lead to the closure of the business or the imposition of unsustainable costs. On the contrary, it is important to note that an injunction need not operate as an inflexible instrument which expunges one land use in favour of another. Injunctions can be effective in forcing polluters to investigate cleaner technologies which enable the activity to continue at less cost to the environment. McLaren (1972) argued that producers are often reluctant to take this step of their own accord:

> There is little doubt that industrialists will often ignore technological reality and resist making adjustment in their processes to accommodate pollution control, unless they are forced to think and to act.[644]

As evidence for this assertion he cited an extract from an interview with a manufacturer of pollution abatement equipment:

> … we have found it very hard to place our equipment out in the field, mostly because industries refuse to spend any money for this cause. The attitude towards cleaning up the waste water is very negative, and they feel that they are paying for something in which there is no profit available to them. Therefore, unless they are forced into doing something about it, my opinion is that they are going to continue to stall, either by pulling political strings or denying that there is any purification equipment available.[645]

McLaren concluded that injunctions are the most effective means of forcing operators to adopt cleaner technologies. Once damages have been awarded the pollution may continue unabated, however, an injunction enables the court to influence the manner in which the plant is operated:

> The choice of an injunction shows clearly that the court is serious about dealing with the root of the problem which has given rise to the plaintiff's claim. Moreover, when a court grants injunctive relief it undertakes a supervisory role in seeing that the terms of the injunction are satisfied, and thus can guarantee that the polluter takes the appropriate action.[646]

As technology advances it is becoming increasingly difficult for operators to argue that the technology does not exist to abate the pollution. Indeed, as long ago as the turn of the Century, Dewees empirical study of tort litigation arising out of sulphur dioxide emissions in the United States and Canada[647] demonstrates that injunctions were extremely effective in encouraging operators to develop new abatement technology. In

---

644. J.P.S. McLaren, *Nuisance Actions and the Environmental Battle*, 10(3) Osgoode Hall L. J. 505, 557 (1972).
645. J.C. Esposito, *Air & Water Pollution: What to Do While Waiting for Washington*, 5 Harv. Civ. Rights – Civ. Lib. L. Rev. 32 (1970).
646. McClaren (n. 644) 557.
647. See D. Dewees, *Sulphur Dioxide Emissions from Smelters: The Historical Inefficiency of Tort Law* (University of Toronto 1996); D. Dewees and M. Halewood, *The Efficiency of the Law: Sulphur Dioxide Emissions in Sudbury*, 42 U. Toronto L. J. 1 (1992).

States where courts granted injunctive relief in preference to damages copper and lead smelter operators quickly adopted the latest available abatement technology known as the electro-static precipitator (ESP).[648] Dewees concludes that:

> [I]n general the abatement undertaken at these smelters represented either pioneering work or at least best practice at the time it was installed. This litigation, with its injunctive relief, seems to have been reasonably effective in pushing abatement near to the state of the art at the time.[649]

Far from imposing a burden on operators, in some cases it was found that new abatement technology actually led to cost savings; for example, ESP technology enabled metal particles to be recovered which would otherwise have been expelled with the flue gases. In another example quoted by Dewees, smelter owners in Tennessee who installed acid plants to remove sulphur dioxide from emissions found that the sulphuric acid produced as a by-product of the process was more profitable than the copper produced. Furthermore, the principal market for sulphuric acid was in the production of fertilizer, thus, the substance which had originally killed crops was converted into a form which enabled them to thrive. This was just a few years after a court had refused to enjoin smelter operators in Tennessee from producing sulphur dioxide emissions on the grounds that to do so would lead to the closure of the smelters.[650] The case demonstrates the difficulties in conducting an accurate cost – benefit analysis between competing land uses.

Furthermore, it is possible to attach conditions to injunctions which allow the activity to continue whilst reducing the harmful effects on the plaintiff. Such conditions may be tailored to take account of technical feasibility.[651] In the US case of *R.L. Renken v. Harvey Aluminium, Inc.*,[652] fruit growers sought injunctive relief in respect of crop damage caused by fluoride emissions from the defendant's aluminium reduction plant. Aluminium is produced in cells by an electrochemical process; this gives off gases and particulates which must be treated before being released in to the environment. There are usually several stages involved in the cleaning process. In this case the defendant had installed 'aprons' around the cells which collected the fumes at source and directed

---

648. The flue gases were passed through a chamber which was fitted with electrically charged wires and oppositely charged plates. The wires charged the particles passing into the chamber which were then attracted to the plates through electromagnetic attraction.
649. Dewees (n. 647).
650. *Madison* et al., *v. Ducktown Sulphur, Copper & Iron Co. Ltd.* (1904) 83 S.W. 658, 660: 'It is found ... that if the injunctive relief sought be granted, the defendants will be compelled to stop operations and their property will become practically worthless, the immense business conducted by them will cease, and they will be compelled to withdraw from the State. It is a necessary deduction from the foregoing that a great and increasing industry in the state will be destroyed, and all of the valuable copper properties of the State will become worthless ... If these industries be suppressed, these thousands of people will have to wander forth to other localities to find shelter and work.'
651. For an example of such an approach see *Jordan v. Norfolk County Council and another* [1994] 1 W.L.R. 1353; see §3.05[B][3], above. In the US Restatement of Torts it is stated at § 941 Comment that courts may require operators to experiment with alternative processes or procedures as a means of reducing the harm. Thus conditions may be attached to injunctions requiring operators to investigate cleaner production processes.
652. United States District Court, District of Oregon, 1963. 226 F.Supp. 169.

them to burners. The exhaust gases were sucked through a humidifying chamber and thence into the 'scrubbing towers' where the fumes were washed by several layers of water sprays; this trapped particulates and heavier elements in the exhaust gases. A final line of defence was provided by a mist eliminator at the top of the towers. Despite these measures some 1,300 pounds of fluorides escaped into the atmosphere each day. It was found that the aprons failed to catch 20% of the emissions at source. Of the remaining 80%, which were directed through the burn chambers and into the scrubbing towers, a further 10% of the finer particles escaped.

Closing the plant was not a realistic option; it employed 550 persons and produced 80,000 tons of aluminium per year for industrial and defence purposes. Relocation would have been difficult, if not impossible, as some USD 40,000,000 had been invested in setting up and developing the plant. However, it was generally accepted that it would be possible to improve the abatement measures employed at the plant. Other facilities had installed hoods over the cells, which captured a far greater proportion of the emissions at source. In addition, ESP, of the type described above, were often fitted in order to capture those finer particles which evaded the water sprays. Kilkenny, District Judge, was satisfied that the defendant could and should bear the costs associated with implementing these additional measures:

> While the cost of the installations of these additional controls will be a substantial sum, the fact remains that effective controls must be exercised over the escape of these noxious fumes. Such expenditures would not be so great as to substantially deprive defendant of the use of its property. While we are not dealing with the public as such, we must recognize that air pollution is one of the great problems now facing the American public. If necessary, the cost of installing adequate controls must be passed on to the ultimate consumer. The heavy cost of corrective devices is no reason why plaintiffs should stand by and suffer substantial damage.

Thus an injunction was granted which enabled production at the plant to continue, provided that hoods and ESPs were fitted within one year of the date of the decree.

To grant injunctive relief against a large and influential industrial concern demands courage on the part of the court. However, the larger and more successful the enterprise the more likely it is to have the resources to comply with the terms of an injunction. Where, an enterprise cannot comply with the terms of an injunction, even in circumstances where it has been tempered to take account of technical feasibility and cost, McLaren draws the harsh conclusion that such enterprises are not worth saving:

> If in the final analysis, the practical result is the shutting down of the offending operation, then, in the writer's opinion, that has to be faced by the polluter and the community with what fortitude they can muster. It can well be argued that in the contemporary scale of social values endeavours to improve the state of the environment are more important than the continued existence of marginal or struggling industrial concerns. Apart from anything else it is not beyond the ingenuity of society and particularly governments to compensate for the adverse community consequences of the demise of a local employer. New non-polluting industries may be brought in or encouraged to set up. Workers may be absorbed in other plants or relocated. The consequences are remediable. However, pollu-tion, by definition, has no other solution than to restrict or remove its sources. If

155

it continues, then the sure result is further and perhaps irremediable corruption of the environment.[653]

Many years have elapsed since McLaren made this assertion but his argument still holds true today. Courts are now in a far better position than they were forty years ago to critically evaluate arguments to the effect that a technology is too costly, impracticable or unobtainable. The growth of environmental regulation, which has increased exponentially since the latter part of the twentieth century, has led to a proliferation of technical standards and guidance notes. For example, in the EU environmental regulations are underpinned by the Best Available Technique (BAT) standard[654] which requires operators to utilize modes of operation which are as close as possible to the state of the art. The bare standard is fleshed out by reams of technical guidance notes which stipulate precisely what constitutes BAT in a particular industrial process.[655] On occasion, in the context of judicial review proceedings challenging licensing requirements, the courts have been prepared to enforce the standard in the light of the accompanying guidance.[656] There is no reason why such evidence should not be used in the context of proceedings in tort. Thus, where a clear technical solution is available the courts are clearly in a position to make a finding to the effect that a particular technique should be used. If a company is not capable of adopting such a measure then McLaren's argument that such an enterprise should be allowed to fail may still have merit.

However, matters are rather less clear cut where no obvious and cost effective technological solutions falls readily to hand. In such cases the court may very quickly find itself straying into political waters and the issue of how an entire industry should be regulated. In such circumstances the use of an injunction, which amounts to a form of judicial regulation of an activity, may prove exceedingly problematic. This problem is highlighted by the climate change litigation issue. In the US cases the issue of injunctive relief is inextricably bound up in the 'political question' issue. The courts have struggled with the issue of whether the imposition of liabilities flowing from contribution to climate change is essentially a political question which should not be determined in the judicial arena. Abate[657] notes that in US case law the courts are more likely to encounter the political question issue where the plaintiff seeks an injunction as opposed to damages. It is for this reason that the district court found against the

---

653. McLaren (n. 644), 559.
654. See European Parliament and Council Directive (EC) 2008/1 concerning integrated pollution prevention and control (IPPC), O.J. L24/8 (the IPPC Directive).
655. In the EU these take the form of BAT Reference (BREF) documents which are formulated by the European IPPC Bureau (a division of the EU Comission's Directorate General Joint Research Centre) pursuant to Article 17 IPPC Directive. In the UK many of these standards are incorporated in sector guidance notes published by the Environment Agency.
656. See *R. (on the application of Rockware Glass Ltd) v. Quinn Glass Ltd (and another)* [2006] EWCA Civ 992; [2006] All ER (D) 151 (Jun) in which the terms of an industrial emissions permit, issued to a glass bottle manufacturer, were successfully challenged on the grounds that they did not reflect what emission levels could be achieved through the application of well established BAT standards for the industrial sector.
657. R.S. Abate, *Public Nuisance Suits for the Climate Justice Movement: the Right Thing and the Right Time*, 85 Wash. L. Rev. 197 (2010).

plaintiff in the climate change public nuisance case of *Connecticut v. American Electric Power Co.*[658] It was held that the decision as to whether or not to grant an injunction and if so upon what terms would embroil the court in the 'identification and balancing of economic, environmental, foreign policy, and national security interests'[659] which were all clearly non-justiciable political questions. Nevertheless, the district court was overturned on the political question issue by the Court of Appeal for the Second Circuit[660] which emphatically rejected the notion that an injunction would require the 'court to fashion a comprehensive and far-reaching solution to global climate change, a task that arguably falls within the purview of the political branches.'[661] Rather the decision would be confined to limiting emissions from six specific power stations.[662]

Whether this view of the problem fully appreciates the economic reality of the power generation industry is open to debate. Indeed, it is difficult to conceive of a more politically contentious topic than energy policy. Imposing severe limits on a coal-fired power station may require the adoption of carbon capture and storage (CCS) technology.[663] However, CCS technology has yet to be developed to a state whereby it can be regarded as fulfilling the BAT criteria i.e., available and affordable.[664] The adoption of CCS technology requires the establishment of a national infrastructure of pipelines, pumping stations and reservoirs. This is not something which can be achieved by the operators of individual plants in isolation. Furthermore, strict emission limits for coal imposes may increase reliance on alternative sources such as nuclear or renewable. Once again, this raises crucial issues of national energy policy pertaining to the safety of nuclear energy and the viability of renewable. Thus, notwithstanding the findings of the Court of Appeal for the Second Circuit in *American Electric Power*, it would take an extremely bold court to blunder into this political territory using the blunt instrument of an injunction. In such circumstances the pluralistic objectives of tort may better be served by an award of damages whilst the more complex distributional issues are shifted into the political arena.

---

658. 406 F. Supp. 2d, 265 (S.D.N.Y. 2005). See Abate (n. 657) 216.
659. 406 F. Supp. 2d, 265, 274 (S.D.N.Y. 2005).
660. *Connecticut v. American Electric Power* 582 F.3d 309 (2d Cir. 2009).
661. *Ibid.*, 325.
662. See Abate (n. 657) 217–18.
663. CCS encompasses various techniques by which CO2 emissions are removed at source and condensed into a transportable form before being piped or shipped to underground reservoirs such as depleted oil and gas fields. For an overview of the legal impications associated with regulating this technolgy see M. Schurmans & Van A. Vaerenbergh, *The New Proposed EU Legislation on Geological Carbon Capture and Storage (CCS): A First Impression of the Commission's Proposed Framework on CCS*, 17(2) Eur. Energy. Envtl. L. Rev. 90, 95–6 (2008).
664. Certain national governments and the EU have adopted various 'technology-forcing' measures, such as financial incentives, in an attempt to establish several demonstration schemes capable of proving the viability of the technology; however, progress has been slow. For details of the UK demonstration programme see Department of Energy and Climate Change, *UK Demonstration Programme*, http://www.decc.gov.uk/en/content/cms/emissions/ccs/demo_prog/demo_prog.aspx (accessed June 8, 2011).

The pluralistic analysis provides a sound and practicable theoretical basis for the use of tort in an environmental context. It is possible for liability to remain firmly anchored in the harm principle whilst preserving the ability of the law to take account of distributional issues. The law of tort has always absorbed social and political preferences regarding where loss should fall. Economic efficiency is only one criterion which can be applied and, as Posner appears to concede, may provide little guidance in determining the desirability of protecting a natural resource. The issue of where losses should fall must be determined in accordance with a broader range of criteria including 'the deciding authority's moral and political philosophy'.

A useful example of the manner in which the law of tort may be developed, so as to reflect changing social and political preferences regarding the distribution of losses, is provided by industrial accident law. In an early edition of Dias and Markesinis it was argued that liability based upon fault 'suited Victorian morality and cushioned growing industries at a time when insurance was in its infancy'.[665] However, it eventually became 'politically unacceptable to let the loss lie on injured workmen'.[666] Furthermore, the development of insurance and the realization that costs could be passed to consumers through the pricing of goods 'led to the conviction that employers were best equipped to carry such losses'.[667] Thus elements of loss distribution were introduced into industrial accident law.

The political and social climate is now such that the focus of tort, in an environmental context, should be directed to the issue of 'who should bear the loss'. If one applies general principles of environmental law it seems clear that the polluter should pay; hence the inclusion of the 'polluter pays' principle as a basic tenet of environmental law.[668] However, the fact that tort is conceptually capable of accommodating such distributional objectives does not mean that it would necessarily augment regulatory responses already in place. This gives rise to the issue of what role the law of tort should play, if any, in an environmental context.

§4.03   THE ROLE OF TORT IN AN ENVIRONMENTAL CONTEXT

[A]   Private Enforcement of Environmental Standards

The bulk of environmental law consists of licensing regimes which permit emissions up to a certain limit;[669] these may be tightened in accordance with improvements in abatement technology.[670]

---

665. R.W.M. Dias and Basil S. Markesinis, *Tort Law*, 14 (Clarendon Press 1984).
666. *Ibid.*
667. *Ibid.*
668. See, for example, Article 191 of the Treaty on the Functioning of the European Union (TFEU).
669. In the UK there has long been an environmental-permitting system the current version of which is governed by the Environmental Permitting Regulations 2010 S.I. 2010/675.
670. Conditions in permits must ensure that operators adhere to the BAT requirement as set out in the IPPC Directive (n. 654). See Enviornmental Permitting Regs (n. 669) reg. 3 and Sched. 7, para. 5.

The regulator[671] polices these limits and may have recourse to criminal penalties[672] where they are breached. Historically regulators adopted a conciliatory approach and regarded prosecution as a last resort.[673] However, in the 1990s the Environment Agency adopted a far more assertive enforcement strategy.[674] The Agency now publishes an enforcement strategy document[675] which is regularly updated. Although there is still a preference for non-confrontational approaches in the initial stages, such as the provision of advice and guidance, the current strategy plots a clear course through escalating penalties culminating in criminal sanctions. Furthermore, there is a new focus on pre-emptive powers where serious damage is imminent.

These developments are welcome and will no doubt increase the deterrent effect of criminal sanctions which, in the past, have not been viewed as 'proper' offences; although this perception may now be changing.[676] However, no system of environmental regulation can rely entirely upon one mechanism; each method has strengths and weaknesses according to the circumstances. The use of licenses, backed by criminal sanctions, leaves gaps in enforcement which tort may have a useful role in reducing. For example, due to limited resources, regulators must inevitably be selective in terms of choosing which cases to pursue in the criminal courts.[677] Furthermore,

---

671. In the UK complex or particularly hazardous activities fall within the jurisdiction of the Environment Agency, whereas, local authorities regulate atmospheric emissions of a less complex or hazardous nature. As regards the Environmental Permitting Regs (n. 669) these activities are divided into Part A and Part B processes divided between the Environment Agency and Local Authorities respectively.

672. As regards breaches of environmental permitting requirements in the UK a range of enforcement powers are available to the regulator under Part 4 of the Environmental Permitting Regs (n. 669). These include enforcement notices and criminal sanctions.

673. See Keith Hawkins, *Environment and Enforcement: Regulation and a Social Definition of Pollution* (Clarendon 1984); R. Baldwin and C. McCrudden, *Regulatory Agencies: An Introduction*, in *Regulation and Public Law* (R. Baldwin & C. McCrudden eds., Weidendeld and Nicolson 1987).

674. See O. Lomas & R. Fairley, *The Long Arms of the Environment Agency*, 80 Legal Bus. Supp. 8–9 (1997); S. Tromans and M. Doring, *Convictions for Environmental Offences*, 5(8) Envtl. L. M. 10 (1996).

675. Environment Agency, *Enforcement and Sanctions Statement* (Policy 1429_10) (25/02/11) http://publications.environment-agency.gov.uk/PDF/GEHO0910BSZJ-E-E.pdf (accessed 9 June 2011).

676. In *Sherras v. De Rutzen* [1895] 1 QB 918 it was stated that administrative offences, 'are not criminal in any real sense but are acts which in the public interest are prohibited under a penalty', per Wright J. at 922. In an environmental context this view was clearly reflected by Viscount Dilhorne in *Alphacell v. Woodward* [1972] 2 All ER 475: 'This Act is, in my opinion, one of those Acts...which...deals with acts which are not criminal in any real sense, but are acts which in the public interest are prohibited under a penalty.' More recently, however, Bell & McGillivray have detected a hardening in judicial attitudes regarding the seriouness of environmental crimes: see Simon Bell and Donald McGillivray, *Environmental Law*, 44–45 (7th ed., OUP 2008). Indeed, certain environmental offences, such as 'fly-tipping', are now routinely attracting jail sentences where the culprits are shown to have blatently flouted the law with a view to profit; see N. Parpworth and K. Thompson, *Fly-tipping: a real environmental crime*, 9 J. Plan. Envtl. L. 1133 (2009).

677. Thus there is an inevitable gap between the number of reported incidents and the number of successful prosecutions. At the time of writing the most up to date statistics on Environment Agency prosecutions was for 2008; see – *Datafile: Environmental Offences 2008*, Environment in Business (Jan/Feb) 6 (2010).

criminal sanctions are not designed to remediate the harm or secure compensation for those affected.[678]

A further potential benefit of tort is that, whereas the standard of proof in criminal law is beyond reasonable doubt, in civil law the court must be satisfied on the balance of probabilities. As Burnett-Hall points out:

> To avoid convicting a defendant on a criminal charge unfairly, he is, quite rightly, afforded a whole range of evidential and other procedural safeguards, notably the appreciably heavier criminal burden of proof. This protection inevitably means either that there are more acquittals than would otherwise be the case or – no doubt much more often – that proceedings are never brought in the first place.[679]

This burden is reduced where the offence is of strict liability, however, this only relates to the state of mind (*mens rea*) of the defendant; it is still necessary to show, beyond reasonable doubt, that the damage was attributable to the defendant (*actus reus*). It can be difficult to establish causation according to the civil test; this task is even more onerous under the criminal test.[680]

In the UK the difficulties of utilizing the criminal process in the context of certain forms of environmental harm have led to the introduction of civil penalties.[681] These operate rather like parking fines in that the penalty is administered by administrative law and does carry with it the stigma of a criminal conviction. From an enforcement perspective it is hoped that the mechanism will prove to be much cheaper to apply and lead to a greater degree of enforcement.[682] This is flanked by the expansion of administrative enforcement powers designed to secure the clean-up of pollution or to

---

678. Although substantial fines may exert some deterrent effect on other operators. One of the largest penalties imposed in respect of a breach of the UK Environmental Permitting regime concerns a cement plant which was fined EUR 250,000 in respect of excessive dust and noise; see Environmental Data Services (ENDS), *Failings at Castle Cement plant lead to record fine*, 421 ENDS 5 (2010).

679. R. Burnett-Hall, *Enforcement through civil proceedings*, 2 Amicus Curiae 24 (1997).

680. This is clearly illustrated by the Australian case of *EPA v. Barlow* (Unreported, Land & Environment Court of New South Wales, 23 April 1993). In this case there seemed to be overwhelming prima facie evidence that fish had been killed as a result of a crop spray, known to be harmful to fish, used by the defendant on his cotton plants. The dead fish were found the day after the spray had been used and tests on the carcasses revealed traces of the chemical. However, the judge threw out the case on the grounds that there was a possibility, albeit improbable, that the contamination may have washed down from another plantation upstream. Hemmings, considers that there is a greater likelihood that the evidence would have been sufficient to establish causation under the civil test. (See N. Hemmings, *The New South Wales Experiment: The Relative Merits of Seeking to Protect the Environment though the Criminal Law by Alternative Means*, 19(4) Cmmw. L. Bull. 1987 (1993). This would certainly be the case according to the position adopted by the House of Lords in *McGhee v. N.C.B.* [1973] 1 W.L.R. 1. Recall that, where it cannot be established whether a specific breach of duty led to the harm, there may be a presumption of causation provided the identity of the causal agent is not in doubt. In *EPA v. Barlow* there was no doubt that the chemical was only used by the cotton industry in that region; therefore, it seems likely that a civil court would have been in a position to make a presumption of causation in these circumstances.

681. Pursuant to the Regulatory Enforcement and Sanctions Act 2008.

682. See R. Macrory, *Reforming Regulatory Sanctions – a Personal Perspective*, 11(2) Env. L. Rev. 69 (2009).

prevent it from occurring in the first place.[683] Thus, the regulator may require the polluter to remove a hazard before harm is caused or to remediate the damage if it has already occurred. The regulator may take action itself and recover the costs *ex poste* from the polluter if there is an immediate threat of harm or the polluter is tardy in taking action. These measures are to be welcomed; nevertheless, they cannot provide a complete alternative to tort. There are still resource implications associated with the powers which means that they cannot be invoked in all circumstances. Furthermore, although individual harm may appear serious from the victim's perspective it might not reach the threshold of significance needed to invoke such powers. Moreover, individual losses suffered as a result of a polluting incident, such as personal injury, may fall outside the definition of environmental harm for the purposes of these measures.[684]

[B]   Private Law and the Public Interest in the Environment

Above, it was noted that, in a system of tortious liability which is characterized by corrective principles, a plaintiff cannot be viewed as a private enforcer of a public interest. However, it was then explained that there is a sound theoretical basis for admitting public interest issues into substantive tort rules and the remedies available to the courts. An important issue concerns whether it would be possible to take this approach one step further and allow private bodies to undertake actions, related to environmental damage, on the publics' behalf.

Such an approach would greatly increase the number of participants in the enforcement of environmental standards and reduce the need to rely upon enforcement agencies to take the initiative. A polluting incident which affects a limited number of individuals may not prompt a regulatory authority to take action. Nevertheless, from the perspective of the individuals concerned, the incident may appear to be of great importance and cause them to initiate their own proceedings. Thus, civil liability may penetrate a far greater range of activities than regulatory responses where regulatory authorities are constrained in the matters which they choose to pursue by issues such as staffing shortages, policy considerations and limited resources.

To a limited extent, those statutes which impose civil liability (in addition to criminal penalties), by way of the tort of breach of statutory duty, facilitate a degree of private enforcement. As Rogers argues:

> Provision for public participation and especially by those members who suffer particular loss or damage as a result of legislative non-compliance, would ensure that the public interest in the preservation of the environment was not compromised by governmental inactivity through negligence, political pressure or fiscal

---

683. European Parliament and Council Directive (EC) 2004/35 on Environmental Liability O.J. L143/56; implemented in England and wales by way of the Environmental Damage (Prevention and Remediation) Regulations 2009 (S.I. 2009/995).
684. *Ibid.* See Regulation 4 of SI 2009/995 regarding the definition of damage. This is limited to damage to certain protected species or habitats, water contamination reaching certain thresholds and land contamination resulting in significant threats to human health.

restraints. In the absence of legislative reform in this area, the common law tort of breach of statutory duty would secure public participation in the enforcement process.[685]

A useful case study of how tort actions may result in the private enforcement of environmental standards is provided by 'Fish Legal'[686] which began life as the Anglers' Cooperative Association (ACA) in 1948.[687] Fish Legal is a non-profit organization and its members largely comprise angling clubs throughout the UK. The organization helps its members to bring legal proceedings in respect of damage to fish stocks caused by polluting incidents. It will be recalled that, before one can undertake an action in nuisance, it is necessary to establish a proprietary interest in land. In view of this the organization advises its members to obtain a lease from the riparian owner. The scheme has proved to be extremely successful and the vast majority of actions, supported by Fish Legal and its predecessors, have been won by the angling clubs. In many cases injunctive relief has been granted requiring operators to clean-up pollution.[688]

The Fish Legal example is unusual in that the participants in the scheme have found a means of establishing a proprietary interest in the resource they are seeking to protect. However, the solution to the standing problem adopted by Fish Legal would not be open to most environmental interest groups; save for those which actually own, for example, a nature reserve or a wildlife sanctuary.[689] Thus in order to extend the role of tort as a means of private enforcement it would be necessary to afford standing to such groups. At this point it would be useful to consider whether there is a conceptual basis which would allow this step to be taken. This would entail establishing a community interest in the environment which amounts to some form of proprietary interest.

During the latter part of the twentieth century it has been possible to detect the emergence of a concept of 'environmental rights'. In 1972 the Stockholm UN Conference on the Human Environment resolved in Principle 1 that:

> Man has a fundamental right to freedom, equality and adequate conditions of life, in an environment of quality that permits a life of dignity and well being, and he bears a solemn responsibility to protect and improve the environment for present and future generations.

Some twenty years later, the declaration following the Rio UN Conference on Environment and Development proclaimed in Principle 1 that:

---

685. N. Rogers, *Civil Liability for Environmental Damage: The Role of Breach of Statutory Duty*, 2 (5) Env. Liability 117, 118 (1994).
686. See www.fishlegal.net (accessed July 3, 2011).
687. As regards the work of the Anglers Cooperative Associateion see R. Bate, *Water Pollution Prevention: A Nuisance Approach*, 14(3) Econ. Aff. 13 (1994). Fish Legal's website contains up to date information on its latest victories and campaigns: see (n. 686), above.
688. *Ibid.*
689. See, for example, *League Against Cruel Sports v. Scott* [1986] Q.B. 240 in which deer hounds in pursuit of a stag trespassed upon a sanctuary actually owned by the League Against Cruel Sports.

> Human beings are at the centre of concerns for sustainable development. They are entitled to a healthy and productive life in harmony with nature.

Furthermore, in recent years the European Court of Human Rights has begun to impute certain 'environmental rights' into the European Convention on Human rights although the Convention does not make any express reference to such a concept. In *Lopez Ostra v. Spain*[690] the applicant lived in close proximity to a new liquid waste treatment plant which had been built to deal with the by-products produced by the many leather tanneries in the area. Due to a malfunction on start up, gas fumes, pestilential smells and contamination were released which caused nuisance and health problems to those living in the area and necessitated re-housing. It transpired that the operators of the plant, SACURSA, had not obtained a license and that, furthermore, the regulatory authorities had not taken any steps to enforce the licensing requirements. Having met with little success in pursuing SACURSA in various actions before the domestic courts, Mrs Lopez Ostra resorted to a human rights argument against the State on the grounds that, as a result of its omissions,[691] the State had breached, *inter alia*, Article 8 of the Convention which provides as follows:

> 1. Everyone has the right to respect for his private and family life, his home and his correspondence.
> 2. There shall be no interference by a public authority with the exercise of this right except such as in accordance with the law and is necessary in a democratic society in the interests of national security, public safety or the economic well being of the country, for the prevention of disorder or crime, for the protection of health or morals, or for the protection of the rights and freedoms of others.

The Court upheld this argument on the grounds that:

> Naturally, severe environmental pollution may affect individuals' well-being and prevent them from enjoying their homes in such a way as to affect their private and family life adversely, without, however, seriously endangering their health.[692]

The most interesting aspect of this decision is that a dispute which had the characteristics of a tort problem was converted into a rights issue and pursued against the State. In this respect the *Lopez Ostra* case has proved instrumental in helping to evolve a concept of environmental rights.[693] However, it is not always possible to convert such private disputes into rights issues affecting the state; as the case law of the European Court of Human Rights demonstrates, it is necessary to show an omission on the part of the State to safeguard the rights in question. Furthermore, human rights have a

---

690. (1995) 20 E.H.R.R. (1) 277.
691. The European Court of Human Rights has established that, in addition to placing obligations on states to refrain from breaching human rights, the Convention places a positive obligation on States to protect human rights from interference by others. See *Marckx v. Belgium* (A/31): 2 E.H.R.R. 330, [31]; *Young, James and Webster v. United Kingdom*, Applications Nos. 7601/76 and 7806/77, Series B, No. 39, [168]; *x and y v. Netherlands* (A/91): (1986) 8 E.H.R.R. 235, [23].
692. At [51].
693. For an analysis of the development of environmental rights since Lopez Ostra see O.W. Pedersen, *A Bill of Rights, Environmental Rights and the UK Constitution*, (2011) P.L. 577.

limited horizontal reach which means that they cannot be invoked against private bodies pursuing purely commercial interests; except where a vital public service such as water provision has been privatized. This raises the issue of whether there is any means by which these so-called 'environmental rights' could be brought within the sphere of private law.

In *Lopez Ostra* it is interesting to note that public law mechanisms were used to effectively appropriate certain private interests and link them with a human right in a manner which enabled public law to be engaged. In order to increase the scope of tort in this field it would be necessary to do precisely the opposite; namely appropriate environmental rights and assimilate them with individual interests in a manner which enables private law mechanisms to be engaged. Such an approach is possible in theory, although, it may entail a reassessment of the way in which the concept of property is viewed in this context. It would necessitate expanding the notion of property so as to afford persons a form of proprietary interest in the environment.

A useful starting point for this debate is provided by an article written by Reich in 1964.[694] Reich was deeply concerned by the fact that the well being and livelihoods of citizens in the United States was increasingly dependent upon the 'largess' of government. Largess encompasses state benefits, government contracts, provision of employment in the public sector, the provision of licenses to pursue a trade or profession and so forth.[695] However, he noted that such benefits were perceived as privileges which could be revoked without good reason. Thus, many individuals were needlessly deprived of their livelihoods and status. In certain cases this resulted in gross abuses of civil liberties.[696]

Reich argued that property is an essential component of liberty:

> [T]he Bill of Rights comes into play only at extraordinary moments of conflict or crisis, property affords day-to-day protection in the ordinary affairs of life.[697]

However, during the industrial revolution, the idea of liberty based upon property became increasingly vested in the tangible resource itself; societal constraints on the use of resources were ousted. Thus a person could do as he wished with his land, even if this was at the expense of his neighbours.[698] Reich argued that, as a result of such abuses, powers were increasingly transferred from the private to the public sector during the early part of the twentieth century.[699] However, Government itself became guilty of the same abuses:

---

694. C.A. Reich, *The New Property*, 73(5) Yale L.J. 733 (1964).
695. *Ibid.*, 734–739.
696. Reich was particularly disturbed by the case of *Fleming v. Nestor* 363 U.S. 603 (1960). Nestor had arrived in the U.S. in 1913 and, upon retirement in 1955, became eligible for old age benefits (his employers had made regular contributions). However, following the revelation that he had been a member of the Communist party between 1930 and 1939 he was deported and the payment of benefits to his wife was terminated. The Supreme Court decided that the benefits constituted a gratuity and that the state was under no contractual obligation to maintain them. See Reich (n. 694) 768–769.
697. See Reich (n. 694) 771.
698. *Ibid.*, 772.
699. *Ibid.*, 773.

Government as an employer, or as dispenser of wealth, has used the theory that it was handing out gratuities to claim a managerial power as great as that which the capitalists claimed. Moreover, the corporations allied themselves with, or actually took over, part of government's system of power. Today, it is the combined power of government and the corporations that presses against the individual.[700]

Reich concluded that the only way to safeguard essential benefits conferred by government largess would be to establish proprietary rights in those interests. He also argued that there was no conceptual difficulty with such an approach. The notion of property is an invention of society and may be adapted to suit society's needs.[701] Thus, governments may confer proprietary interests in benefits[702] and stipulate the terms upon which those benefits are held:

Once property is seen not as a natural right but as a construction designed to serve certain functions, then its origin ceases to be decisive in determining how much regulation should be imposed. The conditions that can be attached to receipt, ownership, and use depend not on where property came from, but on what job it should be expected to perform.[703]

Thus, according to this view, property vests in rights and duties associated with use of a resource rather than the resource itself. Macpherson argues that there was originally a much broader conception of property which, apart from the right to exclusive possession, included 'an individual right not to be excluded from the use or enjoyment of things the society had declared to be for common use – common lands, parks, roads, waters'.[704] Hence, the right to exclusive possession of an area of land would have to be balanced against, for example, the grazing rights of others.

In common with Reich, Macpherson argues that it is only since the growth of free market economics that the conception of property has narrowed to the resource itself and the right to exclude others:

[W]ith the predominance of the market, all individual's effective rights, liberties, ability to develop their own persons and exercise their own capacities came to depend so much on the amount of their material property that it was not unrealistic to equate their individual property with their material property.[705]

As the right not to be excluded was not marketable it 'virtually dropped out of sight'.[706]

In earlier époques, individuals enjoyed a form of proprietary interest in certain socially valued resources with the result that a private individual could not appropriate such resources and exclude all others from benefiting from them. Macpherson points

---

700. *Ibid.*
701. *Ibid.*, 771–772.
702. Reich made the point that rights in real property ultimately vest in the state and were originally conferred by the Crown (before US independence). In the UK it is the case that property ultimately reverts to the Crown as *bona vacantia* in the absence of an individual who can show title. See Reich (n. 694) 778.
703. *Ibid.*, 779.
704. C.B. Macpherson, *Human Rights as Property Rights*, 24 Dissent 72, 73 (1977).
705. *Ibid.*, 74–75.
706. *Ibid.*, 75.

out that in pre-market societies there were established 'legal rights not only to life but to a certain quality of life'. Thus:

> the rights of different orders or ranks, guild masters, journeymen, apprentices, servants and labourers; serfs, freemen and noblemen; members of the first and second and third estates. All of these were rights, enforced by law or custom, to a certain standard of life, not just to material means of life, but also of liberties, privileges, honour, and status. And these rights could be seen as properties.[707]

Hence, interests which are currently being developed as human rights issues such as the right to a certain quality of life were viewed as property rights. Furthermore, Macpherson argues that this is a more democratic notion of property than one which merely focuses on the right to exclude others from the use of a resource.

These arguments may seem highly theoretical, however, Gray[708] points to certain areas in which, at least in the United States, there are signs of a return to such a conception of property. For example, he refers to the development of a concept of quasi public places[709] such as shopping centres and parks in which, despite being privately owned, certain test cases have established that the public has a right not to be unreasonably excluded from them.[710] Thus, certain obligations are placed on land holders which may be enforced by the beneficiaries of those obligations with the result that the public gain a form of 'equitable ownership of the resource'. This is exemplified by developments which have taken place in environmental law where, Gray argues that:

> [T]he vital ecological resources of the earth are increasingly seen as governed by a trust for the preservation of environmental quality under conditions of reasonable shared access for all citizens. Meaningful reference can thus begin to be made to the collective beneficial rights of the generalised public in respect of strategically important environmental assets.[711]

It is possible to detect the emergence of this concept of 'stewardship' in the famous dissenting judgment of Douglas J. in *Sierra Club v. Morton.*[712] The case concerned whether the Sierra Club, which undertakes conservation work and promotes outdoor pursuits, had standing to seek injunctive relief in order to restrain environmentally harmful commercial development of the Mineral King Valley in the Sierra Nevada of Northern California. Standing was denied by the majority, however, in his dissenting judgment, Douglas J. appeared to suggest that there could be such a thing as a public trust doctrine in ecological resources. He argued that those persons who have a 'meaningful' or 'intimate' relationship with the resource such as those who 'hike it, fish it, hunt it, camp in it, frequent it, or visit it merely to sit in solitude and wonderment

---

707. *Ibid.*, 77.
708. K. Gray, *Equitable Property*, 47(2) CLP 157 (1994).
709. *Ibid.*, 172-181.
710. See, for example, *Robins v. Prune Yard Shopping Center* 592 P2d 341 (1979), afd sub nom *Prune Yard Shopping Center v. Robins*, 447 US 74, 64 L Ed 2d 741 (US Supreme Court 1980).
711. Gray (n. 708) 189.
712. 405 US 727, 31 L. Ed 2d 636 (1972).

must be in a position to speak for its values.'[713] Unless there was some means of affording indirect standing to ecological resources through the use of representative actions; 'priceless bits of Americana (such as a valley, or alpine meadow, a river or a lake) [would be] forever lost or ... so transformed as to be reduced to the eventual rubble of our urban environment.'[714] At one point Douglas J. appeared to take the radical approach advocated by Stone[715] who argued that the elements which comprise the environment itself such as flora and fauna should be regarded as possessing rights themselves which interested parties should be capable of enforcing in the capacity of a form of guardian *ad litem*:

> inarticulate members of the ecological group cannot speak ... those people who have to frequent the place as to know its values and wonders will be able to speak for the entire ecological community.[716]

Such an approach opens a philosophical debate, however, whether a representative action is viewed as upholding the public interest in an ecological resource or the resource itself the practical result is the same. However, Douglas J. also appeared to recognize that the beneficial interests which he listed may be extremely diffuse and difficult to quantify. For example, how many times must a hiker visit an area before he is regarded as having a beneficial interest in the resource? It is for this reason that Douglas J. was in favour of affording standing to groups with a special interest in the environment such as the Sierra Club.

More recently, in a significant US Supreme Court decision, standing was afforded to NGOs on grounds which reflect the reasoning of Douglas J. in *Sierra Club*. In *Friends of the Earth v. Laidlaw Environmental Services*,[717] the defendants had bought a waste incinerator facility and an associated wastewater treatment plant. They obtained a permit to discharge treated water into the North Tyger River from the South Carolina Department of Health and Environmental Control. Sometime later, levels of certain pollutants, including mercury, discharged into the river were found to exceed the limits stipulated by the permit. A number of environmental pressure groups, including Friends of the Earth (FOE) commenced a private action under the citizen suit provisions of the Clean Water Act 1972. One of the issues which fell to be determined by the Supreme Court concerned whether FOE had standing to commence proceedings under the Act.

Ginsburg J stated that an association would have standing where its individual members would enjoy standing in their own right and had no need to participate directly in the proceedings. Thus it fell to be determined whether any individual members had suffered actionable loss. According to the Court's earlier reasoning in *Lujan v. Defenders of Wildlife*[718] this would require the plaintiff to establish that:

---

713. *Ibid.*, 648f.
714. *Ibid.*
715. C. Stone, *Should Trees have Standing? – Towards Legal Rights for Natural Objects*, 45 S. Cal. L. Rev. 450 (1972).
716. Per Dougals J., 653.
717. (98-822) 149 F.3d 303 US (2000).
718. 504 US 555 (1992).

(1) it has suffered an 'injury in fact' that is (a) concrete and particularized and (b) actual or imminent, not conjectural or hypothetical; (2) the injury is fairly traceable to the challenged action of the defendant; and (3) it is likely, as opposed to merely speculative, that the injury will be redressed by a favourable decision.

The most momentous aspect of Ginsberg J's judgment concerns the broad view which he took of injury. Individual members of the groups who lived in the area were not required to establish that they had suffered traditional forms of actionable loss such as damage to property or personal injury. Instead, Ginsberg J stated that it would suffice to show that the individuals' use and enjoyment of their surroundings and been impaired. For example, one Angela Patterson:

> attested that she lived two miles from the facility; that before Laidlaw operated the facility, she picnicked, walked, birdwatched and waded in and along the North Tyger River because of the natural beauty of the area; that she no longer engaged in these activities in or near the river because she was concerned about harmful effects from discharged pollutants; and that she and her husband would like to purchase a home near the river but did not intend to do so, in part because of Laidlaw's discharges.

Ginsberg J. had no doubt that that such interferences with recreational uses of the river constituted an actionable harm for the purposes of the citizen suit provisions of the Clean Water Act:

> [W]e see nothing 'improbable' about the proposition that a company's continuous and pervasive illegal discharges of pollutants into a river would cause nearby residents to curtail their recreational use of that waterway and would subject them to other economic and *aesthetic harms*. [emphasis added]

As we have seen, in common law jurisdictions, the zone in which one is entitled to the undisturbed use and enjoyment of one's surroundings is limited to the area in which one has a sufficient proprietary interest. Remarkably, the decision in *Laidlaw* extends this zone beyond the boundaries of individual properties and into the general surroundings. Such an approach effectively gives rise to a collective beneficial interest in the immediate environment capable of legal protection.

Thus the recognition in public law that there is a right to an unpolluted environment on the grounds that it is an important aspect of the quality of life is mirrored by developments in private law in the US which recognize that the public has an equitable proprietary interest in the maintenance of a certain quality of life. The use of private mechanisms as a means of protecting rights which are normally considered as belonging to the realms of public law may appear radical. However, as Macpherson has pointed out, there is historical precedent for such an approach. Furthermore, in a society which is dominated by and governed in accordance with the notion of property the only effective way to protect those rights is to assimilate them with the institutions of property. The argument in favour of harnessing the property institutions as a means of protecting fundamental rights is most clearly set out by Gray, who explains (drawing on the work of Macpherson):

It may, of course, be asked why the interests represented in the new equitable property are not merely urged as human or civil rights. The answer must be the one given by Professor Macpherson: 'We have made property so central to our society that any thing and any rights that are not property are very apt to take second place.'[719] In adopting the terminology of equitable property we lock into the insidiously powerful leverage of the primal claim, 'it's mine', and we harness this claim for more constructive social purposes. When important assets of the human community are threatened, we are able to say with collective force, 'You can't do that: those assets are ours.' When you pollute our air or our rivers or exclude us unreasonably from wild and open spaces, we can mobilise the enormous symbolic and emotional impact of the property attribution by asserting that you are taking away some of our property.[720]

Thus, Gray concludes that there is no 'unbridgeable gulf'[721] between public and private law in that it is conceptually possible to harness private law as a means of securing public interest objectives such as environmental protection. As he goes on to state:

The constant imposition of social and moral limits on the scope of 'property' necessarily entails that private property can never be truly private. It has always been one of the fundamental features of a civilised society that exclusory claims of property stop where the infringement of more basic human freedoms begins.[722]

However, there remains the question of how far this rights-based notion of equitable property can be expanded. As previously noted, *Laidlaw* represented a significant departure from traditional notions of standing in that the plaintiffs were freed from the requirement to show a formal property interest in the resources affected. Nevertheless, it must be noted that the damage was localized and that the plaintiffs formed part of a small and well defined class. The more diffuse the pollution and the more diffuse the interests affected, the more difficult it becomes to apply the property analogy in a manner which produces sensible results. In *Laidlaw*, the citizen suit provisions of the legislation were used to address concerns which were redolent of nuisance. Nuisance law itself could not be engaged because the harm did not impinge upon the boundaries of the plaintiffs' homes. Nevertheless, their enjoyment of living in the locality was impaired by the damage to the general surroundings. In this sense the *Laidlaw* decision effectively blurs the boundary between the home and the outside environment. From an English perspective this is significant enough in that it smashes a centuries old common law distinction. Recall that in *Aldred's* case[723] it was held that a landowner has no cause of action in respect of the outlook of his property. No matter how much the countryside is despoiled and no matter how much this ruins the enjoyment of living in a certain place, there can be no cause of action unless the senses are assailed by a tangible element, albeit something as ephemeral as a bad odour. Thus, by crossing this boundary the *Laidlaw* decision is rightly regarded as significant. Nevertheless, others are less impressed and do not regard *Laidlaw* as a 'game changer' when viewed in the

---

719. Macpherson (n. 704) 77.
720. Gray (n. 708) 210.
721. *Ibid.*, 211.
722. *Ibid.*
723. 77 E.R. 816; (1610) 9 Co. Rep. 57. See §2.03[A][1], above.

wider context of environmental protection.[724] The complaints brought by the residents were very much of a nuisance character although, for the above reasons, they could not be addressed using the traditional institutions of property law. It becomes much more difficult to apply the nuisance analogy where the harm is more diffuse and the number of victims is potentially limitless. This inevitably brings us back to the problem of climate change. The notion that we all enjoy an equitable interest in the planet is little more than a slogan in this context in that there is no practicable means of giving expression to the concept. As Mank puts it, in the context of global warming, injury to all becomes injury to none.[725] An equitable rights-based notion of property can certainly be used to justify expanding the range of environmental interests which merit standing. However, we can never entirely escape from the fact that tort is predicated on the basis that interests in a resource must be ascertainable. In a climate change context this entails showing that a specific individual (or group of individuals) has suffered particularized harm which is distinguishable from collective harms and can be causally connected with a particular polluter.[726]

This is not to say that, within the context of a statutory regime on climate change, the notion of actionable harm and requisite standing requirements cannot be expanded. Indeed, in an early version of the ill-fated US Climate Change Bill[727] a draft citizen suit provision was included which may have dramatically expanded the scope for damages claims arising from global warming. The specific nature of this provision will be addressed in due course in the context of standing rights in tort and the definition of actionable harm. Suffice it to say, there were concerns that the draft provision went too far and it was soon dropped from the Bill.[728]

[C]   Tort Law as a Response to Regulatory Failure

So far the analysis has been very much on the extent to which tort can be harnessed as a means of augmenting the enforcement of environmental law. The ultimate expression of this approach is the inclusion of civil liability components in environmental regulations. Thus, the infringement of an environmental standard would give rise to damages claims for breach of statutory duty in addition to any administrative sanctions or criminal penalties.[729] However, this overtly instrumentalist application of tort is distinct from the function of the common law torts.[730] The primary function of the common law is to protect private interests irrespective of whether this also happens to coincide with the protection of a public good such as the environment.

---

724. See H. Elliott, *Congress's Inability to Solve Standing Problems*, 91 Bos. U. L. Rev. 159, 165, fn 26 (2011).
725. See B.C. Mank, *Standing and Global Warming: Is Injury to All Injury to None?* 35 Envtl. L. 1 (2005).
726. *Ibid.*, 80–81.
727. Namely the draft American Clean Energy and Security Act 2009 which would have inserted a new section 336 citizen suit provsion into the Clean Air Act 1970 affording indiviuals a cause of action in respect of certain harms attributable to climate change.
728. See Elliott (n. 724) 184–185.
729. See section §2.07, above, on breach of statutory duty.
730. See P. Cane, *Tort Law as Regulation*, 31(4) C.L.W.R. 305 (2002).

In this respect the common law has a vital role to play as a means of compensating for regulatory failure. For example, no matter how carefully an activity is regulated, there will always remain a possibility that accidents will occur leading to personal injuries, property damage or nuisance. However, the common law is not limited to dealing with the consequences of these *unplanned* harms. Major new projects, such as high speed rail links and power stations, cannot be built and operated without causing some disruption to neighbouring interests. The planning system seeks to anticipate and manage those harms which are the inevitable consequence of such developments. Where the harm cannot be minimized or reduced to acceptable levels compensation may be payable under various statutory regimes. Nevertheless, the system may fail to identify the precise nature and extent of those harms with the result that the interests of certain parties are not taken into account. As previously noted, the circumstances surrounding the litigation in *Allen v. Gulf Oil Refining Ltd*[731] provide a classic illustration of this problem.[732] At no stage were the environmental or health effects of the project fully investigated and no provision was made for compensation in respect of the harms which ensued. However, as has also been noted in respect of this case, Gulf was effectively granted immunity in respect of these harms as a result of a generous interpretation of the statutory authority defence. Thus, the ability of the common law to remedy such regulatory failures has been undermined by doctrinal developments by which the courts have effectively spiked their own guns.

As noted at the beginning of this section, certain statutes establish a private cause of action for breach of statutory duty in addition to administrative sanctions and criminal penalties. This raises complex issues regarding the relationship between these overtly 'instrumentalist'[733] torts and overlapping existing common law torts. In some cases the statutory liabilities operate alongside existing common law torts although there may be a degree of overlap in terms of subject matter.[734] Indeed, from the perspective of regulatory failure, there is a strong argument in favour of preserving existing common law remedies. Under statutory regimes the types of harm giving rise to a cause of action tend to be narrowly defined and linked to regulatory standards. Nevertheless, individual harm can occur irrespective of whether it also constitutes a breach of the regulatory standard. For this reason legislators should be slow to draft statutory duties in a manner which ousts existing common law torts. A case in point concerns the UK Nuclear Installations Act 1965, which, as noted above, expressly excludes the common law from the field.[735] The statute establishes a cause of action in respect of damage caused by nuclear 'occurrences'. However, this is limited to property damage and physical injuries of the sort which would be associated with nuclear

---

731. [1981] A.C. 1001.
732. See §2.03[D][2], above.
733. See Cane (n. 730).
734. See section §2.07., above.
735. *Ibid.*

accidents. At the time the legislation was drafted it was not anticipated[736] that much nuclear contamination would be of a *chronic* nature i.e., low level and prolonged causing nuisance type problems.[737] However, the fact that the regime entirely replaced the common law and confined itself to physical damage of the type associated with accidents effectively prevented the common law from filling this regulatory lacuna.[738]

§4.04   THE EFFECT OF INSURANCE ON THE ROLE OF TORT

As stated above, it is not possible to consider the role of tort in isolation from the issue of insurance; historically, the availability of insurance has affected the development of tort. Thus the extent to which tort may fulfil a useful role, as a means of environmental protection, is partly dependent upon the availability of insurance for environmental damage. However, there are particular problems associated with providing insurance cover in this area.

[A]   Public Liability Policies and the 'Pollution Exclusion'

Claims arising from pollution have usually been indemnified by public liability policies (Comprehensive General Liability (CGL) in the United States). However, following a rapid increase in claims arising from pollution in the early 1970s,[739] insurance companies in the US sought to exclude pollution from CGL policies save for that which was caused by 'sudden and accidental escapes'.[740] In 1991 the Association of British Insurers (ABI) advised British insurers to follow suit and proposed a standard endorsement as follows:

> This policy excludes all liability in respect of Pollution or Contamination other than pollution caused by a sudden, identifiable, unintended and unexpected accident[741]

---

736. This can be gleaned from the Parliamentary debates which took place on the need for special statutory provisions on nuclear liability in the precursor of the 1965 Act, namely, the Nuclear Installations (Licensing and Insurance) Act 1959: HC Deb. vol. 599 cols. 862–938 (9 February 1959).

737. See M. Lee, *Civil Liability of the Nuclear Industry*, 12 J. Envtl. L. 317 (2000).

738. See M.L. Wilde, *Magnohard Ltd v. The United Kingdom Atomic Energy Authority: claiming for the economic and psychologocal 'legacy' of neclear and maritime pollution*, 12(6) Env. Liability 243 (2004).

739. See S. Clark, *Pollution gives general insurers cold feet*, 34 I.C.L. 25 (1994).

740. The ISO pollution exclusion provides: 'This policy does not apply to … property damage arising out of the discharge, dispersal or release or escape of smoke, vapours, soot, fumes, acids, alkalis, toxic chemicals, liquids, or gases, waste materials or other irritants, contaminants or pollutants into or upon land, the atmosphere or any water course or body of water: but this exclusion does not apply if such discharge, dispersal, release or escape is sudden and accidental.' For an overview of the manner in which the exclusion has been interpreted in the US see A. Nyssens, *Pollution Insurance: The Seepage of American Influence*, 4(1) Env. Liability 11 (1996).

741. It should be noted that, in insurance law, accident means any unexpected event from the point of view of the insured; this does not always mean a calamitous occurrence such as a crash. For example, in *Mills v. Smith (Sinclair Third Party)* [1964] 1 Q.B. 30, it was found that damage caused by encroaching tree roots could constitute an accident for the purposes of property

which takes place in its entirety at a specific time and place during the period of insurance.[742]

Some twenty years on such exclusions have become the norm and now govern most environmental liability of a tortious nature.[743] Thus, as regards public liability, the general position is that only costs resulting from an unexpected and temporal event, such as an explosion,[744] can be recovered under the terms of the policy. In the US certain courts have, on occasion, attacked the exclusion by finding that 'sudden' denotes any unexpected event rather than a temporal occurrence.[745] However, these decisions are exceptional and the view that the event should have a temporal quality has now largely been restored.[746]

In the UK, an exclusion of this type was upheld in *Middleton v. Wiggins*.[747] In this case a waste disposal company, which had been found liable in respect of an explosion caused by a build up of methane gas emanating from a landfill site, claimed indemnity under their public liability policy. The insurers sought to rely on an endorsement which excluded liability for damage arising from 'the disposal of waste materials in the way the insured intended to dispose of them unless such claim arises from an accident in the method of disposal'. In the Court of Appeal, Hutchison L.J. held that the accident was not 'in the method of disposal' since the unforeseen events which caused the explosion

---

insurance. In *Trim Joint District School Board of Management v. Kelly* [1914] AC 667 the following test was proposed: 'If, so far as the property is concerned, unexpected misfortune happens and damage is caused, the insured is to be indemnified'. See R.M. Merkin and A. McGee, *Insurance Contract Law*, London, [B.10.6] (Kluwer 1990).

742. ABI, Ref: g/250/065 (23 July 1990).
743. See V. Fogleman, *Plugging the Gap in Cover for Environmental Liabilities in UK Public Liability Insurance Policies*, 17 (1) Envtl. Liability 11 (2009).
744. See *Staefa Control-System=s, Inc. v. St. Paul's Fire & Marine Insurance Co.*, 847 F. Supp. 1460, 1468 (N.D. Cal. 1994), '[T]he 'sudden accident' exception applies only to events that occur quickly, such as an explosion.'
745. See, for example, *Jackson Township Municipal Utilities Authority v. Hartford Accident and Indemnity Company*, 451 A. 2d 990 (N.J. Super. Ct. Law Div. 1982). The plaintiff in this case had been held liable in respect of damage caused by contaminants which had leached from a landfill site into a water supply. Despite the fact that the policy excluded pollution, save for that which was caused by sudden and accidental escapes, and that the pollution had occurred over a twelve year period the court held that the plaintiff could recover its costs under its insurance policy.
746. N.B. Ranney & S. Ardisson, *Recent Developments in California in Respect of the 'Sudden and Accidental' Exception to the Pollution Exclusion*, 2 Intl. J. Innovation Learning 123 (1995). The predominant view is that sudden and accidental connotes a temporal quality. See, for example *Trico Industries Inc. v. Travellers Indemnity Company* 853 F. Supp. 1190 (C.D. Cal. 1944). In this case the plaintiff company sought to recover costs under its general liability incurred under the Superfund Programme as a result of chemical waste contamination at its site caused by the activities of a previous occupier. Trico argued that the term 'sudden' was ambiguous and should be interpreted in its favour so as to read 'unexpected'. However, the court rejected this argument on the grounds that 'most recent decisions ... indicate the emerging majority rule to be that 'sudden' contains a temporal element'. Applying this to the facts of the case in question it was found that 'the decade of continuous pollution at the site was not abrupt, quick or immediate. Since this pollution did not occur suddenly, plaintiff's settlement payments are not covered under the INA policies ... '
747. [1996] Env L.R. 17.

occurred after the waste had been disposed of.[748] McCowan L.J., dissenting, considered that the process of putrefaction and degradation, which causes methane gas, should be regarded as an integral part of the method of disposal.[749]

However, the exclusion may not insulate insurers from 'long tail' risks. A catastrophic event, such as an explosion, may cause immediate property damage and personal injuries, in addition, any chemicals released may lead to long term contamination of the surrounding area. The effects of the contamination may not manifest themselves until years later. As most policies are underwritten on an 'occurrence' basis insurance companies are obliged to meet any claims resulting from accidents, occurring during the period of cover, irrespective of whether the policy has expired.[750] As a result, they may find themselves liable in respect of unforeseen damage. In the US, for example, the unforeseen long term consequences of an intentional act have been found to constitute unexpected events covered by the exception to the pollution exclusion.[751] In the UK this has resulted in an asbestos litigation 'time-bomb' as personal injuries arising from the mishandling of the substance in the 1960s and 70s continue to manifest themselves.[752]

At one time, certain insurers in the US attempted to entirely exclude liability for environmental damage from CGL policies.[753] Although, it would have been more difficult for European Insurers to have taken this step *en masse* due to EU competition rules which would have prevented them from operating as a cartel.[754] Threats of a total withdrawal of cover for environmental damage have evaporated since the early 1990s and the market has evolved considerably since that time. This has largely been due to

---

748. *Ibid.*, 24–25.
749. *Ibid.*, 28.
750. *Knight v. Faith* (1850) 15 Q.B. 649, 667 (Lord Campbell C.J.); *Daff v. Midland Colliery Owners' Indemnity Co* (1913) 6 BWCC 799, 820 (Lord Moulton). See generally, E.R. Hardy-Evamy, *General Principles of Insurance Law*, ch. 37 (Butterworths 1993).
751. In *Waste Management Inc v. Peerless Insurance Co*, 340 S.E.2d (N.C. 1986) the insured were covered because, although the discharge of toxins into a landfill was intentional, the subsequent contamination of a drinking water supply was unexpected and unintended.
752. In various decisions in the UK the courts have held that, as regards employers' liability for asbestos claims, the occurrence should be regarded as the exposure to asbestos in the workplace. Thus, the relevant policies are those employers' liability policies which were in place at the time that the claimant was exposed to asbestos. See *Bolton Metropolitan Borough Council v. Municipal Mutual Insurance Ltd* [2006] EWCA Civ 50, [2006] 1 W.L.R. 1492(CA) and *Durham v. BAI (Runoff) Ltd* [2008] EWHC 2692. [2009] 2 All E.R. 26 (QBD). This has resulted in a major industry involving tracking down what polices were in place forty of fifty years ago and to whom the liabilities have passed during the numerous takeovers and mergers which have occurred in the insurance industry over that time. See Fogleman (n. 743) 15.
753. Nyssens (n. 740) found two decisions in which a total exclusion was upheld by the courts, viz, *Titan Holding Syndicate Inc v. City of Keene*, 898 F.2d 265 (1 Cir. 1990) and *Park-Ohio Industries Inc v. Home Indemnity Co*, 975 F. 2d 1215 (6 Cir. 1992). The Louisiana Supreme Court rejected a total exclusion in *South Central Bell Telephone Co v. Ka-Jon Food Stores of Louisiana Inc and Others*, 93-CC-2926, May 1994, however, this was largely due to the fact that the insurers had misled the insurerd as to the inclusion and effect of the endorsement.
754. Layard argued that a co-ordinated position adopted by the British Insurance Industry as a whole, which affected the competitiveness of other groupings, would have amounted to an abuse ' … of a dominant position within the common market or within a substantial part of it' contrary to Article 82 EC (now Article 102 TFEU). See A. Layard, *Insuring Pollution in the UK*, 4 (1) Env. Liability 17, 18 (1996).

case law and legislative developments clarifying the nature and extent of environmental liabilities. In the UK, for example, the case of *Cambridge Water v. Eastern Counties Leather*[755] was crucial in terms of the defining the extent of polluters' liabilities in respect of historic pollution. However, a number of uncertainties remain regarding the capacity of the insurance market to absorb liabilities arising from environmental torts. It is clear that public liability policies will continue to deal with the bulk of insurance claims arising from specific incidents such as an explosion or a sudden and accidental release of chemicals into a river. Nevertheless, as noted above, since 1991 the ABI has strongly recommended that its members exclude all environmental liabilities from public liability policies save for damage of a sudden and accidental nature. This excludes pollution damage of a chronic nature, that is, harm arising from low level releases of pollutants of an on-going nature caused by everyday operations. Thus, damage of the type at issue in *Cambridge Water v. Eastern Counties Leather* would be excluded on this basis.[756] Given that a not inconsiderable proportion of environmental damage takes this form it is clear that public liability policies alone cannot absorb all tortious liabilities stemming from environmental harm. However, the insurance industry has attempted to fill this gap with a range of alternate specialist policies.

[B] Environmental Impairment Liability

When the first edition of this book was published the specialist environmental insurance market was in its infancy and there was much speculation as to whether the market would be able to absorb the gradually expanding range of environmental liabilities. Only a handful of companies offered products geared to remediating environmental degradation of the type excluded from public liability policies. Today, a cursory search of the internet instantly produces hundreds of brokers and insurance companies offering such policies.[757] The insurance market has grasped the problem of environmental harm and has managed to turn it into a lucrative market. In this respect the insurance market has been driven by expanding liabilities rather than the reverse. However, it should be noted that the new liabilities stem largely from a growth in the use of administrative clean-up powers as opposed to any major expansion of the role of tort.[758] Nevertheless, the fact that the capacity of the market has been boosted in this

---

755. [1994] 2 A.C. 264.
756. Although it should be noted that had Eastern Counties itself been found liable its insurers may well have had to pay under the terms of the public liability policy because the insurance policies in operation at the material time would have predated the exclusion. Furthermore, given that the policies would have been subject to occurrence triggers the insurance company would have been liable notwithstanding the fact that the policies would have long since expired.
757. See, for example, the EAGLE environmental liability insurance product offered by Allianz: Allianz, *Public Good: Environmental Liability Insurance*, http://www.agcs.allianz.com/insights/expert-risk-articles/public-good-environmental-insurance-l/ (accessed Apr. 16, 2012).
758. See for example section 161 and 161D Water Resources Act 1991; Directive 2004/35/EC of the European Parliament and of the Council on environmental liability with regard to the

way may serve to weaken any arguments to the effect that any expansion in tortious liability would be uninsurable and hence unsustainable.

Such policies tend to be more expensive as they are not available 'off the peg' and must be tailor made according to the nature of the environmental hazard at a particular site.[759] To this end the party seeking insurance must first answer a detailed questionnaire regarding the nature of his activities and the history of the site. The insurers may then appoint environmental consultants, at the prospective insured's expense, to conduct an onsite inspection and produce a detailed report. Based upon this information risk engineers will make a recommendation as to whether cover should be offered; if this is favourable the underwriters will draft a policy.

However, EIL policies in the UK do not serve as 'blank cheques' to meet open ended costs. This is because the insurers have chosen to insert 'claims made' triggers rather than the more usual 'occurrence' triggers.[760] Thus, the insured may only seek indemnity in respect of claims made during the currency of the policy or within a specified period after its expiration. This insulates the insurers from the problem of 'long tail' risks. Although claims made policies are legal under English Law[761] they have been ruled illegal in certain European jurisdictions or subjected to statutory controls.[762] These restrictions have been counter-productive in that the development of the EIL market in the UK and US is largely due to the legality of claims made policies.[763]

A further restriction is that the insured may only seek indemnity in respect of fortuitous as opposed to inevitable escapes. This precludes latent damage caused during the normal course of operations without any breach of applicable regulations. To this end a standard clause has emerged in environmental impairment liability (EIL) policies which excludes:

> Any liability arising from Environmental Impairment which is inevitable having regard to the cumulative effects of the normal Business of the Insured and where the harmful nature of any contaminant or irritant was known or should reasonably have been known by the Insured.[764]

This is consistent with general principles of English Law which provide that an insured cannot, at the insurer's expense, purchase the right to continue a nuisance.[765]

---

prevention and remedying of environmental damage O.J. L 143/56 (30 April 2004) and the UK contaminated land regime as set out in Part IIA Environmental Protection Act 1990.

759. See R. Marshall, *Environmental Impairment – Insurance Perspectives*, 3(2/3) R.E.C.I.E.L., 153, 156 (1994). The particular factors to be taken into account include type of activity; materials used; geology of the site; the flow of watercourses; prevailing meteorological conditions; political climate (e.g., media coverage, activity of pressure groups); managerial attitudes; claims history; compliance with regulations etc. This basic methodology has not changed in recent years although for a more recent account see Fogleman (n. 743) 15.

760. *Ibid.*, Marshall (1994) 154–155;Fogleman (2009) 15.

761. *Pennsylvania Co for Insurance on Lives and Granting Annuities v. Mumford* [1920] 2 K.B. 537; *Maxwell v. Price* [1960] 2 Lloyd's Rep. 155. See Hardy-Ivamy (n. 750) 405.

762. See R.G. Lee, *Claims-Made Policies: European Occurrences*, 4(1) Env. Liability 25 (1994).

763. See Lee (n. 762) and Marshall (n. 759) 154–155.

764. See Marshall (n. 759) 156. Thus in a case such as *Cambridge Water* (assuming for the moment that it had been possible to bring a claim during the period of cover) the exclusion would not have precluded Cambridge Water from indemnification. It will be recalled that the hazardous nature of the chemical released was not known at the material time.

765. *Corbin v. Payne*, The Times, (Oct. 11, 1990).

Despite these limitations, EIL policies still afford more scope for the recovery of costs, associated with pollution damage, than claims brought under the sudden and accidental exemption to the pollution exclusion in public liability policies. This is because they are specifically geared to providing indemnity in respect of accidental pollution. For example, in *Middleton v. Wiggins* it will be recalled that a very restrictive interpretation was placed on the exception to the pollution exclusion. Thus the insured could not claim in respect of the on-going hazard caused by the landfill. Such costs are, however, anticipated by the specialist Landfill Cover EIL policy offered by the Swiss Re-insurance Company. This provides cover while waste is being dumped (the 'active' period) and for ten years after the site has been filled in (the 'passive' period).[766] Had such a policy operated in a case such as *Middleton v. Wiggins* the operators would have been indemnified notwithstanding the fact that the site had been closed.

[C]   Effect of Insurance on Risk Management

The existence of insurance does not undermine the element of individual accountability associated with liability in tort. Insurance is principally designed to provide cover in respect of fortuitous events such as accidents. In order to reduce the risk of such events occurring, insurers may exert a great deal of influence on operators to reduce the risk of accidents. This is certainly the case as regards the provision of EIL cover. As described above, detailed site audits must be undertaken and any deficiencies corrected before cover will be offered; this will usually be followed by annual assessments as part of the renewal process. Furthermore, it may be a condition of cover that certain pollution prevention measures are adopted.[767] Thus, far from absolving polluters of liability, insurance companies may be instrumental in requiring polluters to reduce the risk of their activities. As the chief executive of a major insurer has stated:

> We feel insurance and loss prevention go hand in hand with proactive environmental protection. From an economic viewpoint, it is more profitable to employ resources in prevention than in paying insurance claims.[768]

To date, the provision of cover for sudden and accidental escapes under standard public liability policies has not been accompanied by similar incentives for the management of environmental risks. Nevertheless, as a matter economic necessity, insurers will soon have to remedy this situation by introducing measures of the type described above.

---

766. See Marshall (n. 759) 157. The insured's premiums are held in a fund together with an additional lump sum payment. Any liabilities incurred during the passive phase are met from the fund. If no liabilities are incurred, the lump sum payment will be returned at the expiration of the policy.
767. British and European Insurers advocate the establishment of a set of environmental compliance conditions for environmental policies. See D. Lewis-Kirk, *Deterring Pollution*, 29(15) Business Insurance 23 (1995); J. McDonald, *Financial Responsibility Requirements: Liability Insurance as an Environmental Management Tool*, 4(1) Env. Liability 2 (1996).
768. A. Konswold, quoted in Lewis-Kirk (n. 767) fn. 41.

Existing public liability policies do, however, provide an incentive for the insured to limit the consequences of pollution due to the fact that the insured is under a general duty to mitigate the loss. This is demonstrated by the case of *Yorkshire Water Services Ltd v. Sun Alliance and London Insurance Plc*[769] which concerned damage caused by the deposit of sewage sludge into a river. The sewage affected an ICI chemical works which, somewhat ironically, found itself as the victim of pollution. Yorkshire Water settled a claim of EUR 300,000 with ICI and sought to recover this amount under its public liability policy. In addition it claimed costs in respect of alleviation work it had carried out in order to limit the spread of the sewage. Yorkshire Water argued that they should be indemnified in respect of these costs since they mitigated the loss which the insurers may otherwise have had to meet. The Court of Appeal rejected this argument and held that there was no implied term in the policy which would allow the recovery of such costs. A loss which had not yet occurred could not be quantified.

Thus, there is a close link between the conduct of the insured and the availability of insurance. The viability of the insurance contract very much depends upon the ability of the insured to mitigate the losses passed to the insurers. Thus, in this respect, although insurance introduces notions of distributional justice, it also dovetails with the corrective functions of tort in that it is consistent with individual accountability. This limits the availability of insurance, and hence the role of tort, as a means of environmental protection in cases where the insured does not have the opportunity to internalize any of the costs for which he is held liable. This problem is particularly acute in the case of historic pollution.

[D]   The Problem of Historic Pollution

In the past, it was mooted whether tort could play any part in the allocation of responsibility for historic pollution. For example, in its response to the House of Commons Select Committee Report on Contaminated Land, the UK Government stated:

> The Committee have recommended that there should be a clearer position on liability for damage caused by contamination and that urgent attention should be given to the possibility of creating statutory liability. That recommendation has arisen from the Committee's discovery that there appear to be no reported cases in the UK concerning the application of relevant common law principles to contaminated land issues... ...
>
> ... The Government's basic view is that the firm UK common law tradition should only be set aside where it is clearly demonstrated that such principles are inappropriate. Consequently, the case for statutory liability should first depend upon a test of the current principles in the Courts. In particular, *Rylands v. Fletcher* could have extensive implications in its application to questions of contamination.[770]

---

769. [1997] 2LLoyd's Rep. 21.
770. Department of the Environment, *Government Response to First Report of the House of Commons Environment Committee. Contaminated Land*, (Cm. 1161, 1990) para. 4.13.

Soon afterwards, in *Cambridge Water v. Eastern Counties Leather*,[771] the House of Lords made it abundantly clear that there was no prospect of the common law being used to hold operators liable in respect of historic pollution. There were sound policy reasons for adopting this approach which also have some theoretical merit. Applying liability in a retrospective manner divests tort of its corrective functions and converts it into a purely distributional instrument. As the pollution has already occurred the responsible parties are not in a position to internalize any of the costs. Furthermore, due to the existence of occurrence triggers and the fact that the harm would be governed by old policies predating the 1991 gradual pollution exclusion, insurers would bear the brunt of these unmitigated losses. This would no doubt lead to the total exclusion of cover for any form of pollution damage.[772]

The manner in which the Cambridge Water case was decided diffused the potential historic pollution liability time-bomb which otherwise would have gone off in the same manner as the afore-mentioned asbestos time-bomb. The problem of historic pollution was channelled to the administrative field and is the subject of a specialist contaminated land regime under Part IIA Environmental Protection Act 1990 (inserted by the Environment Act 1995). Most other countries have adopted a similar approach.

Uncoupling tort from the problem of historic pollution proved to be a vital step in terms of allowing the insurance industry to develop new policies with a view to meeting future liabilities in a controlled manner rather than conserving resources to meet uncertain liabilities from the past. As Marshall noted in the early 1990s when the matter had yet to be fully resolved: 'Is there any incentive for a buyer of insurance to invest in the future, particularly when the focus is on the past and the problems of today?'[773]

§4.05 CONCLUSIONS

It is conceptually possible to harness private law in pursuit of public interest objectives. The pluralistic view of tort, perhaps grounded in England's interpretation of the theory of complementarity, provides a sound philosophical basis for the use of tort in an environmental context. The manner in which tort has developed, particularly since the nineteenth century, shows that it is no longer possible to isolate a private dispute from the distributional objectives of society. However, it is equally unrealistic to determine these distributional objectives in accordance with narrow wealth maximization criteria. As Posner now seems to admit, the market may no longer be regarded as providing a reliable indicator of the value of natural resources. These determinations must now be made by reference to wider criteria including the predominant moral and political

---

771. [1994] 2 A.C. 264.
772. Prior to the Court of Appeal judgment in *Cambridge Water v. Eastern Counties Leather*, the ABI issued a press release which stated that, if the Court found in favour of Cambridge Water, its members would be forced to withdraw cover for pollution altogether. See Layard (n. 754) 18.
773. Marshall (n. 759) 158.

philosophy; this clearly includes recognition of the desirability of environmental protection.

The law of tort has the capacity to augment regulatory responses by affording each member of society the ability to participate in policing the environment. At present, this depends upon whether an individual, or organization, can establish a direct proprietary interest in the resource affected. However, as the arguments put forward by Reich, Macpherson and Gray suggest, it may be possible to extend this approach one step further and confer a form of 'equitable property' in the environment upon each member of society. This would open the way for representative actions undertaken by an environmental interest group on the publics' behalf.

However, although tort can accommodate distributional objectives, it must always be borne in mind that its correctional functions serve an important purpose. The element of individual accountability associated with tort provides incentives for risk management. If tort liability is extended into areas in which there is no opportunity to internalize costs, such as historic pollution, insurance becomes unworkable and costs unsustainable.

Despite these limitations, there has been much consideration of the extent to which tort can be harnessed in pursuit of public interest environmental objectives without undermining its corrective functions and rendering it a means of blunt-loss allocation. A number of individual states have introduced special environmental liabilities regimes and various European and international bodies have given active consideration to adopting supranational environmental liability regimes based upon tortious principles.

CHAPTER 5

The European and International Dimension

---

§5.01 INTRODUCTION

The greatest limiting factor of the common law, as explored in depth in the preceding chapters, is the fact that it must evolve gradually in response to the emerging problems of society. There is an inevitable time lag while the courts wrestle with the adaptation and re-interpretation of antique principles which were invented centuries before there was any conception of the problems facing us today.

However, in recent decades the problem of transboundary pollution has come to the fore and it is now a truism to assert that pollution does not respect national frontiers. The problem was first demonstrated very clearly in the events leading to the Trail Smelter Arbitration concerning the deposition of pollution in the US from Canadian smelters just north of the border. More recently scientific research has demonstrated that certain pollutants can be carried many thousands of miles and far beyond the immediate border regions between neighbouring states. Attempts have been made by individuals suffering loss as a result of transboundary pollution to seek compensation in tort. This immediately gives rise to jurisdictional and conflict of laws problems due to the wide divergences in liability rules in different states. This raises the issue of whether some degree of harmonization would be desirable.

The EU (and under its former guise as the EC) was been at the forefront of early initiatives on the introduction of a specialist environmental civil liability regime. However, no actual legislation on the introduction of a special tort based environmental liability regime was ever implemented. Instead of a civil liability regime designed to augment private rights in tort, the EC (as it then was) opted to expand the role of administrative pollution prevention and remediation powers under the Environmental Liability Directive (ELD). Nevertheless, arguments to the effect that some form of harmonization of private law mechanisms may be necessary, in the interests of the single market, remain pervasive and the issue remains open. The need for the EU to revisit the issue may become of more pressing importance as a number of Member

States have already pressed ahead with their own regimes. Clearly, if such regimes create major differences in terms of the liabilities faced by operators in different Member States there will be implications for the single market.

Aside from the EU initiatives, which so far have come to nought, there has been international cooperation on tort based environmental laws in limited areas including nuclear contamination, maritime oil pollution and, to a much lesser extent, transboundary contamination caused by the escape of GMOs. In addition, there have been abortive attempts by the International Law Commission to devise a broader system of tort based liability rules for transboundary environmental harm.

Aside from an analysis of the conflict of laws problems engendered by divergent liability rules, this chapter provides a broad overview of the types of initiative which have emerged both at an EU and International Level. Particular attention is focused on the extent to which such regimes have the capacity to augment civil liability for environmental damage without underpinning the corrective functions of tort. In the following chapters there is consideration of the extent to which some of the themes emerging from these initiatives, such as strict liability, have been reflected in actual laws and policies at a domestic level.

§5.02   SUPRANATIONAL ASPECTS OF ENVIRONMENTAL HARM: 'EXPORTING' POLLUTION

There is a strong international dimension to environmental liability in that pollution is not constrained by national borders. As the scale of industrial operations has increased so has the reach of pollutants. The most obvious manifestation of this problem is the issue of transboundary pollution whereby pollutants emitted in one state are carried by wind or tide and currents to other states. This has raised conflict of laws issues regarding the ability of an injured party to seek a private law remedy in respect of harm stemming from a facility under the jurisdiction of another state. As we shall see, this largely depends upon what international treaties or conventions have been agreed between the states concerned. However, modern business practices enable pollution to be 'exported' in a less obvious manner. Many large multinational companies set up industrial operations in all parts of the globe under the auspices of subsidiary enterprises. In some cases companies may take advantage of laxer local environmental laws in order to pursue practices which would not be tolerated closer to home. Thus, severe damage may be caused to the environment surrounding the plant and the interests of the local population. This constitutes a form of exporting pollution in that the costs (or externalities) of 'dirty' plants are imposed upon those local populations as opposed to the consumers of the end product or the population of the state in which the main 'seat' of the organization is located. Where liability mechanisms in the state in question are weak, it may prove extremely difficult for affected parties to seek redress against the polluter in the domestic courts. Furthermore, multinational companies may be able to shelter behind the 'veil of incorporation' with the result that claimants are precluded from attacking the parent company on its 'home turf' where standards may be more stringent. This has given rise to the concept of the 'alien tort' and the extent to which such multinational companies may be held to accountable under the law of the home state in respect of harm caused in other parts of the world.

Transboundary pollution and alien torts raise extremely complex and technical legal issues and it is not proposed to offer any more than a brief overview of these areas in order to establish their relationship with the issue of environmental liability in private law. Our main focus is on the broader issues raised, namely, the extent to which in a 'global commons' it is possible to reduce such jurisdictional conflicts through the adoption of common standards and legal mechanisms. As we shall see, states guard their sovereignty very closely in such matters and progress towards establishing liability mechanisms in respect of certain types of environmental harm has been slow and piecemeal to say the least.

[A] Transboundary Pollution

The problem of transboundary pollution emerged as a serious environmental issue in the early part of the twentieth century; largely in the context of long running disputes between the United States and Canada regarding cross-border emissions from the latter's mineral smelting industries. The small city of Trail in British Columbia, just 11 miles from the US border, emerged as the focal point for these disputes in the 1920s and 30s.[774] US farmers across the border in Washington State complained about substantial crop damage which they attributed to atmospheric emissions of sulphur dioxide (and other noxious elements) carried downwind from the Consolidated Mining and Smelting Company of Canada's smelter in Trail. Following representations made by the US through diplomatic channels, the International Joint Commission (IJC) was engaged, by mutual agreement with the Canadian Government, to investigate the matter. The IJC had originally been established by the US and Canada to facilitate cooperation regarding the management of the great lakes and watercourses which straddle the long border shared by the two nations. The Commission reported in 1931 proposing the payment of compensation and setting out various recommendations for reducing emissions from the Trail smelter. However, the terms of the settlement were not acceptable to the US and the parties agreed a new Convention in order to set up a special tribunal to resolve the matter. The process became known as the 'Trail Smelter Arbitration' which is still celebrated as a successful early example of international cooperation on transboundary pollution. The Tribunal did not make its final ruling until 1941,[775] as the storm clouds of the Second World War gathered over North America. The Tribunal ruled in favour of a more generous compensation package and introduced a host of further requirements regarding the future management of the industry. Most significantly, in terms of the development of international law, the Tribunal asserted that:

---

774. For a detailed account of the Trail Smelter dispute by one of the lawyers involved see, J.E. Read, *The Trail Smelter Dispute*, 1 Can.Y.B. Int. L. 214 (1963).
775. *Trail Smelter (U.S. v. Can)*, 3 R.I.A.A. 1905 (1941).

> ...no state has the right to use or permit the use of its territory in such a manner as to cause injury by fumes in or to the territory of another or the properties or persons therein, when the case is of serious consequence and the injury is established by clear and convincing evidence.[776]

This wording near enough exactly expresses the private nuisance maxim *sic utere tuo ut alienum non laedas* (so use your property as not to injure your neighbour) and directly transposes it to an international context. Thus nuisance type problems between neighbouring states are regarded as a form of infringement of sovereignty rights in the same manner that a private nuisance between individuals is regarded as a form of interference with property rights. As we shall see below, the principle has now become firmly established as a part of customary international law.

There has been a recent postscript to the Trail Smelter Arbitration in the shape of the decision of the US Court of Appeals (Ninth Circuit) in *Pakootas v. Teck Cominco Metals Ltd*[777] concerning the current operator of the Trail Smelter site. Pollution stemming from the operation of the site in less enlightened times has continued to cause transboundary damage. This case, which has inevitably been dubbed 'Trail Smelter II', concerned contamination of the Columbia River by slag deposited in the river from the Trail Smelter plant over many decades and carried downstream. Despite the fact that Teck was on the point of reaching an agreement with the US EPA regarding the clean-up of the river, the Confederated Tribes of the Colville Reservation invoked the citizen suit provisions of the US Comprehensive Environmental Response and Liability Act (CERCLA) so as to hasten the resolution of the matter. CERCLA is designed to bring about the remediation of land and bodies of water which have been contaminated by historic pollution. The Act can impose liability for clean-up costs on a range of potentially liable parties including the current incumbent of the site from which the pollution stemmed. Had Teck been situated in the US it would have been a clear candidate for CERCLA liability. However, the fact that Teck was a Canadian company situated across the border raised the issue of whether CERCLA could have any international reach. The District Court[778] held that the 'effects doctrine', a principle of international law to the effect that jurisdiction arises where the harm is manifested, could be applied to CERCLA. However, the Court of Appeals for the Ninth Circuit interpreted the statute in a manner which denied that there was any transboundary element to the dispute at all. The slag and sediments at the bottom of the Columbia River continue to leach pollutants into the water. CERCLA contains a very broad definition of 'facility' which includes sites where wastes have been 'stored, disposed of, or placed, or otherwise located.'[779] Given that the materials were still present on the river bed and still leaching pollutants they could be regarded as a 'facility' – a bastardization of the English language if ever there was one! By this dubious sleight of hand the Ninth Circuit rendered the pollution an entirely domestic matter which

---

776. *Ibid.*, 1965.
777. 452 F.3rd 1066 (9th Cir. 2006). The decision has effectively been affirmed by the US Supreme Court which declined to hear an appeal in January 2008; 128 S Ct. 858 (U.S. 2008).
778. 35 Envtl. L. Rep. 20083 (E.D. Wash. 2004).
779. CERCLA § 9601(9).

precluded transboundary elements. Nevertheless, as Battista and Stedwill have pointed out, the decision may have long term implications regarding the ability to seek redress in respect of transboundary pollution.[780] Despite the foundations laid by the original Trail Smelter Arbitration, there has been little progress on the issue of transboundary pollution in the public law arena. States are reluctant to agree laws which impinge upon sovereignty and their right to regulate their own industries as they see fit. Trail Smelter involved two friendly states sharing the world's longest international border, a long history and shared values. Yet the Trail Smelter affair necessitated the passing of a new convention, the establishment of a special Tribunal and some fifteen years of investigation and deliberation. The significance of the Teck case is that the action commenced by the native tribes transferred the matter from the world of international diplomacy to private law. This had the effect of dramatically expediting proceedings, although private international law can only be successfully engaged where there is a high degree of mutual recognition between states regarding jurisdictions and where laws share common values.

Transboundary pollution is also a particularly serious problem in Europe due the number of neighbouring industrialized states. Airborne pollutants do not respect boundaries and do not have to travel far before crossing a European frontier. Furthermore, many European States share common watercourses, which can carry pollutants into the territories of downstream riparian states. One of the most serious incidents occurred in 1986 near Basle, Switzerland following a fire at an agrochemical warehouse owned by Sandoz. Run-off water, used to fight the fire, washed 30 tonnes of chemicals into the Rhine including fluorescent dye and organophosphorus pesticides. The incident resulted in massive fish kills and affected organisms along a 400 km stretch of the river.[781] Indeed, this was one of the disasters which focused the Commission's attention on environmental liability issues.[782] A number of EC Member States have concluded their own regional agreements on shared watercourses,[783] however, these agreements have often proved difficult to enforce.[784] As a result, transfrontier pollution of this nature has, on occasion, been the source of civil litigation between private parties in neighbouring states; a notable example is provided by the *Rijnwater* litigation.[785]

---

780. G.J. Battista & H.R. Stedwill, *Choosing Pragmatic over Polite: should International Transboundary Pollution be a Matter for Courts or Consul? The Case of Pakootas v. Teck Cominco Metals, Ltd,* 16(2) Env. Liability 35 (2008).
781. See Robin Clarke, *Europe's Environment: The Dobris Assessment: An Overview* (Earthscan Publications 1994).
782. O. McIntyre, *European Community Proposals on Civil Liability for Environmental Damage – Issues and Implications,* 3(2) Env. Liability 29, 30–31 (1995). 29.
783. For example, the Rhine Commission, established in 1950, is charged with harmonisation of emission limits and regulations between riparian states. However, to date it has only adopted two Conventions, namely, the Rhine Chemicals Convention and the Rhine Chlorides Convention.
784. Although the Rhine Commission has established a compulsory unilateral arbitration procedure for dispute resolution, the mechanism has hardly been utilised.
785. Further examples concern discharges of PAHs by Belgian plants into rivers causing environmental damage in the Netherlands. This resulted in actions being brought against the Belgian

This long running dispute stemmed from the dumping of 12 million tonnes of salt per year into the Rhein by potassium mines in Alsace. The pollution was carried to the Netherlands where it posed a threat to the safety of drinking water. As a result the Dutch Government was required to adopt expensive purification measures. Damage caused to crops eventually prompted growers to pursue civil litigation against the potassium mines. In reasoning which is strongly redolent of the Trail Smelter arbitration, The Dutch Courts expressed the view that those inhabitants of a riparian state, who have suffered loss as a result of unlawful emissions from another riparian state, have a cause of action against the polluters in question. Even if this duty could not be said to have attained the status of a customary principle of international law, it was stated that the maxim *sic utere tuo ut alienum non laedas* (so use you property as not to injure your neighbour) could be applied as a general principle of law recognized by civilized nations under Article 38(l)(c) of the Statute of the International Court of Justice:

> If what is considered above is applied to the case postulated above, this leads to the following conclusions: [a] that the general principles of law recognised by civilised peoples are binding on citizens [b] that it is settled that the damage is caused by the salt discharges [c] that the injury is established by clear and convincing evidence [d] that the discharge of the saline waste into an international river by a legal person under national law in this case constitutes a violation by the latter of a general principle binding upon it, *sic utere tuo ut alienum non laedus.*[786]

This reasoning is strongly redolent of that which was applied in the Trail Smelter Arbitration dealt with above.

Despite the acceptance of certain internationally accepted principles in this context, some scope for jurisdictional conflict or 'forum shopping remains';[787] especially in the light of the fact that certain states are pressing ahead with more rigorous regimes than others. Of particular note in this respect is the Austrian system of liability for damage caused by escapes of radiation introduced under the Act on Third Party Liability for Nuclear Damage (*Atomhaftungsgesetz* 1999 (*AtomHG* 1999)).

---

plants in the Dutch Courts by NGOs. For a discussion see G. Betlem, *Cross-border Water Pollution: two Paradigmatic Dutch Cases*, 4(2) Eur. Rev. Priv. L. 159 (1996). Developments in the Netherlands regarding increased standing for NGOs in civil proceedings in respect of environmental damage are discussed in chapter 8.

786. Case 4320/74 *Handelskwekerij G.J. Bier BV & Stichting Reinwater v. Mines de Potasse d'Alsace SA* and Case 3789/77 *Handelskwekerij Firma Gebr. Strik BV & Handelskwekerij Jac. Valstar BV v. Mines de Potasse d'Alsace SA* [1979] E.C.C. 206.

787. The scope for jurisdictional conflict in Europe was greatly reduced by Article 5(3) of the 1968 Brussels Convention on Jurisdiction and the Enforcement of Judgments in Civil and Commercial Matters. This provides that in cases of non-contractual liability, the matter can be tried by the courts exercising jurisdiction over the territory of 'the place where the harmful event occurred'. From an environmental perspective, Betlem (n. 785), 161–164 notes that one possible limitation of the provision is that it has been construed narrowly in a manner which precludes *imminent* harm from the scope of the Article. This would prevent a claimant from seeking a precautionary remedy such as a *quia timet* injunction.

The Act has introduced a particularly stringent liability regime, which is far more rigorous than international requirements under the Paris[788] and Vienna[789] Conventions. This may seem curious in the light of the fact that Austria does not generate any of her electricity by means of nuclear power; indeed, this is expressly prohibited under Austrian law (a measure of the Austrian peoples' scepticism regarding the safety of nuclear energy). However, as Pelzer explains, it seems that the Act was passed largely in order to facilitate civil actions in respect of contamination caused in Austria by activities in neighbouring states.[790] According to section 23(1) non-contractual claims relating to damage in Austria shall, at the request of the claimant, be dealt with in accordance with Austrian law. Judgments may be executed against any assets of foreign based operators in Austria and any Austrian firms which have supplied foreign operators with equipment and expertise. Furthermore, it would be possible to enforce the judgments of the Austrian Courts under the Act in other jurisdictions.

For these reasons the Act has been very controversial and has raised concerns that it could fetter the ability of Austrian suppliers to engage in contracts with foreign operators. Although no state is under any international obligation to promote the use of nuclear energy, it is clear that no state has the right to impede the use of nuclear energy in neighbouring states.[791] At an EU level, any steps which restrict the interstate flow of nuclear technology and equipment could amount to a breach of Member State obligations under European Atomic Energy Community (Euratom). As Pelzer points out, Article 192 Euratom places the contracting parties under an obligation to: '[A]bstain from any measures which could jeopardise the attainment of the objectives of the Treaty.'[792] These objectives, as set out in the preamble to the Treaty, focus on encouraging the peaceful use of nuclear energy through the establishment of a free market in nuclear technology and components. Thus:

> It is open to question whether it would be in line with the obligations under the Euratom Treaty to use national legal means simply and perhaps excessively with a view to hampering the peaceful use of nuclear energy in other contracting parties to the Euratom Treaty.[793]

Transboundary pollution is an acute problem in Europe which gives rise to complex jurisdictional issues. It is understandable that states such as Austria which, due to its topography, is particularly vulnerable to transboundary pollution[794] may wish to take

---

788. Paris Convention on Third Party Liability in the Field of Nuclear Energy, 29 July 1960, revised 28 January 1964 and 16 November 1982 (UNTS vol. 956, 251).
789. Vienna Convention on Civil Liability for Nuclear Damage, May 21, 1963 (UNTS vol. 1063, 266).
790. N. Pelzer, *Focus on the Future of Nuclear Liability*, 17(4) J. Envtl. & Nat. Res. L. 332, 344–348 (1994).
791. See Article IV of the 1968 Treaty on the Non-Proliferation of Nuclear Weapons (UNTS vol 729, p. 161), which declares the 'inalienable right of all Parties to the Treaty to develop research, production and use of nuclear energy for peaceful purposes.'
792. Pelzer (n. 790) 348.
793. *Ibid.*
794. The Alps trap atmospheric pollution and act as a barrier to its dispersion. Furthermore the dense vegetation and Alpine forests are particularly vulnerable to pollutants. See E. Brandl and C. Schmelz, *Environmental Civil liability Schemes: Do they make sense for Austria?*, 3(1) Eur. Pub. L. 1 (1997).

a proactive stance. However, the potentially divisive nature of such measures, in terms of international obligations, provides a further source of conflict. Accordingly, the issue of transboundary pollution provides a strong justification for assimilating liability rules.

[B]   Multinational Corporations, Conflict of Laws and Alien Torts

As noted in the introduction to this section, the other means by which an operator can effectively export pollution to other parts of the world is to step up a subsidiary in countries (usually the developing world) where the same environmental standards may not apply. This is facilitated by the privilege of incorporation which means that subsidiaries have their own legal personality and are accountable for their own actions according to local laws. Such business practices are highly damaging to the reputation and image of Western business and contribute to the exporting of externalities, such as pollution, rather than the internalization of such costs. In many cases the environmental harm would give rise to a cause of action in tort were it to occur in the home state of the parent company. However, it may be difficult to pursue such claims against the subsidiary in the state where the damage occurs. In some cases substantive local laws may simply not be equal to the task of holding certain industries to account. More frequently, there may be procedural obstacles to bringing such claims due to lack of public funding for civil claims, lack of a 'civil society' and NGOs with the wherewithal to advise litigants, corruption, or inefficiencies and under capacity in the court structure. This raises the issue of to what extent claims in respect of these 'alien torts' can be 'brought home' to the jurisdiction in which the parent company resides. In recent years the problem has been highlighted by the saga of the Anglo-Dutch corporation Shell's exploits in Nigeria.

The Niger Delta region in southern Nigeria is rich in oil and gas reserves and has been exploited by Western oil interests for many decades; Shell has been active in the region since the 1950s. Oil exploration and production is this region is conducted by a Nigerian registered subsidiary company, namely, Shell Petroleum Development Company of Nigeria (SPDC). Shell has become synonymous with poor environmental management in the region and spillages have been a frequent occurrence. The impact on the local environment and the health and well-being of local populations has been devastating.[795] A number of cases have been brought against Shell's Nigerian subsidiary over the years with variable results. It has been difficult to secure redress in the Nigerian courts due to procedural obstacles of the nature described above.[796] However, significant efforts have been made to bring such claims before the UK and US courts, albeit with varying success.

---

795. The extent of the oil pollution damage in one of the most heavily contaminated areas (Ogoniland) has been the subject of a much publicized study undertaken by the United Nations Environment Programme (UNEP); UNEP, *Enviornmental Assessment of Orgoniland*, (UNEP 2011) available for download at http://www.unep.org/nigeria/ (accessed Sept. 8, 2011).
796. See K.S.A. Ebeku, *Judicial attitudes to redress for oil related environmental damage in Nigeria*, 12(2) Rev. Eur. Community. Intl. Envtl. L. 199 (2003).

In private international law there are two issues which need to be determined, namely, which state should enjoy jurisdiction and which law should apply. As regards the first issue all EU States are governed by the 2001 Brussels Regulation on jurisdiction and the enforcement of judgments in civil and commercial matters[797] – which supersedes the 1968 Brussels Convention of the same name. In the UK the European requirements are distilled into domestic law by way of the Civil Jurisdiction and Judgments Act 1982 (as heavily amended on numerous occasions). In most cases jurisdiction turns upon the domicile of the defendant; thus, if a defendant has retreated to his home state, having committed a tort in another state, the claimant may pursue the matter in the defendant's home state. This issue becomes problematic in the case of Multinational Corporations (MNCs) with a complex structure involving subsidiary companies, parent and indeed grandparent companies. A claimant may wish to by-pass the local subsidiary, ostensibly charged with the day-to-day running of the operation, and pursue the parent company in its home state. Alternatively, he may wish to hold the subsidiary company to account in the jurisdiction of the parent company. However, due to the fact that the parent company has a separate legal personality to that of the subsidiary, the parent company may be able to argue that it has had no involvement in the commission of the tort. Similarly, the subsidiary may be able to argue that, as it is entirely domiciled in the same state as the claimant, the courts in the home state of the parent company cannot claim jurisdiction. At this point it is necessary to scrutinize the issue of 'domicile', as set out in the legislation, in more detail. As regards corporations the 1982 Act provides that a corporation is domiciled in the UK if it is registered in the UK, *or*, its central management and control is exercised in the UK.[798] The fact that these two tests are set out as alternatives is of vital importance in that it means that a company may be domiciled in the UK notwithstanding the fact that it may be registered overseas. There is case law to the effect that, where the parent company exercises a high degree of control over the subsidiary, the central management and control may be regarded as situated in the jurisdiction of the parent.[799] Thus, the claimant could sue the parent as being directly implicated in the tortious conduct; alternatively, it could sue the subsidiary in the home state of the parent on the basis that that is the true domicile of the subsidiary company. As regards choice of law, the basic rule is that the law of the state where the damage occurs should apply,[800] although in some cases the parties are free to negotiate which law should be

---

797. Regulation (EC) 44/2001, [2002] O.J. L12/1. The 1968 Brussels Convention was enacted pursuant to Article 220 (subsequently Article 293 and now Article TFEU) so as to harmonise arrangements for the recognition and enforcement of judgments. Intervention of this nature was deemed necessary in the interests of the proper functioning of the internal market. For example, difficulties would arise if a German Court refused to participate in the enforcement of a judgment obtained by a claimant in a UK court, in respect of a matter occurring outside the EU, on the grounds that the matter was outwith its jurisdiction. For more detailed background see A. Briggs, *The Conflict of Laws*, 56–58 (2d ed.,OUP 2008).
798. See section 42.
799. See James Fawcett & Peter North, *Cheshire and North's Private International Law*, 172–173 (13th ed., OUP 1999).
800. See European Parliament and Council Regulation 864/2007 on the law applicable to non-contractual obligations (Rome II) O.J. [2007] L 199/40, Article 4; as regards the UK see section 11 of the Private International Law (Miscellaneous Provisions) Act 1995.

used.[801] Thus, if a Polish smelter situated near the German border caused crop damage in Germany, German law would apply unless the parties agree otherwise.

As regards the European position it is possible to see these principles at work in the afore-mentioned on-going litigation concerning the giant oil corporation Shell's exploits in the Niger Delta oilfields of Southern Nigeria. Current litigation in the UK courts stems from two incidents occurring from 2008 to 2009 whereby major oil pollution was caused by fractured pipelines in Bodo, Ogoniland. It is estimated that some 10 million gallons were spilt with a devastating effect on the environment and the livelihoods of the local fishing communities amongst others.[802] A group action involving 69,000 claimants was launched against both Royal Dutch Shell (RDS) and its Nigerian subsidiary, Shell Petroleum Development Company of Nigeria (SPDC). In August 2011 an agreement was reached whereby SPDC admitted liability under Nigerian law but submitted to the jurisdiction of the English Courts. In return the claims against RDC were discontinued.[803] In the light of the above analysis of private international law it is interesting to speculate as to what legal arguments may have been raised so as to achieve this settlement. The choice of law issue is relatively straightforward in that the damage occurred in Nigeria with the result that the law of that state should apply. Rather more surprising is the fact that SPDC, a foreign based subsidiary of RDC with operational control of the Nigerian facilities, submitted to the jurisdiction of the English courts. As noted above, a foreign based subsidiary may be considered as domiciled in the UK if its parent company exercises a very high degree of control. However, in order for the separate identities of parent and subsidiary to be eroded in this way, one would normally expect to find a very high degree of involvement by the parent in operational matters. For example, direct involvement in the management of facilities rather than mere participation in corporate governance matters such as appointment of directors, management of share capital etc. Had Shell resisted the jurisdiction of the English courts, the degree of control exercised by RDC over SPDC would have been subject to close scrutiny in the courts. One can only speculate as to whether Shell accepted jurisdiction on the basis that there was compelling evidence of a very high degree of involvement of RDC in the affairs of SPDC; or whether the decision to settle the matter in this way was a purely pragmatic one based upon economic, political and public relations considerations.

Given the power and reach of MNCs, and the extent to which they often become enmeshed in the politics of the states in which they operate, arguments have been to the effect that MNCs should be rendered liable for breaches of universally recognized human rights.[804] This would be a highly significant development in that it would dramatically extend the jurisdiction of US courts under the Alien Tort Claims Act

---

801. *Ibid.*, see Rome II Regulation, Article 14.
802. See R. Hall, *Shell admits liability for huge oil spills in Niger Delta*, The Independent (Business News) (Aug.4, 2011) http://www.independent.co.uk/news/business/news/shell-admits-liability-for-huge-oil-spills-in-niger-delta-2331551.html (accessed Sept. 8, 2011).
803. *Ibid.*
804. See B. Mostajelean, *Foreign Alternatives to the Alien Tort Claims Act: the Success (or is it Failure) of Bringing Civil Suits Against Multinational Corporations that Comit Human Rights Violations*, 40 The Geo. Wash. Intl. L. Rev. 497 (2008).

(ATCA).[805] The Act is far-reaching in the sense that it affords US court's jurisdiction in respect of breaches of fundamental human rights, such as the right to life, irrespective of the domicile of the parties and where the incident occurred. There are two key issues, however, which need to be resolved before ATCA can be utilized in respect of the activities of an MNC. First, it must be possible to frame the infringement of a basic human right in terms of a corresponding tort. Second, there is the issue of the extent to which such rights and obligations have horizontal reach; in other words, can they be enforced by an individual against a private corporation in addition to the state itself? As regards the first issue, breaches of the right to life[806] or to be free from torture or unlawful imprisonment[807] are easily converted into torts to the person such as assault, battery and false imprisonment. One might be forgiven for questioning the relevance of such actions to a corporation accused of environmental abuses. Nevertheless, such claims are at the heart of litigation again arising out of the activities of Shell in the Niger Delta. In the case of *Kiobel v. Royal Dutch Shell Petroleum Corporation*,[808] it was alleged that Shell was complicit in human rights abuses including the imprisonment, torture and even killing of environmental campaigners opposed to the environmental degradation of the Delta region.[809] This raises the second issue, namely, the extent to which such fundamental human rights have horizontal reach. In *Kiobel* the 2nd Circuit Court of Appeals rejected the notion that such international norms could be enforced against private companies as opposed to states or emanations of the states. In other words, human rights only have vertical as opposed to both vertical and horizontal effect. However, the *Kiobel* decision has not resolved this question in that it differs from earlier judgments.[810] Most significantly, it has been heavily criticized by the Court of Appeal 7th Circuit in *Boimah Flomo, et al. v. Firestone Natural Rubber Co. LLC.*[811] It was claimed that workers at a Liberian rubber plantation were induced into enlisting child labour by unrealistic production quotas. It was held that there is no logical reason to confine liability for breaches of human rights law to states. Judge Richard Posner advanced an argument to the effect that the only reason why human rights law had hitherto been restricted to vertical disputes was simply that historically human rights infringements had been associated with misuse of state powers. In his view there has never been a conscious decision to specifically preclude the horizontal reach of human rights norms. Furthermore, it is clear that private actors can be criminally liable for certain breaches of customary international law; thus, it is difficult to exclude the application of civil liability. Alluding to the Nuremburg war crimes trials he asserted:

> If a corporation complicit in Nazi war crimes could be punished criminally for violating customary international law, as we believe it could be, then a fortiori if

---

805. 28 U.S.C. § 1350 (2006).
806. As set out in, for example, Article 3 UN Universal Declaration of Human Rights http://www.un.org/en/documents/udhr/ (accessed Sept. 8, 2011).
807. *Ibid.*, Articles 5 and 9.
808. 621 F.3d 111 (2nd Cir. 2010).
809. Including the well known Nigerian author and environmentalist Ken Sar-Wiwa.
810. *Sarei v. Rio Tinto plc* 456 F.3d 1069, 1074 (9th Cir. 2006); see Mostajelean (n. 804) at pp. 502-503.
811. 643 F.3d 1013 (7th Cir. 2011).

> the board of directors of a corporation directs the corporations' managers to commit war crimes, engage in piracy, abuse ambassadors or use slave labor, the corporation can be civilly liable.[812]

This is an entirely logical conclusion if one considers the extent to which state powers are now delegated to private agencies. Moreover, the power wielded by large multinational companies, especially those involved in energy production, means that they may play a crucial role in the political arena. However, given the disagreement in evidence between the various appeal circuits in the US the matter seems rife for consideration by the US Supreme Court.

It should be noted that such extreme and overt human rights abuses are likely to be atypical in an environmental context. As has been previously explained, nuisance type problems have sometimes been the subject of human rights claims under Article 8 of the ECHR on the sanctity of the family home. However, the issue of whether there is a sufficiently developed and universally accepted human right to a clean environment is debatable. As matters currently stand, it seems unlikely that the Alien Torts Act could be utilized in respect of a pollution incident un-associated with extreme human rights abuses of the type described above. It is for this reason that the *Kiobel* litigation focused on the abuse of environmental activists rather than the pollution itself.

As noted at the outset of this section, the need to resort to such complex jurisdictional arguments would be reduced if there was greater consistency between domestic legal systems regarding how liability is determined in respect of cross-border environmental damage. Whilst there are a number of international agreements on transboundary pollution, and other types of environmental harm with an international dimension, few contain measures addressing liability issues. Nevertheless, there have been some developments of note at both a European and international level.

§5.03   THE EU AND CIVIL LIABILITY: FALSE STARTS AND POLICY CHANGES

The EU (including its previous incarnations as the EEC and EC) has been at the forefront of environmental protection for forty years and must be credited for helping to develop the subject of environmental law as we know it today. The early priority of the EEC was to develop the common market (later to become the single market) thus it is no surprise to find that early measures focused on harmonizing technical product standards. Some of these technical standards had an environmental dimension in that they related to the emissions of polluting products such as car engines.[813] However, any environmental benefit arising from such standards was purely fortuitous and not the main objective. In the early 1970s the first in a continuing series of Action Programmes[814] was passed which formally adopted environmental protection as a legitimate objective of the Community. Environmental protection was not enshrined in

---

812. *Ibid.*, 1019.
813. See, for example Directive 70/220/EEC on gaseous emissions from cars with petrol engines O.J. [1970] L 76/1.
814. Council Resolution on the First Environmental Action Programme O.J. [1973] C 112/1.

the actual Treaties until the Single European Act (SEA) 1987 which inserted a new Environmental Title into the EC Treaty. These provisions remain largely unchanged in most respects and can now be found in Articles 191–193 of the TFEU.

EU environmental law has gone through a number of phases and twists and turns since the early 1970s. Much EU environmental law comprises technical measures and policies designed to reduce the volume of pollutants released into the environment. To this end, emission limits place numeric values on the level of specified pollutants which can be released at source (such as a factory chimney). A notable example includes the Large Combustion Plants Directive[815] which controls emissions of certain atmospheric pollutants, such as sulphur dioxide, from Large Combustion Plants which include fossil fuelled power stations, refineries, steelworks and other heavy industries. As regards the technical response to environmental harm the other major element comprises quality objectives which focus on reducing the total levels of pollutants in the environment. This approach looks at the aggregate emissions from particular sectors with a view to formulating strategic responses to reducing those levels. In addition, the EU has sought to underpin these strategies with the concept of IPPC.[816] The basic elements of this strategy are that specified industrial activities must be subject to a permitting system and that regulators must take a holistic view of pollution. Thus technical requirements pertaining to atmospheric emissions should not place undue loads on other environmental media such as water. Pursuant to this policy of integration the Large Combustion Plants and IPPC Directives are due to be merged, along with a range of other measures, into a giant new Industrial Emissions Directive.[817]

Thus, EU environmental law has developed into a multi-faceted and sophisticated system which has endeavoured to tackle all the great pollution issues of our age from the pollution of a stream to climate change. However, the problem of how to enforce these laws has been a constant thorn in the side of the EU Commission's DG for the Environment.[818] To put it bluntly, the Commission simply does not have the resources to enforce environmental law in a hands-on and direct manner.[819] One means of reducing this enforcement deficit is to place enforceable rights in the hand of private individuals. This empowers individuals to take action to protect their own interests (which may intersect with a public good such as environmental protection) irrespective of whether a regulator is minded to act. The development of direct effect is the most obvious and celebrated manifestation of this approach in the context of EU

---

815. European Parliament and Council Directive (EC) 2001/80 on the limitation of emissions of certain pollutants into the air from large combustion plants [2001] O.J. L 309/1.
816. European Parliament and Council Directive (EC) 2008/1 concerning integrated pollution prevention and control [2008] O.J. L 24/8.
817. Commission (EC), 'Proposal for a Directive of the European Parliament and of the Council on industrial emissions (integrated pollution prevention and control)' COM (2007) 844 final, Dec. 21, 2007.
818. For an in depth analysis of the problem see Pál Wennerås, *The enforcement of EC environmental law* (OUP 2007).
819. This is in marked contrast to the somewhat draconion investigative powers enjoyed by the DG for Competition under Article 105 TFEU which inlcudes the notorious power to launch dawn raids and take away inciminating documents.

law. However, although direct effect has a useful role to play where the enforcement problem stems for failings on the part of the Member State, it has limited reach in horizontal disputes between non-state actors. Building a civil liability component into environmental measures provides one means of increasing the horizontal reach of environmental laws.

In the late 1980s the EC began considering the introduction of a European wide civil liability scheme for environmental damage. In essence, such a regime would have incorporated civil liability components into existing environmental measures. Thus, aside from any administrative or criminal penalties, private individuals suffering loss would be afforded a cause of action for 'breach of statutory duty'. This idea was certainly not new; as we have already seen, there are certain long standing examples of such statutory duties including section 12 of the Nuclear Installations Act 1965[820] which affords private parties a cause of action in respect of individual losses arising from breaches of the nuclear safety regime. However, an EC regime would have made such mechanisms the norm. A proposal for a directive on civil liability for caused by waste emerged in 1989[821] but was never adopted. During the course of the next twelve years or so the debate trundled on and yielded a green paper[822] and eventually a white paper[823] which considered a more generally applicable environmental liability system. The green and white papers never culminated in legislation extending the role of tort as a means of environmental protection. Instead the EU changed tack and promulgated a Directive designed to increase the use of administrative powers as a means of securing the clean-up or prevention of pollution.[824] Although the Directive is referred to as the ELD, it sets out a very different type of 'environmental liability' to the tort based system envisaged by the earlier discussion documents. Nevertheless the discussion exercise yielded much interesting material and debate. Many of the proposals which emerged,[825] such as strict liability as a default position, relaxing causality tests, broadening standing rights, refining the definition of damage and so on feature in some of the domestic laws discussed in the following chapters. In this respect the green and white papers are of more than historic value and continue to shed light on the debate. Furthermore, although the ELD deals with a very different type of liability, it addresses certain issues, such as causation, which are also relevant to any tort based system. In any event, there remains the possibility that the EU may yet revisit the issue and dust off these documents.

---

820. See disccussion of breach of statutory duty, above, at §2.07.
821. [1989] O.J. C 251/3; as amended by proposal [1991] O.J. C 192/7.
822. *Communication from the Commission to the Council and Parliament on Environmental Liability*, COM(93) 47 final.
823. EC Commission, *White Paper on Environmental Liabiltiy*, COM(2000) 66 final.
824. European Parliament and Council Directive 2004/35/EC on environmental liability with regard to the prevention and remedying of environmental damage [2004] O.J. L 143/56.
825. For an in depth analysis of the proposals which emerged from the 2000 White Paper see M. Wilde, *The EC Commission's White Paper on Environmental Liability: Issues and Implications*, 13(1) J. Envtl. L. 21 (2001).

§5.04 THE COUNCIL OF EUROPE CONVENTION ON CIVIL LIABILITY

In a broadly European context it is also necessary to have regard to a Council of Europe initiative, namely, the Council of Europe Convention on Civil Liability for Damage resulting from Activities Dangerous to the Environment (the *Lugano* Convention). The Convention has been open for signature for many years but has yet to gain the requisite ratifications necessary for it to come into force.[826] It is gradually accumulating dust and has not gained any new signatures since 1997. Thus, despite the fact that the Convention remains open for signature, it now seems doubtful whether it will ever come into force. Indeed, given the large overlap in membership between the Council of Europe and the EU, the fortunes of the Convention were always destined to be closely yoked to EU policy on the issue. Indeed, at one time the EC, as it then was, contemplated adopting the Convention as opposed to drafting its own environmental liability regime.[827] Nevertheless, the Convention is still worthy of consideration in that it provides a template for a tort based environmental liability regime and has doubtless inspired some of the initiatives which are reviewed in later chapters. In short, the Convention requires signatories to adopt strict liability regimes for environmental damage subject to certain defences and affords considerable standing to NGOs to pursue claims.

§5.05 INTERNATIONAL INITIATIVES ON ENVIRONMENTAL LIABILITY SCHEMES

It has proved exceedingly difficult to obtain international consensus on the issue of environmental liability. As previously noted, states are typically reluctant to alter domestic liability rules in a manner which may undermine sovereignty and may expose domestic industries to additional costs. Given these difficulties, it will come as little surprise to find that liability regimes have only been established in very limited areas, namely ship-source maritime pollution and the nuclear industry. There is outline agreement for a Convention on civil liability for damage caused by the transport of GMOs although, despite extensive studies, these plans have yet to reach fruition. The following gives a broad overview of each of these initiatives with a view to teasing out common themes such as strict liability and the provision of compensation themes. This will provide the backdrop for a more detailed analysis of some of these themes in subsequent chapters.

---

826. The Council of Europe Convention on civil liability resulting from activities dangerous to the environment; agreed in March 1993 and opened for signature at Lugano, Switzerland on 21 June 1993. To date, the Convention has been signed by Cyprus, Finland, Greece, Iceland, Italy, Liechtenstein, Luxembourg, Netherlands and Portugal. However, it will not come into force until it has been ratified by three states. As regards history and ratification status see Council of Europe website for the Convention at http://conventions.coe.int/treaty/Commun/ QueVoulezVous.asp?NT=150&CL=ENG (accessed Aug. 2011).

827. According to Mr Chris Clark, an official of the Environmental Directorate of the Commission, DGXI), addressing a seminar on environmental liability held by *Simmonds & Simmonds* on 27th September 1996. Reported by Environmental Data Services (ENDS), *Bjerregaard poised for fresh move on environmental liability*, [1996] 260 ENDS Report 38.

[A]   Maritime Pollution

Maritime oil disasters, from *Torrey Canyon* to *Deepwater Horizon*, have come to symbolize environmental degradation in its most extreme form. Images of oil slicks, stricken wildlife and contaminated beaches are now deeply embedded in the public consciousness and have become emblematic of the worst excesses of modern industrial society. To this rogues gallery can be added, the *Amoco Cadiz*, the *Exxon Valdez*, the *Erika* and the *Prestige*. In fact the *Torrey Canyon* disaster was largely responsible for pushing environmental concerns up the political agenda. The *Torrey Canyon* was one of the new breed of super-tanker with a capacity of 120 thousand tons of crude oil. It foundered off the coast of Cornwall on 18 March 1967. The scale of the oil slick and the futile attempts of the RAF and Royal Navy to burn off the oil by dropping bombs attracted worldwide attention and a fair amount of ridicule. The disaster proved to be the catalyst which brought about one of the first examples of international cooperation in environmental matters. In 1969 the ICCOP (1969 Civil Liability Convention)[828] was established under the auspices of the International Maritime Organization (IMO). This established strict liability for oil pollution damage, subject to certain defences, and harmonized the types of damage claim and clean-up costs which could be met. The 1969 Convention was soon followed by the 1971 International Convention on the Establishment of an International Fund for Compensation for Oil Pollution Damage (1971 Fund Convention).[829] This supplemented the 1969 Civil Liability Convention with a compensation fund so as to meet a proportion of the claims which could not be met under the liability regime.

The essence of this system, namely a two pronged regime comprising a liability system supplemented by a compensation fund, remains in place to this day. Although in 1992 the regime was amended by two Protocols; the amended measures are known as the 1992 ICCOP (1992 Civil Liability Convention)[830] and the 1992 International Convention on the Establishment of an International Fund for Compensation for Oil Pollution Damage (1992 Fund Convention).[831]

As regards the 1992 civil liability regime, the main aspects include the imposition of strict liability – although certain defences are available.[832] It covers 'pollution damage' which is defined as loss or damage caused outside the ship although costs associated with rectifying environmental impairment are subject to a test of reasonableness.[833] Overall, 'pollution damage' is not defined in any great detail and there is still much scope for interpretation in domestic courts. As we have seen in Chapter 3, in

---

828. 9 ILM (1970) 45.
829. 11 ILM (1972) 284.
830. See International Oil Pollution Compensation Fund (IOPC), *Liability and Compensation for Oil Pollution Damage:Texts of the 1992 Conventions and the Supplementary Fund Protocol* (2005 edition), http://www.iopcfund.org/npdf/Conventions%20English.pdf (accessed Sept. 13, 2011).
831. *Ibid.*
832. 1992 Liability Convention, Article III.
833. *Ibid.*, Article I(6).

the English and Scottish cases there has been much debate as to whether this definition encompasses economic losses.[834] In any event, it is clear that the extent of an operator's liability may vary hugely dependent upon in which jurisdiction the vessel came to grief; although, it must be noted that the Convention enables the operator to cap his liability in accordance with a calculation based upon the tonnage of the vessel.[835]

The 1992 Fund Convention is financed by a levy on persons, whether governments, public bodies, or private enterprises, which import more than 150,000 tonnes of oil per year.[836] This clearly encompasses all states which are reliant upon oil imports and private enterprises such as downstream oil refiners dependent upon overseas supplies of crude. The fund has its own governing and administrative mechanisms including an assembly comprising the parties to the convention and an executive committee.[837] Following amendments in 2000 the total amount payable under the fund in respect of a particular incident is capped at 203 million Special Drawing Rights (SDR)[838] which roughly equates to USD 260 million. This amount can be increased if contributions to the fund have been augmented by three or more parties importing more than 600 million tonnes per year (which of course increases the levies payable into the fund).[839] In 2003 a final 'backstop' was introduced to establish a third tier of compensation where limits are exhausted under both the liability and fund conventions. The 2003 Protocol to the 1992 Fund Convention (the 2003 Supplementary Fund Protocol) establishes another pot of money although there is a *total cap*, comprising all sums payable under the liability and both fund regimes combined, of 750 million SDR.[840]

Although less dramatic than accidental spillages of crude oil from super-tankers and the like, pollution damage from bunker oil (the heavy fuel oil used in ships engines) causes major environmental damage. Furthermore, much of the pollution stems from deliberate releases associated with the illegal washing out of empty fuel tanks at sea. Accidental spillages may arise from the grounding or sinking of a ship. The 2001 International Convention on Civil Liability for Bunker Oil Damages[841] closely resembles the 1992 Civil Liability Convention in that it imposes strict liability and contains a similar definition of damage and liability may be capped. Key additional features include a requirement to obtain compulsory insurance in respect of this type of harm and the right to pursue claims directly against the insurer.

---

834. See §3.05[A][2], above. This issue shall be returned to below (see §10.04[C]) in the context of the extent to which economic loss should be regarded as a component of environmental harm.
835. 1992 Liability Convention, Article V.
836. 1992 Fund Convention, Article 10.
837. *Ibid.*, Article 16.
838. *Ibid.*, Article 4(4)(a),(b). An SDR is a form of credit unit issued by the International Monetary Fund (IMF); its value is determined on the basis of a basket of currencies and the idea is that it can be traded without one party losing out due to the vageries of exchange rates.
839. *Ibid.*, Article 4(4)(c).
840. *Ibid.*, Article 36(4).
841. 40 ILM 40 (2002).

As noted at the beginning of this section, most recently the name *Deepwater Horizon* was added to the list of the world's worst maritime oil pollution disasters. However, it is important to note that oil spillages from oil exploration are not covered by the maritime oil pollution conventions described above. In the event, the absence of such a regime had little effect on the liability issues arising from *Deepwater Horizon*. As we have seen, the political ramifications of the disaster resulted in BP agreeing to a compensation package which far exceeds the caps set by domestic law.[842] Neverthe-less, the disaster demonstrates the risks associated with deepwater drilling and the potential for transboundary pollution is clear. Deepwater Horizon could well serve as the touchstone for an international agreement on civil liability for damage caused by oil exploration and drilling in the same way that the *Torrey Canyon* proved to be the catalysts for the original 1969 Liability Convention on oil pollution from ships.[843]

To date international cooperation on liability for maritime oil pollution damage has been focused upon oil pollution; this is hardly surprising given the high profile nature of oil pollution damage arising from spectacular disasters. However, a great many other hazardous substances, such as chemicals and waste, are also transported around the world in bulk. Yet it is only in recent times that attempts have been made to establish a liability and compensation fund along the lines of those discussed above. The 1996 International Convention on Liability and Compensation for Damage in Connection with the Carriage of Hazardous and Noxious Substances (HNS Conven-tion)[844] seeks to plug this gap. The Convention follows the above models in that it establishes liability rules supplemented by a compensation fund (capped at 250 million SDR) financed by certain recipients of bulk hazardous cargoes; the chemicals industry is an obvious example.

[B]   Liability for Nuclear Accidents

In the post war years nuclear energy was seen as a panacea for solving the world's energy requirements. It is significant that the founders of the European integration project saw fit to devote an entire Treaty (Eurotom) to the technology.[845] It was not long, however, before the hazardous nature of the technology became apparent. In 1957 a fire in a nuclear reactor at the Windscale plant caused substantial localized damage and contamination of neighbouring farmland; a more widespread nuclear calamity was narrowly avoided.[846] In 1979 a core melt down occurred at the Three Mile Island plant near Harrisburg in the US leading to the release of approximately 2.5

---

842. See §3.05[A][2], above.
843. For an analysis of the gaps in the international oil pollution liability regimes highlighted by the Deepwater Horizon see J. Allen, *A Global Oil Stain – Cleaning up International Conventions for Liability and Compensation for Oil Exploration/Production*, 25(1) A. & N. Z. Mar. L.J. 90 (2011).
844. 35 ILM 1415 (1996).
845. Treaty Establishing the European Atomic Energy Community (Euratom).
846. See R. Batten, *A Significant Moment in the Development of Nuclear Liability and Compensation: Dealing with the Consequences of the Windscale Fire 1957*, 3 Ex Historia 79 (2011).

million curies of radiation.[847] This was followed by the worst accident in the history of the industry, namely, the notorious Chernobyl disaster in 1986. A reactor exploded as a result of a botched experiment which placed the reactor in an unstable state. The explosion resulted in massive localized contamination and transboundary pollution stretching as far as Western Europe.[848] Most recently the disaster at the Fukushima plant, which was stricken by a tsunami, has again highlighted the perils of the technology should all safety mechanisms fail.[849]

In the UK the damage to the local farming industry, caused by the Windscale fire, highlighted the need for a compensation scheme.[850] Parliament responded with the Nuclear Installations (Licensing and Insurance) Act 1959 which was soon superseded by the Nuclear Installations Act 1965. In a simultaneous development, which may also have been prompted in no small measure by the Windscale Fire, the 1960 Convention on Third Party Liability in the Field of Nuclear Energy[851] was signed in Paris under the auspices of the OECD (the Paris Convention). Key features of the original Paris Convention include strict liability for personal injuries and property damage and the channelling of liability to the operators of nuclear plants and the transport of nuclear material. Liability is capped[852] and claims are subject to limitation periods. In addition there is a requirement for the operators of nuclear plants to carry appropriate insurance. In 1963 the Convention Supplementary to the Paris Convention (Brussels Convention) established a compensation fund (financed by public funds from the signatory states) to meet claims which could not be met under the Paris Convention. Thus, the basic elements of the system are identical to the mechanisms already discussed in relation to maritime pollution, namely, a liability regime based upon strict liability supplemented by compensation funds. In 2004 amendments were introduced to the Paris/Brussels Conventions with a view to massively raising the ceiling on liabilities[853] and broadening the definition of damage so as to include environmental

---

847. Not surprisingly there is a huge amount of historical literature and articles on the disaster; however, for a particularly gripping and detailed account see J.S.Walker, *Three Mile Island: A Nuclear Crisis in Historical Perspective* (University of California Press 2004).

848. For the most comprehensive account to date on the extent of the environmental damage stemming from Chernobyl see A.V. Yablokov, V.B. Nesterenko & A.V. Nesterenko, *Chernobyl: Consequences of the Catastrophe for People and the Environment*, vol. 1181 (Annals of the New York Academy of Sciences 2009).

849. As an on-going situation at the time of writing there are continual developments which can be followed on the International Atomic Energy Authority (IAEA) webpages on the subject: IAEA, *Fukushima Nuclear Accident*, http://www.iaea.org/newscenter/focus/fukushima/ (accessed Sept. 24, 2012).

850. See Batten (n. 846).

851. 29 July 1960, in force 1 April 1968; UKTS 69 (1968). For the full text of the treaty and ratification status etc. see webpages maintained by the Nuclear Energy Agency (a branch of the OECD) at http://www.oecd-nea.org/law/paris-convention.html (accessed Sept. 20, 2011).

852. As regards the operators of nuclear plants liability is capped at 15 million Special Drawing Rights (SDR) and 5 million SDR for the transporters of nuclear material; see Article 7 Paris Convention.

853. 2004 Protocol to Amend the Paris Convention, para H. This raises the liability of operators of nuclear operators to ¤700 million; those engaged in 'low risk' nuclear activities to ¤70 million; and those engaged in the transport of nuclear material to ¤80 million. See OECD (NEA) website http://www.oecd-nea.org/law/paris-convention-protocol.html (accessed Sept. 20, 2011).

impairment.[854] It is noteworthy that the changes were prompted by the Chernobyl disaster despite the fact that a protocol was not adopted until 2004. At the time of writing, on the 25th anniversary of the disaster, the changes are still not in force.

The Paris Convention is a regional convention in that it only comprises twelve Western European States. In 1963 the International Atomic Energy Agency (IAEA) secured the adoption of a broader based treaty open to all other states – the 1963 Vienna Convention on Civil Liability for Nuclear Damage.[855] Initially, the treaty focused on property damage and personal injuries although it allowed some flexibility for competent courts to adopt broader definitions in accordance with domestic laws. However, in the wake of the Chernobyl disaster, a 1997 Protocol was introduced which broadened the definition of damage to include economic loss arising from death, personal injury and property damage and costs associated with remediating environmental impairment.[856] The fact that there are two similar treaties governing the same issue is clearly unsatisfactory. In order to reduce duplication and uncertainty a 1988 Protocol was introduced with a view to coordinating the treaties and clarifying jurisdictional matters.[857] Nevertheless, there is still a major difference between the Paris and Vienna Conventions in that the latter does not establish a compensation fund for settling those claims which cannot be met through the application of liability rules. In 1997 a further instrument, the Convention on Supplementary Compensation for Nuclear Damage, was agreed, again under the auspices of the IAEA.[858] Assuming that it eventually comes into force, it will establish a single compensation fund linked to both the Paris and Vienna Conventions. As with the current fund operated under the Paris/Brussels Conventions, the fund will be financed by state contributions from public monies. The formula for calculating the contributions to the fund from each contracting state is complex. In short, the basic starting point is 300 SDR for each 'unit of installed capacity'; in other words 300 SDR for each megawatt produced by nuclear energy.

From the above it is apparent that there is a long standing internationally agreed system for meeting civil claims arising from cross-border nuclear contamination. However, there is little evidence to suggest that these instruments have had a major

---

854. *Ibid.*, see para B 2004 Protocol.
855. 21 May 1963, in force 12 November 1977; 2 ILM 727 (1963). For the full text of the treaty and ratification status etc. see webpages maintained by the IAEA at http://www.iaea.org/ Publications/Documents/Conventions/liability.html (accessed Oct. 6, 2011). For example, the protocol provides that the operator of a nuclear facility in a state which is party to the Vienna Convention may be liable for damage to a state which is party to the Paris convention and vice versa. Thus an operator in the Russian Federation (party to the Vienna Convention) would be liable in respect of damage caused in Finland (part to the Paris Convention) and vice versa. Liability shall be determined in accordance with whichever convention applies in the state where the plant is located.
856. Protocol to Amend the Vienna Convention on Civil Liability for Nuclear Damage, 29 September 1997, in force 4 October 2003, 36 I.L.M. 1454, 1462 (1997). See A. Layard, *Nuclear Liability Damage Reform after Chernobyl*, 5(3) Rev. Eur. Community Intl. Envtl. L. 218 (1996).
857. Joint Protocol Relating to the Application of the Vienna Convention and the Paris Convention (Vienna) of 21 September 1988, in force 27 April 1992; 42 Nuclear Law Bulletin 56 (1988).
858. Convention on Supplementary Compensation for Nuclear Damage (Vienna) of 12 November 1997, not yet in force; 36 ILM 1473 (1997).

effect on the allocation of losses arising from nuclear accidents. This is largely due to the fact that nuclear accidents, on a scale which gives rise to transboundary pollution, are thankfully rare. The Chernobyl disaster occurred some ten years before the former Soviet states at the heart of the incident, Ukraine and the Russian Federation, acceded to the Vienna Convention. In any case, the scale of such a disaster calls into question whether such liability rules could have dealt with more than a fraction of the total claims. Furthermore, it has become increasingly apparent that spectacular disasters are not the greatest risk associated with nuclear plants. Experience has demonstrated that much nuclear contamination is of a chronic nature, that is to say, low level and gradual releases accumulating over many years. The fact that much of the nuclear liability legislation is based upon the catastrophic disaster scenario means that it is not well suited to dealing with claims of this nature. These are issues which shall be returned to in due course in the context of the role and limitations of civil liability.

[C] Liability for Damage Caused by Transboundary Movements of Hazardous Wastes

Waste is a valuable commodity and is frequently shipped over large distances thereby increasing the risk of accidents and escapes of harmful elements. The 1989 UNEP Basel Convention[859] seeks to control the transboundary movement of wastes and introduced a system of prior-informer consent so as to ensure that all movements are carefully logged and tracked. In 1999 a Protocol was added with a view to introducing a liability and compensation system in respect of transboundary damage caused through the international movement of hazardous waste.[860] The Protocol is still not in force although its key features are worthy of note. Damage is afforded a wide definition and includes loss of life, personal injury and certain forms of economic loss arising from a direct interest in a damaged natural resource.[861] In addition it provides for the recovery of costs associated with preventing environmental damage[862] or remediating damage which has already occurred.[863] Strict liability is initially imposed on the person who notifies the state to which the waste is to be shipped (according to the prior-informed consent system set out in the main Basel Convention). Liability passes from the transferor of the waste to the disposer in the destination state once the latter is in possession of the material.[864] In addition, certain other parties who deal with the waste may incur fault based liability.[865] Liability is capped[866] although all parties who may be

---

859. Basel Convention on the Control of Transboundary Movements of Hazardous Wastes and their Disposal of 22 March 1989, in force 5 May 1992; 28 ILM 657 (1989).
860. Basel Protocol on Liability and Compensation for Damage Resulting from Transboundary Movements of Hazardous Wastes and their Disposal (Basel) of 10 December 1999, not yet in force; EMuT 989:22/B. For full text of the Protocol and ratification status etc. see webpage maintained by UNEP at http://basel.int/pub/protocol.html (accessed Nov. 4, 2011).
861. *Ibid.*, Article 2(1)(c).
862. *Ibid.*, Article 2(1)(e).
863. *Ibid.*, Article 2(1)(d).
864. *Ibid.*, Artcile 4.
865. *Ibid.*, Article 5.
866. *Ibid.*, Article 12 and Annex B.

potentially liable for loss under the Protocol are expected to adopt financial security measures such as insurance.[867] The Protocol does not establish a new oil pollution type compensation fund in respect of damage costs which exceed the cap on liability. Rather, it refers to 'existing mechanisms'[868] which, according to the explanatory manual, means the Technical Cooperation Trust Fund set up under the main Basel Convention.[869] The parties to the Convention are required to continually review the need for further compensation mechanisms.

[D]   GMOs and Transboundary Pollution

Transboundary pollution arising from the escape of GMOs constitutes the only other substantive area in which moves have been made towards establishing internationally recognized liability rules. Although, as we shall see, the results have been modest to say the least.

On 29 January 2000 the Cartagena Protocol on Biosafety[870] was adopted as an additional measure to the Convention on Biological Diversity. In short the Cartagena Protocol seeks to control the transfrontier shipments of GM material in a manner which prevents unplanned releases into the environment. Article 27 of the Protocol required the contracting parties to establish liability rules for dealing with the consequences of such unplanned releases. An obvious example would include an accidental spillage at a location where transboundary pollution is likely; such as a lorry laden with GM seed overturning near a national frontier. Having carried out an extensive study of liability rules pertaining in different states the Conference of the Parties (the body charged with implementing Article 27) adopted a liability regime similar to the EU ELD.[871] As previously noted,[872] the ELD utilizes public law mechanisms, as opposed to private law, and stipulates that environmental regulators must be empowered to effect the clean-up of pollution and to recover the costs from the polluter. The mechanism adopted pursuant to Article 27 of the Cartagena Protocol is enshrined in the Nagoya – Kuala Lumpur Supplementary Protocol on Liability and Redress to the Cartagena Protocol on Biosafety.[873] The Supplementary Protocol is highly redolent of the ELD Directive in that it requires a competent authority to be charged with the task of dealing with the consequences, or the imminent risk of GM contamination. The competent authority may take action itself and recover the costs *ex poste* from the operator. Alternatively, it may require the operator to take preventative or remedial measures itself. Presumably, the authorities in the state where the operator is based are required

---

867. *Ibid.*, Article 14.
868. *Ibid.*, Article 15.
869. Instruction Manual for the Implementation of the Basel Protocol on Liability and Compensation for Damage Resulting from Transboundary Movements of Hazardous Wastes and their Disposal, 17–18 http://basel.int/protocol/instmanual/index.html (accessed Nov. 4, 2011).
870. 29 January 2000, in force 11 September 2003; 39 ILM 1027 (2000).
871. European Council and European Parliament Directive 2004/35/EC on environmental liability with regard to the prevention and remedying of environmental damage OJ L 143/56.
872. See §5.03, above.
873. 15 October 2010, opened for signature 7 March 2011 (not yet in force); http://bch.cbd.int/protocol/supplementary/ (accessed Oct. 21, 2011).

to cooperate with the authorities in the state where the damage occurs with a view to ensuring that these remediation costs can be recovered; although this issue is not dealt with in any detail.

However, the Supplementary Protocol has very little to say on the issue of civil liability. Extensive research was undertaken into how tortious liability issues arising from GM contamination was dealt with in various states.[874] It was noted that some states dealt with such issues under existing laws on tortious or non-contractual liability. Other states dealt with the issue under general environmental liability regimes whereas a number had introduced specific civil liability rules on GM contamination. Rather than seeking to harmonize these differing approaches, Article 12 of the Supplementary Protocol effectively maintains the status quo by enabling signatory states to adhere to existing approaches. Thus, states may continue to apply their existing laws, including general civil liability rules; adopt new laws specifically geared towards damage caused by GM contamination; or adopt a combination of the two approaches. All that can be said about the Supplementary Protocol is that it does at least provide that states must have some form of liability mechanism in place for providing injured parties with compensation in respect of GM damage. However, as we shall see in the forthcoming chapters, liability rules vary enormously in different states in terms of the standard of liability, causation, definition of damage and so forth. In this respect the Supplementary Protocol will do nothing to alleviate conflict of law problems and 'forum shopping' as parties endeavour to resolve disputes in the jurisdiction which is most amenable to their case.

[E]   The International Law Commission's Draft Principles

One further instrument is worthy of note in this context, namely, the International Law Commission's (ILC) 'Draft Principles on the Allocation of Loss in the case of Trans-boundary Harm Arising out of Hazardous Activities.'[875] From the above analysis it is apparent that initiatives in this area have all been sector specific. Circa 2001 the ILC was charged with the task of establishing a much broader international liability system in respect of transboundary harm caused by hazardous activities. Initially there had been talk of establishing an ambitious new Treaty in order to set the rules in concrete.[876] However, given the difficulty experienced in securing international agreement on liability regimes which are very narrow in scope, this objective looked

---

874. Intergovernmental Committee for the Cartagena Protocol on Biosafety, 'Liability and Redress for Damage Resulting from Transboundary movements of Living Modified Organisms' (Report) UNEP/CBD/ICCP/3/3, 6 March 2002. For a more detailed account of the contents of the report see M. Wilde, *Liability Issues Associated with Genetically Modified Organisms: EU and International Developments*, in *Environmental Liability in the EU: the 2004 Environmental Liability Directive compared with US and Member State Law*, 292–298 (G. Betlem & E. Brans eds., Cameron May 2006).
875. International Law Commission (ILC), *Yearbook of the International Law Commission* vol. 2 Part 2 (United Nations, 2006).
876. For a detailed account of the background to the ILC proposals see A.E. Boyle, *Globalising Environmental Liability: The Interplay of National and International Law*, 17(1) J. Envtl. L. 3 (2005).

unattainable from the outset and was quickly abandoned in favour of a soft law approach.

In short the 2006 Draft Principles encourage states to cooperate in resolving disputes arising from transboundary pollution and to adapt existing domestic laws where necessary. It also operates as a template for any new international legislation on liability in specific areas, although, as we have seen, such initiatives are few and far between. Notwithstanding the limited prospects for international agreements, there is also an expectation that they could form the basis of bilateral agreements between neighbouring states. In many respects the principles do little more than restate the long established principle of customary international law at issue in Trail Smelter, namely, that cross-border polluting emissions constitute an infringement upon the sovereignty of the state in which the harm occurs. However, this basic duty is fleshed out with a number of more detailed principles setting out how such disputes should be resolved.

The key elements of the Draft Principles include imposition of strict liability on the operator and the provision of prompt and efficient compensation mechanisms including insurance and state backed compensation funds of the type which we have already met. It is also provided that the state in which the operator is based should take certain steps to ensure that states at risk of transboundary pollution are notified and that the operator is made to comply with its obligations. Furthermore, it is provided that injured parties should have access to legal remedies in the state of origin in addition to the state where the harm occurred. This could conceivably open the way for victims to choose the forum which is most amenable to its claim. However, it is difficult to see how this could be achieved without the conclusion of an international treaty between the parties concerned. In this respect it is possible that the ILC would hold up the Brussels II Convention[877] as a model which, as has been seen, allows some scope for moving the forum to a state other than where the damage occurred.

Whether the ILC draft principles will have a profound effect remains to be seen; nevertheless, it is hoped that, by influencing law and policy makers in different states, they may contribute to the glacially slow process of eroding the distinctions between jurisdictions in the field of environmental liability.

§5.06   CONCLUSIONS

Rules on tortious liability initially arose as a response to localized harm. In recent decades the phenomenon of transboundary pollution has become better understood and it is clear that there must be international cooperation in terms of harmonizing liability rules in this context. Otherwise, jurisdictional disputes will continue to inhibit attempts to seek redress in respect of this type of harm. The first edition of this book heavily concentrated on EU initiatives commencing with the late 1980s and early 1990s proposals for Directives on liability for damage caused by waste. Although it must be noted that single market considerations may have carried more weight in early initiatives. The EU continued to drive the debate for the next twenty years; however,

---

877. See n. 797, above, Article 14.

the ELD which eventually emerged from this protracted process was a very different beast to the tort based system which had been eagerly anticipated. In short the ELD adopted a public law approach as opposed to a private law approach and relies upon administrative powers conferred on public authorities. However, this measure does not pretend to provide a complete solution to the problem and does not attempt to secure redress for individual victims. In this respect there remains a need for greater international cooperation in this field.

As we have seen, international attempts to harmonize tort based liability rules in respect of certain forms of transboundary environmental harm span fifty years. However, such initiatives are extremely narrow in scope and the only established systems cover nuclear contamination and maritime oil pollution. Recent attempts to harmonize liability rules for GM contamination have resulted in a somewhat anaemic provision which allows states to apply existing domestic laws. Attempts by the International Law Commission to introduce a more wide-ranging system of civil liability for transboundary harm met with considerable resistance from states keen to protect their sovereign rights. It now seems most unlikely that any new treaty will emerge from this initiative.

Thus, it seems that tort based liability rules in different jurisdictions will continue to diverge sharply in terms of standards of liability, causation, definitions of damage and so on. Nevertheless, a number of states have pressed ahead with their own liability regimes. As regards conflict of laws, it now seems well accepted that liability must be determined according to the state in which the harm was manifested. In this respect it is possible to argue that states may be provided with an indirect incentive to improve the robustness of their domestic regimes. For example, imagine a scenario in which there are two neighbouring states; one has especially stringent liability rules and one has lax liability rules. An operator in the state with more stringent liability rules may be induced to site his factory near the border at a location where prevailing winds and river currents transport the pollution into the neighbouring state. Such a scenario may encourage the neighbouring state to tighten its liability rules so as to avoid becoming a dumping ground for cross-border pollution. Unless, of course, the state has so little regard for its environment that it is willing to use its lack of environmental controls as a means of attracting unscrupulous operators with a view to gaining a competitive advantage. Although, within the EU, the market integration project is designed to eradicate such practices by means of raising the standard of environmental protection in all states.

In any event, despite the fact that EU initiatives on a tort based system of environmental liability have petered out for the moment at least, the issue is still very much alive and worthy of detailed consideration. If liability rules within Member States continue to diverge sharply the EU may be forced to look at the issue afresh in the interests of the proper functioning of the internal market. Moreover, the enlargement of the EU has brought the issue of transboundary pollution to the fore as many new Eastern European states struggle to replace crumbling Soviet era infrastructure. The following part of this book shall be devoted to an analysis of substantive liability rules and the extent to which they can be adapted so as to facilitate a greater role for tort in an environmental context.

Part IV: Increasing the Role of Tort as a Means of Environmental Protection: A Comparative Analysis of Substantive Rules in Certain EU States and their Common Law Counterparts

CHAPTER 6

Strict Liability

§6.01   INTRODUCTION

As we have seen, liability in tort is often contingent upon the need to establish some degree of fault on the part of the operator. From an Anglo-American perspective, negligence provides the basis of liability in most cases and is the cornerstone of the tort system. However, as the foregoing analysis has demonstrated, negligence increases the evidential burden on claimants thereby resulting in higher transaction costs. In certain cases, tort systems may replace fault based liability with strict liability. This may occur where it has been determined that the need to safeguard the public and provide adequate compensation outweighs the need to establish any form of moral culpability on the part of the defendant. For example, where a hazardous activity is concerned, it may be determined that the party who creates the risk and derives certain economic benefits from it is in the best position to bear any losses resulting from that activity. As noted in previous chapters such policy considerations lie behind the judgment in *Rylands v. Fletcher* which established strict liability in respect of 'non natural' land uses in the UK. More recently, the EC determined that strict liability should be imposed on producers of defective goods[878] since producers are in a better position to bear such losses than the consumer. Furthermore, consumers could face insurmountable difficulties in attempting to establish that a producer was at fault in failing to identify a defect in a new product.

For similar reasons, it seems that strict liability is usually regarded as an automatic prerequisite of any environmental liability regime. Certainly, strict liability is a feature of most environmental liability systems already introduced in certain EU Member States. However, strict liability is by no means a fixed or universal standard. Strict liability is not the same as absolute liability in that strict liability affords scope for

---

878. Council Directive 85/374/EEC on the approximation of the laws, regulations and administrative provisions of the Member States concerning liability for defective products O.J. L 210/29.

defences. The strictness of the duty can be raised or lowered depending on the range of defences which may be built into the regime. As will be seen below, there are significant differences between the regimes implemented in Member States on this issue. Further important issues concern the scope of strict liability; for example, should strict liability be triggered by the nature of the activity causing the harm or the nature of the harm itself? These are important issues which any specialist liability system needs to address.

§6.02   THE NATURE OF LIABILITY UNDER THE GENERAL LAW OF TORT IN EU MEMBER STATES

Continental civil jurisdictions are no different to their common law world counterparts inasmuch as general tort laws may be used in respect of environmental damage. The law of negligence (or its equivalents) is a universal constant and is normally the default remedy in most jurisdictions. However, stricter forms of liability may be adopted within existing legal frameworks. In some cases fault based rules may be applied in a more stringent manner which blurs the boundaries with strict liability. Moreover, property based torts are less preoccupied with issues of fault and the focus is on the protection of certain rights in land. In other cases special rules, akin to *Rylands v. Fletcher*, may apply to hazardous activities which cause various types of loss including pollution damage.

The ubiquitous tort of negligence may be used where a polluter has breached a duty of care owed to a specific party. For example §823 of the German Civil Code *Das (Burgerliches Gesetzbuch*: BGB)[879] establishes fault based liability in respect of physical harm. German law draws a rigid distinction between tangible injuries of this nature and the more ephemeral or nebulous nuisance type harms which must be dealt with under §906 BGB. Thus, in the leading *Kupolofen* (or Smelting Oven) case,[880] which concerned damage to the paint-work of cars caused by emissions from the smelter, the claimants were compelled to seek damages under §823 BGB which necessitated establishing fault.

As we have already seen in respect of common law jurisdictions, the need to establish a breach of the duty of care is one of the main factors which have limited the use of negligence based remedies in an environmental context. However, it is interesting to note that courts in some jurisdictions have managed to alleviate these difficulties within the confines of existing tort laws. For example, in the afore-mentioned *Kupolofen* case, it was held that the burden of proof could be reversed in

---

879. '(1)A person who, intentionally or negligently, unlawfully injures the life, body, health, freedom, property or another right of another person is liable to make compensation to the other party for the damage arising from this. (2)The same duty is held by a person who commits a breach of a statute that is intended to protect another person. If, according to the contents of the statute, it may also be breached without fault, then liability to compensation only exists in the case of fault.' (official translation published by *Bundesministerium de Justiz* at http://www.gesetze-im-internet.de/englisch_bgb/englisch_bgb.html (accessed Nov. 23, 2011)).
880. (1985) BGHZ 92, 143. See B. Markesinis and H. Unberath, *The German Law of Torts: A Comparative Treatise* (Hart Publishing, 2002).

such cases thus placing the onus on the defendant to exculpate himself. This suggests that, where damage has been caused by excessive emissions, there is an assumption that the emissions must have resulted from a breach of duty. It seems that an overtly policy based justification was adopted for this approach based upon the importance of environmental protection. An analogy was drawn with products liability law in which the burden may be reversed on the grounds that the defendant is in a better position to produce evidence than the claimant.[881] In the UK this would be regarded as 'judicial legislation' and the courts would recoil from implementing such radical new rules for unashamedly policy based reasons. The nearest equivalent principle which may lead to an assumption of fault in English law is res ipsa loquitur[882] which may lead to an assumption of fault in some cases. Although, as the courts have been at pains to point out, the principle does not reverse the burden of proof. It merely enables the court to make a finding of fault on the available evidence if an alternative explanation is not forthcoming. Aside from reversing the burden of proof on the lines of the German model, the imposition of a very high standard of care may result in de facto strict liability. Hinterleggar notes that this is the case in Spain 'where scholars already speak of an "objectivisation" of fault liability, which, in its practical application, comes close to strict liability.'[883] This blurring of the line between negligence based and strict liability is also exemplified in Belgium and France where the foreseeability requirement may be dispensed with where there has been a breach of a statutory duty.[884]

Fault plays a lesser role in the torts to land such as trespass and private nuisance. Liability is triggered by an interference with certain interests in land rather than fault on the part of the polluter. Nevertheless, as has been explained with regard to the common law cases, this 'strict' standard of liability has been watered down by the need to establish foreseeability of harm in some cases. Laws equivalent to the common law of nuisance (variously described as 'laws of the neighbourhood' or 'troubles de voisinage')[885] can be found in most continental jurisdictions. These mirror the common law position inasmuch as the standard of liability is stricter than under the general law of negligence. For example, §906 BGB (German Civil Code)[886] establishes liability for

---

881. See M. Hinteregger (ed.), *Environmental Liability and Ecological Damage in European Law*, 579–580 (CUP 2008). Hintergger makes that a similar approach was adopted in an Austrian decision and that it would also be possible under the Greek civil code.

882. See §2.06[B][1], above.

883. *Ibid.*, 579.

884. *Ibid.*, 580.

885. *Ibid.*, 70 and 104 (pertaining to the position in French Law).

886. See § 906 BGB (official translation published by Bundesministerium de Justiz at http://www.gesetze-im-internet.de/englisch_bgb/englisch_bgb.html (accessed Nov. 23, 2011)), '(1)The owner of a plot of land may not prohibit the introduction of gases, steam, smells, smoke, soot, warmth, noise, vibrations and similar influences emanating from another plot of land to the extent that the influence does not interfere with the use of his plot of land, or interferes with it only to an insignificant extent. An insignificant interference is normally present if the limits or targets laid down in statutes or by statutory orders are not exceeded by the influences established and assessed under these provisions. The same applies to values in general administrative provisions that have been issued under section 48 of the Federal Environmental Impact Protection Act [*Bundes-Immissionsschutzgesetz*] and represent the state of the art.'

interferences with a neighbour's use of land provided that such interferences are not 'insignificant.' As noted above, the *Kupolofen* case precludes claims arising from physical damage and channels them to §823 BGB on negligence based liability. The nuisance provision of the BGB is very similar to the English common law of nuisance in that express reference is made to the nature of the locality. However, there is a crucial difference to the common law position in that it is acknowledged that the fact that an activity is consistent with the character of the neighbourhood does not necessarily lessen the impact on the claimant. Thus, the polluter may still be required to make a compensatory payment in return for continuing his activities.[887] Another crucial aspect is that the provision makes express reference to the fact that interferences may not be regarded as significant if they stem from industrial emissions which are consistent with regulatory limits. In English law emission limits and the like normally operate without prejudice to existing common law rights. Moreover, it seems that in most jurisdictions a degree of foreseeability is normally required in the sense that an operator knew that his activity was harmful or at least potentially harmful.

Finally, most jurisdictions contain special strict liability rules pertaining to hazardous activities which closely resemble the English common law principle of *Rylands v. Fletcher*.[888] Special liability rules of this nature can be used in respect of pollution damage although such loss may not be the specific focus of the tort. For example, Articles 6:175–178 of the Dutch Civil Code (Burgerlijk Wetboek:BW) establish strict liability where a person uses dangerous substances for professional purposes and damage is caused as a result of that activity.[889] Aside from personal injuries and damage to property the provisions may be used to seek compensation in respect of wider environmental harms including the pollution of air, water and soil. However, it is necessary to show that the harm was foreseeable which mirrors the application of *Rylands v. Fletcher* following the House of Lords decision in *Cambridge Water v. Eastern Counties Leather*.[890] Here, it will be recalled, the House of Lords determined that *Rylands* did not impose absolute liability, rather, the hazardous properties of the substance and its propensity to escape must have been foreseeable. A similar provision can be found in Article 1384 § 1 of the French Civil Code which imposes strict liability on the 'custodian' of a 'dangerous object.'[891]

From the foregoing it is apparent that fault based liability tends to be the default position in most European states although de facto strict liability may be introduced by establishing a very high duty of care in some cases. Strict liability exists under general

---

887. *Ibid.*, '(2)The same applies to the extent that a material interference is caused by a use of the other plot of land that is customary in the location and cannot be prevented by measures that are financially reasonable for users of this kind. Where the owner is obliged to tolerate an influence under these provisions, he may require from the user of the other plot of land reasonable compensation in money if the influence impairs a use of the owner's plot of land that is customary in the location or its income beyond the degree that the owner can be expected to tolerate.'
888. See §2.04, above.
889. See Hinteregger (n. 881) 138–139.
890. [1994] 2 A.C. 264. See §2.03[C], above.
891. *Ibid.*, 73.

civil laws concerning neighbourhood disputes and hazardous activities. However, whilst such torts may offer some scope for holding polluters strictly liable for environmental damage, their capacity to do so may be limited. As we have already seen in common law jurisdictions, neighbourhood disputes are typically governed by the 'property torts' and are only open to those with a sufficient interest in land. Special strict liability rules pertaining to hazardous activities are limited by the need to show that the defendant's activities were unusual or exceptionally dangerous. Thus, in order to establish strict liability for a wide range of environmental harms arising from everyday industrial activities, it is usually necessary to introduce specialist environmental liability legislation. Consumer protection legislation is commonly cited as a model for such an approach.

Nevertheless, strict liability is not a fixed concept and the stringency of the standard varies greatly according to the types of harm to which it applies and the extent to which specific defences are permitted. Clearly, the more defences that are made available the more the strictness of the standard is diluted. As a result, it is instructive to consider how strict liability has been used in environmental liability regimes in EU Member States.

§6.03 INTRODUCTION OF STRICT LIABILITY REGIMES IN EU MEMBER STATES

Whilst the EU cogitated on the issue of whether to introduce an EU wide tort based environmental liability regime, a number of Member States pressed ahead with their own schemes, a key feature of which is strict liability in most cases. In fact some States have liability schemes which pre-date the EU interest in the topic by many years. As regards the rationale for introducing strict liability, it must be noted that there is no clear evidence to suggest that it exerts a superior deterrent effect to liability based upon fault.[892] However, it can be argued that deterrence should not be regarded as the main consideration in this context in that tort is primarily concerned with the allocation of costs *ex poste* – although the outcome of a large case, such as *Exxon Valdez*, may have some wider implications regarding the manner in which an industry is operated in future. When viewed as an *ex poste* mechanism it is possible to argue that strict liability channels more of the damage costs to the polluter than fault based liability. In this respect strict liability would appear to accord more closely with the polluter pays principle.

---

892. For a brief summary of some of the handful of empirical studies which have been carried out see S. Shavell, *Foundations of Economic Analysis of Law*, 206 (Harvard 2004). One of the only empirical studies to tackle the deterrent effect of strict liability in an environmental context concerned accident and spill data in US states which had introduced various forms of strict liability for pollution. However, no clear pattern emerged from the results as it seems that the imposition of strict liability may have a very complex effect on corporate behaviour; for example, the increased sub-contracting of hazardous activities in a manner which may simply redistribute the harm. See A. Alberine and D.H. Austin, *Strict Liability as a Deterrent in Toxic Waste Management: Empirical Evidence from Accident and Spill Data*, 38 J Envtl. Econ. Mgt. 20–48 (1999).

The following section is by no means a comprehensive analysis, however, by focusing on a sample drawn from the most well established systems, it is possible to identify the main themes associated with this issue.

[A]   Sweden

Sweden has the longest standing and most comprehensive strict liability regime with the result that this form of liability is the norm for most forms of environmental damage.

The principle of strict liability for environmental damage was first established by the Environmental Protection Act 1969 and was subsequently extended by the Environmental Civil Liability Act 1972 (which only covered damage to real property) and the Environmental Civil Liability Act 1986 which extended cover to roads and airfields in addition to real property. In 1999 these, together with certain other measures, were consolidated by Chapter 32 of the Environmental Code Ds 2000:61.[893] The consolidated provisions give rise to strict liability in respect of pollution to watercourses, lakes or other bodies of water; groundwater; activities which change the water level (e.g., excessive abstraction); air pollution; noise or vibration. In addition, damage caused by blasting work and excavation carried out in a manner which is likely to result in damage is also covered. The legislation also establishes liability for bodily injury, damage to personal property and economic losses associated with such polluting incidents. Given that the 1999 is largely a consolidation measure, much of the earlier case law is still relevant.

The legislation is far-reaching in that, unlike legislation introduced in certain other states, strict liability is not reserved for the most hazardous activities giving rise to the most serious forms of damage. Rather, strict liability is applied in circumstances where 'the damage is not acceptable in view of local conditions or of the extent to which such disturbance normally occurs in similar conditions.' To some extent this is redolent of the locality doctrine which is a central feature of the common law of nuisance. Thus, strict liability can be utilized in order to deal with disputes involving relatively minor amounts of damage. For example, in one case,[894] the plaintiff was able to obtain compensation in respect of damage caused to the plaster facade of his house caused by vibrations resulting from blasting works carried out by the municipality. In an earlier case,[895] smallholders succeeded in claiming compensation in respect of noise pollution caused by a new road which was judged to have adversely affected the market values of their properties.

It is noteworthy that the 1999 legislation does not set out any specific defences, which means that, provided that the claimant can show that the damage exceeds the 'acceptability threshold', it is difficult for an operator to escape liability. However, it is

---

893. For official English translation see Swedish Government website at http://www.sweden.gov.se/sb/d/2023/a/22847 (accessed Jan.10, 2012). For an overview of the liability provisions of the statute see Hinteregger (n. 881) above, 159–160.
894. Supreme Court NJA 1992 s. 896.
895. Supreme Court NJA 1977 s. 376.

also interesting to note that there are extensive provisions on 'future compensation.' Moreover, in some cases the claimant may require the operator to purchase his property outright. This provision brings to mind the UK case of *Allen v. Gulf Oil Refining Ltd.*[896] In this case the local residents living in the shadow of the oil refinery were in favour of Gulf purchasing the village and paying for a new settlement some distance away. However, Gulf rejected the proposal for reasons which are unclear. A provision of this type could have enabled the villagers to compel Gulf to have proceeded with the transaction. Overall it seems that, although the Swedish legislation establishes a very strict standard of liability, it is anticipated that economically important industries may continue to pollute in return for the payment of compensation.

[B]   Germany

Strict liability for water pollution was introduced in Germany as early as 1960 under the Water Resources Act[897] which covered property damage, personal injury and pure economic loss resulting from any change in the physical, chemical, or biological composition of a water source. Various other sector specific strict liability regimes have been introduced in limited areas including mining,[898] nuclear reactors,[899] electricity and energy production[900] and other industries which are capable of releasing particularly harmful substances into the environment.[901] It was the Sandoz fire of 1 November 1986 which caused transboundary pollution of the Rhine from Basle to Rotterdam in the Netherlands which prompted the German Government to consider the extension of strict liability to pollution of all environmental media resulting from a wide range of land use activities, not just the most hazardous; the intension to draft appropriate legislation was announced in 1987. This eventually resulted in the passing of the ELA of 1990 (*Gesetz über die Umwelthaftung*) which came into force as from the 1 January 1991.[902] § 1. of the Act provides that:

> If a person suffers death or injury to his body or health, or if property is damaged, due to an environmental impact that issues from one of the facilities[903] named in

---

896. [1981] A.C. 1001; see §2.03[D][2], above.
897. Wasserhaushaltsgesetz s. 22(1).
898. Bundesberggesetz s. 114.
899. Atomgesetz ss. 25 et seq.
900. Haftpflichtgesetz s. 2.
901. Bundes-Immissionsschutzgesetz s. 14.
902. The Act complements existing sector specific civil liability regimes as opposed to replacing them. See generally Hinteregger (n. 881) above.
903. ELA s. 3(2) 'Facilities are permanent structures such as plants or storage facilities ... (3) Facilities include: (a) machines, instruments, vehicles and other mobile technical structures, and (b) ancillary structures.' Appendix 1 of the Act lists 96 types of facility which are covered by the regime, viz, those involved in (1) mining, energy and heat production; (2) the manufacture of products from stone; (3) the processing and manufacture of steel, iron and other metals; (4) the manufacture of chemical, pharmaceutical, or petroleum products or their further processing; (5) treatment with organic materials and the manufacture of artificial materials; (6) the processing of wood and wood pulp; (7) the production of food, feed and

Appendix 1, then the operator of the facility shall be liable to the injured person for the damage caused thereby.

This imposes strict liability in that, provided a causal link can be established between the facility and the 'environmental impact', the operator of the facility *shall* be liable to the injured person. There is no mention of a need to establish any form of culpability on the part of the operator, as Hoffman states:

> [C]ausation alone provides the basis of liability. This means that polluters are strictly liable for damage caused by their pollution regardless of whether the pollution was intended negligent, known, unknown, 'sudden and accidental' or gradual.[904]

Liability is only excluded on very limited grounds; the principal exclusion is for damage caused by Force Majeure (*höhere Gewalt*).[905] Despite intensive lobbying from industry, a development risk defence[906] was not included with the result that an operator cannot escape liability on the grounds that the state of scientific knowledge at the time did not allow the defendant to appreciate the potential risk to the environment. Hence, if the facts of *Cambridge Water v. Eastern Counties Leather* were repeated in Germany (after the effective date of the ela), the tannery would not be able to succeed on the basis that the pce chemicals were not perceived as a hazard until the introduction of monitoring under the EC Directive. Furthermore, there is no provision for a defence based on the fact that the operator complied with all applicable regulations, licensing conditions etc. at the time the pollution occurred. In this respect the Act differs from the Water Act, paragraph 22 of which provides that, 'a claim for compensation for detrimental effects suffered cannot be brought if the person who caused such effects had obtained an approval under the law on water and he is meeting the requirements of that authorization.' A further significant limitation on liability is the fact that the Act does not have any retroactive effect[907] which rules out its use in respect of historic pollution occurring before the effective date of 1 January 1991. Moreover the Act only applies to specified industrial activities set out in Annex 1 of the legislation.

It is important to note that, although strict, the standard of liability under the Act is not absolute. The limited restrictions on liability referred to above emphasize the fact that the operator must have been in a position to exercise control over the plant at the time the pollution occurred before liability can be established.

---

agricultural products; (8) the treatment of waste; (9) the storage and disposal of certain materials; and (10) other facilities, including paint, printing ink, asphalt etc., production.'
904. W.C. Hoffman, *Germany's New Environmental Liability Act: Strict Liability for Facilities Causing Pollution*, 38 Neth. Intl. L. Rev. 27, 32 (1991).
905. ELA s. 4.
906. Such a defence is provided in s. 1(2) of the Products Liability Act (*Gesetz über die Haftung für fehlerhafte Produkte*).
907. ELA Article 5.

[C]   Finland

Strict liability for all forms of pollution is established by section 3 of the Environmental Damage Compensation Act, 737/1994.[908] Immediately prior to the introduction of the Act, the concept of strict liability under the Tort Act 412/1974 had been accepted by the Finnish Courts in respect of activities hazardous to the environment thereby developing a principle analogous to the rule in *Rylands v. Fletcher.* Thus in Supreme Court decision 1995: 108, which concerned soil contamination caused by leakage of petroleum from an underground storage tank, the owner of the tank was held strictly liable for the pollution on the grounds that storage of petroleum creates a special duty of care due to its self-evidently volatile and potentially harmful properties. The 1994 Act had the effect of extending this principle to all forms of environmental harm occasioning actual damage from whatever source. In this sense the Act goes further than its German Counterpart in that it is not limited to pollution emanating from 'facilities.'

The 1994 Act is comprehensive in that it is not limited to actual damage resulting from the most hazardous activities, it also covers lesser forms of environmental harm giving rise to nuisance types problems. Matters of this nature were formerly dealt with under the Neighbour Relations Act 26/20 which, under section 17, gives rise to strict liability for certain types of 'enduring and unreasonable nuisance' affecting neighbours. Examples of activities found to be nuisances by the Supreme Court include noise caused by granite quarrying[909] and soot from a coke plant[910] which caused damage to the stock of a timber merchants. It seems that the courts also applied a test somewhat analogous to the character of the neighbourhood test. In case 1936 II 87 noise and smell from a poultry house was held not to be unreasonable due to the rural setting of the premises.

The Act does not provide for any defences and does not even refer to force majeure as a possible grounds for excluding liability. However, it is likely that the courts will interpret the Act so as to imply such a defence in accordance with the general law of tort in Finland.

[D]   Denmark

Denmark introduced a strict liability regime for environmental damage under the Act on Compensation for Environmental Damage, 225/1994.[911] However, the Act differs significantly from its equivalent in Finland in that it is restricted in scope to pollution caused by a fixed list of the most potentially harmful activities.[912] This list can only be

---

908. For an overview of the Act see P. Wetterstein, *The Finnish Environmental Damage Compensation Act – and some Comparisons with Norwegian and Swedish Law,* 3(3) Env. Liability 41 (1995).
909. Case 1982 II 109.
910. Case 1962 II 26.
911. Act No. 225 of 6 April 1994. The Act was implemented following the Report of the Committee constituted by the Minister of Justice No. 1237/1992.
912. The Annex to the Act lists the following types of activity: manufacturing, processing, surface treatment of iron, steel, metal, wood and plastic; processing of certain listed types of raw

added to with the assent of Parliament and the passing of an appropriate statutory instrument. Only commercial operators and public utilities are covered and compensation can only be sought in respect of damage caused by the particular activity covered by the Act. Furthermore, damage resulting from transportation or movement of substances is excluded from the Act with the result that compensation cannot be sought under the Act in respect of damage caused by leakage from a pipeline or transit accidents involving vessels or vehicles. The Act does not have retroactive effect which means that it does not apply to any damage occurring before July 1994; accordingly its use in respect of establishing liability for historic pollution is out of the question.

As a result of the limited application of the Act, the case law of the Courts will continue to be of importance. As regards strict liability, the Danish Courts have developed *Rylands v. Fletcher* type strict liability in respect of hazardous land uses. For example, in *Helsingor v. Jonsbo*[913] a gas supply company was held liable for damage resulting from a leak in its pipeline even though it was accepted that it would have been impossible to detect the leak. A similar conclusion was reached in *Copenhagen Water Supply Company v. Uniform*[914] which concerned damage caused by a leak from a water main. However, unlike the position in the UK following the decision in *Cambridge Water v. Eastern Counties Leather*, the standard of liability in these cases has not been diluted by the inclusion of foreseeability as a requirement for establishing liability. Thus in *Melbyhus Water Purifying Plant*,[915] which concerned damage to houses caused by drainage work carried out during the course of constructing a water purification plant, the defendant was found to be liable despite the fact that the court emphasized the fact that the damage was not foreseeable. However, the courts have declined, so far, to apply strict liability in respect of historic pollution; as we have seen above,[916] this type of environmental harm remains subject to fault based liability. Thus although the strict liability standard for certain land uses remains intact under Danish case law, unlike the standard of liability under *Ryland v. Fletcher* following the *Cambridge Water v. Eastern Counties Leather* Decision, the fact that the Danish Courts have elected not to apply it to cases of historic pollution means that the position is essentially the same as in the UK, namely, that historic pollution is not as a rule actionable in that it is not foreseeable. It is possible that the Danish Courts share the opinion of the House of Lords in that they consider that liability for historic pollution is a special case which requires statutory intervention.

---

material; winning and treatment of mineral oil, mineral oil products, asphalt and natural gas; manufacturing of chemicals and glue; processing of vegitable raw materials; manufacture of feedstuffs; printing works; processing of animal raw material; generation of power and heat; motor racing circuits and airfields; manure storage tanks; fish-farms; manufacturing of protein, pectin and enzymes; crematoria; companies posessing an underground oil tank of more than 6000 litres; and plants for storage, deposit, treatment, destruction and recycling of waste.

913. UfR.1983.895H.
914. UfR.1983.866H.
915. UfR.1983.714H.
916. See *Gram-Case* and *Purhus v. Minister of Defence*, *supra*.

[E] Key Commonalities and Differences in European States

Although strict liability is a common feature of these schemes, as this brief overview demonstrates, the manner in which the principle is applied varies considerably. One difference occurs in the range of activities which are covered by legislation. In Denmark and Germany, for example, strict liability is reserved for those activities which pose the greatest threat to the environment. In contrast, the schemes in operation in Sweden and Finland[917] are not limited to specified hazardous activities; the type of damage is the determining factor rather than nature of the activity which caused it.

Another difference occurs in the range of defences available. In Germany Liability is only excluded on very limited grounds; the principal exclusion is for damage caused by force majeure (*höhere Gewalt*).[918] Despite intensive lobbying from industry, a development risk defence[919] was not included with the result that an operator cannot escape liability on the grounds that the state of scientific knowledge at the time did not allow the defendant to appreciate the potential risk to the environment. In Finland and Sweden the standard of liability is even more rigorous in that no defences at all are provided; this would suggest that liability is absolute rather than strict.[920] The Spanish Draft Act is, in contrast, more lenient in that it provides for defences on the basis of force majeure, necessity, and where the damage results from the malicious act of a third party.[921]

Strict liability is clearly not a universal concept which has the same meaning in all jurisdictions. The effects of strict liability vary greatly depending upon the range of the activities to which it is applied and the extent of defences made available. These are important considerations which any new EC initiative would have to take on board. Allowing Member States to adopt their own interpretations of strict liability could result in major divergences in the application of Community law.

§6.04 EUROPEAN AND INTERNATIONAL LIABILITY REGIMES

Strict liability is a key feature of the European and international liability regimes reviewed in the previous chapter such as the Lugano Convention[922] and the conventions relating to maritime oil pollution[923] and nuclear accidents.[924] There is a clear

---

917. See Wetterstein, P., *The Finnish Environmental Damage and Compensation Act – and some Comparisons with Norwegian and Swedish Law*, Env. Liability 41.
918. ELA s. 4.
919. Such a defence is provided in s. 1(2) of the Products Liability Act (*Gesetz über die Haftung für fehlerhafte Produkte*).
920. The terms 'strict' and 'absolute' liability are often used interchangeably, however, liability should only referred to as absolute where no defences of any sort are available: see W.V.H. Rogers, *Winfield and Jolowicz on Tort*, 424 (13th ed., Sweet & Maxwell 1989). A rare example of a statutory provision imposing absolute liability in tort occurs under section 14 of the Gas Act 1965.
921. Article 4.2 (draft Act).
922. See §5.04, above.
923. See §5.05[A], above.
924. See §5.05[B], above.

assumption that, irrespective of whether strict liability has a deterrent effect, it is the best way of requiring operators to internalize a greater proportion of the damage costs associated with their activities. The early EC Green and White papers[925] on the subject made much of the fact that strict liability is the most effective means of giving effect to the polluter pays principle.[926] However, as the foregoing analysis of strict liability in the context of specialist environmental liability regimes makes clear, the nature of strict liability may vary greatly according to two key factors. These focus on the scope of liability, meaning the range of activities to which the standard applies, and the extent to which the strictness of the duty is offset by the provision of defences. Given the centrality of these issues to the debate it is worth considering them in some depth.

§6.05   SCOPE OF STRICT LIABILITY

[A]   Activities Covered

When considering the implementation of a strict liability regime the most basic consideration concerns the issue of which activities should be covered. For example, in Sweden strict liability is triggered by the type of damage,[927] whereas, in Germany strict liability under the *UmweltHG* is imposed on specified industries.[928]

At an early stage in the environmental liability debate the European Environmental Law Association argued that the draw-back of linking strict liability to the type of damage is that it risks creating uncertainty as to whether a person is subject to the regime.[929] However, it is impossible to draft an exhaustive list of harmful activities or harmful substances. An otherwise harmless substance may cause serious pollution if deposited in large quantities in a river.[930] Thus, in drafting a list of activities the legislator would need to be aware of three broad classes of potentially liable persons. Namely those engaged in inherently hazardous activities; those who handle substances which are potentially harmful in large quantities; and those whose activities may be environmentally harmful in sensitive locations.[931] It is interesting to note that the EU ELD,[932] which, it will be recalled, introduced a public law based system of pollution

---

925. See §5.03, above.
926. See in particular EC Commision Environmental Liability White Paper COM(2000) 66 final, 16–17.
927. See §6.03[A], above.
928. See §6.03[B], above.
929. European Environmental Law Association (EELA), *Repairing Damage to the Environment – A Community System of Civil Liability* (Position paper submitted to the Commission of the European Communities), 14, at para. 7.1.
930. The EELA, above, use the example of an overturned milk tanker depositing its cargo in a river.
931. There is a precedent for such an approach in Directive 85/377 on environmental impact assessment (OJ 1985 No. L 175/40). This distinguishes between schedule 1 projects, which are inherently hazardous, and schedule 2 projects which may be hazardous as a result of their nature size or location. A schedule 1 project would include an oil refinery whereas a schedule 2 project would include a major construction project such as the building of a bridge near a nature reserve.
932. European Parliament and Council Directive (EC) 2004/35 on Environmental Liability with Regard to the Prevention and Remedying of Environmental Damage OJ L143/56.

prevention and environmental remediation, focuses on the nature of the damage rather than the activity. Liability is triggered where environmental damage is caused by occupational activities.[933] Occupational activities are further defined as any activity of an economic nature irrespective of whether it is conducted with a view to profit.[934] This definition is not quite as open as it first appears, in that it is further elucidated by a long list of activities in Annex III. Nevertheless, the Directive casts the liability net wide and catches undertakings which may not necessarily regard themselves as undertaking environmentally hazardous activities. This approach raises another fundamental question, namely, the issue of what types of loss should be regarded as environmental harm attracting strict liability.

[B]   Type of Harm Subject to Strict Liability

Environmental damage is most closely associated with the property torts such as nuisance and trespass to land. Thus nuisance to an individual property caused by emissions from an industrial plant may be symptomatic of a wider environmental problem. However, as has been clearly demonstrated by the Corby litigation in the UK,[935] pollution can also cause personal injuries and property damage unconnected with rights in real property. Most specialist environmental liability regimes take a broad view of environmental harm and facilitate personal claims of this nature. For example, both the Swedish[936] and German[937] systems allow claims for damage to personal property and personal injuries, provided such losses are connected with wider environmental harm caused by the facility. Moreover, economic losses may be recovered, to a greater or lesser extent, depending upon the nature of the regime. As regards international initiatives, all the regimes considered in the previous chapter make provision for personal injuries, property damage and economic losses.[938] This raises the interesting point that the environmental dimension of harm, which would otherwise constitute purely *conventional* loss, may place the claimant in a stronger position. For example, an individual who suffers respiratory problems as a result of exposure to a toxic element in the work place would need to establish a breach of duty on the part of the employer. If the toxic element escaped into the wider environment, and a local resident contracted a similar disease, strict liability would be engaged as a result of the environmental nature of the exposure. Cane[939] has argued forcefully that this would constitute an invidious state of affairs in that there is nothing special about environmental harms. This is a compelling argument if one looks at the issue purely in terms of the individual losses sustained. However, in the context of an environmental liability regime, an individual loss is regarded as one constituent part of damage to the environment as a whole. In other words, environmental damage is characterized as a

---

933. *Ibid.*, Article 3.
934. *Ibid.*, Article 2(7).
935. See §2.05[C] and §2.06[B][2], above.
936. See §6.03[A], above.
937. See §6.03[B], above.
938. See §5.05, above.
939. P. Cane, *Are Environmental Harms Special?*, 13(1) J. Envtl. L. 3 (2001).

collection of individual losses. The imposition of strict liability plays a vital role in giving practical effect to the polluter pays principle. Adjusting tortious principles so as to achieve instrumentalist objectives in this manner inevitably results in differing standards of liability depending upon whether the individual harm is associated with some greater societal evil. Thus, the use of tort in an instrumentalist manner unavoidably renders certain harms 'special'. This may appear unjust on a case by case basis; however, when viewed in the light of the overall public interest objects such an approach appears entirely consistent with the idea of distributional justice described in Chapter 4.

Certain environmental harms may be unconnected with damage to real or personal property or personal injuries. A further issue concerns the extent to which the so-called 'un-owned' environment should be covered by a strict liability regime. The term 'un-owned' needs further explanation in this context in that it is difficult to conceive of any part of the environment which is truly un-owned. Rather, the concept entails looking at the environment as a separate entity from the property interests which vest in it. This enables one to view the environment as a 'common good' for the benefit of all as opposed to a collection of private property rights. In fact an Austrian proposal on civil liability for environmental damage, which never came to fruition, encompassed harm to 'common goods' of this type.[940] Thus damages could have been sought in respect of the destruction of habitats and the extinction of species. Of course, damages would hardly be an adequate remedy in such circumstances; ecological damage is often irreversible. As will be discussed in more detail in Chapter 9, in order to be effective in such circumstances, civil liability must be underpinned by effective 'precautionary' remedies such as injunctive relief.

The Commission White Paper[941] also favoured the inclusion of ecological damage of this type within the scope of an environmental liability regime. However, the ELD[942] has had the effect of drawing a distinction between ecological damage and other types of conventional loss such as damage to property and personal injuries.[943] The Directive regards ecological damage as falling within the realm of public law which is why the measure utilizes administrative mechanisms such as the conferral of cost recovery powers on regulators. This raises the issue of whether tort based environmental liability regimes should focus on conventional loss and eschew ecological damage. A regime which concentrated purely on damage to property and personal injury would be open to the criticism that it took an overly anthropocentric approach to environmental protection.[944] As noted in Chapter 1, the main problem with the anthropocentric approach to environmental regulation is that it suggests that the environment can be exploited to the extent that this does not have an immediate impact on the welfare of humans. Protection of the environment in the widest sense of the term, and the

---

940. Draft Bill JMZ 7720 – 1/2/91. See E. Brandl & C. Schmelz, *Environmental Civil Liability Schemes: Do they Make Sense for Austria?*, 3(1) Eur. Pub. L. 1 (1997).
941. EC Commision Environmental Liability White Paper COM(2000) 66 final, 16–17.
942. See n. 932, above, Article 2(1) and Article 3.
943. See Draft Directive on Environmental Liability (explanatory memorandum) COM(2002) 17, 16.
944. See A. Gillespie, *International Environmental Law, Policy and Ethics*, Ch. 1 – *Anthropocentrism* (Clarendon Press 1999).

conservation of species within it, is neglected by an anthropocentric analysis. As argued in Chapter 4, one of the main benefits of private law it can be used to compensate for lack of enforcement by regulators. However, its capacity to do so, in an environmental context, is severely limited if its role is confined to purely personal loss.

Moreover, it was further argued in Chapter 4 that it is appropriate to use principles derived from tort in pursuit of public interest objectives such as environmental protection. To recap briefly, this is because the public can be regarded as having a form of equitable interest in the environment and that this interest invites the application of tort based remedies. To this extent, a liability regime should also reflect the public interest in the protection of the wider environment and the conservation of species. This is a theme which shall be returned to in Chapter 8 on the role of NGOs.

[C] Defences

The nature of strict liability varies enormously according to the extent to which the strictness of the duty is offset by defences. If no defences at all are provided liability is more akin to absolute liability. However, if a multitude of defences are provided the distinction with fault based liability becomes blurred.

[1] Conventional Defences

In Chapter 4 it was argued that strict liability increases the distributional functions of tort, however, strict liability is also consistent with the corrective functions of tort in that it allows for certain defences. This is where strict liability differs from absolute liability which serves as a purely distributional device. A difficult balance has to be struck between maximizing the proportion of the damages costs which must be met by the polluter whilst retaining incentives to take care. Thus it is appropriate to admit defences in respect of events which were entirely beyond the control of the polluter such as force majeure. In the UK most environmental regulations, which impose strict criminal liability, allow for defences in respect of natural phenomena (Act of God)[945] or third party intervention.[946] Similarly, most national and international environmental liability regimes contain defences of this nature. For example, as regards national regimes, §4 of the German ELA includes the defence of *höhere Gewalt* relating to matters beyond the control of the operator.[947] As regards international measures, Article III of the 1992 Convention on Liability and Compensation for Oil Pollution Damages[948] establishes a range of defences associated with acts of war and natural phenomena. Similarly, Article IV of the Vienna Convention on Civil Liability for

---

945. The defendant is, however, expected to take precautions against foreseeable natural phenomena such as heavy rain. See *Southern Water Authority v. Pegrum* [1989] Crim L.R. 442; *Alphacell v. Woodward* [1972] C.L.Y. 3549.
946. See *Impress (Worcester) Ltd v. Rees* [1971] 2 All E.R. 357; *Welsh Water Authority v. Williams Motors (Cwmdu) Ltd*, The Times, (Dec. 5, 1988).
947. See §6.03[B], above.
948. See n. 830, above.

Nuclear Damage[949] relieves the operator of liability in respect of nuclear damage 'directly due' to armed conflicts or 'grave natural disasters of an exceptional character' – although domestic regimes are free to provide otherwise.

The phrase 'directly due' is of crucial significance here in that operators must be expected to take certain precautions against events of this nature. For example, the Fukushima plant was damaged by a tsunami which would certainly fall with the category of 'grave natural disasters.' However, if it transpires that tsunamis were a predictable, albeit remote, risk in the location and that more could have been done to mitigate the damage in terms of the design of the plant, there would be an argument for saying that the nuclear damage was not 'directly due' to the tsunami. In fact, as regards the Fukushima disaster itself, it seems that a rather different tack may be adopted regarding the liability of the operator. In most parts of the world a tsunami on the scale of the one which struck the Fukushima plant would be regarded as an example *par excellence* of a 'grave natural disaster of an exceptional character'. However, in Japan the bar may be set very high in terms of the magnitude of disasters deemed to fall within this category. Claims arising from the Fukushima disaster are governed by the Japanese Act on Compensation for Nuclear Damage which enshrines the exceptional grave natural disaster exception to the general rule of strict liability for nuclear facilities.[950] During the course of enacting the legislation, however, the Congress stated that 'only a huge natural disaster beyond the expectations of humankind' would suffice to invoke the defence. Given that Japan is situated in a volatile area where earthquakes are likely, it could be argued that the tsunami was not of sufficient magnitude to exceed human expectations in this manner. The courts have yet to rule on the issue of whether the Fukushima disaster falls within this category. Nevertheless, it has been pointed out that not even the 1995 earthquake which struck Kobe, measuring 6.9 on the Richter Scale and killing 5,000 people, was regarded as meeting this threshold.[951]

[2] Regulatory Compliance Defence

A rather more controversial issue concerns whether a defence should be available where the operator has carried out an activity in accordance with the terms of a license. In other words, should the existence of a license be regarded as a form of statutory authority? In Chapter 3, it was noted that it would be difficult to argue such a defence under existing tort rules in the UK; especially in the light of the Court of Appeal decision in *Barr v. Biffa Waster Services Ltd.*[952] As regards other EU Member States, the Austrian Supreme Court has adopted a similar approach. In a landmark case the plaintiffs were awarded compensation in respect of damage to the paint-work of their cars caused by

---

949. See n. 855, above.
950. X. Vásquez-Maignan, *Fukushima: Liability and Compensation* (*NEA News* No 29/2, 2011) http://www.oecd-nea.org/nea-news/2011/29-2/nea-news-29-2-fukushima-e.pdf, 10 (accessed Jan. 17, 2012).
951. *Ibid.*
952. [2012] EWCA Civ 312, [2012] All ER (D) 141 (Mar); see §2.03[D][4], above.

emissions of iron oxide dust from the defendant's facility, which had been licensed since 1979. The Austrian General Civil Code of 1811[953] imposes strict liability in respect of nuisances emanating from neighbouring property.[954] The decision is significant for a number of reasons, not least of which is the fact that the plaintiffs' vehicles had been damaged whilst on a parking lot in which they had no proprietary interest. For present purposes the decision was notable in that the Supreme Court held that the defendant could not escape liability simply by relying upon the fact that it had held a license for fifteen years.

Furthermore, the Court stated, *obiter*, that, where the 'state of the art' had changed since the grant of the license, a plaintiff would be able to seek injunctive relief. It is difficult to reconcile this approach with the nuisance provisions of the Austrian Civil Code. Paragraph 364a (abgb) provides that the plaintiff's remedies are restricted to compensatory damages where harm arises from factors, which were not mentioned at the time of the application.[955] It seems that the Court was of the opinion that there is a qualitative distinction between information which was available at the time of the application but was not considered, and information which could not have been known at the time. One possible justification for this distinction is that paragraph 364a (ABGB) is an equitable provision intended to prevent the operator from being unduly burdened by a failure of the regulatory authority to take into account all relevant considerations. Where new factors come to light, such as new scientific information regarding the effect of an industrial activity on the environment, there is an assumption that the authority would have taken such considerations into account had they been known at the material time. The license is thereby reopened to challenge.

The issue of regulatory compliance raises difficult issues in that the effect of licenses and permits on third party rights differs from state to state. As noted above, a license to pollute in the UK merely removes an administrative obstacle to pursuing an activity and is without prejudice to third party rights In the Netherlands, operators are allowed to operate in accordance with the terms of a permit even though this may result in some interference with third party rights.[956] German law draws a distinction between a permit (*Erlaubnis*) and a license (*Bewilligung*). Whereas a permit is issued

---

953. *Allgemeines Bòrgerliches Gesetzbuch* (ABGB).
954. § 364(2) (ABGB): 'An owner of real property may prevent a neighbour from issuing from the latter's ground waste water, smoke, gases, heat, odours, noise, explosions and other nuisances insofar as they exceed the usual issuance according to local standards and are essentially prejudicial to the usual local use of this real property. Direct conduct upon the property of another without a special legal title is not permissible under any circumstances.'
955. § 364a (ABGB): 'If, however, the encroachment is caused by a mine or another installation duly licensed upon the neighbour's ground which exceed the issuance set above, the owner of the affected real estate is entitled to demand in court only compensatory damages, even if the damage originates from factors which were not mentioned during the administrative licencing proceedings.'
956. In *Sopar*, Appeals Court of the Hague, 19 November 1992, TMA 1993, nr 5, 131–132 it was held that the right to emit pollutants in accordance with the terms of a permit even extended top a neighbouring state, in this case Belgium, provided that there were no directly applicable emission limits in place.

without prejudice to third party rights, licenses amount to a form of statutory authority thereby authorizing some interference with private interests.[957]

In its early proposals the EC Commission was attracted to the inclusion of a regulatory compliance defence as it viewed civil liability as a means of underpinning and enforcing environmental standards in other EC legislation. Thus, as Bergkamp et al., noted, such a defence 'would promote the liability regimes stated objective of providing an additional sanction for violations of EC environmental law.'[958] Such an approach uses tort in an overtly instrumentalist manner in order to secure public interest objectives. However, closely linking actionable harm with regulatory compliance creates a severe risk that tort may lose its capacity to correct regulatory failure.[959] For example, the regulatory standards may not address the specific type of harm suffered by an individual or may simply prove to be inadequate in the light of subsequent scientific developments. Thus, as has already been noted,[960] there are dangers associated with closely yoking liability in tort with public mechanisms.

Nevertheless, the Commission expressed some support for a regulatory compliance defence in its White Paper. In fact it went so far as to say that, where damage was caused by emissions sanctioned under a permit, a proportion of the damage costs ought to be recoverable from the regulator:

> some room might be granted to the court ... to decide – for instance in cases where the operator who caused the damage can prove that this damage was entirely and exclusively caused by emissions that were explicitly allowed by his permit – that part of the compensation should be borne by the permitting authority.[961]

This approach would have been highly problematic in that that it would have enabled the operator to join the regulatory authority in proceedings and thereby led to further protracted and technical arguments regarding whether the standard set by the authority was adequate. In this respect such a provision would have greatly increased transaction costs.

In fact the Commission appeared to recognize the risk that such a provision could be used for 'buck passing' between the operator and the regulatory authority. The White Paper suggested that the onus should remain on the operator to avert pollution, notwithstanding compliance with an administrative standard. Thus, in allowing courts a discretion to apportion damages in this manner, the White Paper stated that 'further criteria would need to be defined for such a provision, for instance that the operator has done everything possible to avoid the damage.'[962] However, the Paper did not define

---

957. For example, Article 11 of the Water Management Act (*Wasserhaushaltgesetz*) provides that a third party has no remedy against a license holder in respect of damage caused by emissions into a water course provided that the terms of the license have been complied with. See Horst Schlemminger and Claus-Peter Martens, *German Environmental Law for Practitioners*, 118 (Kluwer Law International 2004).
958. Bergkamp et al., *The Commission's White Paper on Environmental Liability: A Weak Case for an EC Environmental Liability Regime (Part 2)*, Eur. Envtl. L. Rev. 141, 142 (2000).
959. See §4.03[C], above.
960. *Ibid.*
961. Environmental Liability White Paper, n. 941, p. 18.
962. *Ibid.*

what it meant by 'everything possible'. Precisely what steps would an operator have to take in order to merit having some of the damage costs shared with the regulatory authority?

One solution would have been to place the license holder under an obligation to keep abreast of the latest scientific evidence regarding the effects of his activity and to report significant new data to the appropriate regulatory authority. Provided that such steps were taken, the operator would be absolved of a proportion of his liability in respect of pollution caused despite compliance with an emission limit, even where the authority failed to act on this information by altering the terms of a license. However, the operator would not escape liability where he failed to put in place systems designed to keep him up to date with latest the scientific developments.

In fact there is a precedent for such an approach in the field of the regulation of the uncontained use of GM crops. Any consent granted under the licensing system may stipulate conditions[963] such as a requirement to maintain a 'buffer zone' around the crops in order to reduce the possibility of cross-pollination with conventional crops. However, these are only minimum requirements. The consent holder is also placed under an obligation to keep himself up to date with the latest developments regarding the risks of environmental damage. If he should come across new information, or circumstances at the site change, he is expected to take additional preventative measures and to inform the Secretary of State.[964] The latter has the power to vary or revoke consents in the light of this information.[965] It would be easy to link such a provision with a civil liability component. Thus, failure to comply with this duty would preclude the license holder from relying upon the regulatory compliance defence.

Nevertheless, the approach adopted by the White Paper, whereby the regulator is effectively joined as a defendant on the grounds that the emissions were in accordance with the permit which it granted, seems overly complex and unnecessary. If an operator was relieved of part or all of the damage costs on the grounds of regulatory compliance it is likely that the regulator would have to meet the balance in any case using tax payers' money. This is the assumption upon which the ELD operates. A polluter may avail himself of a regulatory compliance defence provided that he was not otherwise at fault.[966] If the costs cannot be recovered from the polluter the tenor of the Directive establishes a clear expectation the regulator will effect clean-up using funds drawn from the public purse.

[3] The Development Risk Defence

The above discussion raises another important issue concerning which, if any, defences should be available under a strict liability regime. An operator may argue that a particular hazard could not have been discovered in the light of the current state of

---

963. S. 112(1) EPA 1990.
964. S. 109(7) EPA 1990.
965. S. 112(1) EPA 1990.
966. Environmental Liability Directive, n. 932, Article 8(4)(a).

scientific knowledge at the time the harm occurred. This raises the issue of whether a 'development risk' defence should be included.

The issue of whether a 'development risk' defence should be included raises complex issues. The main problem with the development risk defence, which has been developed in the field of products liability, is that it relates to the manner in which the operator has managed his activities. Accordingly there is a risk that the defence may equate the standard of liability with negligence and undermine the distributional function of strict liability. This is because the development risk defence is based upon a 'risk-utility' analysis; such an approach is now frequently adopted in negligence for the purpose of determining whether the defendant has taken due care.[967] Nevertheless, Terry points out that there is a distinction inasmuch as negligence judges the conduct of the defendant whereas the development risk defence judges the product.[968] Thus, in US products liability cases, the courts have adopted objective tests for determining whether a producer should have been aware of a risk. Where knowledge of a defect exists, prior to the marketing of a product, the knowledge is imputed to the producer irrespective of whether he was in possession of the knowledge. In other words, there is a presumption that he ought to have been in possession of the knowledge. Compliance with regulatory standards and independent assessments of industry capability have been admitted as sufficiently objective tests to invoke the defence.[969] In contrast, evidence relating to industry practice and standards set by the industry itself is regarded with suspicion.[970] Tests based on industry custom are subjective and focus attention on the conduct of the producer rather than the safety of the product;[971] such evidence has, therefore, been dismissed by the US courts on a number of occasions.[972]

In Europe, Directive 85/374/EEC[973] on product liability required Member States to introduce strict liability in respect of certain types of harm caused by defective

---

967. English court have long since become accustomed to weighing the magnitude of the risk against the practicality of precautions. See, for example, *Latimer v. A.E.C.* [1953] A.C. 643.
968. N.P. Terry, *State of the Art Evidence: From Logical Construct to Judicial Retrenchment*, 20(3) Anglo-Am. L. Rev. 285 (1991).
969. *Ibid.*, 296.
970. See *Lewis v. Coffing Hoist Div., Duff-Norton Co.*, 515 Pa. 334, 528 A.2d 590, 595 (1987): 'The injection of industry standards into a design defect case would be not only irrelevant and distracting, but also, because of the inherently self-serving nature of 'industry standards', would be highly prejudicial to the consumer/plaintiff. By our determination today, we have made it clear that a manufacturer cannot avoid liability to its consumers that it injures or maims through its defective designs by showing that 'the other guys do it too''. (Larsen J.).
971. 'Introducing evidence of industry and/or manufacturer's customs and practices shifts the jury's focus from what the consumer expects to what the manufacturers are doing. By focusing the jury's attention on the custom of the industry, implicitly the jury's attention is focused on the defendant's design choice and the reasonableness of that choice. In effect, such evidence incorporates negligence concepts and the seller orientated approach we [have] rejected.' *Lenhardt v. Ford Motor Co.*, 102 Wash.2d 208, 683 P.2d 1097, 1098 (1984).
972. Thus, in *Lewis v. Coffing Hoist Div*, above, the court was not prepared to find that the absence of basic safety features in a control panel for a hoist was excusable on the basis of the development risk defence merely because the practice in the industry was not to incorporate such safety features.
973. [1985] O.J. L210/29.

products. Member States were, however, afforded the option of incorporating a development risk defence which provides as follows:

> The producer shall not be liable as a result of this Directive if he proves ... that the state of scientific and technical knowledge at the time when he put the product into circulation was not such as to enable the existence of the defect to be discovered.[974]

This formulation of the defence entails establishing that the knowledge existed at the material time and was discoverable by the producer concerned. Furthermore, in order to make out the defence, the producer must show that any available knowledge would not have enabled him to identify the defect.[975] It is not enough to show that there had been no previous reports of defects or no studies which identified the exact nature of the problem. Rather, it must be shown that there were no readily available means, such as a safety test, by which existing background knowledge could have been used to highlight the risk.[976] In this respect the courts have avoided adopting an overly subjective approach which looks at the matter solely from the perspective of the producer. Such an approach risks over reliance on industry practices which, as noted above, may be self-serving and myopic in their appreciation of risk.

A contentious issue has concerned whether a 'state of the art' or 'development risk' defence of this type should be included in environmental regimes establishing strict liability. For example, it is possible to envisage a scenario in which emissions from an industrial facility, which were hitherto thought to be harmless, are found to be damaging in the light of new scientific evidence. The example of *Cambridge Water*[977] springs to mind in which it could not have been known that the leather tannery's mode of operation was storing up long term environmental damage. In this case a foreseeability requirement was introduced which watered down the strictness of the duty under nuisance and *Rylands v. Fletcher*.[978] Had this incident occurred in a jurisdiction where environmental harm was subject to strict liability it is likely that the operator would have been held liable unless the regime included a state of the art defence. However, it seems that few, if any, environmental liability regimes incorporate a defence of this nature. This is no great surprise when one considers that few states adopted the development risk defence available under the Product Liability

---

974. *Ibid.*, Article 7(e).
975. For a review of the relevant case law on the interpreation of the defence see C. Pugh & M. Pilgerstorfer, *The Development Risk Defence – Knowledge, Discoverability and Creative Leaps*, 4 J. Pers. Injury L. 258 (2004). See also P. Sheers, *The EU Product Liability Directive – Twenty Years on*, J. Bus. L. 884 (2007).
976. *Ibid.*, a clear example is provided by the case of *Abouzaid v. Mothercare*, The Times (London, Feb. 20, 2001) in which a toddler was injured by a metal clip on the end of an elasticated bungee cord attached to an accessory designed for a pram. Although there had been no reports of similar incidents a rudimentary knowledge of the laws of physics and a simple test would have sufficed to reveal the risk.
977. See n. 890, above.
978. (1868) L.R. 3 H.L. 330.

Directive.[979] There is a risk that the development risk defence may undermine the strict nature of the duty in that attention focuses on whether the producer took reasonable steps to apprise himself of the latest scientific evidence and took sufficient precautions to identify and alleviate risks. This is more redolent of liability based on the duty of care in negligence that strict liability where liability should primarily rest upon causation.

Moreover, it is difficult to anticipate how the development risk defence might be applied in cases where the nature of the risk is uncertain due to scientific disagreement. A clear example of this problem is provided by the issue of GMOs. According to the product liability type formulation of the defence it is not clear whether it should be available where one body of scientific evidence rejects the existence of a risk but another body of evidence supports the existence of a risk. Is an operator entitled to argue that, due to the inability of science to deliver a definitive answer, he could not reasonably be expected to have avoided the risk? Such an approach hardly seems to accord with the precautionary principle which requires operators to guard against risks which have yet to be scientifically proven. Furthermore, it undermines the generally accepted rationale of strict liability which is that losses should fall on the person who creates a risk and benefits from it economically. Thus, should it one day transpire that GM technology was unsafe all along, should operators be absolved from all liability on the basis that the risk was not scientifically known at the time?

It is far from clear whether this difficulty would be solved by the formulation of the development risk defence set out in the ELD. This provides that the operator may be absolved of liability if he can demonstrate that an emission or activity 'was not considered likely to cause environmental damage according to the state of scientific and technical knowledge at the time when the emission was released or the activity took place.'[980] This begs the question of how much scientific evidence is needed before damage is considered 'likely'. In this respect one has to differentiate between two types of harm which may be caused by the spread of GMOs. It is known that GMOs can cross-pollinate with conventional crops and that such cross-pollination may be regarded as 'damage' in that it alters the characteristics and value of the contaminated crop.[981] Thus, it is unlikely that a development risk defence could be used where neighbouring crops were contaminated by GM crops being grown as part of a field trial. However, scientific knowledge cannot yet deliver a definitive answer on the wider question of the long term effects of such releases on the ecosystem and biodiversity. A biotech company might have a better chance of arguing that, according to the current state of scientific knowledge, one cannot say that damage of this nature is likely. In fact,it seems that such damage is excluded from the scope of strict liability

---

979. See n. 973, above.
980. Environmental Liability Directive, n. 932, Article 8(4)(b).
981. See §2.03[B], above, and the discussion of *R. v. Secretary of the State for the Environment, ex parte Watson* [1999] Env. L.R. 310.

under the ELD in any case.[982] This suggests that a political decision was taken to absolve biotech companies from such widespread liability provided that they showed due diligence. However, as regards tort based liability regimes adopted in certain Member States, it seems that a similar decision has not been taken to limit the liability of operators in this manner. For example, the Finnish and Swedish environmental liability regimes do not include a state of the art defence nor does the German Umwelt HG. In Austria neither the Gene Technology Act nor the Nuclear Liability Act include such a defence.[983]

It must be acknowledged that a development risk defence in an environmental liability regime could provide an incentive to constantly review procedures and investigate new technology. In fact, even where liability is based upon fault, the need to keep abreast of the latest technological developments, with a view to meeting the duty of care, may be an onerous requirement. However, this would have to be balanced against the underlying requirements of the polluter pays and precautionary principles. The inclusion of a development risk defence in any environmental liability may severely curtail its capacity to hold the operator liable for the full damage costs.

An additional consideration is that, in an environmental context, there would have to be a distinction between knowledge of harmful emissions and knowledge of a defect in process. The defence should only be available in respect of the former. The facts of *Graham and Graham v. Re-Chem International*,[984] which concerned emissions from a toxic waste incinerator,[985] can be used to illustrate the significance of this distinction. Let us assume that there had been a strict liability regime in place and the issue of liability rested on a development risk defence. If the defence was only available in respect of knowledge of harmful emissions the defendant would have failed in this case. The judge stated that, at the material time, it was well known that the burning of PCBs could cause the emission of dioxins and furans.[986] As the defendant was engaged in a hazardous activity, he would have had difficulty in refuting the presumptions of knowledge under both the EC and UK versions of the defence. However, if the defence was also available in respect of defects in process the outcome could be different. The process by which the pollutants were produced was not known until after the incinerator had been closed. Therefore, Re-Chem could have argued that the state of scientific knowledge was such that the emissions could not have been prevented. This would equate strict liability far too closely with negligence and undermine its distributional objectives. According to the polluter pays principle, once knowledge of the

---

982. See Article 3(1)(b) Environmental Liability Directive, n. 932, which provides that operators will only be liable in respect of damage to protected species or natural habitats in cases where fault can be established. See M. Wilde, *Liability Issues Associated with Genetically Modified Organisms: EU and International Developments*, in *Environmental Liability in the EU: the 2004 Environmental Liability Directive compared with US and Member State Law*, 292–298 (G. Betlem & E. Brans eds.,Cameron May 2006).
983. See Hinteregger, n. 881, above, 315–317.
984. [1996] Env. L.R. 158.
985. The full facts are set out in Ch. 3.
986. [1996] Env. L.R. 158, 167.

existence of harmful emissions becomes known, the onus must be on the polluter to find a solution.[987]

Taking the above considerations into account, a possible form of words, based upon the products liability defence, could be as follows:

> The operator shall not be liable ... if he proves that the state of scientific and technical knowledge during the time when he carried on the process was not such as to enable the existence of harmful emissions to be discovered.

§6.06 CONCLUSION

Strict liability is generally regarded as a prerequisite of any tort based environmental liability system. As the Commission White Paper stated, 'there is an assumption that environmental objectives are better achieved that way'. As noted above, this has proved to be an extremely difficult assumption to justify despite having been the subject of a substantial amount of academic research. Nevertheless, as has also been, there is some evidence to suggest that strict liability may have a subtle effect on business behaviour in the longer term. To recap, this is because it requires operators to recognize environmental damage costs as costs of production which must be reduced in order to increase efficiency.

However, it is important to bear in mind the theoretical basis of strict liability as discussed in Chapter 4. Strict liability is not the same as absolute liability since it allows scope for the inclusion of defences. In the absence of any defences, the liability system would lose its corrective functions and become a purely distributional device. In Chapter 4 it was noted that there are number of advantages associated with maintaining corrective functions in tort. The main advantage is that strict liability typically only holds defendants liable for costs over which they had control and were in a position to mitigate. Thus, defences are normally available in respect of events entirely outside the control of the defendant such as force majeure. However, if the scope for defences is too great the standard of liability is watered down and the distinction between strict and fault based liability is lost. For this reason, defences must strike a balance between the distributional and corrective functions of tort. Thus, although there are strong arguments in favour of including defences in respect of events entirely beyond the control of the operator, care should be taken when deciding whether to admit adevelopment risk defence. For the reasons stated above there is a risk that such a defence could be interpreted in a manner which equates strict liability with fault based liability.

---

987. It is interesting to note that this mirrors the definition of strict liability which has now been established in nuisance. Once a nuisance has been discovered the defendant must abate it, irrespective of whether he was at fault in causing the nuisance in the first place. See Ch. 3, above.

As regards the scope of a regime, once again certainty is an important consideration and liability regimes must be clear as to what types of harm and what activities are covered.

CHAPTER 7

Reducing the Burden of Proof on Causation

---

§7.01 INTRODUCTION

The difficulties faced by a plaintiff in establishing causation are formidable and were discussed at length in Chapter 3 with regard to examples drawn from recent English case law and other common law based jurisdictions. There have been various attempts to overcome causation difficulties within the context of environmental liability regimes. However, the difficulty which must be overcome concerns how this objective can be achieved without holding operators liable for damage costs to which they did not contribute. Once again, this could give rise to open ended and hence unsustainable liability.

§7.02 GENERAL CONSIDERATIONS

Causation is closely associated with the corrective functions of tort in that it seeks to hold the tortfeasor accountable for the loss flowing from his actions; thus the parties concerned are locked into a 'normative embrace'.[988] From an environmental perspective, causation fulfils a useful function in that it links the harm with the person who is in the best position to internalize costs, this is generally the polluter. Without a test of causation tort would be rendered a purely distributional device which is not linked to patterns of conduct. This would lead to collective responsibility, rather than individual accountability, and reduce incentives for risk management.[989] Furthermore, such an approach would cause insurers to withdraw cover in that, as has been explained in Chapter 4, the viability of insurance is dependent upon the ability of the insured to limit

---

988. Izhak Englard, *The Philosophy of Tort Law*, 45 (Dartmouth Publishing 1993).
989. G. Teubner, *The Invisible Cupola: From Causal to Collective Attribution in Ecological Liability* in *Environmental Law and Ecological Responsibility – The Concept and Practice of Ecological Self-Organization*, 29 (G. Teubner, L. Farmer & D. Murphy, eds., John Wiley & Sons 1994).

the costs passed to the insurers. As Huber has pointed out, 'neither businesses or insurers can or will provide such assistance for very long if payments are not systematically and predictably linked to specific patterns of conduct.'[990] In the United States, a lax application of causality tests by the courts augmented the difficulties faced by insurers in assessing risk under CERCLA.[991]

Thus the difficulty which has to be overcome concerns the extent to which the burden of causation may be eased without giving rise to unsustainable liability of the nature described above. It is necessary to establish a framework which enables the court to draw common sense conclusions based upon the circumstances of the case without the need to show with scientific certainty that a substance, emanating from the defendant's facility, caused or contributed to the harm. In certain English and American cases there has been an attempt to award damages on a proportionate basis calculated upon the increase in risk caused by the defendant's activity.[992] These are often referred to as 'lost chance cases' in that the cause of action is the chance of avoiding the harm which was lost as a result of the defendant's actions.[993] The problem with this approach is that in many cases it may be impossible to quantify the extent to which the defendant's conduct increased the risk thereby lessening the plaintiff's chances of escaping the harm. Furthermore, it may lead to a situation in which, although all plaintiffs receive some compensation, none receive damages which in any way reflect the true costs which they have endured and some may receive damages to which they are not entitled. For these reasons Huber is dismissive of solutions of this type and describes them as 'an edifice of compromise'.[994] Indeed, it is for similar reasons that the House of Lords eventually decided to firmly reject the notion that causation could be determined on this basis under English Law.[995] Nevertheless, as has already been explained at some length, the material increase in risk test has had some

---

990. P. Huber, *Environmental Hazards and Liability Law*, in *Liability Perspectives and Policy*, 147–148 (R.E. Litan & C. Winston eds., The Brookings Institution 1988).
991. This has largely been due to the fact that in many States cases are still decided by civil juries which are capricious by nature and more likely to be swayed by sympathy for the alleged victim than complex arguments relating to causation. For a review of the more outlandish decisions see Peter Huber, *Galileo's Revenge: Junk Science in the Court Room* (Harper Collins/Basic Books 1991).
992. In England this approach was adopted by the Court of Appeal in *Hotson v. East Berkshire Health Authority* [1987] 1 All E.R. 210, 219 where it was stated: 'The fundamental question is: what is the damage which the plaintiff suffered? Is it the onset of the avascular necrosis or is it the loss of chance of avoiding that condition? In my judgment it is the latter.' (Dillon L.J.). In the United States the United States Court of Appeals for the Fourth Circuit defined the 'lost chance' cause of action in the case of *Waffen v. U.S. Department of Health and Human Services* 799 F.2d 911, 919 as follows: 'The confusion that has persisted is based upon confusing 'causation' and 'harm' … it is better to consider the loss of a substantial chance of survival as a different type of loss with a different measure of damages than the loss of life, instead of treating the former as a variation on the burden of proving causation in a claim for negligently causing the patient's death. The destroyed chance is itself the compensable loss.'
993. D.P.T. Price, *Causation – The Lords' 'Lost Chance'*, 38 Intl. Comp. L.Q. 735 (1989).
994. Huber (n. 990) 145.
995. See *Greg v. Scott* [2005] UKHL 2, [2005] 2 A.C. 176. Although the strong dissenting judgments of Lords Nicholls and Hope should be noted. Furthermore, in a similar Australian case the lost chance approach succeeded on the basis that it was the only means of enforcing the doctors' duty of care in such circumstances; see *Rufo v. Hosking* (2004) NSWCA 391.

success in extending the scope of liability for asbestos related diseases.[996] Although, as has also been explained, it would entail a quantum leap in legal reasoning to apply this technique to environmental problems on the scale of climate change related losses.[997]

An alternative solution would be to set up a rebuttable presumption based upon the circumstances of the case. Thus, if circumstantial evidence, such as prevailing wind direction and breaches of duty pointed to the defendant's facility, there would be a presumption that the harm was attributable to the defendant's activity. It would, of course, be possible to rebut the presumption on the grounds that the cause of the harm emanated from elsewhere; however, the onus would be on the defendant to adduce evidence in support of this contention. As will be seen below, this is the approach which has been adopted in Germany.

§7.03 APPROACHES TO CAUSALITY IN EU MEMBER STATES

Conventional liability rules in all jurisdictions tend to place a heavy evidential burden on claimants in terms of establishing causation. However, despite the absence of specialist statutory rules on causation, courts in a number of states have evolved means of reducing the evidential burden in certain circumstances through case law developments. For example, in certain jurisdictions, the onus of proof may be shifted onto the defendant if there have been breaches of duty or excessive emissions.[998]

As regards those states which have introduced special environmental liability regimes, there is little consistency regarding how the issue of causation is dealt with. Certain States have not included any special rules on causation in their legislation. For example, in Denmark, the rules on causation under normal civil law remain unaltered by the Act of Compensation for Environmental Damage 225/1994 and the Environmental Protection Act, 358/1991. Generally speaking, there is no set test in Danish tort law for determining probable cause.[999] Instead, matters are decided on a case by case basis taking into account factors such as the distance between the source of the pollutant and the harm and the time lag between the escape of a pollutant and the materialization of the harm. This latter consideration is particularly unsuited to determining liability in respect of environmental harm as there is often an extensive time lag between the deposition of pollutants and the occurrence of harm. An obvious example concerns landfill sites in which damage often occurs years after waste was originally deposited.

Denmark's Scandinavian neighbours in the EU have included causality tests in their respective regimes although they still place the evidential burden on the claimant. For example, in Sweden, the liability provisions of the Environmental Code provide that liability must be determined on the balance of probabilities taking into account

---

996. See §3.03[B][3], above.
997. See §3.03[B][4], above.
998. See M. Hinteregger (ed.), *Environmental Liability and Ecological Damage in European Law*, 349 (CUP 2008).
999. E.M. Basse, *Environmental Law in Denmark*, 204 (Kluwer 2000).

'other possible causes and any other circumstances.'[1000] This leaves plenty of scope for claims to be defeated on the basis of alternate cause arguments. In Finland, section 3 of the Environmental Damage Compensation Act, 737/1994 provides that the plaintiff has to prove 'a probability of a causal link'; this is expressed as being a likelihood of greater than 50%. The determination must be made by reference to the nature of the activity and the type of damage; the Government Bill which preceded the Act stated that an important consideration would be whether the type of damage in question is commonly associated with the particular activity. Whilst the test appears to reflect a 'balance of probabilities', it is possible that, where the damage pathways are particularly complex, the Courts may be drawn to the 95% scientific standard of proof as has occurred in the UK. The reasons for this have been extensively discussed in Chapter 3.

In reviewing the Scandinavian legislation in the mid-1990s, Wetterstein opined that the causality tests included in the Swedish and Finnish Acts constituted an improvement to the extent that they crystallize the causality tests which should be applied. Generally speaking, as regards the general law of tort, causation in those jurisdictions is decided on a case by case basis and there has been no attempt to set out universally applicable principles. However, Wetterstein[1001] made the point that these tests still place a fairly heavy evidential burden on the claimant, although they make it clear that probability of a link will suffice rather than scientific certainty. Nevertheless, in the UK, where the courts developed similar balance of probability tests in the common law many years ago, it has proved difficult for claimants to satisfy these tests in cases concerning environmental damage. In Chapter 3 it was noted that claimants encounter particular difficulties when multiple causes are involved. For reasons which were extensively discussed in that chapter common law refinements of causality tests, such as 'material contribution', have done little to alleviate the evidential burden in an environmental context.

Wetterstein[1002] considered that these states should have gone a step further and introduced a principle by which the evidential burden could be reversed in appropriate circumstances. As an example he cites the system adopted by Sweden's neighbour, Norway, whereby, there is a presumption of causality if there is evidence to suggest that pollutants, emanating from the defendant's facility, may have caused harm damage independently or in combination with other substances.[1003] The presumption can be rebutted by evidence that another unrelated cause is more likely to have caused the damage in question.

Similarly, in Germany measures were taken to ease the burden of causation in cases involving environmental damage, under the ELA 1991 (*Umwelthaftungsgetz* (*UmweltHG*)).[1004] Similar measures have been included in the Austrian Act on Third Party Liability for Nuclear Damage (*Atomhaftungsgesetz* 1999 (*AtomHG* 1999) and the

---

1000. Section 3, Ch. 32 Environmental Code Ds 2000:61.
1001. P. Wetterstein, *The Finnish Environmental Damage Compensation Act – and some comparisons with Norwegian and Swedish Law*, 3(3) Env. Liability 41, 44–45 (1995).
1002. *Ibid.*
1003. Pollution Act 1981, as amended, s. 59.
1004. For an overview of the Act see W.C. Hoffman, *Germany's New Environmental Liability Act: Strict Liability for Facilities Causing Pollution*, 38 Neth. Intl. L. Rev. 27 (1991).

Gene Technology Act (*Gentechnikgesetz* 1994).[1005] In short, these provisions set up a rebuttable presumption of causation which shifts the initial evidential burden onto the defendant. The German mechanism for reversing the burden of proof on causation endeavours to provide detailed guidance on when it is appropriate for the court to make a presumption of causality. Accordingly the provision deserves to be examined in some depth.

As a general principle of German Civil Law it can be extremely difficult to establish causation as the plaintiff is required to prove causation with certainty. The 'balance of probabilities' or 'more probable than not' test which has developed in other jurisdictions is unknown. The strict liability regime introduced by section 22(1) of the Water Resources Act 1960 (WRA)[1006] did not introduce any special rules relating to the establishment of causation with the result that the normal civil rules applied. This meant that it was difficult for plaintiffs to take advantage of the Act. However, the case law flowing from the Act introduced limited grounds for shifting the burden of establishing causation from the plaintiff to the defendant. In case 57 BGHZ 257, 264 (1971) it was held that, where the polluting substance is 'inherently suited' (*geeignet*) to causing the type of harm in question, causation may be presumed. However, this is limited to cases where there are multiple defendants as the principle was designed to relieve the plaintiff of the burden of having to establish precisely how much damage was attributable to each defendant. Where there is only one named defendant the burden of proving causation remains with the plaintiff.

This presumption has been expressly adopted and extended by section 6 of the ELA 1991[1007]. Section 6(1) of the German Act (*UmweltHG*) sets up a rebuttable presumption that the damage in question was caused by the defendant if it can be shown that the defendant's facility is 'inherently suited' to causing that type of harm.[1008] Inherent suitedness is judged by reference to a range of factors relating to the nature of the production process and the circumstances surrounding the release such as meteorological conditions. However, the presumption can only be raised in limited circumstances. Section 6(2) provides that the presumption cannot be raised if the facility has been properly operated. This includes those facilities which have been managed in accordance with 'special operational duties'[1009] and where no disruption of

---

1005. As previously noted the Austrian legislature has also contemplated several Bills on horizontal environmental liability although such a measure has yet to reach fruition. All these proposals have contained provisions on easing the burden of proof on causation.

1006. *Wasserhaushaltsgesetz.*

1007. *Umwelthaftungsgetz.*

1008. § 6(1) ELA 1991, 'If a facility is inherently suited, on the facts of the particular case, to cause the damage that occurred, then it shall be presumed that this facility caused the damage. Inherent suitedness in a particular case is determined on the basis of the course of business, the structures used, the nature and concentration of the materials used and released, the weather conditions, the time and place at which the damage occurred, the nature of the damage, as well as all other conditions which speak for or against causation of the damage in the particular case.'

1009. § 6(3) ELA 1991, 'Special operational duties are those duties imposed by administrative permits, requirements, and enforceable administrative orders and regulatory laws, insofar as their purpose is to prevent environmental impacts that could be considered to be the cause of the damage.'

the business has occurred.[1010] Compliance with all conditions attached to a special operational duty such as a permit, at the time the damage occurred, establishes a presumption that the duty was complied with.[1011] For example, in a case decided by the Upper Regional Court in Düsseldorf[1012] the plaintiff claimed that the paint-work and windows of her car had been damaged by iron oxide dust emitted from a facility operated by her husband's employers. It was alleged that the damage occurred over a two day period when the husband borrowed the car and left it in the company car park. The court held that, whilst there was no doubt that the defendant's plant was capable of producing emissions leading to the type of harm in question in theory (or 'abstract' terms), there could be no presumption that there had been such an occurrence in this particular case (or in 'concrete' terms). At the time the car was left in the car park the plant had been operated in accordance with regulations, regular measurements of emission levels had been taken, and there had been no malfunction which could have led to the emission of iron oxide dust. Operation of the presumption will also be precluded if more than ten years have elapsed since the damage occurred.

To a certain extent, this links liability with whether the operator complied with administrative standards. As a result, it is subject to the same criticisms which have been made against linking fault to the issue of whether or not there has been compliance with administrative standards. Writing shortly after the Act was introduced Hager argued:

> In my view this privilege is not justified. Even if an establishment is legally operated it may create damage to the environment. The victims of those dangers should not be required to provide full proof of causation to be able to recover compensation. Moreover, it should be noted that environmental laws and regulations are not necessarily based on the latest developments of research, they may be more a reflection of economic and political compromise.[1013]

However, this exemption cannot be relied upon in circumstances where there has been an interruption of business;[1014] although this term is not defined it would certainly include an incident such as a major accident. For example, in the case involving damage to the paint-work of a car referred to above, it was significant that there had been no malfunction which could have led to the escape of iron oxide. Thus, plaintiffs

---

1010. § 6(2) ELA 1991, 'Paragraph (1) shall not apply if the facility has been properly operated. A proper operation is present if the special operational duties have been complied with and no disruption of operations has occurred.'
1011. § 6(4) ELA 1991, 'If, for the purpose of supervision of a special operational duty, controls are prescribed in the permit, in requirements, in enforceable administrative orders and regulatory laws, then compliance with this operational duty shall be presumed, if: 1. the controls were carried out during the period in which the environmental impact in question may have issued from the facility, and these controls give rise to no inference of a violation of the operational duty, or, 2. at the time the claim for compensation is made, more than ten years have passed since the environmental impact in question occurred.'
1012. (365) OLG [upper regional court] Düsseldorf, Ruling of 10/12/1993 (22 U 17293).
1013. G. Hager, Umwelthaftungsgetz: The New German Environmental Liability Law, 1(2) Env. Liability 41, 42 (1993).
1014. See n. 1010, above.

would not be able to use this particular ground to prevent operators from rebutting the presumption in cases such as *Cambridge Water v. Eastern Counties Leather*.[1015] This is because the pollution occurred during the ordinary course of business and not as a result of any major incident which interrupted business.

Section 7 sets out the grounds upon which the presumption of causation may be rebutted. It provides that, where either multiple or individual facilities are inherently suited to causing the type of damage in question, the presumption will be rebutted if it can be shown that 'another circumstance' (*Umstand*) was also suited to causing the damage.[1016] This would include pollution emanating from alternative sources.

Taking all this into account we can see that the German provision on reversing the burden of proof is not as far-reaching as it first appears. It is very heavily qualified and is very easy to rebut if there is the slightest suggestion that the harm may have been due to other causes. This may explain why there is a paucity of cases in which the provision has been utilized. In fact the courts have developed far more radical tests through case law developments unrelated to any special liability regimes. In the *Kupolofen*[1017] case, for example, the court held that a duty of full disclosure would arise where the type of damage was consistent with the emissions released. Furthermore, where the disclosure unveiled salient facts, such as an equipment failure or excessive emissions at the material time, the onus would be on the defendant to exculpate himself.

§7.04 EUROPEAN AND INTERNATIONAL INITIATIVES

Whereas strict liability is a common feature of supranational environmental liability regimes, special rules on causation are distinctly lacking. This is inevitable given the complexities of devising a new attest which is acceptable to all. Thus international measures on maritime oil pollution[1018] and nuclear liability[1019] simply refer to the need to establish a causal link between the incident and the damage. The term 'cause' or 'caused' is used frequently throughout the regimes but its meaning is not elucidated or afforded any additional gloss. It is left to the national courts to determine causation in the light of domestic principles. The Lugano Convention makes some attempt to ease the burden of causation faced by the claimant. It appears to have adopted, to a certain extent, the inherent suitedness test in its Convention; Article 10 provides:

1015. [1994] 2 A.C. 264.
1016. § 7(1) ELA 1991, 'If multiple facilities are inherently suited to cause the damage, then the presumption shall not apply if another circumstance is, on the facts of the particular case, inherently suited to cause the damage. Inherent suitedness in a particular case is determined on the basis of the time and place at which the damage occurred, the nature of the damage, as well as all other conditions which speak for or against causation of the damage. (2) If only one facility is inherently suited to cause the damage, then the presumption shall not apply if another circumstance is, on the facts of the particular case, inherently suited to cause the damage.'
1017. BGHZ 92, 143 (1985), 53; see §6.02, above.
1018. See §5.05[A], above.
1019. See §5.05[B], above.

> When considering evidence of the causal link between the incident and the
> damage or, in the context of a dangerous activity as defined in Article 2, paragraph
> 1, subparagraph d, between the activity and the damage, the court shall take due
> account of the increased danger of causing such damage inherent in the dangerous
> activity.

This suggests, that, where the installation in question is particularly suited to causing
the type of damage of which complaint is made, the court should be satisfied with a
lesser standard of proof than would be the case if the damage in question was not
typical of the operation in question. However, the provision is somewhat vague and
does not appear to amount to a reversal of the burden of proof; inherent suitedness is
merely expressed as one of the factors which the court should take into account. In any
case, as has already been explained, it is looking increasingly unlikely that the
Convention will ever see the light of day.[1020]

The various discussion documents which the EU Commission generated during
its deliberations on the need for a European liability regime[1021] vacillated somewhat on
the issue of causation. The 2000 White Paper settled on the need for some easing of the
burden of proof on causation although it did not expand upon how this could be
achieved. It merely referred to the fact that, '[P]rovisions exist in several national
environmental liability regimes to alleviate the burden of proof concerning fault or
causation in favour of the plaintiff.'[1022] As regards a Community regime the White
Paper merely stated that the precise detail of such a provision should be 'defined at a
later stage'.[1023] Bergkamp questioned whether such a provision should be included in
a Community regime at all 'because national courts are able to address any injustice
that may result from the plaintiff's bearing the burden of proof'.[1024] Thus, according to
this approach, under a Community liability regime, the national courts would have
been left to apply existing causality tests under national law. Bergkamp was also of the
opinion that the principle of subsidiarity would restrict the ability of the Community to
impose a unified causality test.[1025]

In this respect it seems that Bergkamp was referring to matters of local policy with
which the issue of causation is deeply imbued. It is certainly true that policy rather than
logic arguably, governs the issue of causation. There is evidence to suggest that the
courts may be prepared to adjust the application of causality tests in order to
accommodate policy considerations. For example, in Chapter 3 it was noted that the
English Courts, as a matter of policy, are reluctant to let the loss lie on injured
employees following industrial accidents. Recall that Lord Wilberforce made comments to this effect in *McGhee v. NCB*.[1026] This could explain why the House of Lords
was prepared to make an assumption of cause and effect on the facts of this particular

---

1020. See §5.04,above.
1021. See §5.03, above.
1022. COM(2000) 66 final, 17.
1023. *Ibid.*
1024. L. Bergkamp et al., *The Commission's White Paper on Environmental liability: A Weak Case
    for an EC Strict Liability Regime, (Part 1)*, 9(4) Eur. Envtl. L. Rev. 105, 110 (2000).
1025. *Ibid.*
1026. [1973] 1 W.L.R. 1.

case. However, as was also noted in Chapter 3, adjusting causality tests on a case by case basis, in order to accommodate policy considerations, can lead to a great deal of uncertainty in the law and may dissuade alleged victims from instigating civil actions. Furthermore, it is far from certain whether there is any judicial consensus on the importance of environmental protection and whether it constitutes an overriding policy objective which could merit some relaxation of causality tests in appropriate circumstances. In *Reay and Hope v. BNFL*[1027] the English High Court conducted a rigorous analysis of the evidence on causality and appeared to err in favour of the defendant where such evidence was finely balanced. Indeed, Holder ventured to suggest that an unarticulated policy objective underlying this decision was the political viability of the Thorp reprocessing plant rather than potential environmental and public health risks.[1028]

Although an EU tort based system of environmental liability never came to fruition, the administrative cost recovery mechanism established by the ELD[1029] raises similar causality issues which are worthy of consideration in this context. In common with the international regimes referred to above the Directive makes liberal use of the term 'cause' or 'caused' without attempting to define the term. This affords national regulators and courts considerable scope to interpret the term in accordance with domestic rules on causation. Nevertheless, the ECJ has ruled that, given the context of the regime and the need to ensure that the polluter pays, domestic courts may adopt a more flexible approach to causation than would ordinarily be the case. In Case C-378/08 *Raffinerie Mediterranee (ERG) SpA .v. Ministero dello Sviluppo Economico*[1030] the Italian authorities had sought to invoke their powers under the ELD to compel a number of petrochemical companies to foot the bill for cleaning up the sea bed in an area where there had been a high concentration of such plants for several decades. The causality difficulties focused on determining the proportion of the damage which was attributable to activities conducted since the Directive came into effect (note that it has no retroactive effect) and apportioning liability amongst multiple operators. The ECJ confirmed that the ELD allowed much scope for interpretation according to domestic laws and practices. The Italian system allowed for a presumption of causation based upon proximity. This was subject to the proviso that the regulator had:

> plausible evidence capable of justifying its presumption, such as the fact that the operator's installation is located close to the pollution found and that there is a correlation between the pollutants identified and the substances used by the operator in connection with his activities.[1031]

As we have seen in the foregoing analysis of domestic liability rules in various EU Member States, it is already the case that courts may be prepared to ease causality tests

---

1027. [1994] Env. L.R. 320.
1028. J. Holder, *Causation in Environmental Law*, 47(2) Current Leg. Probs. 287, 308–309 (1994).
1029. European Parliament and Council Directive (EC) 2004/35 on Environmental Liability with Regard to the Prevention and Remedying of Environmental Damage O.J. L143/56.
1030. [2010] 3 C.M.L.R. 9.
1031. *Ibid.*, at [57].

in cases where there is strong circumstantial evidence pointing to a particular operator or group of operators. Within the context of a specialist environmental regime it is possible that courts may be further emboldened to take such an approach. For example, in the UK there can be no doubt that section 3 of the Compensation Act 2006 has consolidated the attempts by the courts to impose a form of collective joint and several liability on the asbestos industry in respect of the diseases caused by this substance.[1032]

However, the *Raffinerie* case also serves to highlight the difficulties associated with establishing harmonized liability rules in the complex area of causation. The fact that the ELD does not offer a definition of causation and the fact that the ECJ confirmed that the term was open to wide interpretation shows that an EU wide tort based liability regime would not necessarily iron out these differences. The *Raffinerie* case thus demonstrates that differing liability rules may have a profound effect on the extent of the environmental damage costs faced by industries in different states. The continuing implications for the proper functioning of the internal market are clear.

In the light of the above it is clear that any future attempt to harmonize liability rules in the context of environmental damage would need to be cognizant of the following issues. Debate continues to focus on the extent to which viable mechanisms can be implemented for easing the burden of proof on causation.

§7.05   LESSENING THE BURDEN OF PROOF ON CAUSATION: KEY ISSUES

As noted above, to some extent courts in certain EU Member States have already adopted devices which may serve to lessen the burden of proof on causation in certain industries. This normally entails the adoption of a robust view of the circumstantial evidence and the requirement for operators to produce more than speculative or tenuous alternate cause arguments. To date, examples of statutory provisions which expressly reverse the burden of proof remain rare and the mechanism set out in the German UmveltHG remains the prime example. However, raising a rebuttable presumption of causation is not as straight forward as it first appears and may not always achieve the desired result.

[A]   Cases Where There Is Only One Known Causal Agent

The plaintiff would clearly benefit from the presumption where the pollution in question is only associated with the industry in which the operator is involved or where there are no other sources in the area. This is because section 7(1) *UmveltHG* refers to the fact that, wherever there are multiple facilities, all of which are inherently suited to causing the type of damage in question, the presumption can only be rebutted where there is *another circumstance*.

1032. See §3.03[B][1], above.

Thus, in a case such as *Cambridge Water v. Eastern Counties Leather*, where there was no question that PCE was only used by the tanning industry in that area and the only issue was how it travelled from the tannery to the water hole, Cambridge Water would have been relieved of the 'ground breaking' research which it had to undertake in order to establish how the PCE solvents came to contaminate the site.[1033] If there had been other tanneries in the vicinity, section 7(1) would have precluded Eastern Counties Leather from identifying them as other possible sources.

However, the mere fact that an operator is engaged in the industry which is at the source of the pollution is not sufficient to raise the presumption. Section 6(1) narrows down potentially liable parties to those operators whose facilities are 'inherently suited' to causing the type of harm in question. This entails establishing far more than the fact that an operator handled the substance which is known to be the causal agent. For example, it is necessary to take into account all relevant factors such as prevailing weather conditions, whether there had been an incident at a plant and so forth. Where more than one facility meets these criteria paragraph 7(1) provides a second filter by focusing attention on the time and place at which the damage occurred. Thus, fears expressed by Teubner[1034] to the effect that such an approach fails to identify the specific polluter and results in collective responsibility are not entirely justified. The system retains incentives for risk management.

Article 11 of the *Lugano Convention* appears to follow this approach in that it restricts joint liability to those installations where there have been 'incidents'. However, in comparison with the German approach, this restriction is not sufficiently specific in that it makes no provision for consideration of geographic proximity of the plants to the place where the damage occurred and other relevant considerations such as the nature of the incident and the concentrations of harmful substances released.

[B] Cases Where There Is More than One Possible Causal Agent

The extent to which such a provision would be of assistance to a plaintiff in cases where there is more than one possible causal agent very much depends upon the interpretation of the 'alternative cause' ground for rebuttal. In Chapter 2 it was noted that Holder[1035] was of the opinion that, where substances are capable of acting synergistically, the court should be prepared to extend the 'common sense' approach which it already adopts where the nature of the causal agent is known. This accorded with the reasoning of Hager[1036] who argued that, when rebutting the presumption under the *UmweltHG*, the onus should be on the defendant to establish that the

---

1033. This is assuming that the plant had not been 'properly operated'. It will be recalled that s. 6(2) precludes the plaintiff from raising the presumption in cases where the defendant can show that the plant had been properly operated.
1034. See Teubner, *The Invisible Cupola* (n. 989) 27.
1035. J. Holder, *The Sellafield Litigation and Questions of Causation in Environmental Law*, 4 (2) Current Leg. Probs. 278, 302 (1994).
1036. Hager (n. 1013) 42.

alternative causal agent was capable of causing the harm in isolation; otherwise, the defendant could ascribe the harm to environmental pollution.[1037]

However, if it transpires that another substance was capable of causing the harm on its own, this should not automatically rebut the presumption. In other words, the defendant should not be able to use the very uncertainty which the presumption is designed to overcome in order to rebut the presumption; this would defeat the object of the exercise and render the presumption of little benefit. As Price argued:

> If the statistics raised by the plaintiff are sufficient to effect a transfer of the burden of proof it appears ludicrous to allow the defendant to rebut the presumption by using the identical evidence in rebuttal. What purpose does reversing the burden have in such a case?[1038]

The court should be afforded a discretion to consider all the facts of the case including other circumstances which point to the defendant. Thus, if there was a serious accident causing the release of a gas cloud which was borne by winds over a residential area, the court should be in a position to use its discretion to maintain the presumption. However, if there was no such incident and the plaintiff can show no more than a mathematical correlation between the alleged cause and the harm, the court may chose to allow the defence to rebut the presumption.

According to this interpretation of the provision, in a case such as *Reay and Hope v. BNFL*[1039] the judge would have been in a position to infer that, given the fact that there was a breach(s) of statutory duty and given the fact that there was a strong mathematical association between the incidence of cancer amongst the offspring of Sellafield employees, common sense suggested that the parents' exposure to radiation contributed to the harm. This is not to say that the judge was wrong in this case as there were a number of methodological problems with the epidemiological study which cast doubt on its reliability. Nevertheless, as stated in Chapter 3, the current position at English common law unduly restricts the ability of the court to reach a common sense decision.

More recently, the *Corby Group Litigation* case[1040] raised similar issues. Recall that this action concerned claims that birth deformities in children had been caused by their mothers' exposure to teratogens released by the redevelopment of a steelworks site. As noted in Chapter 3,[1041] had the defendants not agreed to settle the claims, each individual claimant would have faced the task of establishing causation in his or her individual case. It was argued that this would have been an uphill struggle had the defendants 'gone to town' on the issue of causation and introduced alternate cause arguments. Given that there were major failings on the part of the developer and assuming that there were no major methodological problems with the epidemiological

---

1037. In this respect s. 59 of the Norwegian Pollution Act 1981 may provide a suitable model in that it specifically refers to the fact that evidence that the pollutant is capable of causing the harm in combination with other substances is sufficient to raise the presumption. See above.
1038. Price (n. 993) 749.
1039. [1994] Env. L.R. 320; see Ch. 3, above.
1040. *Corby Group Litigation v. Corby D.C.* [2009] EWHC 1944 (TCC), [2010] Env. L.R. D2.
1041. See §3.03[B][3], above.

evidence, a presumption of causation of the German type may have served to tip the balance in the claimants' favour. At the very least it would have precluded the defendant from merely asserting that there are other sources of teratogens such as viruses, nicotine or other drugs. It would be necessary to show that the mother was actually exposed to these alternate sources in sufficiently high doses.

Reversal of the burden of causation in this manner does not inevitably lead the court to the conclusion that the defendant was responsible; it merely affords the court the opportunity to depart from the need to establish causation with scientific certainty and enables it to reach a common sense decision based upon the facts of the case. In fact, it can be question whether a special rule is actually needed to achieve this result. As previously noted, in the *Kupolofen* case[1042] the German Court established a rule whereby the onus would fall on the defendant to exculpate himself where there has been an incident and the damage is consistent with the incident. In many respects this is similar to the statutory provision in the *Umvelt HG* which may explain why the latter is little used. At this point it is also necessary to return to the issue of climate change and causation. As noted in Chapter 3, the causation difficulties are likely to prove insurmountable according to orthodox principles – unless there is a major paradigm shift in terms of how the courts or legislature approach the issue of causation.[1043] A reversal of the burden of proof, or a rebuttable presumption, of the type which has been discussed in this section would certainly not constitute such a paradigm shift. An operator would have no difficulty in rebutting the presumption by pointing to a host of other possible causes including other emitters of greenhouse gases. A rebuttable presumption of the type which has been discussed in this chapter is designed to address the *class* causation issue where a number of similar industries are concentrated in a particular area. In such circumstances it is reasonable to raise a presumption of causation against a plant where there has been an 'incident' of some description. Climate change raises causation difficulties of an altogether different magnitude in that the sources are diffused globally and there is no connection between most of these sources. For example, whilst one could argue that there is a sufficient link between electricity generating companies, it would not be possible to disentangle their contribution from unrelated sources such as motor vehicles and agriculture. Thus, as was also noted in Chapter 3, it is likely that liability would have to be attributed according to a different model. This is an issue which shall be addressed in Chapter 11 in the context of financial security mechanisms.

[C]   Retention of Incentives to Abate Pollution

As Hager[1044] argues, compliance with the bare minimum regulatory requirements is not always effective in reducing the risk of pollution. This was clearly demonstrated by the case of *Cockerill Sambre S.A. v. Foundation Reinwater and others*.[1045] Thus, the fact

---

1042. See n. 1017, above.
1043. See §3.03[B][4], above.
1044. Hager (n. 1013) 42.
1045. 3(4) Env. Liability CS62-63 (1995).

that the presumption cannot be invoked where the operator has complied with administrative standards undermines incentives to review existing abatement technologies. Providing a specific ground for precluding the operation of the presumption in such circumstances is unduly restrictive; the issue of whether the plant has been properly operated should merely form one of the general considerations which the court may take into account when considering whether a particular facility was responsible for causing the harm in question. Hence, when there is only one facility in the vicinity which appears inherently suited to causing the harm according to the criteria set out in section 6(1) of the German ELA, it would seem reasonable to infer that the facility was to blame notwithstanding the fact that it was properly operated. Where more than one facility meets the general inherent suitedness criteria, the fact that one of them was not 'properly operated' would focus attention on that particular plant as being the most likely source of the pollution.

§7.06   CONCLUSION

Evidential difficulties in establishing causation greatly increase transaction costs and seriously reduce the role of civil liability as a means of environmental protection. In common with strict liability, causation is central to the theoretical objectives which underlie any system of environmental liability.

Many are suspicious of any attempt to reduce the burden of proof on causation. As Teubner argues, relaxing causation tests may result in collective responsibility rather than individual accountability. Although he recognizes that certain forms of environmental damage may demand a collective response, such as global warming for example, Teubner[1046] argues that it is dishonest to manipulate causation tests so as to render it easier to sue a particular defendant whilst maintaining that individual accountability is the main consideration. In his view any relaxation of existing causation tests creates new 'constellations of collective liability'.[1047] Thus: 'What we find in these constellations is an asymmetric collective responsibility, a kind of "horizontal" vicarious liability'.[1048]

However, the extent to which relaxation of causation tests results in collective responsibility varies greatly according to the mechanism adopted. Such developments are not necessarily incompatible with a tort based liability system which seeks to maintain individual accountability. As has already been stated tort liability is suited to dealing with relatively localized environmental problems. Even those transboundary torts in which successful claims have been brought, typically concern neighbouring states connected by, for example, a common watercourse. Some relaxation of the burden of proof on causation, of the type adopted in Germany, would not, as Teubner seems to fear, create, 'a collective in situations of non-co-operative behaviour'.[1049] The 'inherent suitedness' criteria only enable the claimant to raise the presumption of

---

1046. Teubner (n. 989).
1047. *Ibid.*, 20.
1048. *Ibid.*
1049. *Ibid.*, 27.

causation where local circumstances, such as equipment failure or weather conditions, point to a particular plant. At worst this could create a 'constellation of liability' with other plants engaged in similar activities operating in the locality. This is a very different proposition from the US 'market share' analysis discussed in Chapter 3 whereby such constellations could be created between industries operating in entirely different parts of the country which have no opportunity to cooperate. In order to illustrate the point, it is useful to visualize the objectives of tort as being set out on a spectrum, with corrective functions at one end and distributive functions at the other. If the 'market share' approach is viewed as being at the distributive end of the spectrum, the German rebuttable presumption approach would be found far closer to the opposite corrective end of the spectrum. Thus Teubner's assertion that although, 'the German doctrinal developments do not lead to exactly the same results as their American counterparts … they have one thing in common', in that 'liability law artificially creates a collective in situations of non-co-operative behaviour'[1050] is, perhaps, a little misleading.

Thus, in conclusion it must be noted that the issue of causation has always been bound with policy considerations. It provides one of the mechanisms by which the courts can seek to control the reach of the net of liability. In common with strict liability, discussed in the previous chapter, the mechanism can be adjusted so as to achieve a balance between the corrective and distributive functions of tort discussed in Chapter 4.

1050. *Ibid.*

CHAPTER 8

Access to Justice I: Liberal Conferral of Standing

---

§8.01   INTRODUCTION

As noted in Chapter 2, a major limitation of tort is that liability is contingent upon personal loss. Thus, in many cases of pollution, there may not be an individual or other legal person who is in a position to institute civil proceedings. Even in circumstances where environmental damage does co-coincide with personal loss or interference with property rights, the individual concerned may choose not to pursue the matter. This precludes the operation of civil liability as a means of protecting the so-called 'un-owned environment', as the Commission stated in its early deliberations on the need for an EU regime:

> [A]n important characteristic of environmental law is the frequent lack of a private interest as an enforcement driving force. The environment is often characterised as our 'common heritage'. This also implies that more often than not there is no private appropriation of many parts of it, such as air, seas, wild flora and fauna. Therefore, it is often the case that deterioration of the environment does not cause immediate reaction, and that even if a problem does arise, there is no means by which individuals can use the law to remedy the problem, or there are no appropriate legal remedies available. Even for Community environmental law, it can be the case that important general principles cannot be enforced by individuals (e.g. polluter pays, preventative and precautionary principles).[1051]

This raises another recurrent theme in the environmental liability debate, namely, the extent to which the concept of standing (or *locus standi*) in tort should be expanded to as to enable interested parties to act as form of *guardian ad litem* for the environment.

1051. Communication from the Commission, *Implementing Community Environmental Law*, COM(96) 500 final, para. [38].

Such a development would be of particular interest to environmental NGOs which would then be in a position to pursue polluters through the civil courts. Such actions would be especially useful to an NGO where the damage has not affected a private individual with the wherewithal to pursue his own action. Moreover, even where private actions could be brought, they would focus on individual losses which would not necessarily equate with the full extent of the environmental harm. However, as will be seen below, this issue raises fundamental questions regarding the relationship between public and private law.

§8.02   DEVELOPMENTS IN EU MEMBER STATES

[A]   *Locus Standi* of NGOs

In certain continental jurisdictions the distinction between the public interest and the interests of the individual has been eroded so as to afford standing to NGOs in environmental matters.

For the most part, it is not possible for NGOs to bring claims in respect of the environment as a separate entity from any private interests. In cases where private interests have in fact been affected, in certain jurisdictions, standing may be afforded to associations comprising members who have suffered direct loss as a result of the pollution. For example, in Denmark, section 34(3) of the Freshwater Fisheries Act provides that the Danish Angling Association and the Association of Commercial Fisheries may claim compensation for the cost of restocking polluted lakes and rivers.

Until recently this was also the position in France where persons who have suffered loss as a result of a criminal act may initiate civil proceedings with a view to recovering damages. Formerly, the only interest groups which were allowed to rely upon this right were organizations which represented the individual victims who had suffered direct loss. For example, in the *Protex*[1052] case, the Chairman of the Board and head manager of the Protex group were convicted of offences relating to a fire at a chemicals plant which led to the contamination of the Loire. Interest groups which represented those directly affected, such as local federations of fishermen and fish breeders, were able to recover damages in respect of various expenses to which they had been put. However, general conservation groups which had incurred indirect costs, such as an ornithological group which had endeavoured to rescue birds, were excluded from this category. However, since the *Protex* case the right to recover damages following a criminal conviction has now been extended to interest groups which have incurred such indirect costs.[1053] Thus, an operator who has sustained a criminal penalty in respect of a polluting incident may also find himself liable in damages to any interest groups which have incurred clean-up costs.

This provision was put to good effect in litigation stemming from the Erika oil spill off the coast of Brittany. In December 1999 the super-tanker, Erika, ran into heavy

---

1052. TGI Tours, ch. correctionelle, 13 Janvier 1992, ministère public c/M et R. No. 106.
1053. Article 5 III of Law 95/101 of 2nd February 1995. This was later absorbed by Article L142-2 of the Environmental Code.

252

storms in the Bay of Biscay and broke in two. A considerable quantity of oil washed ashore on the beaches of Brittany and had a devastating effect on wild life. Various environmental organizations, including the *Ligue pour la Protection des Oiseaux*, incurred considerable expense in treating birds and cleaning up the damage. In 2008 the *Tribunal Correctionnel de Paris* found the ship's owners, charterers and classification society guilty in respect of a number of criminal offences associated with the spillage. A number of the French environmental groups, which had joined the proceedings by way of the civil party petition procedure, were awarded damages in respect of the costs which they had incurred.[1054] Thus, it seems that economic losses of this nature are clearly regarded as recoverable within the context of the special regime enshrined in the Environmental Code.[1055] Indeed, according to the approach adopted by the Court in the Erika case, such loss is regarded as direct and immediate and can be equated with damage caused to those with a proprietary interest in a damaged resource. Interestingly, however, damages went beyond the direct financial loss suffered by the environmental groups and reflected 'moral loss' associated with the disaster and the damage to the marine and coastal environment.[1056] In English law this can be equated with non-pecuniary 'general damages' which are normally awarded in respect of pain and suffering or the unquantifiable upset suffered by the victim of a tort. The basis for making such an award in the Erika case is the subject of some debate. It could be interpreted as reflecting the impact of the disaster on the collective feelings of the members of the groups. Alternatively, it could reflect the damage to the objects of the organizations all of which had long standing and deep rooted involvements in the affected locations.[1057] Whatever the precise justifications for the approach, it clearly signifies the endorsement of French environmental organizations as guardians of the environment. This facilitates the protection of the environment as a distinct entity in its own right as opposed to a collection of private interests. There appears to be strong judicial enthusiasm for this approach in France in that a liberal interpretation of the rules has been adopted and it seems that it is no longer necessary to launch such an action on the back of criminal proceedings. Rather, civil actions have now been brought in the civil courts independently of any criminal proceedings.[1058]

The best known example of a system in which the *locus standi* of public interest groups has been extended in an environmental context can be found the Netherlands. In the late 1980s and early 1990s NGOs gained substantial standing rights in civil cases concerning both actions in tort and judicial review. Although, as regard the latter, there

---

1054. For a detailed overview of the Erika litigation see D. Papadopolou, *The Role of French Environmental Associations in Civil Liability for Environmental Harm: Courtesy of Erika*, 21(1) J. Envtl. L. 87 (2009).
1055. See n. 1053, above.
1056. See Papadopolou (n. 1054) 98.
1057. *Ibid.*
1058. *Ibid.*, 102.

has latterly been some hardening of the rules on *locus standi*.[1059] Nevertheless, the position in the Netherlands is still worthy of careful consideration.[1060]

At one time the position under Dutch Law as regards standing was similar to that under English Law in that there was a clear distinction between the realms of public and private law. Thus, whilst an interest group would be afforded standing in judicial review proceedings, it would not be afforded standing in tort actions. However, in 1986 the Dutch Supreme Court ruled in the case of *De Nieuwe Meer*[1061] that the Civil Code's tort law provision[1062] was capable of affording protection to general environmental interests and that organizations who represented those interests (according to their articles of association) should be entitled to seek injunctive relief in order to safeguard them. This decision was affirmed in the *Kuunders*[1063] case in which various environmental foundations sought an injunction against a farmer who was operating a pigsty in breach of licensing requirements. The Supreme Court took the opportunity to expand upon the rationale for extending standing to NGOs in such circumstances:

> 4.1.2 (...) In the present case – which concerns combating the impairment of the environment by causing damage to a protected nature reserve – an exception is to be accepted to the rule that the description of the purpose of a legal person alone does not entitle it to institute proceedings before the civil courts with respect to infringements of the interests which it is promoting according to that description. This exception is justified by the fact that the interests of the Foundations are promoting – ecological interests which are served by the [designation] of the Deurnse Peel as a nature reserve – concern interests of citizens which are not suitable for protection against infringements as *in casu* by individual actions. Consequently, efficient protection of these interests against such an infringement by proceedings before the civil courts – which may be needed next to the protection which must be provided by the public authorities – requires 'joining' as constituted by the legal proceedings by the Foundations. Furthermore, the interests in hand are of a kind as protected by Article 1401 (old) Civil Code and Article 6:162 Civil Code.[1064]

Thus, it seems that the court viewed increased standing for NGOs as a means of aggregating the diffuse ecological interests of citizens.

The approach adopted by the Dutch Supreme Court on the issue of standing in tort actions was later codified by the Dutch legislature; to this end the Collective Actions Act 1994 inserted two new Articles into Book 3, Title 11, of the Civil Code on Rights of Action which provide as follows:

> An association or foundation with full legal capacity is entitled to entertain an action for the purposes of protecting interests of other persons that are similar

---

1059. See H. Tolsma, K. De Graaf & J. Jans, *The Rise and Fall of Access to Justice in the Netherlands*, 21(2) J. Envtl. L. 309 (2009).
1060. For a general overview of the Dutch system see, See M. Hinteregger, (ed.) *Environmental Liability and Ecological Damage in European Law*, 460–472 (CUP 2008).
1061. Supreme Court 27 June 1986, *Nederlandse Jurisprudentie* 1987, 743, note by Heemskeerk.
1062. Article 162 of Book 6.
1063. Supreme Court 18 December 1992, *Nederlandse Jurisprudentie* 1994, 139 note by Scheltema and Brunner.
1064. Extract reproduced in Gerrit Betlem, *Civil liability for Transfrontier Pollution* (Kluwer 1993).

in kind, inasmuch as it promotes these interests according to its articles of association.[1065]

This is subject to a number of limitations which include the need for the NGO to establish that it has made sufficient attempts to settle the matter out of court.[1066] Furthermore, an NGO would not be able to insist upon pursuing an action against the will of the landowners affected.[1067] This limitation protects the freedom to contract in that it prevents an NGO from undermining the property rights of a landowner who may have reached his own settlement with the polluter and elected not to pursue any action before the courts. In addition, as a general principle of Dutch law, vexatious claims are prohibited by Article 3.13 of the Civil Code on abuse of rights.

The Dutch Supreme Court and the legislature have developed a principle whereby NGOs are regarded as representing the ecological interests of citizens. Thus, in seeking injunctive relief the NGO can be considered as acting on behalf of those collective interests. However, it is difficult to apply this logic in cases where damages are sought as opposed to injunctive relief. As the NGO is not acting on behalf of a fixed class of specified individuals it would be impossible to make an award of damages. As a result the amended Civil Code expressly precludes the recovery of damages where the NGO is acting on behalf of the public interest in this manner.[1068] However, as Betlem[1069] pointed out when reviewing the system in its early years, this does not prevent NGOs from recovering damages in respect of costs which the NGO has sustained itself as a result of a polluting incident. In the *Kuunders* case the court stated that ecological damage could be regarded as 'unlawfulness' towards those organizations which have as their object the protection of such interests. In the *Borcea*[1070] case the Dutch Society for the Protection of Animals sought to recover the costs it had incurred in cleaning and nursing sea birds which had been caught by an oil spill. It was held that, although sea birds could not be regarded as anyone's property, their conservation must be regarded as a public interest deserving of protection in the Netherlands. Furthermore, this public interest could be viewed as the 'individual interest' of the Society as its very purpose was to undertake the conservation of such animals. Accordingly, the court could see no reason why the Society should not be able to recover damages 'in so far as the Society's claim relates to the damage which it itself has suffered.'[1071] This mirrors the approach adopted in France where, it will be recalled, organizations my now recover clean-up costs which they have incurred as a result of pollution.

1065. Article 3: 305a(1).
1066. Article 3: 305a(2): 'A legal person within the meaning of section 1 shall not have standing if and when it has insufficiently attempted, in the circumstances of the case, to reach the result sought be the action by way of consultation with the defendant'.
1067. Article 3:305a(4): 'An act cannot form the basis of an action within the meaning of section 1 to the extent that the person affected by it objects to the action'.
1068. Article 3:305a(3): An action as referred to in section 1 cannot relate to damages in money.
1069. G. Betlem, *Standing for Ecosystems – Going Dutch*, 54(1) Cambridge L.J. 153, 165 (1995).
1070. District Court Rotterdam Mar. 15, 1991, N.Y.I.L. (1992) 513.
1071. *Ibid.*

The logic applied by the court in this case was ingenious in that, by regarding the general interest in bird protection as the Society's own interest, a link was provided between ecological damage and a private interest which could provide the basis of an action in tort. Thus, as Betlem stated, once this step has been taken:

> A public interest group can ... 'play the legal' game like any other player and claim compensation for harm done to its own interest.[1072]

[B]   The Right of Public Authorities to Pursue Actions in Tort

In certain States, public authorities have the right to pursue a polluter in tort rather than relying upon regulatory powers. For example, an authority could find that its powers are inadequate in a particular matter or would not achieve the desired result. Of course, the State may have a direct proprietary interest in, for example, an area of land or a body of water contaminated by pollution. In this case the State would be in a position to seek damages or injunctive relief in the same manner as a private litigant. However, the matter is rather less clear where the State has no direct proprietary interest in the resource affected, but wishes to pursue the matter in tort on behalf of the public interest in environmental protection. This raises rather similar issues to those discussed above in respect of affording standing to NGOs in such matters. The theoretical arguments for affording standing to interested bodies as representatives of the publics' equitable private interest in the environment have already been discussed. It would seem logical to assert that if standing can be conferred on an NGO, which can demonstrate a sufficient interest in the matter, a public authority charged with protecting the environment by law should be in a similar position. However, as regards the ability of public authorities to bring actions in tort, there is an added complication in that such bodies are already equipped with regulatory powers which are not available to an NGO. An issue which has arisen in certain Member States concerns whether an authority should be able to bring actions in tort in place of, or in addition to, the use of any public enforcement powers available to it. This issue is likely to become of increasing importance due to the widening of administrative clean-up powers under the ELD.[1073] Given that the ELD focuses on a relatively narrow type of harm[1074] it is possible that authorities may wish to use alternative actions in tort as a means of recovering damages in respect of other types of losses. However, this raises difficult issues regarding the duplication of powers and the extent to which public law mechanisms should be construed as replacing alternative actions in tort. These issues are discussed below.

1072. Betlem (n. 1069) 166.
1073. European Parliament and Council Directive (EC) 2004/35 on Environmental Liability with Regard to the Prevention and Remedying of Environmental Damage O.J. L143/56.
1074. See §6.05[B], above.

In certain jurisdictions, a public authority cannot pursue an action in tort in order to recover the costs of a service which it is bound to provide.[1075] Thus, a fire brigade would not be able to recover the costs of fighting a fire.[1076] This principle, common to Anglo-American jurisdictions in addition to France and Germany is sometimes referred to as the 'free public services doctrine' or *'gratuité des services publics'*.[1077] The oil company Amoco successfully invoked the principle in proceedings brought against it following the Amoco Cadiz oil slick. Thus certain authorities, which had incurred considerable expenditure in cleaning up the oil, were barred from recovering these costs via the tort route.[1078] On occasion there may be statutory exceptions to the general doctrine which enable authorities to seek remedies against the polluter in tort. However, in most cases public regulatory powers will contain a mechanism for recovering clean-up costs from the polluter. Once again one can refer to the ELD as an especially apposite example of such an approach.

However, other States in Western Europe do not maintain a rigid demarcation between the realms of public and private law with the result that authorities may have recourse to remedies in tort.[1079] Nevertheless, it has proved necessary to formulate underlying principles for determining when it is appropriate for an authority to pursue an action in tort as opposed to using its public powers. In terms of legal certainty it would seem inappropriate for an authority to circumvent its statutory powers by the use of tort. Once again, a particularly clear case study of the development of these principles is provided by the experience in the Netherlands. Although Dutch authorities have a general right to pursue actions in tort,[1080] the courts have limited this right in order to avoid unnecessary duplication of public enforcement powers.

In the *Beckiser* case,[1081] the issue arose as to whether a public authority had *locus standi* to seek injunctive relief in order to secure the removal of large quantities of gypsum from Dutch territory. The gypsum had been exported to the Netherlands by the German company *Beckiser* for reprocessing by a Dutch company, Bos, at a very low price. Rather than reprocessing the substance, Bos dumped the gypsum at eight sites in

---

1075. Stewart argues that it is inappropriate to rely upon standard principles of tort in this context. The principles of corrective justice which apply to relations between private individuals cannot apply in the same manner as regards the relationship between the individual and the state. Thus, to borrow a concept from EC law, corrective justice normally operates on a horizontal plane as opposed to a vertical plane. This is because the government and its agencies have duties and competencies which are not enjoyed by citizens. See R.B. Stewart, 'Liability for Natural Resource Damage: Beyond Tort' in Rene Foque et al. (eds.), *Geinte-greerde rechtswetenschap*, 460 (Gouda Quint 1994).

1076. See, for example, the French cases of *Chausson v. Prefect de Valice* (Cass. 10 January 1866) and *X v. Pompier des Bouches-du Rhône*, 87, 10-3-1959 (Cass. 10 January 1990).

1077. See P.F.A. Bierbooms & P.A. Kottenhagen-Edzes, *Environmental Damage and a Public Authority's Right to Sue*, 4 Eur. Rev. Priv. L. 145 (1996).

1078. 954 F2d 1279 (7th Circ. 1992): 'In both nations (France and the US), courts decline to require tortfeasors to compensate the government for the cost of services (such as police protection or fire-fighting) that a public body supplies.'

1079. Bierbooms and Kottenhagen-Edzes (n.1077) 156–157.

1080. Under Art 6:162 of the *Burgerlijk Wetboek* (Dutch Civil Code(BW)), public authorities have the right to seek injunctive relief or to sue for damages in order to prtect certain interests.

1081. *Hoge Raad* 14 April 1989, NJ 1990, 712. Discussed by Bierbooms and Kottenhagen-Edzes (n.1077) 151–152.

the Netherlands in clear breach of the Chemical Waste Act; this posed a major environmental and public health threat as gypsum contains cyanide. The Dutch authorities sought a mandatory injunction against Beckiser requiring it to recover the gypsum and return it to Germany. Although the Dutch authorities had no direct proprietary interest in any of the sites where the substance had been dumped, it was found by the Hoge Raad (Dutch Supreme Court) that the authorities had a general interest in environmental and public health protection. Furthermore, this interest was of a type which could be classed as a 'tort protected interest'. In other words, the interest was sufficiently concrete to be afforded protection in tort. It can be argued that this decision reflects the view that in this context the State can be regarded as guardian of the publics' equitable ownership of the environment. Furthermore, the Hoge Raad stated that it was appropriate for the authorities to utilize tort in this case as the same result could not have been achieved by means of the administrative powers contained in section 49 of the Chemical Waste Act.

Thus the Court recognized that it would be advantageous for an authority to pursue an action in tort in certain circumstances and that this avenue should not be barred to it. However, it was also clear that it would be necessary to develop principles for determining when it would be appropriate for an authority to pursue an action in tort. The 'tort protected interest' test enunciated in *Beckiser* was found somewhat lacking in this respect as there was no general consensus on how one defines a 'tort protected interest'.[1082] Furthermore, it did little to resolve the problem of overlap between tort based remedies and statutory powers and when it would be appropriate to use tort in place of such powers.

In subsequent decisions the Dutch Courts have developed the 'encroachment test' according to which authorities may have recourse to remedies in tort provided that they do not unacceptably encroach upon regulatory enforcement mechanisms. The principle was formulated in the *Windmill* case[1083] in which the Dutch State instigated tort proceedings against Windmill in respect of discharges of waste plaster slurry into a waterway owned by the state. Windmill objected to making further payments on the grounds that it had obtained all requisite licenses under the Rivers Act and the Pollution of Surface Waters Act. The Hoge Raad held that the issue of whether the use of tort by the state unacceptably encroached upon statutory powers should be determined by the application of three criteria relating to the content and purpose of the regulation; whether citizens' interests are adequately protected under public law; and whether a comparable result could be attained through the use of public powers. In applying these criteria to the present case the Court found that allowing the state to obtain compensation in tort would encroach upon the public law system to an unacceptable degree. Allowing the State to challenge in tort discharges which it had itself sanctioned would have entirely undermined the licensing system and would have

---

1082. *Ibid.*, 152.
1083. *Hoge Raad*, 26 January 1990, NJ 1991, 393. Discussed by Bierbooms and Kottenhagen-Edzes (n. 1077) 153–154.

had serious implications for legitimacy, democracy and legal certainty in the Dutch legal system.[1084]

The criteria were subsequently applied in *State v. Magnus Metals International*[1085] in which a rather different conclusion was reached. In this case the Dutch authorities sought injunctive relief against Magnus in order to prevent soil contamination by zinc residue and the importation of further consignments of this substance. Once again the issue arose as to whether the Dutch authorities were entitled to seek a remedy in tort in place of their statutory powers under section 49 of the Chemical Waste Act. Recall that in Benckiser the authority's action succeeded on the grounds that the same result could not have been attained through the use of this particular statutory provision. However, in the interim the powers in section 49 had been strengthened and a new section 49(a) included which enabled the authority to carry out remediation works and recover the costs from the polluter. Despite this improvement the authority still sought injunctive relief in tort on the grounds that in this particular case there would be practical difficulties associated with recovering the clean-up costs from the operator. Reversing the decision of the Hof (Dutch Court of Appeal) the Hoge Raad concluded that it was appropriate to take into account practical difficulties when applying the 'comparable result' criterion of the encroachment test. As previously noted, the ELD has significantly increased the scope of such clean-up powers under administrative law. However, the approach adopted by the Hoge Raad demonstrates that, whilst regulators should be required to use the public power whenever possible, they should maintain some discretion to pursue actions in tort when this is the most efficacious solution.

§8.03 EUROPEAN AND INTERNATIONAL DEVELOPMENTS

For the most part international agreements on environmental liability do not specifically extend *locus standi* to bodies such as environmental interest groups. However, the 1992 Convention on Liability for Oil Pollution Damage[1086] provides that any person can recover the costs of reasonable preventative measures and measures of reinstatement. Given that it is reasonable for a conservation or wildlife protection group to incur such costs in cleaning up birds and beaches etc., it seems that the Convention is capable of bearing an interpretation which would afford such parties a cause of action. This is in accordance with the approach adopted by the French courts in litigation stemming from the Erika oil spill.[1087]

1084. *Ibid.*,152. It is for this reason that the Hoge Raad has retreated from the 'dual track' approach whereby authorities had unfettered rights to bring actions in tort irrespective of whether they also enjoyed adequate public enforcement powers.

1085. Hoge Raad 22 October 1993, NJ 1995, 717. Discussed by Bierbooms and Kottenhagen-Edzes (n. 1077) 154–155.

1086. See definitions under Article 1 of the IOPC, 'Liability and Compensation for Oil Pollution Damage:Texts of the 1992 Conventions and the Supplementary Fund Protocol'(2005 edition), http://www.iopcfund.org/npdf/Conventions %20English.pdf (accessed Sept. 13, 2011). See §5.05[A], above.

1087. See §8.02[A], above.

Article 18 of the Council of Europe Convention addresses the issue more directly and affords standing to '[a]ny association or foundation which according to its statutes aims at the protection of the environment' provided that it complies with 'any further conditions of internal law.' This enables such organizations to seek injunctive relief in order to; prohibit dangerous and unlawful activities which pose a threat to the environment; require that the operator takes measures to prevent an incident or damage from occurring (similar to a *quia timet* injunction); require that the operator takes measures to prevent damage after an incident has occurred; require that the operator takes reinstatement measures where the damage has already occurred. However, the Convention leaves domestic jurisdictions free to decide the circumstances in which such a request should be denied and the court or tribunal before which such requests should be made.

As regards the earlier EU policy debates about the need for a tort based environmental liability regime the Commission eventually decided in favour of extending standing to NGOs. The 2000 White Paper regarded this as a means of empowering civil society to share the burden of enforcing environmental law:

> there are limits to the availability of public resources for this, and there is a growing acknowledgement that the public at large should feel responsible for the environment and should under circumstances be able to act on its behalf.[1088]

However, the Paper also seemed to be aware of the fact that there is a risk that persuading NGOs to take a proactive role by affording them *locus standi* to seek injunctive relief, for example, could encourage public authorities to stand back and shirk their responsibilities. In this respect it is significant that the Paper referred to the setting up of a 'two tier' approach whereby 'Member States should be under a duty to ensure restoration of biodiversity damage and decontamination in the first place (first tier), by using the compensation or damages paid by the polluter'.[1089] Public interest groups would act on a subsidiary basis (second tier) where the authority does not act at all or responds in an inadequate manner.[1090] In such circumstances the public interest group would be in a position to instigate civil proceedings against the polluter. Thus it seems that the White Paper envisaged some form of *vertical integration* in the enforcement process between the State and public interest groups. The ELD, which replaced the tort based approach envisaged by the White Paper with a public law based cost recovery system, affords no special status to NGOs. Rather, they are confined to a weak power to request the authority to exercise its powers. This right is shared with all other interested parties such as local residents.

Given that the ELD focuses on public powers it is not surprising that the role of NGOs is very limited. It is difficult to say whether the more extensive role proposed by the 2000 White Paper would have been retained in any tort based regime. Delegating public enforcement powers to bodies which are not part of government and which espouse partisan views would have been problematic and fertile ground for judicial

---

1088. Com(2000) 66 final, para [4.7].
1089. *Ibid.*, para. [4.7.1].
1090. *Ibid.*

review proceedings. However, as we have seen, environmental damage can be closely equated with individual costs sustained by such bodies. Thus, there are still strong arguments for adopting a broader view of *locus standi* where liability in tort is concerned. Nevertheless, this still raises some difficult issues regarding the relationship between public and non-governmental bodies in the protection of the environment. These difficulties shall be addressed in the final section of this chapter.

§8.04 MAIN CONSIDERATIONS

Increased standing for NGOs would be a vital component of any civil liability regime designed to reduce the risk of ecological damage. As the Dutch Supreme Court reasoned in the *Kuunders* case, unless there is some mechanism for aggregating the diffuse costs of this form of pollution, tortious liability cannot play any useful role in this context. One method of aggregating these costs is to allow NGOs to undertake representative actions on behalf of the public interest. Environmental interest groups have made considerable progress in gaining standing rights in tort actions in both the Netherlands and France. Moreover, it seems likely that the EU Commission would have adopted a similar approach had it decided to pursue the implementation of a tort based environmental liability regime. However, increased standing rights for bodies such as NGOs also raises a number of difficult issues which require careful consideration.

[A] Usurpation of Private Bargaining Rights

A particularly difficult issue concerns the need to balance the objective of environmental protection against the freedom of a private individual to reach his own settlement with a polluter. The Dutch system prohibits NGOs from taking action where this would be contrary to the wishes of individuals directly concerned. This gives rise to a dilemma in that, whilst such agreements may be in the short term interests of the landowners concerned, they may not be in the best interests of the environment. If public interest issues demand that pollution should, notwithstanding any such private agreements, still be halted by means of injunctive relief, it could be argued that only a governmental organization with statutory powers should be in a position to override the landowners freedom to contract. This is the approach adopted in Italy where public authorities, as trustees for the community, are afforded sole responsibility for bringing civil claims for environmental damage.[1091] However, the increased standing afforded to public authorities has been at the expense of the standing rights afforded to NGOs which have been entirely precluded from instigating proceedings.[1092] The problem with this approach is that it prevents any other organization from acting in default of the public authority which may be fettered by, for example, policy considerations or lack of

---

1091. Law 349/1986. For an overview of the Italian system see, A. Bianchi, *The Harmonization of Laws on Liability for Environmental Damage in Europe: An Italian Perspective*, 6(1) J. Envtl. L. 21 (1994).
1092. *Ibid.*, Article 13.

resources. As argued in the previous chapter, the EU wishes to increase the role of civil liability in order reduce reliance upon public authorities. The solution to this problem may be to adopt elements of both the Dutch and Italian systems; thus whilst an NGO would be prevented from instigating proceedings where the individuals concerned object, it would nevertheless remain open to a public authority to instigate its own proceedings in the public interest. This would augment the regulatory powers, such as those set out in the ELD, which enable certain authorities to carry out preventative or remedial measures in default and to recover the costs from the polluter.

[B]   The Role of Public Authorities

The 2000 White Paper suggested that public authorities should enjoy *locus standi* to pursue actions in tort in order to protect environmental media in which they may have no direct proprietary interest. However, the Paper did not acknowledge the difficulties associated with conferring private rights of action upon regulatory authorities in addition to existing public enforcement powers; indeed, it seemed wholly unaware of this potential problem. As we have seen, many environmental regulations already contain provisions which allow authorities to carry out remediation works and recover the costs from the polluter or occupier. This approach has been radically expanded under the ELD. Including a civil liability component, which affords standing to public authorities, in existing regulations could result in duplication of public enforcement powers. This may lead to uncertainty of the nature described above in relation to developments in certain EU Member States. Indeed, even those States, which do permit authorities to pursue claims in tort in the exercise of their public functions, wish to limit this right and improve public enforcement powers. As we have seen, the Dutch courts have limited recourse to tort through the development of the encroachment test.[1093] Moreover, certain regulations allow authorities to recover remediation costs through the use of regulatory powers[1094] whilst other regulations confer specific standing rights on authorities to pursue actions in tort.[1095] This reflects the fact that different environmental problems demand the use of different regulatory techniques and regulators must be afforded flexibility in determining which method to employ in particular circumstances. For example, the definition of damage under the ELD is rather narrow. It may be necessary to have recourse to tort in order to recover damages in respect of other types of harm such as property damage.

1093. The right to pursue actions in tort is also limited in other jurisdictions. In Belgium, for example, the existence of a statutory duty is said to break the chain of causation between the tortious act and the harm. However, certain statutes expressly confer standing rights on public authorities which serve as an exception to this general principle. In Germany, § 677 of the Civil Code (BGB) afford authorities the right to seek damages in respect of the costs of services. However, German academic opinion is highly critical of this provision on the grounds that it interferes with public law powers and can lead to problems of certainty and legitimacy of the nature described above. See Bierbooms and Kottenhagen-Edzes (n. 1077), 156–157.
1094. See, for example, section 49(a) Chemical Waste Act referred to above in the Magnus litigation.
1095. See Article 75 Soil Protection Act.

In the UK, however, it is difficult to conceive of a situation in which a public authority would feel compelled to pursue an action in tort as opposed to using administrative powers. This is because *statutory nuisances*[1096] cover many of the types of harm which normally provide the subject matter of tort actions in an environmental context. Although statutory nuisances sound in the public sphere and are subject to administrative powers and criminal penalties, they were originally created by directly importing concepts drawn from the private law of nuisance into the early Public Health Acts.[1097] In fact the courts usually call upon common law authorities on the definition of private nuisance to help define the scope of statutory nuisances.[1098] In addition, local authorities can bring proceedings in public nuisance which may afford certain individuals a private cause of action in respect of harm which exceeds that suffered by the general population.[1099] Thus, administrative powers are likely to cover most types of harm beyond the reach of the ELD.

[C] Respective Roles of the State and Public Interest Groups

The two tier enforcement strategy advocated by the 2000 White Paper, whereby a public interest group would only be able to act in default of a public body, could also give rise to some difficulties. As noted above, the Paper was clearly of the opinion that the primary responsibility for environmental protection should remain with the State and its regulatory authorities. For this reason the Paper made the point that the role of public interest groups should be *subsidiary* to that of the state. However, the Paper did not explain how this could be achieved in practice. It is easy to envisage a situation in which the State, perhaps for the sake of saving resources, may decline to act in a matter in the hope that a public interest group would take up the cause. This would shift enforcement responsibilities onto public interest groups, which in many cases only have very limited resources themselves, to an unacceptable degree.

Any system, which attempted to allocate responsibility between the State and public interest groups, would need to ensure that pressure is maintained upon the state to take the lead role. For example, public interest groups could be afforded a formal right to request the authority to act in a certain matter. If the authority declined to act it could be required to supply the public interest group with a full written explanation of its reasons within a set time limit. If the interest group then decided to press ahead with its own proceedings the Court could be required to consider the authority's decision not to pursue the matter when apportioning costs. If it considered that the authority's reasons were inadequate the Court could be afforded a discretion to make the authority bear a proportion of the public interest groups costs. Similarly, where, in an urgent case, the public interest group has obtained an injunction prior to any

---

1096. See Part III of the Environmental Protection Act 1990.
1097. For historical analysis see N. Morag-Levine, *Is Precautionary Regulation a Civil Law Instrument? Lessons from the History of the Alkali Act*, 23(1) J. Envtl. L. 1 (2011).
1098. See *National Coal Board v. Neath BC* [1976] 2 All E.R. 478
1099. See §2.05, above.

consultation with the relevant authority, the Court could once again be afforded a discretion to require the authority to bear some of the costs.

As we have seen, the right of bodies, such as NGOs, to request action on the part of regulators appeared in a very watered down form in the ELD. It has already been noted that there are good reasons for this in that there are difficulties associated with bestowing public enforcement powers on non-governmental bodies. However, in the context of the tort based regime advocated by the 2000 White Paper, where damage would have been more closely equated with the interests of the organization, the reasons for adopting a two tier approach still hold good.

[D]   Remedies

The other main issue which deserves careful consideration concerns which remedies should be available to an NGO. Injunctions are most commonly sought to prevent the continuance of, for example, harmful emissions, or to prevent an activity from proceeding which constitutes an immediate threat. Where damage has already oc-curred the issue is rather more complicated in that it must be ensured that any payments made benefit the environment as opposed to the NGO. An award of compensatory damages is clearly appropriate where an organization has incurred expenses as a result of carrying out remediation works. This is the approach followed in Holland; the 1991 Draft Directive on Civil liability for Damage Caused by Waste also allowed interest groups to recover expenses which they have incurred as a result of clean-up operations.[1100] A further consideration is that costs which have actually been incurred by interest groups may only represent part of the full costs of the pollution in that the organization may not have had the expertise or resources to effect a full clean-up; further measures may be necessary in future. The European Environmental Law Association suggested that the most obvious solution would be to pay damages, calculated upon the basis of the full cost to the environment, into a trust fund.[1101] This would ensure that the money could only be used for the purpose of on-going remediation works resulting from the original escape. In England such an approach is already common place in personal injuries cases where a person has been left with a long term disability. Periodic payments are made into a trust fund from which the trustees may, from time to time, authorize payments in order to pay for nursing or further treatment.[1102]

1100. Article 4(3): 'Common interest groups or associations, which have as their object the protection of nature and the environment, shall have the right either to seek any remedy under paragraph 1(b) … ' Paragraph 1(b) provides for: ' … the reimbursement of costs lawfully incurred in reinstating the environment and in taking preventative measures (including costs of damage caused by preventative measures)'.

1101. European Environmental Law Association, *Repairing Damage to the Environment – A community System of Civil Liability* (submission to the Joint Public Hearing of the European Parliament and the Commission of the European Communities on Preventing and Remedying Environmental Damage), para. [11.13] (Brussels Nov. 3/4, 1993).

1102. See The Law Commission Consultation Paper No. 125, *Structural Settlements and Interim and Provisional Damages* (Stationary Office Books 1992).

An alternative solution would be to enable NGOs to seek mandatory injunctions requiring the polluter to effect clean-up measures. In response to the Commission Green Paper the European Environmental Law Association argued:

> Given the inclusion in the Green Paper of discussion on the restoration of the environment, we see no reason why it should be beyond the scope of a system of civil liability to allow persons to bring proceedings to seek an order from a court requiring a defendant to repair environmental damage, or to pay the cost incurred by others in so doing.[1103]

Article 4(3) of the 1991 draft Directive on Civil Liability for Damage Caused by Waste provided that interest groups should be in a position to obtain any remedy; this would include mandatory injunctions in those jurisdictions where they are available. It will be recalled that Article 18 of the *Lugano* Convention identifies the different forms of injunctive relief which should be available to an interest group. Article 18(1)(d) provides that an interest group should be able to request 'that the operator be ordered to take measures of reinstatement.' The 2000 White Paper retained the right for NGOs to seek injunctive relief in urgent cases.[1104]

§8.05 CONCLUSION

It has been noted on a number of occasions that one of the main limitations of tort as a means of environmental protection concerns the fact that it is geared towards the protection of the private interests which vest in the environment rather than the environment as a distinct entity. An environmental liability regime cannot have any useful role to play unless access to remedies in tort is opened to those who do not have a direct proprietary interest in the resource in the traditional sense. In other words, it is necessary to recognize the existence of an equitable public interest in environmental protection. In Chapter 4 it was explained that a conceptual basis is beginning to emerge which can support this notion and that, furthermore, this public interest can be equated with a form of proprietary interest in the environment. Developments in United States case law support the emergence of this notion as demonstrated in the case of *Friends of the Earth v. Laidlaw Environmental Services*[1105] discussed in Chapter 4. These interests can be represented by the state itself or NGOs as the White Paper envisages.

The Dutch and French systems provide clear examples of how these diffuse interests in environmental protection can be aggregated and conferred upon a single body which is deemed to have a direct interest in the resource affected. There can be no doubt that liberal conferral of standing rights is a vital ingredient of any environmental liability regime which seeks to provide redress in respect of the so-called 'un-owned environment.'

1103. European Environmental Law Association (n, 1101), para. [11.3].
1104. See n. 1088, above, para. [4.7.2].
1105. United States Supreme Court (98-822) 149 F.3d 303, (2000).

CHAPTER 9

Access to Justice II: Class or Group Actions

---

§9.01 INTRODUCTION

Class actions, or group actions, constitute an alternative means of aggregating diffuse environmental costs to the representative action undertaken by the State or NGOs. Transaction costs are high where a single polluting incident affects a great number of parties with the result that many claims may be brought in connection with the same incident. This gives rise to transaction costs in the form of aggregation costs; these represent the costs of aggregating all the claims so that the damages payable represent the true overall cost of the damage caused. Where many separate actions are brought aggregation costs are high due to the fact that proceedings are duplicated. This is an inefficient solution which benefits the polluter since, due to the expense of legal proceedings, only those who have been most severely affected are likely to bring civil claims with the result the polluter is not required to internalize the full aggregate costs of the pollution. As Balen succinctly put it:

> Pitted against Goliath industries and their insurers the consumer David's only chance of success may be to combine together nationally and internationally with other similarly affected individuals. The concept of group actions has therefore evolved in order to provide an arena in which the injured party can obtain redress.[1106]

In an environmental context, group or class actions are most likely to be brought in the event of an environmental disaster causing personal injuries or property damage to a large group or class of persons. For example, many forms of airborne pollutants can be carried over large distances. Where the pollutant is particularly toxic, even a small amount can cause widespread loss. Within the EU the most notable example of such a

---

1106. P. Balen, *Group Actions, Aims, Aspirations and Alternatives: A Historical Global Perspective*, J. Pers. Injury Litig. 196, 199 (1995).

catastrophe concerns the Seveso disaster of 1976 in which the failure of a safety valve and small explosion resulted in the release of a gas cloud, containing the highly toxic tetrachlorodibenzo-p-dioxin (TCDD). This spread over 1800 ha of densely populated land and caused personal injuries to local inhabitants in the form dermal lesions known as chloracne. Aside from the personal injuries sustained many farmers lost their businesses, as some 77,000 animals had to be destroyed. A mere 2 kg of the toxic substance caused this mass destruction.[1107] However, the insidious effects of chronic pollution occurring over a protracted period of time can also generate large numbers of claimants. This is clearly demonstrated by the Corby litigation in the UK whereby a group action was brought by many parties in respect of birth defects allegedly attributable to toxic emissions from the defendant's contaminated land reclamation project.[1108] Moreover, Kimblin and Wignall anticipate that in the event of a *Deepwater Horizon* scale disaster in the North Sea oilfields, some means of grouping the claims would prove vital in order to expedite proceedings.[1109]

§9.02   DEVELOPMENTS IN MEMBER STATES

In the UK, aggregation costs can be reduced to a certain extent by the use of group actions in cases where there is a commonality of interests or issues. By allowing all affected parties to join in the same proceedings the number of lawyers involved can be reduced and the facts of the case can be heard at a single trial and any subsequent appeal hearings.[1110] The group action procedure has been used in a number of well known environmental cases, namely, *A.B. & others v. South West Water Services Ltd*[1111] which, it will be recalled, concerned personal injuries claims following the release of aluminium sulphate into the public drinking water supply. Another notable example is provided by the case of *Hunter v. London Docklands Development Corporation*[1112] which, as we have seen, concerned public and private nuisance claims brought by local residents during the main phase of the redevelopment of the London Docklands area. As previously noted, the procedure facilitated a number of personal injury claims concerning the redevelopment of a former steelworks site in Corby.[1113] One of the largest group actions to date concerns the claims brought by some 69,000 alleged

---

1107. See European Environment Agency, *Europe's Environment: The Dobris Assessment*, Pt III, Ch. 18, Box 18B (Office for Official Publications of the European Community 1995).
1108. *Corby Group Litigation v. Corby District Council* [2009] EWHC 1944 (TCC); [2010] Env. L.R. D2. For the main facts see §2.05[C], above.
1109. R. Kimblin and G. Wignall, *Slick operators*, 98 Eur. L. 20 (2010).
1110. GLOs are governed by Part 19 of the Civil Procedure Rules 1998 SI 1998/3132. Once an order has been made, a register is compiled containing details of like claims and a number of test cases are selected to be taken forward to full trial. Any party included on the register will be bound by the outcome of the test case although an individual claimant may apply to be removed from the register at an earlier stage in the proceedings.
1111. [1993] 2 W.L.R. 507.
1112. [1996] 2 W.L.R. 348.
1113. See n. 1108, above.

victims of oil pollution damage in the Niger Delta region associated with Shell's oil exploration and refining activities.[1114]

Nevertheless, group actions are still relatively costly in that they are often more time-consuming than individual actions. This is due to the fact that, although the facts of the case can be heard at a single trial, there must be an individual assessment of each damages claim. Furthermore, the GLO may only focus on a narrow range of legal issues. For example, in the Corby litigation the court was confined to determining the nature of the failings on the part of the defendant and the nature of the liability under various causes of action including negligence, breach of statutory duty and public nuisance. However, each individual claimant was left to establish causation in his or her particular case in subsequent proceedings – although in the event this did not prove necessary as the defendant agreed to settle the claims.[1115] Where causation difficulties are less acute it would probably not be necessary to hear all individual claims in this manner. However, generally speaking there still needs to be an individual assessment of damages.

In the United States, this problem may be avoided by the use of class actions in which a single case is taken to be representative of all those with similar claims.[1116] A single award is made which is applicable to all those within the class. However, in Europe, class actions are largely unknown although the matter is under consideration in Finland. The main objection to the procedure is that damage claims normally vary considerably in each individual case and it would be arbitrary and artificial to impose a uniform award on all parties. In the United States, some provision is made for such variances in that classes are defined according to the nature of the loss they have suffered; thus, those suffering personal injury would be grouped into a separate class from those who have suffered property damage.[1117] It should also be noted that the class action procedure is different to the GLO procedure adopted in the UK. The UK procedure requires each claimant to instigate his or her own proceedings in order to join the group. Whereas, in the US class action procedure, all potential claimants are automatically included in the class and need not instigate individual proceedings. In some cases claimants will merely be required to register their interest. The GLO system

---

1114. See §5.02[B], above.
1115. As regards the causation issues stemming from the Corby case see §2.06[B][2]. , above.
1116. See Rule 23 of the Federal Rules of Civil Procedure. This empowers the court to 'certify' a class where the criteria of numerosity, commonality, adequacy and typicality are satisfied. According to Rule 23(b)(3) any claimants included in the class must be given notice and afforded the opportunity to opt out. However, if the court considers it expedient to do so, it may make a 'mandatory' class certification under Rule 23(b)(1) or (2), which litigants may not opt out of. This occurred in the Exxon Valdez litigation in which the Federal District Court certified five classes, namely, cannery workers, commercial fishermen, area businesses, Alaskan natives, and property owners.
1117. For example, plaintiffs who took part in litigation following the accident at the Three Mile Island Nuclear Power Station were divided into three classes. The first two classes concerned individuals and businesses within 25 miles of the plant who had suffered ordinary economic loss as a result of the turmoil and mass evacuation which occurred following the accident. The third class included all those who had 'suffered personal injury, incurred medical expenses, [or] ... suffered emotional distress.' See *In re Three Mile Island Litigation*, 557 F. Supp. 96 (M.D. Pa. 1982).

has drawn unfavourable comparisons with class actions on the basis that the latter does not require claimants to take potentially onerous proactive steps.[1118] However, such criticisms fail to take account of advances in technology and the ability of claimants in the UK to instigate claims on line. In very large cases the solicitors handing the claims will normally establish a website where potential claimants can register their interest. The solicitors will then deal with much of the 'form filling' and the filing of claims. From the point of view of the claimant, therefore, joining a group action in the UK may appear little more onerous than joining a class action in the US.[1119] Nevertheless, it must be conceded that there is less scope for hearing cases in a manner which obviates the need for an individual assessment of damages.[1120]

As regards environmental damage it will come as little surprise that one of the largest class action suits brought to date in the US courts stems from the *Deepwater Horizon* disaster in the Gulf of Mexico. This caused economic loss to many thousands of claimants whose livelihoods depend on the fishing, tourism and related industries. Other losses were suffered by rescue workers and those involved in the clean-up operation. At the time of writing BP announced that it had agreed to settle claims amounting to some USD 7.8 billion representing the losses suffered by 110,000 claimants falling within the above categories.[1121] A multitude of other claims stemming from the costs incurred by local government bodies and a variety of agencies remain outstanding. As previously noted, BP established a USD 20 billion escrow account for the purpose of settling such claims, an amount which is far in excess of the legal minimum demanded by legislation.[1122]

In France, the rules on standing rights for NGOs facilitate a form of class action. To this end limited provision for class actions for environmental damage was introduced by law 95/101 of 2 February 1995 which allows recognized environmental pressure groups to pursue civil claims on behalf of an affected class of individuals. Article 5 IV inserted a new law into the Rural (or Environmental) Code[1123] which provides as follows:

> Where several identified individuals have suffered personal damage by the same person (individual or legal entity) and had a common origin, in the fields mentioned in L252-3, any interest group which is authorised (*agrée*) in accordance with Article L – 252 – 1 may, if it has been commissioned by at least two of the

1118. See R. Mulheron, *Some Difficulties with Group Litigation Orders – and Why a Class Action is Superior*, 24 Civ. Just. Q. 40 (2005).
1119. In the UK the largest on-going litigation undoubtedly involves asbestos related personal injuries. A number of solicitors have established specialist websites for garnering claims. See, for example, the website operated by Macks Solicitors, http://www.asbestosclaims.co.uk/claim-form (accessed Mar. 4, 2012).
1120. *Ibid.*, 47. This may in part be due to the distinct lack of detail in the legislation and the extent to which such matters are left to the judge in accordance with established practice. In other commonwealth and US jurisdictions such matters are precisely set out in detailed legislation.
1121. See R. Peston, *BP's Deepwater Horizon settlement*, http://www.bbc.co.uk/news/business-17243914, 3 March 2012 (accessed Mar. 4, 2012).
1122. For a full account of the liability issues raised by the Deepwater Horizon disaster see §3.05[A][2] above and §5.05[A].
1123. See §8.02[A], above.

affected individuals, bring an action before any jurisdiction in the name of those individuals.

The fields referred to by Article L – 252 – 3 constitute those:

> acts concerning a direct or indirect damage to the collective interests that the authorised interest groups have to protect and constituting a violation of the laws relating to the protection of nature and the environment, the improvement of standards of living, the protection of water, air, soils, sites and landscapes, town planning or the purpose of which is the prevention of pollution and nuisances, as well as of the texts enacted for the application of such laws.

Accordingly, aggregation costs are substantially reduced by allowing an interest group to pursue a single claim in respect of the collective costs of the damage as opposed to separate claims in respect of the damage suffered by each individual.

§9.03   EUROPEAN INITIATIVES

Despite the above developments, as a general rule, class actions remain an unpopular concept in Europe. This is reflected in the fact that none of the European initiatives on civil liability recommended their use in an environmental context. The *Lugano* Convention does, however, expressly permit the use of class actions subject to the proviso that such actions would ordinarily be permitted within the jurisdiction of the signatory; to this end Article 22 provides:

> A court other than the court first seised may also, on the application of one of the parties, decline jurisdiction if the law of that court permits the consolidation of related actions and the court first seised has jurisdiction over both actions ... [F]or the purposes of this Article, actions are deemed to be related where they are so closely connected that it is expedient to hear and determine them together to avoid the risk of irreconcilable judgments resulting from separate proceedings.

§9.04   MAIN CONSIDERATIONS

From the point of view of individual victims the class action has certain advantages over the representative action in that it allows for the compensation of individuals. However, the primary focus of such actions is on personal loss which, as has been discussed above, does not always coincide with environmental harm; thus, whilst damages awarded may provide a more accurate reflection of the true costs of the activity than isolated actions, it may still be the case that such damages are insufficient to effect full environmental remediation. Nevertheless, there can be no doubt that some of the greatest and most publicized damages settlements have resulted from class or group actions.[1124] There is also some evidence to suggest that such actions, or even the threat of such actions, have often marked key turning points in industry practices and

---

1124. Not least of which, from an environmental perspective, is the damages settlement in *Exxon Valdez* amounting to some USD 5 billion.

have resulted in the implementation of major improvements in plant or product safety. For example, as Stanton points out: 'It is unlikely that many car ferries leave harbour with their bow doors open after the Zeebrugge disaster.'[1125] To give a more topical example, it is inconceivable that the oil exploration companies operating at the vanguard of technological capability of deep sea drilling would fail to take on board the lessons of the *Deepwater Horizon* disaster.

It must also be borne in mind that class or group actions relate to civil procedures rather than the substantive principles of tort. There has already been on-going debate at an EU level regarding the issue of whether the Product Liability Directive[1126] should be modified so as to facilitate increased use of class or group actions in respect of liability claims for defective products. However, the Commission[1127] initially expressed the view that there were formal objections to harmonizing civil procedures in this context on the grounds there was a lack of competence under Article 95 (now Article 115 TFEU) and that rules on legal proceedings should not be created for specific sectors. Since this time the EU has gained increased competence in the field of civil procedure although it is an area in which Member States are still very unwilling to cede sovereignty and it is doubtful whether a legislative solution could be imposed.[1128] Nevertheless the Commission has pressed ahead with various policy initiatives on 'collective redress' which seek to encourage Member States to facilitate product liability claims through the adoption of such measures on an EU template.[1129]

Similar observations could be used in respect of any measures designed to set up an EU an environmental liability regime. Although, as will be abundantly clear by now, a measure of this nature is now further away than it has ever been.

§9.05   CONCLUSION

Although class or group actions form part of civil procedure in the domestic jurisdictions of certain EU Member States and do not form part of the substantive law of tort itself, their importance and relevance to the debate cannot be overlooked. Where environmental damage is diffuse, with many individuals bearing a small part of the overall loss, the ability to bring such actions greatly enhances the chances of success by

---

1125. K. Stanton, *Modern Law of Torts*, 15 (Sweet & Maxwell 1994).
1126. Council Directive of 25 July 1985 (85/374/EEC), O.J. No L 210 of 7.8.1985 on liability for defective products.
1127. Report from the Commission on the Application of Directive 85/374 on Liability for Defective Products, COM(2000) 893 final, at [3.2.10].
1128. The Lisbon Treaty brought the area of Judicial Cooperation in Civil matters within the scope of the main treaties (the Treaty on the Functioning of the European Union) where it is now subject to the 'ordinary legislative procedure'. Thus it is at least theoretically possible to harmonize aspects of civil procedure. However, it seems that the ability to use the ordinary legislative procedure was bought at a cost in that the wording on the competence of the EU to adopt such measures is somewhat vague. Article 81(2)(f) TFEU merely refers to measures which promote the compatibility of the rules on civil procedure applicable in the Member States; the operative word here is clearly 'promote' which appears to suggest something far less than the imposition of a uniform EU rule.
1129. See D. Fairgrieve & G. Howells, *Collective Redress Procedures – European Debates*, 58(2) I.C.L.Q. 379 (2009).

reducing transaction costs. Furthermore, it focuses attention on the wider, or global impact, of an activity rather than its immediate and localized aftermath. In this sense, class actions provide one means of overcoming the central objection to the use of tort in an environmental context, namely, the now familiar assertion that tort is concerned with individual justice rather than the impact of an activity on society as a whole. As an American writer has stated: 'class actions are an alien force in the tort system which focuses on individual justice.'[1130] Procedures designed to cope with traditional forms of individual loss are incapable handling mass litigation resulting from some of the great environmental disasters of recent times:

> the principles that are being applied in attempting to cope with the regulation and resolution of disputes surrounding Chernobyl, Bhopal, and the Exxon Valdez essentially flow from the breadth of mind that considered what was to happen in merry old England if your dog crossed onto someone else's property.[1131]

To this long list of environmental disasters we can now add Deepwater Horizon.

Thus, although harmonization of civil procedure rules on this issue could not be imposed under any supranational regime, it is to be hoped that civil procedures in individual states will be commensurate with these objectives. For this reason, the adoption of such mechanisms in the UK, and certain other European states, providing a statutory basis for group actions is a timely development.

1130. D. Rosenburg, *Class actions for Mass Torts*, 62 Ind. L.J. 561 (1987).
1131. J. London, *Exponential Change: Today is Already Tomorrow*, 3 Loyola Annals Health L. 155 (1994).

CHAPTER 10

Remedies for Environmental Damage

§10.01 INTRODUCTION

One of the main limitations of tort as a means of environmental protection concerns the fact that remedies usually reflect private loss as opposed to environmental damage. An environmental liability regime would also need to make provision for damages in respect of environmental impairment. This raises two complex issues, namely the definition of environmental damage and the extent to which damages should reflect the costs of restoring the environment to its former state.

As regards injunctive relief, it has been argued that injunctions provide an extremely effective remedy in an environmental context. However, their efficacy as a means of environmental protection may be severely undermined if courts exercise their discretion to award damages in lieu too freely. Although, as has also been argued, it must be acknowledged that there are circumstances in which such an approach may constitute the best solution.[1132] These issues have been highlighted by developments in certain European States and EU initiatives.

It should also be noted that this issue is closely related to the definition of harm. For example, if a legal system does not recognize pure economic loss as a recoverable harm, it follows that damages cannot be awarded and the liability of the tortfeasor is limited as a result.

1132. See §3.05[B][4], above on damages in lieu of an injunction.

§10.02   DEVELOPMENTS IN MEMBER STATES

[A]   Recoverable Damages

As regards the position in the UK it has been explained how it is possible to recover restoration costs provided that they are foreseeable. The prime object of damages is to restore the claimant to the position he was in prior to the occurrence of the harm. This may entail awarding damages which enable him to restore his land to the state it was in prior to the incident. However, where such costs would be out of proportion to the value of land damages are calculated on the basis of the diminution in the market value of the land caused by the pollution. A similar rule occurs under the German Civil Code (BGB). Paragraph 251(2)BGB[1133] provides that the defendant will be liable for the full costs of remediation unless such costs are unreasonable in relation to the value of the object impaired. An unreasonable relation between restoration costs and the value of the land is considered to exist where restoration costs exceed the value of the land by approximately 30%.

However, calculating damages on the basis of the diminution in market value of the property may not provide sufficient funds to undertake restoration work. Thus, it is necessary to consider whether there is some alternative basis upon which damages for environmental impairment may be calculated.[1134]

Of course, the ideal solution would be to restore the environment to its exact former state and to reinstate the intricate ecosystems which have been disrupted. However, in many cases it would be prohibitively expensive, or even technically infeasible to attain this level of perfection. The next stage down seeks to reduce contaminants to a level whereby flora and fauna can re-establish themselves in a self-sustaining system and hopefully adapt to their impaired surroundings.[1135]

The third, and perhaps most pragmatic approach, entails the calculation of damages on the basis of the amount it would cost to restore the environmental media to a level which would enable it to be used for a certain purpose.[1136] This approach allows for considerably more flexibility than calculating damages on the basis of loss of market value alone, although it may not result in the environment being restored to anything like its former state. Rather, natural resources are restored to a level which enable them to be used by humans for recreational, leisure, or business purposes. Of course, this is very much an anthropocentric solution and reflects an economic approach in that it focuses on how an economic function can be restored to the damaged resource. As such it is not an ideal solution from an environmental perspective in that it overlooks the role which the resource played in the ecosystem. For example, a lake could be restored to a

---

1133. This provision is applied under s. 16 of the Environmental Protection Act 1991 (*UmweltHG*).
1134. For an overview of the different methods of valuing environmental damage see, P. Sands and R.B. Stewart, *Valuation of Environmental Damage – US and International Law Approaches*, 5 (4) Rev. Eur. Community Envtl. Intl. L. 290 (1996).
1135. *Ibid.*, 292.
1136. *Ibid.*

level which would enable it to be used for sailing and swimming. It could even be re-stocked with certain types of hardier fish so that angling could be reintroduced. However, residual pollution could still render the lake incapable of supporting more delicate life forms thereby preventing it from fulfilling its full role in the ecosystem.

Nevertheless, in many cases there may be no practical alternative to a use based approach. An obvious example concerns the vast areas of land which have supported heavy industrial activity since the dawn of the industrial revolution. Throughout Europe, landscapes have been irreversibly scarred by steel works, mines and factories. Industrial activity conducted on this scale and over such a long period of time renders the land sterile and beyond any hope of restoration to its former state. Following the demise of heavy industry in many regions the only viable solution has been to reduce pollution to a level whereby certain cleaner land uses can be introduced such as housing, shops, leisure facilities or light industry. This normally entails removing the most heavily contaminated topsoil, sealing the deeper contaminated soil under a thick concrete raft and covering it with clean replacement topsoil.

However, this in turn raises the issue of whether property should be restored to a standard which enables it to be used for a specific or limited number of end uses as opposed to all possible end uses. The former approach is referred to as the 'suitable for use' method and is firmly established as the favoured technique in the UK.[1137] A similar approach is adopted in most other EU states[1138] although the Netherlands once attempted to apply an ambitious 'polished earth' approach under its Soil Protection Act 1987. This demanded that land should be restored to a standard which rendered it suitable to accommodate all, or at least as many as possible, potential end uses. Article 38(1) introduced the concept of *multifunctionality* which meant that the functional properties of the soil for man, plant or animal had to be maintained or restored.[1139] However, the standard was watered down by exceptions which considerably eased the burden. The multifunctionality requirement could be abandoned if there were special environmental, technical or financial circumstances which rendered the approach infeasible or unrealistic. Special environmental circumstances would be deemed to exist if, for example, the clean-up operations would have resulted in the escape of hazardous substances. Technical and financial circumstances existed if the cost of restoration was out of proportion to the cost of cheaper yet effective alternatives. In such circumstances section 38(1) of the 1987 Act allowed for the use of isolation, containment and monitoring measures.[1140] Formulas existed for calculating when

1137. Guidance is provided in various policy documents including, Office of the Deputy Prime Minister, *Planning Policy Statement (PPS) 23: Planning and Pollution Control* (HMSO, 2004). Note that this function now rests with the Department for Communities and Local Government. See also DEFRA Circular 01/2006, *Contaminated Land* (DEFRA, 2006).

1138. See M. Hinteregger (ed.), *Environmental Liability and Ecological Damage in Europe*, 437–438 (CUP 2008).

1139. See C. Van der Wilt, *Multifunctionality of Soil: the rise and fall of a Dutch principle*, 6(1) Env. Liability 18 (1998). Section 38(1) Soil Protection Act 1987 provides: 'Anyone cleaning up the land shall do so in such a way that the functional properties it has for humans, plants or animals are retained and restored, unless circumstances obtain as referred to in paragraph 3 below.'

1140. 'It shall be laid down by general administrative order in what circumstances related to special characteristics of the case of pollution in question measures can be taken to isolate and control

these alternatives should be employed in place of multifunctionality.[1141] In this sense the Dutch system seemed to have subverted the multifunctionality approach by introducing a 'lessor of' rule of the type typically applied in other jurisdictions. It is little surprise that the Dutch Government eventually abandoned the pretence of adopting a multifunctionality approach and amended the 1987 Act accordingly[1142] Thus, according to the current law, the proposed end use of the land shall determine the nature of the clean-up measures which are to be instigated; in other words, a *functional*, rather than a *multifunctional* approach is applied. However, it is important to note that the concept has not been entirely abandoned. Although the objective has been discarded in respect of historic pollution, that is pollution occurring prior to the introduction of the 1987 Act, it has been maintained in respect of pollution occurring after that date.[1143] Thus, if an accident occurs leading to land contamination it is likely that the multifunctionality requirement would still come in to play. This because anyone wishing to clean-up land must comply with the requirements of the 1987 Act. Thus it is likely that any damages settlement, following a civil claim, would reflect the remediation costs which the victim would incur in restoring the land to a standard which complied with the requirements of the Act. Nevertheless, it should also be borne in mind that, even where contemporary pollution is concerned, multifunctionality is still qualified by the environmental, technical and financial considerations referred to above.

Another difficult issue concerns the extent to which pure economic loss should be recoverable. In Chapter 3[1144] it was explained that, under English Law, liability for economic loss is restricted to damage which flows directly from damage to property. Thus businesses which have lost trade as a result of environmental damage may not claim in respect of lost profits.[1145] In contrast, certain liability regimes introduced in other European States have made provision for economic loss.[1146] This is the case under the new systems in Spain,[1147] Norway,[1148]

---

the pollution and monitor the effects of such isolation and control. Rules on isolation, control and monitoring as referred to in the first sentence shall be laid down by ministerial regulation.'

1141. For example, for clean up costs up to 10,000 Dutch Guilders, costs are deemed excessive if they are nine times greater than the alternative measures. Where clean-up costs amount to up to 100 million Dutch Guilders, these costs will be considered excessive if the alternative measures would be one and a half times cheaper: see Appendix 9 to the circular in the entry into force of the Soil Protection Act clean-up provisions, second phase, December 1994. Reports show that this has been the most frequently used ground for departing from the multifunctionality requirement. See Van der Wilt (n. 1139), at 20.

1142. Although multifunctionality was a 'nice ideal' it seems that the expenditure involved was just too great. Certain estimates put the figure at 100 billion Dutch guilders. At the current rate of expenditure, it would have taken 100 years to clean up existing contaminated land to a standard which complied with multifunctionality. In fact, only 8% of sites were cleaned to a standard which complied with this standard.

1143. See van der Wilt (n. 1139) 18.

1144. See in particular §3.05[A][2],

1145. See, for example, *Weller & Co. Ltd. v. Foot and Mouth Disease Research Institute* [1966] 1 Q.B. 560.

1146. See generally Hinteregger (n. 1138), 625–626.

1147. See J.M. Barrenetxea, *The Spanish Draft Act on Liability for Environmental Damage*, 5(6) Env. Liability 115 (1997).

1148. Pollution Act 1981, as ammended, s. 57.

Sweden[1149] and Finland.[1150] However, in order to avoid opening the 'floodgates' it has been recommended that only those with a direct commercial interest in the resource affected should be able to recover economic loss.[1151] Thus, if, for example, chemicals leaked from a plant situated on the coast and washed ashore near a resort, fishermen would be able to claim in respect of lost profits. However, tourists would be precluded from claiming damages in respect of the impairment of their holidays. This is entirely in accordance with the common law examples explored in Chapter 3.

[B]   Injunctive Relief

In Chapter 2 it was argued that injunctions are the most effective remedy in an environmental context in that they compel the polluter to investigate cleaner technologies. In the UK it was noted that the courts have a discretion to award damages in lieu of an injunction. It was argued that the injunction is a powerful tool in terms of securing the remediation or prevention of environmental harm; thus, the discretion must be used sparingly. However, it was also noted that the courts have proved reluctant to entertain public interest arguments as a ground for exercising the discretion in favour of awarding damages. This has led to unsatisfactory results in those cases where damages would arguably have provided the best solution.[1152] This contrasts with the position in the Netherlands[1153] where, although there is a general presumption in favour of injunctive relief and the power to grant damages in lieu is very strictly controlled,[1154] damages may be substituted if societal interests would be harmed.[1155]

§10.03   EUROPEAN AND INTERNATIONAL INITIATIVES

The right for injured parties to recover damages are at the core of the international regimes referred to in Chapter 5 such as the Conventions on nuclear accidents and maritime oil pollution. As has already been explained in respect of the scope of liability under those regimes, recoverable loss includes property damage, personal injuries and the costs of environmental remediation.[1156] However, they tend to leave issues, such as

---

1149. Environmental Code 2000, Ch. 32, s. 1(2); note that 'pecuniary loss', which is not caused in circumstances which would also give rise to criminal liability, is only recoverable under this section 'where the loss is not inconsiderable.'
1150. See P. Wetterstein, *The Finnish Environmental Damage Compensation Act – and some Comparisons with Norwegian and Swedish Law*, 3(3) Env. Liability 41 (1995).
1151. See Barrenetxea (n. 1147) 117–118; Wetterstein, (n. 1150) 45. Wetterstein points out that this is the approach adopted in Norway.
1152. See §3.05[B][4].
1153. See Gerrit Betlem, *Civil Liability for Transfrontier Pollution – Dutch Environmental Tort Law in International Cases in the Light of Community Law*, (Graham & Trotman/Martinus Nijhoff 1993); G. Betlem, *Transboundary Enforcement: Free Movement of Injunctions*, in, *Environmental Rights – Law, Litigation and Access to Justice*, (S. Deimann & B. Dyssli eds., Cameron May 1995).
1154. See Article 3:296 Civil Code.
1155. Article 6:168 Civil Code.
1156. For discussion of the maritime and nuclear regimes see §5.05[A] and §5.05[B], above, respectively.

the recoverability of pure economic loss, to be assessed according to domestic law. As we have seen, this can lead to wide divergences in terms the amount of compensation recoverable in different jurisdictions.[1157]

[A]   Lugano Convention

Article 7 of the Lugano Convention allows for the recovery of damages in respect of death, physical injury, damage to property or environmental impairment. Environmental impairment is defined as:

> loss or damage by impairment of the environment in so far as this is not considered to be damage within the meanings of sub-paragraphs a or b above provided that compensation for impairment of the environment, other than for loss of profit from such impairment, shall be limited to the costs of measures of reinstatement actually undertaken or to be undertaken; the costs of preventive measures and any loss or damage caused by preventive measures.

The term 'environmental impairment' is nebulous, however, it seems that it relates to damage which is capable of being rectified by means of an injunction to prevent the continuation of the offending activity or damages amounting to the costs of restoring the property affected to its former state. However, according to Article 2(7)(c) this does not encompass economic loss resulting from such impairment.

As noted above, Article 18 of the Convention also makes specific provision for environmental interest groups to seek injunctive relief in order to prevent damage or to compel operators to 'take measures of reinstatement'.

[B]   EU Developments

The discussion documents[1158] which mooted the possibility of a tort based EU environmental liability regime devoted considerable attention to the scope of damages under such a regime. Although the proposals were never pursued, they contain some useful observations on the problem which are worthy of note. The Green Paper recognized that it is difficult to place a monetary value on certain environmental attributes and focused on the cost of remedying tangible environmental which could be rectified:

> [I]f there is an obligation to maintain those elements of the environment in a healthy state, a concurrent obligation arises to restore these elements to that state

---

1157. See, for example, discussion of the case of *Merlin v. British Nuclear Fuels Ltd* [1990] 2 Q.B. 557 discussed at §3.05[A][2], above. Here the statutory regime governing nuclear liability was interpreted according to common law definitions which had the effect of precluding pure economic loss. Similarly, it will be recalled that the UK courts have adopted a restrictive interpretation of the recoverability of economic loss under the maritime oil pollution liability regime. See *Algrete Shipping Co. Ltd. v. International Oil Pollution Compensation Fund* [2003] 1 Lloyd's Rep. 327 also discussed at §3.05[A][2], above.
1158. For general background to the Green and White Papers on environmental liability and the subsequent change in tack to an administrative law based approach see §5.03, above.

whenever they are damaged. This obligation carries with it the right to claim the costs of restoration from the party who caused the damage. *The amount of compensation the liable party is obliged to pay is computed in terms of the actual cost of environmental restoration.*[1159] [emphasis added]

The Green Paper did, however, point out that in certain cases it may be difficult to identify the threshold of damage in cases of environmental impairment. In other words, the point at which the environment becomes sufficiently degraded by pollution to warrant remediation:

> Actual physical destruction or gross contamination is generally considered damage, but what about lesser impacts? All human activities result in emissions, but the point at which these emissions are to be considered 'pollution' is not clear. Nor is it clear at which point 'pollution' causes actual damage.[1160]

As noted earlier, the White Paper suggested linking a liability regime with existing EU environmental legislation so as to provide an additional means of securing compliance with environmental standards.[1161] Thus, breaching an environmental standard prescribed by a directive would trigger civil liability in addition to sanctions under public law.

Moreover, the White Paper recognized that, although the restoration of the environment to its exact former state would be the ideal, in reality this may not be a technically realistic or financially viable option. In such circumstances the Paper accepted that it may be necessary to adopt a functional approach of the type already applied in most Member States.[1162] It is possible that the Commission took on board the difficulties experienced in the Netherlands in the application of a multifunctional approach.

As regards the issue of economic loss, at no stage did the Commission recommend the inclusion of an express provision in a liability regime allowing for the recovery of damages in respect of this type of harm. The White Paper dealt with this under the heading of 'Traditional Damage' which it stated would 'remain under the Member States' jurisdiction'.[1163] Thus national courts would have been left to apply existing principles deriving from domestic tort law when determining whether such loss should be recoverable. Due to the complexity of national laws on this issue and the variety of differing approaches adopted in domestic tort law, it is understandable that the Commission was reluctant to make express provision for the recovery of economic loss in a tort based regime. However, as will be argued below, in certain circumstances, there are strong arguments in favour of allowing limited recovery for economic loss. Furthermore, such losses have the potential to greatly increase the liability of operators. If Member States continue to adopt radically different positions on this issue the need for some form of EU harmonization on this issue may need to be revisited.

1159. COM(93) 47 final, [2.1.10].
1160. *Ibid.*, [2.1.7].
1161. COM(2000) 66 final, 12, [3.3].
1162. *Ibid.*, 19, [4.5.1].
1163. *Ibid.*, 21, [4.5.3].

The White Paper also dealt with the issue of measuring 'non-use' values relating to ecological damage under, for example, the Wild Birds Directive.[1164] The Paper referred to various economic methods which have evolved as a means of quantifying this type of loss in monetary terms. However, as will be argued below, there is little to be gained by attempting to fix a value on the extinction of a species, for example. No amount of damages could reverse a loss of this magnitude. Any damages awarded would serve a purely punitive function. Where sensitive ecological habitats are concerned remedies should focus on preventing the harm from occurring in the first place by, for example, increasing the availability of injunctive relief. As argued below, where damage has already occurred, damages should focus on the concrete and readily identifiable costs involved in restoring the media to a standard whereby wildlife could be reintroduced.

Some indication as to what approach a tort based EU liability regime would have adopted can be gleaned from the scope of the ELD[1165] although, as has been explained at length, the ELD adopted an administrative as opposed to a tort based approach. As previously noted, the Directive covers damage to protected species and wildlife habitats, water and land. Article 8 provides that operators shall be liable for the full costs of preventative action or environmental remediation. However, 'the competent authority *may* decide not to recover the full costs where the expenditure required to do so would be greater than the recoverable sum or where the operator cannot be identified.' [emphasis added]. It should also be recalled that certain defences operate which have the effect of absolving the operator of liability and shifting the costs to the tax payer.

§10.04   MAIN CONSIDERATIONS

[A]   The Threshold of Damage

Most environmental liability proposals cover standard heads of damage including personal injury and property damage. However, defining the point at which general environmental impairment should become actionable is rather more difficult. For the sake of certainty, one approach entails linking the threshold of damage with standards established under other environmental legislation. Thus damage would be deemed to have occurred where levels of specified elements exceed levels set by, for example, EU Directives. The EU Commission certainly favoured such an approach in its earlier White Paper on environmental liability.[1166] As Carnwath J. noted in *Blue Circle Industries Plc v. Ministry of Defence*, in cases of doubt, regulatory standards can be useful in determining whether a change is significant:

1164. *Ibid.*, 19, [4.5.1].
1165. European Parliament and Council Directive (EC) 2004/35 on Environmental Liability with Regard to the Prevention and Remedying of Environmental Damage OJ L143/56, Article 8.
1166. COM(2000) 66 final, 4.2.2.

> Given the sophistication of the regulatory systems now covering most areas of human activity, the views of the regulatory authorities are often critical ... in the *Cambridge Water* case [1994] 2 A.C. 264 the damage was caused because the contamination rendered the water unusable in accordance with the standards prescribed pursuant to the relevant EEC directive, not because it was in fact dangerous to health (see per Lord Goff, p. 249G). Thus, although the existence of a statutory regulatory system cannot alter the requirement that there should be some physical change, *it may be relevant in considering whether the physical change is of any practical significance.*[1167] [emphasis added]

However, the problems of linking the definition of damage with quality objectives or emission limits have also been highlighted; it will be recalled that standards have only been set in respect of a limited number of substances. As a result, such limits should operate as minimum requirements in cases or doubt and not preclude those who can show that they have been adversely affected by lesser concentrations from seeking redress.

[B] Restoration Standards

One of the most difficult issues concerns the extent to which remedies should seek to restore damaged environmental media to their original status.. As regards common law systems, it was explained in Chapter 4 that this entails balancing the right to full compensation against the technical feasibility and cost of environmental remediation. In many cases this involves assessing damages on the basis of the lost use of a natural resource and the costs of restoring that use. Thus in *Cambridge Water v. Eastern Counties Leather,*[1168] had the damage been foreseeable, *Cambridge Water* would have been able to recover the costs of relocating the pumping station so as to enable it to continue abstracting drinking water. If the water had been abstracted for another purpose, for use in the manufacture of paper for example, then clearly the contamination would not have affected the use of the resource.

However, Steele[1169] expressed concern that the linking of damages to the use of a natural resource risks partitioning the environment into tradable assets in which the value of a natural resource resides in its commercial use. Once natural resources are priced in this way they become vulnerable to becoming the subject of market transactions. This is because the market exerts a pressure to trade resources so that they eventually vest in the person who values them most highly (the 'transformative economy'),[1170] as Steele explained in her 1995 article:

> [T]he market approach to private law clearly treats property as having value because of its role in a human, not a natural economy. More than this, it derives

---

1167. [1997] Env. L.R. 341, 347–348.
1168. [1994] 2 W.L.R. 53.
1169. J. Steele, *Remedies and Remediation: Foundation Issues in Environmental Liability,* 58(5) Modern L. Rev. 615 (1995).
1170. See J. Sax, *Property Rights and the Economy of Nature: Understanding Lucas v. South Carolina Coastal Council,* 45 Stan. L. Rev. 1433 (1992).

the value of land from human preferences, which can be maximized only through exchange and use.[1171]

Thus, where the polluter's use appears to be more profitable, according to economic criteria, the court may, for example, be persuaded to grant damages in lieu of an injunction calculated upon the basis of the plaintiff's use of the resource. Such an approach leaves 'little space for the concept of environmental protection and would essentially tend to enhance the risk of environmental damage'.[1172]

This raises the issue of the extent to which damages should be recoverable in respect of 'non-use' or 'non consumptive' values. These values relate to the worth which individuals place on protecting or restoring a natural resource even though they may not use it or visit it. As noted in Chapter 3, economists have been grappling with the issue of how best to measure these intangible environmental values for many years. Of the various methodologies which have emerged, CVM is the most widely used although it is still highly controversial and has been the subject of much criticism.[1173] To recap, the method relies upon survey techniques in order to ascertain how much a sample section of the public would be prepared to pay in order to safeguard an environmental asset.[1174] Despite the shortcomings of the method it has been accepted by the US courts, most notably in the *Exxon Valdez* litigation, as a legitimate means of assessing quantum in respect of non-use values. It will be recalled that this was despite the best efforts of Exxon's lawyers to discredit the method. It seems likely that the method will also form a major component of liability arising from the *Deepwater Horizon* disaster.[1175]

At this point mention should also be made of another tool developed by environmental economics, namely, the 'ecosystem services' approach.[1176] This attaches a monetary value to the direct benefits which ecosystems provide to mankind. Obvious examples include fresh food and water in that it reduces the costs associated with purification. Another example includes bees which provide an invaluable service to agriculture through pollinating crops and cannot survive in the absence of a favourable environment. Other examples include cultural services such as recreation and tourism which are facilitated by a clean environment. The ecosystem services approach is being used alongside CVM as a means of assessing the long term damage costs associated with the Deepwater Horizon oil spill. The US National Academy of Sciences has made an extensive evaluation of the technique in respect of the disaster

---

1171. Steele (n. 1169), 630.
1172. *Ibid.*, 631.
1173. See Sands and Stewart (n. 1134) 293. As noted in chapter 3 principal difficulties relate to overcoming bias and validating responses. The fact that the exercise is hypothetical means that the participants are free to place inflated values on environmental media.
1174. See N. Hanley, J.F. Shogren and B. White, *Environmental Economics in Theory and Practice* (MacMillan 1997).
1175. See J. Corkindale, *Resolving environmental disputes and providing remedies for environmental damage: the use of environmental damage: the use of environmental valuation research in court proceedings in England and Wales*, 23(2) Envtl. L. Mgt. 63, 63 (2011); R. Force, M. Davies & J.S. Force, *Deep Trouble: Legal Ramifications of the Deepwater Horizon Oil Spill*, (2011) 85 Tul. L. Rev. 889 (2011).
1176. *Ibid.*, 66.

and has concluded that it could be a useful tool for assessing, by way of example, the impact on the storm defence capabilities of wetlands and the ocean as a source of seafood.[1177]

Although methods such as CVM have now gained legal status in the United States, these developments do not appear to have been replicated in Europe. Indeed, it seems highly unlikely that courts would take it upon themselves to invent a new head of damage based upon interference with abstract non-use values.[1178] However, due to the controversy which continues to surround the concept, it would be unwise to impose an obligation on states to make specific provisions in a liability system requiring the inclusion of non-use values as a component in damages claims. In any case, the effect of such damages is purely punitive in that they cannot lead directly to the restoration of the media affected. They merely reflect loss of enjoyment caused by a reduction in wildlife, for example. It is the actual restoration costs which facilitate remediation works designed to restore the environment to a state in which wildlife may return. Sands and Stewart noted that there is a certain 'embarrassment of logic' associated with the CVM technique:

> The basic rationale for rejecting the private law 'lesser of rule' in favour of recovery of the reasonable costs necessary to protect and reinstate the injured environment is the difficulty of placing a proper monetary value on environmental injury. To afford recovery, in addition, of impaired environmental value necessarily presupposes that such impairment can be reliably measured. If so, why should the 'lesser of' rule not be followed, in order to ensure that society does not commit more in the way of its resources to reinstating an injured environment than it is worth to society?

It is difficult to escape the central problem that environmental damage is usually greater than the sum of the individual losses incurred by specific parties. Private law has limited capacity to incorporate the new methodologies developed by environmental economics so as to reduce this gap.

Nevertheless, when considering the quantum of damages under an environmental liability system, it would be necessary for the courts to take a broad view of 'use' which takes account of the role of the resource in the ecosystem. As Corkindale argues: 'In such circumstances, it is hard to see how the courts can avoid the need to use the results of environmental valuation research in order to determine the extent of such damages'.[1179]

The courts have demonstrated a willingness to adopt a broad view of use which goes beyond the attributes of property which are of direct and immediate value to the landholder. In *Blue Circle Industries Plc v. Ministry of Defence*, the radiation contaminated a small area of marshland near the boundary of the site where no one generally

---

1177. National Research Council of the National Academies, *Approaches for Ecosystem Services Valuation for the Gulf of Mexico After the Deepwater Horizon Oil Spill*, (National Academies Press 2012).
1178. At an international level, the Executive body of the IOPC Fund is unwilling to entertain claims in respect of such values. See IOPC Fund Resolution No 3 10 October 1980, FUND/A/ES 1/13, para 11(a) and Annex.
1179. Corkindale (n. 1175), 67.

had cause to go. Furthermore, although levels of contamination exceeded statutory limits, they were insufficient to constitute a health risk. Nevertheless, in the High Court, Carnwath J. was prepared to take a broad view of use which encompassed impairment of the enjoyment of property:

> That the contamination rendered the property less useful or less valuable is ... to my mind self evident. The matter can be looked at narrowly, simply on the basis that, from the time the contamination was made known until it had been dealt with by removing the earth, that part of the estate could not be used as freely as it had been. Indeed, during the course of the works it could not be used at all.[1180]

It should also be noted that the extent to which a legal settlement is capable of absorbing these factors may be dependent upon which remedy is being sought. The threat of an injunction may induce the parties to reach a bargain in which case they have free rein to use whichever criteria they wish for the purposes of reaching a financial settlement. However, if an injunction cannot be obtained the courts must impose their own damages settlement and are more constrained in terms of how compensation is assessed.

However, even if environmental damage can be reduced to an economic value, it does not necessarily follow that this loss can be linked with the personal losses suffered by the claimant such as loss of amenity and loss of use and enjoyment. The full environmental damage costs cannot be recovered in the absence of a system which facilitates claims by 'public trustees', such as the state itself or NGOs, in their capacity as custodians of the environment. As we have seen in Chapter 4[1181] certain items of US legislation, including CERCLA[1182] and the Clean Air Act, incorporate the public doctrine which facilitates public interest suits of this nature. The OPA 1990 enables various public bodies including the state, federal agencies and Indian tribe trustees appointed by the President to pursue damages in respect of natural resource damage.[1183] This is likely to be a major component of the on-going *Deepwater Horizon* litigation.[1184] In Europe there is no direct equivalent of these powers which greatly limits the scope to use private law in this context.[1185]

Nevertheless, one piece of legislation which reflects the public trust doctrine to a certain extent is the ELD;[1186] although, as has now been noted on innumerable occasions, this adopts a public law based approach. Nevertheless, it is worthwhile briefly considering how the ELD approaches the issue of environmental remediation and the manner in which natural resources are valued. To a large extent the ELD was modelled on the US OPA 1990 and shares the same basic techniques and methodologies regarding the assessment of damage to

---

1180. [1996] Env. L.R. 341, 346.
1181. See §4.03[B], above.
1182. Comprehensive Environmental Response Compensation and Liability Act.
1183. 33 U.S.C. § 2702(b)(2)(A).
1184. See M. Davies, *Liability Issues Riased by the Deepwater Horizon Blowout*, 25 A.N.Z. Mar. L.J. 35, [3.4] (2011).
1185. See Corkindale, (n. 1175), above.
1186. European Parliament and Council Directive (EC) 2004/35 on environmental liability with regard to the prevention and remedying of environmental damage OJ L143/56.

natural resources.[1187] According to Annex II of the Directive, wherever possible the objective must be to restore the damaged environmental media to its baseline condition – that is, the condition it was in prior to the incident; this is known as primary remediation. However, potential liabilities extend still further in that the responsible party may also be held accountable for the loss of the resource pending its full restoration – this is referred to as compensatory restoration. Where primary remediation is not possible because, for example, the damage is irreparable or the costs are disproportionate, then measures may be taken to provide an alternative elsewhere. For example, if a particular wildlife habitat has been lost, plants could be established in an alternative site some distance away from the contamination; this is known as complementary restoration.

The guidance offered under Article II of the ELD is broad and it seems that the Member States have been left to devise specific methodologies for putting these concepts into effect. It seems likely that they will draw upon the experience in the United States where the use of economic methodologies, for calculating the value of a natural resource, has been sanctioned by the courts. The eco-services approach, which has been outlined above, provides a likely candidate for calculating damage costs under the compensatory restoration method. However, it must be reiterated that the ELD differs greatly from its US counterparts in that it establishes a solid partition between the costs of environmental remediation and damage to private interests.[1188] Whereas measures such as the US OPA make specific provision for certain private losses, the ELD expressly excludes such claims.[1189] Thus, EU law maintains a clear dividing line between environmental damage and the private interests which vest in it.

[C] Economic Loss

European initiatives and international proposals have declined to delineate the precise circumstances in which private parties should be in a position to recover damages in respect of pure economic loss; this is understandable. The extent to which the net of liability can be cast beyond those directly affected by the damage is bound with policy considerations; such as the classic 'floodgates argument'.[1190] Accordingly it is difficult to set a rigid legal test. To this end the courts have traditionally enjoyed a discretion to widen and draw-back the net in accordance with such considerations. In English

---

1187. See E.H.P. Brans, *Liability for damage to public natural resources under the 2004 EC Environmental Liability Directive: standing and assessment of damages*, 7(2) Env. L. Rev. 90, 99–105 (2005).
1188. See 33 U.S.C. § 2702(b)(2)(E) which affords private parties a right to claim damages in respect of the earning capacity of a damaged natural resource. This provides a clear cause of action for the tourism injury which relies upon pristine beaches and fishermen who depend upon clean water.
1189. See ELD (n. 1186) Annex II(1)(d).
1190. As Cardozo C.J. stated in *Ultramares Corp. v. Touche* 174 N.E. 441, 444 (1931) the defendant should not be held liable 'in an indeterminate amount for an indeterminate time to an indeterminate class.'

common law the test of remoteness of damage has been used as the control mechanism which regulates the extent to which economic loss may be recovered.[1191]

Other regimes are more sympathetic to the recoverability of pure economic loss.[1192] However, it cannot have been the intention of those legislatures to allow an unfettered right to recovery by all those who have suffered inconvenience and disruption as a result of pollution. Once such losses are multiplied they can very easily give rise to unsustainable liability. Those economic loss provisions, which have already been implemented in certain states, only contain limited guidance for the courts on which types of claim should be excluded. For example, only claims for 'significant' economic loss should be entertained under the Finnish Act and in Norway claims are expressly limited to those who have incurred economic losses in the pursuit of a commercial activity.

However, even if the recoverability of economic loss was prescribed by a requirement that only those with a commercial interest in the matter may claim damages, the 'floodgates' could still be opened. Let us consider an example in which an area of coastline has been polluted by chemicals released from a coastal plant. In addition to commercial fishermen, those who operate pleasure cruises could equally claim a commercial interest in the matter. Once claims are admitted by those who rely on tourism the floodgates are thrown wide. Shops, restaurants, hotels, bus companies, taxi firms etc. could all argue that their businesses have been affected. Liability of this type would make it extremely difficult to calculate risk and could have an adverse effect on the availability of insurance.[1193]

Thus, it seems likely that the courts would still need to fall back on tort based concepts such as foreseeability and remoteness in order to limit recoverability of economic loss.[1194] It is conceivable that certain courts could limit recoverability to those whose livelihoods depend solely and directly upon a natural resource such as fishermen or farmers. However, it is inevitable that at some point the courts would have to draw an arbitrary cut off point based on policy rather than logic. For example, to return to the coastal pollution example referred to above, it is possible that a court

---

1191. See R.W.M. Dias, *Remoteness of Liability and Legal Policy*, 20(2) Cambridge L.J. 178 (1962).
1192. For example, in Belgium, the Netherlands, Finland, Sweden and Spain damages are readily available in respect of the diminution in the market value of property, even if there is no actual damage to the fabric of the property itself. See M. Hinteregger (ed.), *Environmental Liability and Ecological Damage in European Law*, 440–441 (CUP 2008).
1193. There is some suggestion that the courts have restricted recovery of damages in respect of economic loss for negligent mis-statement, the 'high water mark' of which was *Anns v. Merton London Borough Council* [1978] A.C. 728, partly in response to the insurance implications. In *Caparo v. Dickman* [1989] Q.B. 653, in which the class of persons to whom one may be liable for negligent mis-statement was limited, Bingham and Taylor LJJ, at 688–689 and 703 respectively, referred to the fact that their decision should not affect the availability of insurance for company auditors. In *Smith v. Bush* [1990] 1 AC 831, at 858–859 Lord Griffiths considered that the availability of insurance was relevant to the issue of whether a valuer should be liable to the purchaser of a property. See Peter, *Tort Law and Economic Interests*, 423–424 (2d edn., Clarendon Press 1996).
1194. See Wetterstein (n. 1150) 45.

would find that an operator of pleasure boats would suffer a direct and immediate loss as a result of pollution in that he would be precluded from trading. However, it is possible that a general reduction in trade suffered by hoteliers and cafe owners in the town would be regarded as too remote. This is not to say that the inclusion of an economic loss provision would have no effect. It will be recalled that in the UK the recovery of pure economic loss is extremely limited in that the loss must be rooted in physical damage to a resource in which the claimant has a direct proprietary interest. This is merely the arbitrary 'cut off' point, chosen by the UK courts, on policy grounds. An express provision allowing for the recovery of pure economic loss would free the courts from the need to show a direct link with physical damage. Recall that in the *Braer* litigation, discussed in Chapter 4, certain litigants were precluded from obtaining damages on the grounds that they could not establish a sufficient proprietary interest in the coastline affected.[1195] Freeing the courts from the common law constraints on recoverability of economic loss would have enabled the courts to consider a wider range of criteria.[1196] For example, a range of criteria for determining whether economic loss should be recoverable have emerged in the so-called 'fund jurisprudence' of the Executive body of the IOPC 1971.[1197] The 1998 edition of the IOPC 1971 claims manual states that, where claims are brought in respect of economic loss, the key criterion must be 'proximity'. This can be established by consideration of:

> [1] the geographical proximity between the claimant's activity and the contamination; [2] the degree to which a claimant was economically dependant on an affected resource; [3] the extent to which a claimant had alternative sources of supply or business opportunities [4] the extent to which a claimant's business formed an integral part of the economic activity within the area affected by the spill.

1195. See, for example *Smith v. Braer Corp* [1999] GWD 21-1023.

1196. The Scottish Courts in the *Braer* litigation felt unable to entirely abandon common law constraints on the recoverability of economic loss as the ICCOP 1969 is silent on the issue. The IOPC 1971 is equally unhelpful. Thus, as noted in chapter 4, Cullen LJ declined to determine the matter solely on the basis of a 'but for' causation test as this would open the floodgates. However, it is significant that, for the purposes of the IOPC, the Court had no difficulty in accepting that Shetland fishermen should be in a position to claim in respect of loss of profits. Thus, in this context, a direct economic interest in a natural resource will suffice. Such a claim could not have been entertained according to a strict application of common law principles. See *Landcatch Ltd v. International Oil Pollution Compensation Fund* [1999] 2 Lloyd's Rep. 316. See G.M. Gauci, *Ship-Source Oil Pollution Damage and Recovery for Relation Economic Loss*, J.B.L. 356 (2000).

1197. The Convention establishes a fund against which claims can be made in respect of oil pollution damage where such claims cannot be brought against an individual operator under the 1969 Convention. As liability is not an issue, each claim is decided upon its individual merits with the result that the Executive Body is not restricted by traditional legal limitations on the recoverability of economic loss. In *Landcatch*, the Scottish Court of Session did not feel that it could go beyond the wording of the International Conventions when interpreting the compensation provisions of the Merchant Shipping (Oil Pollution) Act 1971 and that the 'fund jurisprudence' did not provide an authoritative source as to how the Convention should be interpreted.

This demonstrates that it is in fact possible to admit claims for pure economic loss whilst holding back the floodgates by applying sensible criteria.[1198] It may, however, be advisable to make specific provision for the recovery of clean-up costs incurred by organizations afforded standing under any regime. Given the fact that the object of the exercise is environmental remediation, it seems entirely reasonable to allow for the recovery of such costs.[1199]

The Deepwater Horizon disaster has provided the greatest challenge to date regarding the use of existing legal mechanisms for the recoverability of economic loss. Indeed, the bulk of the claims arising from the spillage concern economic losses incurred by businesses which relay upon the quality of water and shorelines in and around the Gulf of Mexico.[1200] However, the waters have been greatly muddied by the unprecedented scale of the disaster and the fact that liability has been determined by political intervention rather than strict adherence to legal principles.[1201]

In the immediate wake of the disaster and following the establishment of the USD 20 billion dollar escrow account, following the application of thumb screws to the BP executives in Washington, the Gulf Coast Claims Facility (GCCF) was established to handle claims.[1202] Offices were set up in various locations and standards claim forms and procedures were instigated. It is important to emphasize that this is a form of alternative dispute resolution (ADR) which operates outside the formal legal frame-work.[1203] In this respect it is free to develop its own practices and criteria and need not be hidebound by the manner in which economic loss claims are determined in the courts. In many respects the body has similarities with the executive body of the IOPCF. As noted above, the IOPCF executive develops its own fund jurisprudence which differs somewhat from established legal principles. The initial guidance issued by the GCCP related to initial emergency payments and adopted a restrictive approach based upon geographic proximity, the nature of the industry and its reliance upon the

---

1198. This approach has enabled the Executive body of the IOPC to consider a far wider range of claims than would have been possible under UK common law. In one decision, for example, fish processing plants deprived of fish due to an exclusion zone were able to claim in respect of loss of profits. See Gauci (n. 1196) 360.

1199. Recall that, whereas in the Netherlands such costs would be regarded as losses flowing from harm to the interests of an environmental pressure group, in the UK they would probably be regarded as economic loss; see G. Betlem, *Standing for Ecosystems – Going Dutch*, 54(1) Cambridge L.J. 153, 166–167 (1995). This is also the position adopted under the ICCOP (1969) Article 1 (7) of which provides: ''Preventative' measures' means any reasonable measures taken by any person after an accident has occurred to prevent or minimise pollution damage'. See also the 1988 Wellington Convention on the Regulation of Antarctic Mineral Resource Activities, Convention of 2 June 1988, 27 ILM 859 Article 8(2)d: 'An operator shall be strictly liable for: reimbursement of reasonable costs by whomsoever incurred relating to necessary response action, including prevention, containment, clean-up and removal measures, and action to restore the status quo ante where Antarctic mineral resource activities undertaken by that Operator result in or threaten to result in damage to the Antarctic environment or dependant ecosystems.'

1200. See §3.05[A][2], above.

1201. *Ibid.*

1202. For analysis of how the system works see Davies (n. 1184), 38–39.

1203. Although the body is financed by BP it is administered by an independent lawyer, Kenneth Feinberg.

natural resource affected.[1204] This closely reflects the narrow legal test adopted under the *Robins Dry Dock* rule.[1205] Thus legalistic tests such as 'geographic proximity' and 'proximate cause' were very much to the fore. Given the need to conserve the fund it is understandable that initial emergency payments were directed towards those most directly affected by the spillage such as fishermen and waterfront hoteliers. However, the criteria were subsequently broadened so as to facilitate claims by those without direct interests in the damaged natural resources, but whose businesses are nevertheless heavily intertwined with the Gulf of Mexico economy. Those who service the fishing industry and waterfront businesses are obvious examples. To this end the next set of GCCF guidance dropped references to 'geographic proximity' and proximate cause.[1206]

It is important to reiterate the fact that the GCCF system is a means of private ordering which operates independently of the legal liabilities established by the OPA 1990. This is underscored by the fact that Professor John Goldberg of Harvard Law School, who was commissioned by the US Government to provide an expert opinion on the recoverability of economic loss under the OPA 90, emphasized that his findings did not extend to how the GCCF should determine its claims. Professor Goldberg's report[1207] indicates that a more restrictive view of recoverable economic loss is likely to be taken by the courts in respect of claims brought directly under the Act. This has caused some surprise in that the OPA was passed in the wake of the Exxon Valdez disaster and there was an assumption that it was intended to broaden the scope of recoverable economic loss beyond those with a direct interest in the damaged resource. The OPA 90 provides that the following economic losses shall be recoverable:

> Damages equal to the loss of profits or impairment of earning capacity due to the injury, destruction, or loss of real property, personal property, or natural resources, which shall be recoverable by any claimant.[1208]

Professor Goldberg concluded that under the terms of the Act:

> Only those economic loss claimants who can prove that they have suffered economic loss because a spill has damaged, destroyed or otherwise rendered physically unavailable to them property or resources that they have a right to put to commercial use.

This conclusion has drawn some criticism in that it appears to run counter to the notion that the OPA 90 was intended to extend the scope of liability for economic loss. In fact, the need to show some form of direct interest in the damaged resources, albeit something less than a legal interest, marks somewhat of a return to the Robins Dry Dock rule. Davies, amongst others, has strongly argued that this interpretation is not

---

1204. Protocol for Emergency Advanced Payments, 23 August 2010; see Davies (n. 1184), 39.

1205. *Robins Dry Dock & Repair Co v. Flint* 275 U.S. 303, 48 S Ct. 134 (1927).

1206. Protocol on Interim and Final Claims, 22 November 2010; see Davies, (n. 1184), above, 39.

1207. John C. P. Goldberg, *Liability for Economic Loss in Connection with the Deepwater Horizon Spill* (Nov. 22, 2010), http://nrs.harvard.edu/urn-3:HUL.InstRepos:4595438 (accessed Mar. 30, 2012).

1208. 33 U.S.C. § 2702(b)(2)(E).

supported by the language of the section. Such an approach appears to facilitate claims by fishermen but not those who service the industry.

In conclusion, it seems that the ever present fear of the floodgates exerts a continual pressure to adopt a restrictive view of the recoverability of economic loss.

[D]   The Availability of Injunctive Relief

In the context of environmental protection, a difficult issue concerns the fact that the rationale for granting injunctive relief differs from when it is granted to protect private interests. As regards the protection of private interests, it will be recalled that an increasingly popular view of the role of injunctions stems from the economic analysis of law outlined in Chapter 4. To recap, the theory provides that injunctions should not be viewed as a once and for all prohibition against the continuance of an activity, rather, they should be regarded as an instruction to the parties to bargain.[1209] Thus, according to this view, the injunction serves to prevent a polluter from interfering with a person's use and enjoyment of his property without first attempting to negotiate an easement. This analysis appeals to economists in that the injunction serves to channel the land use decision to the market[1210] which they regard as being a more accurate indicator of land use preferences than the courts.[1211] However, it is also recognized that, in certain circumstances, the granting of an injunction may not have the effect of inducing the parties to bargain.[1212] In such circumstances it is argued that the court should award damages in lieu thus compulsorily purchasing the claimant's right to the undisturbed use and enjoyment of his property.[1213]

Such an outcome is hardly commensurate with the objective of environmental protection and it is a discretion which should be used sparingly. Although, it must be acknowledged that there may be circumstances in which it offers the best practicable solution.[1214] It is difficult to see how such a discretion could form part of a specialist liability regime of the type which has been adopted in certain Member States and which was at one time contemplated by the EU Commission. This provides a strong argument in favour of using alternative mechanisms or procedures to focus on the environmental damage as opposed to the personal cost. In the Netherlands, for example, NGOs may

---

1209. See, for example, Robert D. Cooter &Thomas Ulen, *Law and Economics*, 176 (Addison-Wesley 1997); C. Veljanowski, *Legal Theory, Economic Analysis and Tort*, in, *Legal Theory and Common Law*, 229–230 (W.L. Twining ed., Basil Blackwell 1986); Cane (n.1193), 54–55.
1210. William M. Landes & Richard A. Posner, *The Economic Structure of Tort Law*, 31 (University of Chicago Press 1988).
1211. *Ibid*. See also A.I. Ogus & G.M. Richardson, *Economics and the Environment*, 36(2) Cambridge L.J. 284, 321 (1977), '[O]ne important respect in which the court may fail to achieve efficiency is in its jealous preference for an injunction over damages.'
1212. This may occur in circumstances where there are many parties involved in that it would be impractical for the polluter to reach a different settlement with each individual; see Cooter and Ulen, (n. 1209), 171.
1213. Landes and Posner (n. 1210), 31: Cooter and Ulen (n. 1209), 176; G. Calabresi and D.A. Melamed, *Property Rules, Liability Rules, and Inalienability: Our view of the Cathedral*, 85 Harv. L. Rev. 1089 (1972).
1214. See §3.05[B][4], above.

seek an injunction in respect of the environmental damage in a separate action from any individual remedies sought by private parties in respect of personal losses.[1215]

§10.05   CONCLUSION

The nature of available remedies strikes at the heart and purpose of an environmental liability regime. In previous chapters it has been argued at length that, in order to be effective, such a regime would have to focus on the environmental damage costs in addition to any harm suffered by private interests vesting in the environment. Due to the breadth and diversity of domestic legal traditions on this issue, international initiatives on environmental liability have tended to leave detailed issues of quantum to be determined according to national law. In the absence of special provisions on the quantification of environmental loss, there is a danger that any funds recovered could be absorbed into the public purse and used for general spending purposes. The costs of environmental remediation should remain at the forefront of such regimes. Moreover, since the first edition of this book was published, efforts have continued apace to find viable means of attaching a pecuniary value to environmental damage. These techniques are currently undergoing rigorous testing in the context of the Deepwater Horizon disaster.

Existing national legal principles also vary greatly on the issue of the recoverability of economic loss. Most legal systems have accumulated complex bodies of case law on this issue as courts have striven to achieve coherent principles for determining at which point such losses should be deemed too remote or unforeseeable. On occasion, courts have abandoned the search for principle and have drawn arbitrary cut off points on policy grounds. Do to the wide divergence in domestic legal traditions on this issue, it has proved difficult to establish unified principles in the context of international regimes. Once again, this is an issue which is normally interpreted in the light of existing domestic laws. However, it is an issue which should not be neglected. As the major oil pollution disasters have shown, economic loss claims often constitute the lion's share of private losses stemming from a major incident.

In conclusion it must be noted that the issue of remedies is prone to be neglected in most specialist environmental liability regimes and existing laws are often used as the default position. However, such regimes are only as effective as the remedies which they apply. Should the EU at some point elect to return to the issue of a European system of tort based remedies for environmental damage, it would need to pay more attention to the need for harmonization on this issue.

1215. See Hinteregger (n. 1192).

CHAPTER 11

Financial Provision for Extended Civil Liability

§11.01 INTRODUCTION

As stated in Chapter 4, it is not realistic to consider the role of tort in isolation from insurance or other financial security mechanisms such as compensation funds. The financial implications arising from extended civil liability for environmental damage are never far from the surface in any debate on this topic. It is generally accepted that there is little point in extending liability if the means of absorbing those additional costs do not exist. Moreover, as has already been discussed in some depth, the possibility of potentially open ended liability has major implications for the rationale of tort based liability and the insurability of risk. This raises the issue of the extent to which liability should be capped and to what extent it should be linked with other mechanisms for meeting the costs of environmental remediation.

European and international initiatives on environmental liability have all made some attempt to link tort based liability with some form of financial security such as compulsory insurance or compensation funds. The greatest challenge remains how best to ensure that the environmental remediation costs are met without undermining the element of personal accountability resulting from tort based liability.

§11.02 DOMESTIC LAWS IN EU STATES

In common with the United States and the United Kingdom, the insurance industry in most EU States excludes coverage for pollution damage save for that which is caused by 'sudden and accidental' escapes.[1216] This raises the issue of whether adequate financial security mechanisms are in place capable of meeting the additional costs of environmental liability.

The German ELA (*UmweltHG*) makes provision for compulsory insurance under section 19, although the legislature was slow to activate the provision due to a lack of suitable products in the insurance market.[1217] However, over the course of the last twenty years the expertise of the insurance industry and the availability and sophistication of products has grown exponentially.[1218] As regards insurance for environmental liability, the ELD has served as a key driver for the development of suitable policies.[1219]

After some hesitation,[1220] the German insurance industry[1221] decided to exclude pollution cover from general liability policies whilst simultaneously offering new EIL policies.[1222] These policies differ somewhat from their counterparts in the UK. Whereas UK EIL policies contain 'claims made' triggers to avoid the problem of 'long tail' risks,[1223] the German version comprises 'manifestation' triggers: 'The insurance case is the first discovery of bodily injury or material damage by the injured party or a third party or by the policyholder.'[1224] This does not preclude the possibility of exposure to long tail risks; thus, it seems that the industry is confident that detailed site surveys can reduce this risk to manageable proportions. This corresponds with the findings of Holmes and Broughton who, it will be recalled,[1225] argue that, those UK insurers who choose to continue providing pollution cover under public liability policies, can reduce exposure to long tail risks by introducing EIL type site surveys. In addition, the German EIL policies provide limited indemnity in respect of gradual pollution arising from incidents other than sudden and accidental escapes. This would include, for example, pollution caused by oil drips from a broken down machine but not emissions resulting from the normal operation of a plant. However, this type of indemnity has been capped at DM 20 million.[1226]

1216. See P. Wetterstein, *The Finnish Environmental Damage Compensation Act – and some comparisons with Norwegian and Swedish Law*, 3(3) Env. Liability 41, 47 (1995); and J.M. Barrenetxea, *The Spanish Draft Act on Liability for Environmental Damage*, 5(6) Env. Liability 115, 124 (1997).
1217. See W.C. Hoffman, *Germany's New Environmental Liability Act: Strict Liability for Facilities Causing Pollution*, 38 Neth. Intl. L. Rev. 27, 39 (1991).
1218. See §4.04[B], above.
1219. *Ibid.*
1220. See Hoffman (n. 1217), 40–41. For a time the industry was unsure whether to adapt existing general liability policies or to entirely exclude cover and offer new stand alone EIL policies.
1221. For a general overview of the insurability of environmental risks in Germany see Haust Schlemminger & Claus Peter Martens (eds.), *German Environmental Law for Practitioners*, Ch. 6 (Kluwer 2004).
1222. See R. Woltereck, *New Environmental Impairment Liability Policy Introduced into the German Insurance Market*, 5 Intl. Ins. L. Rev. 202, 203 (1994). The industry has stated that cover will only be offered to the 100,000 plants subject to the *UmweltHG* under new conditions.
1223. See §4.04[B], above.
1224. See Woltereck (n. 1222) 204.
1225. See §4.04[B], above.
1226. See Woltereck (n. 1222) 204.

Insurance companies in certain states have endeavoured to increase capacity by forming insurance pools such as Assurpol in France.[1227] By pooling resources and expertise in this manner the industry is better able to absorb unexpectedly large claims resulting from, for example, long tail risks.[1228]

Certain states have adopted a horizontal approach to liability whereby costs which cannot be recovered through tort rules and insurance may be drawn from a compensation fund financed by, for example, a tax or premium on industry. In Sweden, recourse may be had to such funds where the identity of the polluter is unknown, where civil action is statute barred or where the polluter is insolvent.[1229]

§11.03 EUROPEAN AND INTERNATIONAL INITIATIVES

Compulsory insurance is a component of most of the supranational liability schemes which have been mooted or implemented at a European or international level. Article 12 of the Lugano Convention requires operators to take part in a compulsory financial security scheme to cover the costs of liability incurred under the Convention. This does not amount to compulsory insurance in that it allows for alternative mechanisms. The Article is rather vague as to the proportion of the damage costs which should be covered. It merely refers to the fact that a financial guarantee should be agreed up to a certain limit in accordance with internal law. As regards international regimes, compulsory insurance is a central component of the conventions governing maritime pollution[1230] and nuclear accidents.[1231] These regimes are also closely linked with compensation funds designed to meet costs which exceed the caps on liability.

The insurability of environmental damage costs, arising from extended civil liability under an EU regime, was also a major preoccupation of the EU Commission during its deliberations on the subject. The 1992 Commission Green Paper recited the familiar arguments relating to the difficulties of quantifying risk and lack of capacity in the insurance market.[1232] However, as the developments reviewed above indicate, the market has expanded considerably over the past twenty years. The Green Paper also proposed that there should be a simultaneous introduction of clean-up funds for use

---

1227. This has proved necessary in France due to the fact that 'claims made' triggers have been ruled illegal by the *Cour de Cassation* in the case of *Commercial Union v. La Mutuelle des Architectes Francais* (Unreported, 1990). This makes it difficult to insure against long tail risks. Assurpol has started introducing 'manifestation triggers' of the type introduced in Germany, however, it remains to be seen whether these will be acceptable to the courts. See R.G. Lee & S. Tupper, *Claims-made Policies: European Occurrences*, 4(1) Env. Liability 25 (1996); M. Hagopian, *France: Supreme Court Rules that 'Claims Made' Coverage is a Nullity*, 1 I.J.I.L. 52 (1994).

1228. Including Italy, Spain and the Netherlands. See ERM Economics, *The Insurance Sector*, in, *Economic Aspects of Liability and Joint Compensation Systems for Remedying Environmental Damage*, DGXII (European Commission 1996).

1229. Environment Protection Act (1969:387), sections 65–68; Ordinance (1989:365) on Environmental Damage Insurance. Contributions to the fund are calculated upon the basis of the size of the enterprise (in terms of numbers of employees) and the nature of its activity.

1230. See §5.05[A], above.

1231. See §5.05[B], above.

1232. COM(93) 47 final, 13.

where it is not possible to recover costs through liability and insurance.[1233] Thus civil liability and compensation funds are envisaged as constituting two components of a unified system (a 'horizontal' approach) along the lines of the international regimes referred to above.

The subsequent White Paper reiterated the fact that insurance companies cannot provide financial security unless they are able to calculate risk;[1234] indeed, calculation of risk is the essence of the insurance business. It is safe to assume that the fears of the insurance industry were largely responsible for the decision to exclude any possibility of retroactive liability for historic pollution.[1235] Where damage has occurred in the past, insurers would have calculated premiums and drafted policies in accordance with the laws, and state of scientific knowledge, of the day. However, the White Paper acknowledged that the insurance market had yet to catch up with extended environmental liability in Europe.[1236]

As a result, the White Paper suggested 'a cautious approach in setting up the liability regime'. The introduction of an environmental liability regime would provide the impetus for the insurance market to develop. However, the Commission envisaged a gradual introduction of an environmental liability regime so as to avoid swamping existing financial security mechanisms with a spate of environmental liability claims:

> The concerns of the financial sector are one reason for the step-by-step approach mentioned in this paper. The closed scope of dangerous activities, the limitation to those natural resources which are already protected by existing Community law and the limitation to significant damage are all aspects which contribute to making the risks arising from the regime better calculable and manageable.[1237]

Although the ELD which emerged from these deliberations focused on extending the role of administrative cost recovery powers, rather than enhancing the role of tort, it has still had the effect of stimulating the growth of insurance markets in this area.[1238]

1233. *Ibid.*, 23, para. [4.1].
1234. COM 2000(66) final, 24.
1235. Prior to the Court of Appeal judgment in *Cambridge Water v. Eastern Counties Leather* [1993] Envtl. L.R. 287, the ABI issued a press release which stated that, if the Court found in favour of Cambridge Water, its members would be forced to withdraw cover for pollution altogether. See A. Layard, *Insuring Pollution in the UK*, 4(1) Env. Liability 17, 18 (1996).
1236. COM 2000(66) final, 24.
1237. COM(2000) 66 final, 24.
1238. Article 14 of the ELD requires Member States to 'encourage' the development of financial secuirty mechanisms. Moreover, the Commission was required to prepare a report on the development of such mechanims by 30 April 2010. To this end an independent report was commissioned which was submitted towards the end of 2009. This noted that the insurance market was now well developed. See EU Commission Environmental Liability website at http://ec.europa.eu/environment/enveco/liability/index.htm (accessed Apr. 23, 2012), for details of studies undertaken.

§11.04 MAIN ISSUES

The above developments give rise to two main issues, namely, the need for compulsory environmental liability insurance and how liability rules, backed by insurance, should interrelate with alternative compensation mechanisms.

[A] Compulsory Insurance

One of the main objections put forward against the introduction of compulsory insurance for environmental damage is that insurance companies would become licensers of industry.[1239] This argument is somewhat overstated in that operators are already subject to certain forms of compulsory insurance. For example, in the UK, a chemical plant must obtain compulsory employers' liability insurance[1240] and, if it wishes to deliver its products by road, compulsory motor insurance.[1241] Thus, to a certain extent, the ability of an operator to trade is already dependant upon the availability of insurance.

A more compelling argument is simply that in many jurisdictions there is a shortage of specialist insurance products for environmental liability; as noted above, this situation has been experienced in certain states. There is no point in requiring operators to take out compulsory insurance if the market does not provide an adequate supply of suitable products. However, it is also clear that existing public liability policies would not be capable of meeting all the costs associated with environmental damage. The pollution exclusion limits liability to instances where there has been a major accident or catastrophic equipment failure as in the *Seveso* disaster. This does not encompass situations where damage has been caused by a 'drip drip' effect over a number of years as in *Cambridge Water*. Although the environmental insurance market has expanded rapidly over the past twenty years, there are still gaps in cover and it may still be some years before the industry can absorb all the losses stemming from measures such as the ELD.[1242]

This explains why most proposals for environmental liability regimes require operators to establish some form of 'financial security' for increased liabilities, whatever form that may take, rather than imposing a specific compulsory insurance component. Indeed, it could be argued that insurance does not always provide the best solution to the problem of financial responsibility. Faure and Hartleif[1243] have argued that in highly specialized and technical areas, such as nuclear power, the industry itself

---

1239. Roy Marshall of the Swiss Re-insurance Company argued: 'The unavailability of compulsory insurance would in principle mean businesses must be closed. This would unacceptably shift the responsibility to police the enterprise from the public authorities to the insurance industry.' See R. Marshall, *Environmental Impairment – Insurance Perspectives*, 3(2/3) Rev. Eur. Communtiy Intl. Envtl. L. 153, 158 (1994).
1240. Employers' Liability (Compulsory Insurance) Act 1969.
1241. Road Traffic Act 1988 (sections 143 and 145).
1242. See n. 1238, above. For an overview of the current state of the market see §4.04[B], above.
1243. M.G. Faure & T. Hartleif, *Compensation Funds versus Liability and Insurance for Remedying Environmental Damage*, 5(4) Rev. Eur. Community Intl. Envtl. L. 321, 323 (1996).

is best placed to assess risk and finance its own compensation fund.[1244] In the shipping industry this approach has been adopted by tanker owners who have formed Protection and Indemnity Clubs to meet liabilities resulting from pollution.[1245]

A further difficulty is that a compulsory insurance provision would need to specify the proportion of the damage costs which must be met by insurance. It is impossible to generalize on this issue in that it depends upon factors such as the size of the company, the nature of its business and so forth. The *Lugano* Convention recognizes this problem and states that the matter should be left to internal law. It is because of similar difficulties that Germany has been slow to activate the compulsory insurance component of the *UmweltHG*. Given the number of plants covered by the Act and the technical differences between them the Bunderstag considered that it would not be reasonable to require all costs to be met through insurance. However, it is because of these very differences that the German Government has been unable to set mandatory insurance limits.[1246] Due to the range of variable factors involved, the scope of the policy is a matter which should be negotiated between the insurer and the insured. In other words, insurers need flexibility to adapt policies to the circumstances of a particular site.

Provided liability is not imposed in a manner which gives rise to open ended costs, industry and insurance companies are capable of devising financial security mechanisms without compulsory insurance.

[B]   Relationship between Liability Insurance and Compensation Funds

It is clear that not all damage costs can be met through the imposition of tortious liability underwritten by insurance. For this reason it is noteworthy that the regime governing maritime oil pollution adopts a two pronged approach.[1247] A compensation fund operates in parallel with the liability system with a view to providing compensation in respect of a greater proportion of the damage costs than could be met through the application of tort based principles alone. The regime governing nuclear liability adopts a similar approach although it is currently confined to the Paris Convention.[1248]

More recently it has been mooted whether a compensation fund of this nature could be used as a means of establishing liability for damage arising from climate change. Attempts have been made in the US courts to secure compensation for damage

---

1244. See M. Faure, *Economic Models of Compensation for Damage caused by Nuclear Accidents: Some Lessons for the Revision of the Paris and Vienna Conventions*, Eur. J.L. & Econ. 21 (1995).
1245. See T.G. Coghlin, *Protection and Indemnity Clubs*, Loyd's Mar. Com. L. Q. 403 (1994). Indeed, as regards the *Exxon Valdez* disaster, Exxon's insurers only bore a comparatively small part of the overall losses. A far greater proportion of the costs, for which Exxon could be indemnified, were borne by the International Tanker Indemnity Association (ITIA), the Protection and Indemnity Club of which Exxon was a member. It should, however, be noted that there was much legal wrangling over the respective losses which should be met by the insurers and the ITIA under the terms of the insurance policies and the rules of the ITIA. See M.F. Dolin, *An Overview of the Exxon Valdez Insurance Coverage Dispute*, 5(10) Intl. Ins. L. Rev. 313 (1997).
1246. See Woltereck (n. 1222) 203.
1247. See §5.05[A], above.
1248. See §5.05[B], above.

allegedly attributable to climate change although, at the time of writing, no claim has yet come to fruition.[1249] Litigants must overcome considerably difficulties, not least of which is the need to establish causation.[1250] It is conceivable that a compensation fund, operating on the basis of strict liability, could by-pass many of these difficulties.[1251] Such a fund could be financed by a combination of a carbon energy tax on major greenhouse gas emitters, a sales tax on energy intensive products, the insurance industry and public funds. Nevertheless, the establishment of such a fund poses major conceptual and practical difficulties. Conventional funds, such as the IOPCF, maintain close links with tort based liability rules. Claims are triggered by a specific incident such as the grounding of a super-tanker. The fund can then be utilized to meet costs which go beyond the capped liability of the ship owner. As has been explored in depth in earlier chapters, climate changes gives rise to causation difficulties of an altogether different magnitude.[1252] According to the current state of scientific knowledge, it is impossible to pin a specific event, causing particular damage, on an identifiable polluter. It is possible that, freed from the strictures of conventional legal causation tests, the body charged with administering claims under the system could develop a more flexible approach under its fund jurisprudence. However, some form of consistent, rational and coherent test would have to be developed in order to maintain the integrity of the system and to conserve the funds. Otherwise, there is a danger that the fund would operate as yet another green tax unrelated in any way to the conduct of the industries concerned. This would be a formidable task, notwithstanding the freedom to depart from conventional tort based approaches. Farris asserts that causation difficulties could be alleviated by limiting eligible claims to 'readily identifiable impacts';[1253] however, this just begs the question of what constitutes a 'readily identifiable impact.' In Chapter 3 it was argued that it is conceptually possible to develop a model of causation which attaches causative significance to statistical probabilities; even if at first blush they appear insignificant.[1254] However, it was also observed that it is doubtful whether a court would be prepared to adopt such an approach in the near future. As noted above, the body charged with administering a compensation fund may have more freedom to depart from orthodox causality tests. Set against this is the fact that, in order to secure international agreement on the establishment of such a fund, the contracting parties would doubtless seek to clarify precisely what causality tests would be applied. Moreover, a compensation fund has to be managed carefully, otherwise it would be rapidly depleted. The body charged with administering the fund inevitably develops its own 'fund jurisprudence' with a view to achieving consistency and filtering out claims which are deemed too remote. Such concerns are also at the heart of tort; thus it is no surprise that fund jurisprudence is often highly redolent of

---

1249. For an overview of the US litigation see §2.05[E], above.
1250. See §3.03[B][4], above.
1251. For general discussion see D.A. Farber, *Basic Compensation for Victims of Climate Change*, U. PA. L. Rev. 1605 (2007); M. Farris, *Compensating Climate Change Victims: the Compensation Fund as an Alternative to Tort Litigation*, 2(2) Sea Grant L. & Policy J. 49 (2009–10).
1252. See §3.03[B][4], above.
1253. Farris (n. 1251), above.
1254. See §3.03[B][4], above.

case law on tortious liability. Indeed, in some cases fund jurisprudence appears little more generous than tort.[1255] Thus, as regards the possibility of a climate change fund, it is possible that the administering body would adopt a cautious approach to the issue of causation which would undermine its ability to provide a viable alternative to tort.

Finally, it must be acknowledged that, although compensation funds may play a vital role in augmenting the limited reach of tortious liabilities, they too have a finite capacity. The unprecedented Deepwater Horizon disaster swamped all existing legal and compensatory mechanisms. Had the letter of the law been applied then only a fraction of the total damage costs would have been met due to the caps on liability. However, as we have seen, the matter was swiftly moved to the political arena with the result that BP waived any caps on its liability and established an escrow account containing an astronomical amount of funds.[1256] Due to the exceptional nature of the disaster and the ad hoc responses which were adopted, it is difficult to extrapolate general principles of law from this case. Rather, it serves to emphasize the limits of law and conventional mechanisms when society is presented with an environmental disaster of such epic proportions.

§11.05   CONCLUSION

The issue of environmental liability cannot be considered in isolation from the wider financial implications. As has been discussed at length in Chapter 4, the courts have become increasingly aware of the economic realities of their decisions and especially the effects on the insurance industry. Indeed, in most tort actions the original parties appear in name only as the real battle is fought between the respective insurers exercising their subrogation rights.

Once again, it is necessary to view the issue of insurance, and other means of underwriting risks, in the light of the theoretical framework outlined in Chapter 4. It is certainly true to say that the growth of insurance may reduce individual accountability to a certain extent thereby introducing elements of distributional justice. However, if costs are automatically passed to insurers without any account being taken of individual conduct, the industry is likely to withdraw insurance cover altogether, as it threatened to do in the run up to the Cambridge Water decision. Thus any liability system must retain elements of individual accountability. For this reason, it would be important to include defences to strict liability, of the nature described in Chapter 6, which afford operators some opportunity to mitigate their losses. Provided that liability is linked to patterns of behaviour insurance companies are in a position to calculate risk and reward the adoption of cleaner technologies by adjusting premiums accordingly.

1255. See, for example, the manner in which the Scottish Court of Session dealt with economic loss claims brought against the IOPC in *Landcatch v. International oil Pollution Compensation Fund* [1998] 2 Lloyd's Rep. 552; see §3.05[A][2], above.
1256. See §3.05[A][2], above.

As regards the difficulty caused by lack of capacity in the insurance market, it should be remembered that over the years similar arguments have been advanced against increased employers' liability and improved consumer protection legislation.

Ultimately, the market has shown itself to be capable of adapting and exploiting the potential for new business. However, this is provided that liability is extended in a controlled manner. Draconian regimes which swamp existing financial security mechanisms end in disaster and can result in the non cooperation of the insurance industry. Recall that this was the effect of the original Superfund scheme which resulted in many insurers refusing to provide cover for those engaged in environmentally hazardous activities. the 2000 EU White Paper on environmental liability made an important point when it stated that an environmental liability should be introduced in a controlled manner and linked to those industries already subject to EU environmental legislation. Insurers will already have systems in place for assessing risk at such establishments due to existing environmental risks such as contaminated land.

It must be acknowledged that insurance alone cannot provide a complete solution and efforts should continue to develop alternative means of spreading the costs. The IOPCF provides the most highly developed model and is likely to provide the template for other systems. For example, efforts are underway to expand the compensation fund for nuclear damage and a form of compensation fund for the effects of climate change is currently being debated; although the practical difficulties associated with the latter are considerable. Moreover, the Deepwater Horizon saga provides a salutary lesson that there are limits to what can be achieved through the application of conventional liability and cost recovery mechanisms. The unprecedented scale of the disaster resulted in the adoption of a number of ad hoc political responses which were only possible due to the nature of the oil industry and the extent of its resources. A similar approach would not be possible following, for example, the explosion of a nuclear reactor in an impoverished state. Aside from nuclear catastrophes which are thankfully exceedingly rare, the oil industry is associated with the greatest environmental disasters; however, as the wealthiest industry it is unique in having the resources to meet its own costs.

Part V: Conclusions

CHAPTER 12

Conclusion: The Nature of Tort Based Liability in an Environmental Context

§12.01   INTRODUCTION

The purpose of this book has been to establish the role of tort as a component in a system of environmental protection. In the first edition it was concluded that much of the debate on the role of tort, with particular reference to the EU initiatives at the time, failed to address this basic issue focusing instead on the detail of specific proposals. As should be apparent from the foregoing discussion, the debate has moved on and the impetus for change provided by the EU has diminished somewhat. Nevertheless, as recent events demonstrate, interest in the role of tort in this context is unabated and litigants continue to test tort based principles in hitherto uncharted waters such as climate change. Nevertheless, it remains the case that, unless one understands the fundamental nature of tort and the wider arguments concerning its proper function in a modern society, it is impossible to fully appreciate how it should operate in an environmental context. In this regard the foregoing analysis enables one to draw certain conclusions regarding the philosophical basis of tort had how this might define its use in environmental protection.

§12.02   THE PHILOSOPHICAL BASIS OF TORT LAW

One of the main objections to the use of tort as a means of environmental protection has been the assertion that, as a private dispute resolution mechanism, it is conceptually difficult to harness tort in pursuit of public interest objectives such as environmental protection.[1257] However, when one examines the philosophical basis of

---

1257. This view is encapsulated by the Union of Industrial and Employers Confederations of Europe (UNICE): 'Civil liability law protects individuals and, for that reason, civil liability is not suited

tort and its historical development it soon becomes apparent that this is an over simplification.

To recap, the early development of common law was firmly rooted in the protection of private interests in land. Its function was entirely corrective in that it served to restore an interest of which the plaintiff had been wrongfully disseised.[1258] A nuisance was regarded as a misappropriation of an inalienable property right rather than an annoyance or irritation. However, during the course of the nineteenth century the courts began to impute distributional functions into the common law. The view emerged that it was no longer realistic to consider property rights in isolation from social preferences regarding land use.[1259] Thus, from this time tort has been concerned with whether a particular land use is reasonable. To this end liability under English common law, and other common law based systems, has been made contingent upon certain additional considerations including the character of the neighbourhood[1260] and whether an activity constitutes an unnatural use of land.[1261]

Thus, it is clear that from the nineteenth century onwards the law of tort has sought to balance private interests against public interests. Esser explained this duality upon the basis of the Aristotelian distinction between corrective and distributive justice.[1262] Whereas corrective justice focuses on the wrong suffered by the plaintiff and the need to restore the *status quo ante*, distributional justice aims to allocate the loss to the party which is in the best position to internalize it. This has given rise to conceptual difficulties in that the two concepts at first seem incompatible. In the twentieth century academics have been exercised by the problems of how to ground tort in a philosophical basis which enables it to fulfil both functions simultaneously. Englard's application of the theory of complementarity to the problem provides an elegant explanation of how two seemingly contradictory functions can form part of a harmonious totality.[1263] In his view it is possible for a single legal rule to embody both objectives.

The attraction of Englard's approach is that it is possible to apply it to existing tort rules which are relevant in an environmental context. The character of the neighbourhood test, for example, serves distributional functions in that it adjusts the threshold of

---

to compensate damage resulting from activities harmful to the environment as a common good. Only public law can determine what measures the public authorities should take in order to restore the environment as a common good,' See UN1CE, *Position Paper on the Fundamental Options in the Green Paper on Remedying Environmental Damage*, (Brussels July 20, 1993), (written submissions presented to joint EC Commission and European Public Hearing on 'Preventing and Remedying Environmental Damage, Brussels 3–4 November 1993) 20 July 1993, Brussels.

1258. Frederick William Maitland, *The Forms of Action at Common Law: A Course of Lectures* (A.H. Chaytor & W.J. Whittaker eds., Cambridge University Press 1936).
1259. J.P.S.Mclaren, *Nuisance Law and the Industrial Revolution: Some Lessons from Social History*, 3(2) O.J.L.S. 155 (1983).
1260. *St. Helens Smelting v. Tipping* (1865) H.L.C. 642.
1261. *Rylands v. Fletcher* (1866) L.R. 1 Ex. 265.
1262. Josef Esser, *Grundlagen und Entwicklung der Gefährdungshaftung* (2d ed., C.H. Beck 1961).
1263. Itzhak Englard, *The Idea of Complementarity as a Philosophical Basis for Pluralism in Tort Law*, in *Philosophical Foundations of Tort*, 185 (D.G. Owen ed.,Clarendon Press 1995).

damage in accordance with the predominant land use in an area. However, it retains corrective functions in that harm which exceeds this threshold remains actionable.

It is therefore, possible to identify a conceptual basis which justifies using tort rules in pursuit of a public interest objective such as environmental protection. However, the issue of whether there is a need to use tort in this way is, of course, another matter.

§12.03   THE ROLE OF TORT IN AN ENVIRONMENTAL CONTEXT

The major potential benefit of tort in an environmental context is that it affords private individuals, and other bodies with legal personality, the opportunity to take part in the policing of the environment. Where private interests are closely assimilated with environmental interests, a polluting incident may give rise to substantial civil liability in addition to regulatory penalties.[1264] This may have the added advantage of requiring the polluter to internalize a greater proportion of the total damage costs.[1265] A paradigmatic case study is provided by the success of Fish Legal (and its previous incarnation as the ACA in pursuing the polluters of rivers.[1266] Moreover, It was the potential for tort based remedies to operate as an additional enforcement mechanism which first attracted the EU to the idea of an EU environmental liability system.

However, it is important for tort to retain a degree of independence from regulation. As the case of *Blue Circle Industries Plc v. Ministry of Defence*[1267] demonstrates, regulatory standards can provide a useful guide as to whether damage has occurred in cases of doubt. In this case it will be recalled that contaminated soil had to be removed because radiation levels exceeded statutory limits, not because there was necessarily a threat to health. Nevertheless, compliance with such standards should not be regarded as conclusive evidence of harm. The court should retain some discretion to protect private interests in cases where standards set by authorities are inadequate.[1268] Whilst tort should be considered as a means of increasing general

---

1264. This is already the case where a regulation also make provision for civil in addition to criminal liability. See, for example, Nuclear Installations Act 1965, section 12.
1265. Recall that, following the Shell Mersey Estuary Oil spill of 1989, Shell was fined EUR 1m which, up to that point, was the largest penalty ever imposed for environmental impairment. However, clean-up costs amounted to EUR 1.4m and property damage amounted to EUR 2.1m. See R. Holmes and M. Broughton, *Insurance Cover for Damage to the Environment*, 9513 E.G. 123 (1995).
1266. See §4.03[B], above.
1267. [1997] 1 Env. L.R. 341.
1268. Cane points out that the common law can supplement regulatory standards set by, for example, the planning system: 'Although it [the tort of nuisance] cannot overturn the work of the planning system, it can be used to control the detailed use of permitted developments which the planning system does not, on the whole regulate; and it may provide some remedy for the results of planning mistakes.' See Peter Cane, *Tort Law and Economic Interests*, 392 (Clarendon Press 1996). However, the ability of nuisance to fulfil this function has been seriously undermined by the decision in *Gillingham Borough Council v. Medway (Chatham) Dock Ltd* [1993] QB 343 in which a single planning consent was found to be capable of altering the character of the neighbourhood.

private participation in environmental protection it should not be inextricably linked with regulatory standards. Compliance with regulatory standards should continue to be regarded as being of evidential importance.

This raises an important theme regarding the role of tort in an environmental context. Those regimes which utilize tort as an additional means of enforcement, through the establishment of statutory duties, use tort in an instrumentalist manner designed to further the objectives of the legislation.[1269] Thus, the threshold of actionable harm is linked with definitions of harm under the legislation. Furthermore, conduct giving rise to tortious liability may be linked with standards derived from criminal or administrative law. Such an instrumentalist use of tort may serve a useful purpose inasmuch as it provides a means by which individual victims can be compensated. However, it should always be borne in mind that the protection of such interests is not the prime objective of legislation of this nature. As a result, certain statutory duties may be much narrower in scope than general tort based principles of liability. For example, in Chapter 4[1270] it was argued that the definition of damage under nuclear liability legislation excludes many type of harm which are likely to be associated with chronic types of nuclear pollution. Nevertheless, the legislation excludes claimants from pursuing actions under other torts, principally nuisance, which may provide redress in respect of that type of harm. This precludes the general law of tort from operating as a means of compensating for deficiencies in the regulatory regime governing a particular activity.[1271] Thus, tort has two potential roles in an environmental context, which may not always be compatible. On the one hand it may operate as a direct means of enforcing environmental standards. On the other hand, general tort laws may operate as a means of providing redress for private losses which may have been overlooked by the broad sweep of the legislation. This latter function is not directly concerned with environmental protection; however, where a number of parties have suffered loss as a result of pollution, the aggregate effect of multiple actions may account for a substantial part of the damage. A clear example is provided by the Corby litigation[1272] arising from the botched decontamination of a former steelworks site and the current litigation arising from oil pollution in the Niger Delta region.[1273] As a result, where the legislature contemplates the inclusion of civil remedies in an environmental regulation, it should be slow to oust existing remedies.

The Niger Delta case is exceptional given the vast number of claimants.[1274] In most cases the number of litigants involved may be far fewer; this raises the issue of whether individual claims brought by a limited number of parties could exert any deterrent effect upon operators. In this respect it should be noted that individual judgments in high profile matters can attract a great deal of publicity which may result

---

1269. See discussion at §4.03[C], above.
1270. *Ibid.*
1271. *Ibid.*
1272. *Corby Group Litigation v. Corby D.C.* [2009] EWHC 1944 (TCC), [2010] Env. L.R. D2. For main discussion see §2.05[C], §2.06[B][2] and §7.03[B], above.
1273. See discussion at §5.02[B], above.
1274. *Ibid.*

in exemplary deterrence.[1275] Furthermore, a test case can open the way for a multitude of similar claims. This frequently occurs in industrial diseases cases whereby, following a successful representative action, the defendant may agree to settle similar claims out of court.[1276] Thus had Elizabeth Reay and Vivien Hope been successful their action against British Nuclear Fuels Limited (BNFL)[1277] it is likely that BNFL would have been compelled to settle other claims brought by the offspring of Sellafield employees. As regards more recent examples, in the light of the Corby litigation it is most unlikely that a local authority would launch into a major land contamination project without adopting sophisticated precautions[1278] and one can be certain that the operation and maintenance of BOPs has improved immeasurably since the Deepwater Horizon disaster.[1279]

§12.04   THE LIMITS OF TORT

Clearly no system of environmental regulation can rely entirely upon one mechanism. The environmental problem comprises a multitude of issues which range from localized problems to matters of global importance. Liability in tort mainly operates at a local or regional level as it is triggered by specific incidents. Thus tort is suited to dealing with the consequences of accidental escapes or spillages of noxious substances which are well defined in space and time. This type of harm accounts for a significant proportion of total environmental damage costs.[1280] However, it is clearly not realistic to expect tort based mechanisms to be capable of absorbing costs resulting from catastrophic incidents causing long term and widespread damage. As Roman Herzog, then Vice President of the German Federal Constitutional Court said at a symposium on Nuclear Third Party Liability and Insurance:

> If we visualize the very worst possible scenario in the operation of a nuclear power plant, then accidents comparable with the greatest disasters in the history of mankind are no doubt conceivable ... Nonetheless, it came as a surprise to me to find that the legal comparisons offered in illustration of this issue are taken exclusively from the field of liability under civil law – in particular that of absolute

---

1275. Schwarz points out that liability following the Exxon Valdez oil spill was settled according to the common law of negligence. This amounted to an astonishing USD 9 billion; the second largest claim in US legal history. See R. Schwarze, *The Role of Common Law in Environmental Policy: Comment*, 89 Public Choice 201 (1996).
1276. In recent times the asbestos exposure claims provide the clearest example of this process.
1277. *Reay and Hope v. British Nuclear Fuels Plc* [1994] Env. L.R. 320.
1278. For example, the old fashioned 'dig and dump' approach adopted at Corby is in marked contrast to the more recent highly sophisticated land reclamation programme adopted at the Corus Ebbw Vale plant in South Wales. See H. Fox and H. Moore, *Restoration and Recovery: Regenerating Land and Communities* (Whittles Publishing 2010).
1279. See T. Fowler and J.A. Dlouhy, *Blowout Preventer Report could Bring New Designs*, Houston Chronicle (Houston, Mar. 24, 2011), http://www.chron.com/business/energy/article/Blowout-preventer-report-could-bring-new-designs-1599671.php (accessed Apr. 27, 2012).
1280. Estimates supplied by German Insurance brokers show that accidental escapes account for 8–12% of total environmental damage costs. See ERM Economics, *The Insurance Sector*, in, *Economic Aspects of Liability and Joint Compensation Systems for Remedying Environmental Damage*, DGXII, 41 (European Commission 1996).

liability ... However the extreme case which I now wish to invoke in my argument refers to completely different magnitudes. And I trust you will decry when I argue that such an extreme case is really only comparable with disasters such as a gigantic flood; mass unemployment caused by the collapse of entire branches of the economy; diseases of modern civilization; or perhaps even the Second World War ...

... Let us just imagine for a moment that something which we will deem impossible and which each of us in his own way does his utmost to prevent actually happens – a disaster which exceeds the present maximum level of 1 billion DM by 1000 or even 2000 per cent. Can anyone really believe that in such a contingency somebody would invoke section 31 of the Atomic Law or even read it? The Bundestag (Parliament) would convene and call for the largest possible 'unconventional and unbureaucratic' indemnification for all the damage suffered. The same would take place in the government, and not even the Minister of Finance would protest; he would simply nod his head in sympathy. Just think: this is the very same State which does not refuse its help – and quite rightly so in my opinion – when a hailstorm or a flood occurs.[1281]

Interestingly, a mere two years after this statement was made, just such a 'worst case scenario' accident occurred in the former Soviet Union at the Chernobyl nuclear facility. The costs associated with this disaster in terms of human suffering, property damage, and economic loss arising from contaminated farm land and restrictions on produce, extending to countries thousands of miles from 'ground zero',[1282] are incalculable and on-going. Had such an accident occurred in the West, it would have seemed folly to seek to recover the costs through civil liability. Even if an operator in such a case was stripped of its entire assets, through meeting civil claims, only a tiny fraction of the total costs could have been met.

This is not to say, however, that there are no circumstances in which recourse may be had to liability rules in the wake of catastrophic disasters of epic proportions. Aside from the exceedingly rare, albeit spectacular, calamities which occur in the nuclear industry, the most notorious environmental disasters have occurred in the oil industry. In 2010 this culminated in the Deepwater Horizon disaster, the ramifications of which have already been discussed at some length.[1283] In contrast to the nuclear industry, the biggest oil disasters tend to be caused by the biggest industries with the deepest pockets. This enabled a very large amount of political pressure to be brought to bear upon BP with the results that it set aside funds which are far in excess of existing capped liabilities under US law. However, although the assessment of damage costs in this case may have more to do with politics than law, it should be remembered that tort based principles must still be used to apportion liability in the first place.

1281. Roman Herzog, Keynote address, in: OECD/IAEA (ed.), *Nuclear third party liability and insurance – status and prospects* (Munich Symposium 1984), Paris 1985, 13–21 (16), quoted in N. Pelzer, *Focus on the Future of Nuclear Liability Law*, 17(4) J. Energy & Nat. Resources L. 332, 349–350 (1999).
1282. In certain 'hot spots' in Austria, Greece and Scandinavia, levels of caesium-137 deposited exceeded 100 kB/m². See European Environment Agency, *Europe's Environment: The Dobris Assessment*, Ch. 18, Box 18E, (European Environment Agency 1995).
    (Office for Official Publications of the European Community 1995).
1283. See §3.05[A][2] for the main background to the disaster.

For the most part however, tort is more adept at dealing with the less spectacular and localized effects of pollution. Although, as noted above, its ability to do so may be seriously curtailed by statutory regimes which seek to limit the role of existing tort based rules.

Furthermore, tort cannot provide a solution to wider environmental problems which result from the manner in which economies have been managed in the past. A case in point concerns the saga of historic pollution. In this respect it is unfortunate that tort at one point became embroiled in the debate regarding contaminated land. If one accepts the pluralistic view of tort advocated by England,[1284] it is clear that tort rules constantly have to balance corrective and distributional functions. In the case of contaminated land it is impossible to achieve a balance. Where pollution has already occurred, in circumstances where it would not have given rise to tortious liability at the time, tort cannot have any deterrent effect. In such circumstances it must serve as a purely distributional device which allocates responsibility; as Atkinson argued, in the context of contaminated land, there is 'a fundamental inconsistency of the goals of deterrence and compensation which the two seek to achieve'.[1285] Tort has historically governed conduct in accordance with the social values and expectations of the time. It is inappropriate to use it in respect of problems from the past when different standards applied. In this respect tort should not be confused with a system such as CERCLA (Superfund) in the United States which can operate as an arbitrary means of loss allocation.

The example of Superfund and other such no fault compensation and environmental remediation systems leads on to a wider point about the relationship between tort based rules and other forms of financial security such as compensation funds.[1286] These may operate closely with tort based liability and may provide a vital means of extending recoverable costs beyond the comparatively limited reach of tort. In this respect they impose a form of collective responsibility on a particular industry. To some extent conventional tort rules may be applied in a manner which has a similar effect. A very clear example is provided by the manner in which the UK courts have adapted common law causality tests so as to impose a form of collective responsibility on the asbestos industry.[1287] However, this maintains a linkage with the conduct of individual operators inasmuch as the damage may result from failings which are endemic in the industry as a whole. If this link with personal conduct is lost the compensation fund purely operates as a tax on industry and becomes far removed from a liability based approach. This is the greatest problem associated with the idea of a 'Superfund' for climate change liability; unlike asbestos, climate change cannot be attributed to a narrowly defined industry or set of operators. Moreover, there can be no guarantee that the use of such funds will meet all additional costs which exceed any caps on tort based liability. As we have seen, the bodies charged with administering funds often have to

---

1284. England (n. 1263).
1285. N. Atkinson, *The Regulatory Lacuna: Waste Disposal and the Clean up of Contaminated Sites*, 3 J. Envtl. L. 265, 277 (1991).
1286. See discussion at §11.04[B], above.
1287. See discussion at §3.03[B], above.

develop their own fund jurisprudence which may offer little more flexibility than tort based rules. This may be a necessary function of the need to conserve the fund so as to benefit the maximum number of claimants.

Another aspect of financial security concerns the insurability of environmental risks. Thus, the insurance implications of increased environmental liability cannot be excluded from consideration of the limits of tort. Although few judges have attached as much weight as Lord Denning to the existence of insurance when attributing liability,[1288] insurance has undoubtedly affected the development of tort. Thus, the availability of insurance must have a bearing on the decision to proceed with an environmental liability regime. Insurers have made it clear that, following the experience in the United States, they would not be prepared to provide cover in respect of historic pollution. However, provided they are permitted to draft policies which do not leave them exposed to open ended costs, they are prepared to insure against current and future pollution. The availability of insurance will very much depend upon the domestic insurance laws of Member States. The legality of 'claims made' triggers in the UK[1289] and 'manifestation triggers' in Germany[1290] has been instrumental in the development of EIL liability.[1291] In those countries where such terms have been ruled illegal insurers have spread the burden by pooling resources. Furthermore, as Holmes and Broughton pointed out, there is no reason why insurers should not continue to provide pollution cover under standard occurrence based public liability policies subject to more detailed risk assessments and increased premiums.[1292]

It should be noted that these developments have occurred without the introduction of compulsory insurance. In fact compulsory insurance is likely to prove a hindrance to the continued development of insurance in this field due to its inflexibility. It is impossible to set blanket limits on the percentage of damage costs which should be met by insurers due to the range of variable factors involved.[1293] The parties must be left free to determine their own insurance arrangements according to considerations such as the nature of the activity, the size of the enterprise and so forth.

§12.05   AN INCREASED THE ROLE FOR TORT IN AN ENVIRONMENTAL CONTEXT?

Much of the first edition of this book was focused on EU proposals to establish a tort based environmental liability system. As we have seen, there was a sudden change in policy direction and the Directive which emerged established a system for recovering

---

1288. See, for example, *Nettleship v. Weston* [1971] 2 Q.B. 691.
1289. See R.G. Lee and S. Tupper, *Claims-made Policies: European Occurrences*, 4(1) Env. Liability 25 (1996).
1290. See R. Woltereck, *New Environmental Impairment Liability Policy Introduced into the German Insurance Market*, 5 Intl. Ins. L. R. 202, 203 (1994).
1291. It will be recalled that these triggers enable the insurer to fix the period of cover more precisely than the usual occurrence triggers.
1292. See Holmes and Broughton (n. 1265).
1293. See Woltereck (n. 1290).

the costs of pollution, or preventing damage from occurring in the first place, by means of administrative powers.[1294] Although any new EU initiative on a tort based approach looks unlikely in the near future, the debate regarding whether tort should be actively utilized as a means of environmental protection continues. A number of EU Member States have introduced their own regimes and efforts continue at an international level to extend the role of civil liability. This raises a number of issues regarding the extent to which substantive tort rules can be modified, so as to facilitate more actions in an environmental context, without undermining the very essence of tort and its focus on individual accountability. It is noteworthy that certain changes may come about as a result the evolution of case law on existing principles. For example, it was the courts in the UK which eased the burden of proof on causation in asbestos cases.[1295] Similarly, it was the German courts, as opposed to the legislature, which was initially responsible for setting up a rebuttable presumption of causation in respect of certain types of environmental damage case.[1296] However, more radical developments would doubtless require more extensive use of legislative intervention.

Thus, although tort has the potential to fulfil a useful role as a component in a system of environmental protection, as the analysis in Chapter 3 demonstrates, its use is often limited by obstacles to establishing liability (transaction costs). These include the need to establish fault in certain cases, causation, limited standing and limited remedies. Such difficulties face any claimant wishing to pursue an action in tort, however, they are particularly acute where environmental damage is concerned. The technical nature of many polluting processes means that it may be difficult to establish fault. The disperse nature of certain forms of pollution and the complex manner in which it inter-acts with the environment creates difficulties in establishing causation. Furthermore, standing is limited to those whose private interests have been directly affected and remedies reflect private loss as opposed to environmental impairment.

These problems demonstrate that, at present, the English law of tort is characterized by corrective functions. Before tort can fulfil a useful role the focus must be moved from the protection of private interests to the protection of the environment. In other words, if the concepts of corrective and distributive justice are envisaged at two extremes of a sliding scale, there is a need to move tort closer to the distributive end of the spectrum. Of course, if tort is moved to the extreme distributional end of the scale it loses all correctional functions and is converted into an arbitrary means of loss allocation. Therefore, in any system which is designed to harness tort in pursuit of environmental objectives, it is necessary to balance distributive and corrective functions in the manner advocated by England in his theory of complementarity.[1297] The principle means of reducing transaction costs in tort, which were discussed in Part IV, have the capacity to accommodate both objectives.

1294. European Parliament and Council Directive (EC) 2004/35 on Environmental Liability with Regard to the Prevention and Remedying of Environmental Damage OJ L143/56. For an overview of the twist and and turns in EU policy development in this area see §5.03, above.
1295. See §3.03[B][3], above.
1296. See §6.02, above.
1297. England (n. 1263)

Strict liability increases the proportion of the damage costs which must be met by the polluter. However, it retains corrective functions in that it allows for defences; this preserves an element of individual accountability and affords the polluter the opportunity to internalize costs. This is where strict liability differs from absolute liability which is a purely distributional device. Thus it is entirely reasonable to include defences in respect of phenomena which were entirely beyond the control of the plaintiff such as force majeure. As stated in Chapter 6, the development risk defence raises more complex issues in that it relates to the manner in which the defendant conducted his activities. The defence could provide an incentive to review procedures in accordance with the state of the art. This is provided that the onus remains on the defendant to show that the knowledge was not discoverable by the industrial sector in which he operates.

As regards causation, as the experience in the United States demonstrates,[1298] an unduly lax application of causality tests leads to collective responsibility.[1299] The approach adopted under the German ELA 1991 (*UmweltHG*) demonstrates how it is possible to increase the distributional effect of tort whilst retaining corrective functions. A provision of this type could enable the court to reach a common sense decision, based upon the circumstances of the case, without the need to establish a causal link with scientific certainty.[1300] This accords more closely with the requirements of the precautionary principle[1301] than the rigorous causality tests applied under English common law. Furthermore it increases the proportion of the damage costs which must be borne by the polluter in accordance with the polluter pays principle.[1302] In this sense relieving the burden of causality in this way embraces the distributional aspects of EU environmental policy; however, the fact that there must be circumstantial evidence pointing to a particular plant before the presumption can be invoked retains a strong element of corrective justice.

Increased standing for environmental interest groups may also form an important component of any civil liability regime. The fact that liability in tort is contingent upon harm to private interests which vest in natural resources fetters the use of tort as a means of protecting the so-called 'un-owned environment'. This raises certain conceptual and philosophical difficulties. Stone argued that the environment should be regarded as having a form of legal personality which environmental interest groups should be capable of representing as a form of guardian *ad litem*.[1303] This approach

---

1298. P. Huber, *Environmental Hazards and Liability Law* in *Liability Perspectives and Policy*, 147–148 (R.E. Litan & C. Winston eds., The Brookings Institution 1988).
1299. G. Teubner, *The Invisible Cupola: From Causal to Collective Attribution in Ecological Liability* in *Environmental Law and Ecological Responsibility – The Concept and Practice of Ecological Self-Organization*, 29 (G. Teubner, L. Farmer & D. Murphy eds., John Wiley & Sons 1994).
1300. It will be recalled that this is provided that the presumption is not automatically rebutted by the existence of an alternative substance which is capable of causing the harm in synergy with the alleged cause. See G. Hager,*Umwelthaftungsgetz: The New German Environmental Liability Law*, 1(2) Env. Liability 41, 42 (1993).
1301. See Article 174 EC (formerly 130r).
1302. *Ibid.*
1303. C. Stone, *Should Trees have Standing? – Towards Legal Rights for Natural Objects*, 45 S. Cal. L. Rev. 450 (1972).

seemed to receive some support from the dissenting judgment of Douglas J. in the US case of *Sierra Club v. Morton*.[1304] An alternative approach, which may be easier to justify according to existing legal principles, has been adopted by the Dutch Courts in the cases of *Kuunders*[1305] and *Borcea*.[1306] In these decisions, it will be recalled, the courts viewed environmental interest groups as representing the public interest in the protection of natural resources.

Closely associated with this idea is the concept that the remedies awarded by the court, under an environmental liability regime, should reflect the need to protect the environment as a separate entity from the private interests which vest in it. This would necessitate a general presumption in favour of injunctive relief. In Chapter 4 it was argued that injunctions are more effective than damages in requiring the polluter to internalize a greater proportion of the pollution costs associated with an activity. Whereas there is no guarantee that damages will be applied to remedying environmental damage, the court may attach conditions to injunctions which stipulate abatement or remediation measures. These may be adjusted to take account of technical feasibility; as McLaren[1307] argued some forty years ago, it is only in extreme circumstances that an enterprise would be forced to close as a result of an injunction. Thus, by allowing activities to continue whilst simultaneously reducing pollution levels, the remedy embodies both corrective and distributive functions in accordance with the pluralistic view of tort. An approach which favours an award of damages in lieu of an injunction invites an economic approach in which the polluter is allowed to compulsorily purchase the right to pollute.

Where it is necessary to make an award of damages, the quantum should be calculated upon the basis of the cost of restoring the environment as close as possible to its former state. An approach which places undue emphasis upon restoring a natural resource for a specific use prices the resource according to narrow economic criteria. This renders the resource vulnerable to becoming the subject of market transactions.[1308]

Overall, adjusting tort based rules in this manner may serve two basic objectives. First, strict liability and easing the burden of proof on causation increase the accountability of polluters and give rise to duties to protect the environment. Second, increased standing and the application of remedies which reflect environmental damage, as opposed to private loss, allow these duties to be enforced by private individuals and bodies. In this sense an extended role for environmental liability could be instrumental in bringing about a re-evaluation of the relationship between property rights and the environment.

1304. 405 US 727, 31 L. Ed 2d 636 (1972).
1305. Supreme Court Dec. 18, 1992, *Nederlandse Jurisprudentie* 1994, 139. See Chapter 6 at 4.2.
1306. District Court Rotterdam 15 March 1991, (1992) Netherlands Yearbook of International Law (NYIL) 513. See §8.02[A], above.
1307. J.P.S. McLaren, *Nuisance Actions and the Environmental Battle*, 10(3) Osgoode Hall L. J. 505, 557 (1972).
1308. J. Steele, *Remedies and Remediation: Foundation Issues in Environmental Liability*, 58(5) The Modern L. Rev. 615 (1995).

§12.06   CONCLUSION: FROM THE TRAGEDY OF THE COMMONS TO THE GLOBAL COMMONS?

As regards the wider role of tort in an environmental context, a criticism which is often made is the fact that the environment is reduced into a series of individual property rights or interests. Thus, environmental damage is only actionable where it intersects with some private interest. In fact, in a world which is dominated by property rights, this could be considered a strength as opposed to a weakness. Reformulating damage to the environment as an interference with a private right enables the environment to be considered on the same terms as those rights which enable a landowner to use his property in a manner which causes pollution. In a sense this reformulates the environment as a form of commons in which everyone has a stake. However, whereas in Hardin's *Tragedy of the Commons*[1309] everyone is seeking to exploit the resource for similar economic reasons, in an environmental context some of those interests are concerned with conserving the commons. The difficulty arises from putting those conservatory land uses on an equal footing with the economic interests which normally prevail. The language of rights may provide a means of doing this.[1310]

As Macpherson[1311] has explained, ownership of a resource once carried with it duties to use the resource in a certain manner. The dominance of the market has distilled the concept of property to those rights which are tradable, namely the tangible resource itself and the right to exclude others from it. Thus the view of property which has predominated since the eighteenth century confers rights on the owners and duties on all others, namely the obligation to respect the owner's right to exclusive possession. According to this narrow view of property ownership confers rights on the owner but no duties; such a system is open to abuse in that it enables the owner to transfer the costs of his activity to third parties. This gives rise to the externality problem of which pollution is a classic example. As Bromley has argued:

> [T]he concentration of rights in the hands of a few individuals is not of immediate concern in a political sense. What matters is the fear that economic power deriving from this concentration may be put to antisocial uses.[1312]

However, Bromley also pointed out that the lawyer's typical 'bundle of sticks' conception of ownership, in which rights include the right to possess, manage, benefit, secure and alienate in varying degrees, does not denote absolute control.[1313] Control varies according to the extent to which the state permits the owner to disregard the space of others in exercising those rights. This aspect of ownership can be regarded as a privilege rather than an absolute right. As the state maintains the system of property it is in a position to alter the structure so as to restrict the use of such privileges:

1309. G. Hardin, *The Tragedy of the Commons*, 162 (3859) Science 1243 (1968); see §1.02[B]., above.
1310. See discussion at §4.03[B], above.
1311. C.B. Macpherson, *Human Rights as Property Rights*, 24 Dissent 72 (1977); see §4.03[B], above.
1312. D.W. Bromley, *Environment and Economy*, 160 (Blackwell 1991).
1313. *Ibid.*

> For the state to do nothing is to protect those who currently have rights and privileges; to enter the fray in some form of collective action to modify institutional arrangements is to act in the interest of those currently bearing unwanted costs.[1314]

He continued that such a reappraisal of the function of property is inevitable as resources are depleted and new scientific knowledge on causality reveals the extent to which the unfettered right to exclusive possession imposes costs on others:

> As technology advances, and as population pressure continues to increase densities of urbanized areas, we will find new ways to impose unwanted costs on others. New knowledge also contributes in that its allows us to establish cause and effect with more certainty. In the absence of sophisticated scientific evidence many phenomena were simply accepted as part of life. Once we possess the ability to establish definite causality, the matter is thrown into the legislative or judicial arenas. The ultimate outcome of that process is surely a further redefinition of the rights and duties that go with land.[1315]

It is certainly the case that environmental degradation has historically been regarded as 'part of life' as Bromely asserts. Although pollution has always caused anguish and distress to those who value the environment, it has not always been regarded as engaging concrete and enforceable rights. Nevertheless, this view of pollution as an inevitable and inescapable evil began to change as far back as the nineteenth century in industrial England. As the industrial cities spread pollution began encroaching upon the great estates of the landed gentry and nouvelle riche alike. In the worst cases herbage was scorched and livestock was poisoned. Once property damage of this nature had been inflicted pollution crystallized into a concrete form which engaged property based torts such as the law of nuisance.[1316]

Bromley was also correct to assert that causation plays a crucial role in converting general background pollution into a form which engages an actionable right. The establishment of a causal link between particularized damage and a specific source transforms general background inconvenience and annoyance into a direct interference with a private right. The process is slow, however, in that there is an inevitable time lag between the manifestation of damage and the emergence of scientific evidence of a causal link capable of withstanding judicial scrutiny. Arguably, the most celebrated English private nuisance cases, stemming from the effect of nineteenth century industrial pollution on the estates of the wealthy, is *St Helens Smelting v. Tipping*.[1317] A point which is often overlooked is that Tipping had to expend considerable resources in establishing a causal link between the copper smelter emissions and the damage to his property.[1318] However, once this link was firmly established others were able to follow Tipping's example.

Of course, nuisance actions have tended to be the preserve of the wealthy due to the expense of litigation. The greater part of the population had no choice other than to

---

1314. *Ibid.*, 163.
1315. *Ibid.*, 167–168.
1316. See Mclaren (1259).
1317. (1865) 11 H.L.C. 642.
1318. A.W.B. Simpson, *Victorian Judges and the Problem of Social Cost: Tipping v. St Helen's Smelting Company (1865)* in *Leading Cases in the Common Law* (Clarendon 1995).

continue accepting pollution as 'part of life.' Once pollution was recognized as a social ill, a regulatory response emerged under early measures such as the Public Health Acts and Alkali Acts. In many respects this pattern has continued to the present day and we are accustomed to the fact that environmental protection is first and foremost the creature of public law. A system of private law which occasionally steps in to provide redress for a few wealthy landowners in respect of individual harm appears to have little to do with the protection of environmental rights of general application. However, unless such rights are harnessed for the greater good of the general population and the need for a cleaner environment, there shall remain a serious shortfall in the capacity of the law to hold polluters to account for the costs of pollution. To return to arguments advanced by Macpherson and others;[1319] unless we can lock into the language of rights and property, when seeking to protect environmental interests, it is difficult to do battle with polluters on the same terms. Macrory has succinctly set out the problem in the following terms:

> Lawyers traditionally characterize trade freedom as a classical individual right, which should be equivalent to familiar rights of property, and capable of legal protection as such. In contrast, environmental concerns are viewed in law not so much as an aspect of individual freedom or entitlement but rather as an interest which restricts the freedom of what people may or may not do. As such it is an area appropriate for intervention by government but cannot readily be conceived of as a right directly enforceable before the courts in the same way as the freedom to trade.[1320]

The reasons why tort should be developed in a manner which facilitates such actions have already been set out above. To recap, as cases such as *Allen v. Gulf Oil Refining*[1321] and the *Corby Group Litigation*[1322] case demonstrate, public law cannot provide a complete response to all the individual harms which flow from pollution. In some cases there may have been regulatory failure in terms of a lack of enforcement or a deficiency in the regulatory regime itself. In other cases individual harms may simply not have been contemplated by the regulations governing a particular activity.[1323] As has also been noted, it is conceptually and practically possible to develop a model of tort which achieves these objectives without undermining the degree of individual accountability upon which tort depends. To this end, strict liability, modified causation tests, group litigation, increased recoverability for economic loss and other doctrinal developments could all play their part in securing such a public interest model of tort.

Clearly there are limits regarding the extent to which such a public interest model of tort can be pushed. Many of these interests may be diffuse and impossible to quantify; for example, if every passer-by, who was irritated by fumes from a factory, were to be afforded standing to pursue the matter before the courts the floodgates

---

1319. See n. 1311, above.
1320. R. Macrory, *Environmental Citizenship and the Law: Repairing the European Road*, 8 J.E.L. 219, 232 (1996).
1321. [1981] A.C. 1001.
1322. [2009] EWHC 1944 (TCC), [2009] NPC 100.
1323. See §4.03[C], above.

would be opened and liability would become unsustainable.[1324] However, in such circumstances, the collective interests of the community would be aggregated by means of affording standing to NGOs. Such representative actions would amount to an assertion of the collective proprietary interests of society in safeguarding the environmental media concerned. This approach reflects the reasoning of Douglas J. in the *Sierra Club v. Morton*[1325] and the Dutch Courts in *Kuunders*[1326] and *Borcea*.[1327]

In conclusion, an increased role for tort in environmental protection, whether it occurs through case law developments or legislative intervention, serves to emphasize that possessory title to land is not merely a matter of what they *may do* with their property but also what they *may not* do with it. In the years to come it will be interesting to see whether tort may play its part in developing an idea of a public trust doctrine in the environment.[1328] Taking this to its extreme, and assuming that the formidable causality problems could one day be solved,[1329] it is just conceivable that the issue of climate change litigation may finally establish the idea of a 'global commons' in which we all have a proprietary stake.

ADDENDUM

In an important ruling the US Supreme Court ruled in *Connecticut v. American Electric Power*[1330] that, given that the EPA was now in a position to regulate greenhouse gases,[1331] any federal common law rights under public nuisance would be displaced by these regulatory powers. The case is somewhat of a setback for those litigants pursuing claims in tort in respect of climate change; although it remains to be seen how it will affect claims brought by private parties as opposed to states.[1332] The case is significant in that it demonstrates the relationship between private and public law and the reluctance of the courts to develop private law in a manner which may cut across

---

1324. Lord Goff was clearly aware of this problem in *Hunter v. Canary Wharf Ltd* [1997] 2 W.L.R. 684. where he objected extending standing to those without a proprietary interest in property: '[T]he extension of the tort in this way would transform it from a tort to land into a tort to the person, in which damages could be recovered in respect of something less serious than personal injury and the criteria for liability were founded not upon negligence but upon striking a balance between the interests of neighbours in the use of their land. This is, in my opinion, not an acceptable way in which to develop the law,' per Lord Goff at p. 696F-G.
1325. 405 US 727, 31 L. Ed 2d 636 (1972).
1326. Supreme Court 18 December 1992, *Nederlandse Jurisprudentie* 1994, 139. See Chapter 6 at 4.2.
1327. District Court Rotterdam 15 March 1991, (1992) Netherlands Yearbook of International Law (NYIL) 513. See Chapter 6 at 4.2.
1328. See §4.03[B], above.
1329. See §3.03[B][4], above.
1330. 131 S. Ct. 2527 (2011). See discussion at §2.05[E].
1331. Note that in *Massachusetts v. Environmental Protection Agency* 549 U.S. 497 (2007) the US Supreme Court that the EPA was empowered to regulate CO_2 and other greenhouse gases under the Clean Air Act 1970 (as amended). See §2.05[E].
1332. Hari M. Osofsky, AEP v. Connecticut's *Implications for the Future of Climate Change Litigation*, 121 Yale L.J. Online 101 (2011), http://yalelawjournal.org/2011/09/13/osofsky.html. (accessed Nov. 15, 2012).

statutory regimes. This is a cause for concern in that, as has been consistently argued throughout this edition, the job of the common law should be to compensate for regulatory failure or inactivity.[1333] In this respect the courts should be slow to clear the field of tort based remedies where there has been statutory intervention.

1333. See §4.03[C].

Table of Cases

United States

The Netherlands

Sweden

European Convention on Human Rights

Index

ENERGY AND ENVIRONMENTAL LAW & POLICY SERIES

1. Stephen J. Turner, *A Substantive Environmental Right: An Examination of the Legal Obligations of Decision-makers towards the Environment*, 2009 (ISBN 978-90-411-2815-7).
2. Helle Tegner Anker, Birgitte Egelund Olsen & Anita Rønne (eds), *Legal Systems and Wind Energy: A Comparative Perspective*, 2009 (ISBN 978-90-411-2831-7).
3. David Langlet, *Prior Informed Consent and Hazardous Trade: Regulating Trade in Hazardous Goods at the Intersection of Sovereignty, Free Trade and Environmental Protection*, 2009 (ISBN 978-90-411-2821-8).
4. Louis J. Kotzé and Alexander R. Paterson (eds), *The Role of the Judiciary in Environmental Governance: Comparative Perspectives*, 2009 (ISBN 978-90-411-2708-2).
5. Tuula Honkonen, *The Common but Differentiated Responsibility Principle in Multilateral Environmental Agreement's: Regulatory and Policy Aspects*, 2009 (ISBN 978-90-411-3153-9).
6. Barbara Pozzo (ed.), *The Implementation of the Seveso Directives in an Enlarged Europe: A Look into the Past and a challenge for the Future*, 2009 (ISBN 978-90-411-2854-6).
7. Henrik M. Inadomi, *Independent Power Projects in Developing Countries: Legal Investment Protection and Consequences for Development*, 2010 (ISBN 978-90-411-3178-2).
8. Nahid Islam, *The Law of Non-Navigational Uses of International Watercourses: Options for Regional Regime-Building in Asia*, 2010 (ISBN 978-90-411-3196-6).
9. Yasuhiro Shigeta, *International Judicial Control of Environmental Protection: Standard Setting, Compliance Control and the Development of International Environmental Law by the International Judiciary*, 2010 (ISBN 978-90-411-3151-5).
10. Katleen Janssen, *The Availability of Spatial and Environmental Data in the European Union: At the Crossroads between Public and Economic Interests*, 2010 (ISBN 978-90-411-3287-1).
11. Henrik Bjørnebye, *Investing in EU Energy Security: Exploring the Regulatory Approach to Tomorrow's Electricity Production*, 2010 (ISBN 978-90-411-3118-8).
12. Véronique Bruggeman, *Compensating catastrophe victims: A Comparative Law and Economics Approach*, 2010 (ISBN 978-90-411-3263-5).
13. Michael G. Faure, Han Lixin & Shan Hongjun, *Maritime Pollution Liability and Policy: China, Europe and the US*, 2010 (ISBN 978-90-411-2869-0).

14. Anton Ming-Zhi Gao, *Regulating Gas Liberalization: A Comparative Study on Unbundling and Open Access Regimes in the US, Europe, Japan, South Korea and Taiwan*, 2010 (ISBN 978-90-411-3347-2).
15. Mustafa Erkan, *International Energy Investment Law: Stability through Contractual Clauses*, 2011 (ISBN 978-90-411-3411-0).
16. Levente Borzsa´k, *The Impact of Environmental Concerns on the Public Enforcement Mechanism under EU law: Environmental protection in the 25th hour*, 2011 (ISBN 978-90-411-3408-0).
17. Tarcísio Hardman Reis, *Compensation for Environmental Damages under International Law: The Role of the International Judge*, 2011 (ISBN 978-90-411-3437-0).
18. Kim Talus, *Vertical Natural Gas Transportation Capacity, Upstream Commodity Contracts and EU Competition Law*, 2011 (ISBN 978-90-411-3407-3).
19. WangHui, *Civil Liability for Marine Oil Pollution Damage: A Comparative and Economic Study of the International, US and Chinese Compensation Regime*, 2011 (ISBN 978-90-411-3672-5).
20. Chowdhury Ishrak Ahmed Siddiky, *Cross-Border Pipeline Arrangements: What Would a Single Regulatory Framework Look Like?*, 2012 (ISBN 978-90-411-3844-6).
21. Rozeta Karova, *Liberalization of Electricity Markets and Public Service Obligations in the Energy Community*, 2012 (ISBN 978-90-411-3849-1).
22. Sandra Cassotta, *Environmental Damage and Liability Problems in a Multilevel Context: The Case of the Environmental Liability Directive*, 2012 (ISBN 978-90-411-3830-9).
23. Mark Wilde, *Civil Liability for Environmental Damage: Comparative Analysis of Law and Policy in Europe and US*, 2013 (ISBN 978-90-411-3233-8).